DATE OF RETURN
UNLESS RECALLED BY LIBRARY

PLEASE TAKE GOOD CARE OF THIS BOOK

Great Thinkers in Economics Series

Series Editor: A.P. Thirlwall is Professor of Applied Economics, University of Kent, UK.

Great Thinkers in Economics is designed to illuminate the economics of some of the great historical and contemporary economists by exploring the interactions between their lives and work, and the events surrounding them. The books are brief and written in a style that makes them not only of interest to professional economists, but also intelligible for students of economics and the interested lay person.

Titles include:

Esben Sloth Anderson
JOSEPH A. SCHUMPETER

James Ronald Stanfield and Jacqueline Bloom Stanfield
JOHN KENNETH GALBRAITH

Julio Lopez and Michaël Assous
MICHAL KALECKI

G.C. Harcourt and Prue Kerr
JOAN ROBINSON

Alessandro Roncaglia
PIERO SRAFFA

William J. Barber
GUNNAR MYRDAL

Paul Davidson
JOHN MAYNARD KEYNES

Peter D. Groenewegen
ALFRED MARSHALL

Michael Szenberg and Lall Ramrattan
FRANCO MODIGLIANI

Gavin Kennedy
ADAM SMITH

John E. King
NICHOLAS KALDOR

Gordon Fletcher
DENNIS ROBERTSON

John E. King
DAVID RICARDO

Barbara Ingham and Paul Mosley
SIR ARTHUR LEWIS

Forthcoming titles include:

Nahid Aslanbeigui and Guy Oakes
ARTHUR C.PIGOU

Warren Young and Esteban Perez
ROY HARROD

Robert Dimand
JAMES TOBIN

Albert Jolink
JAN TINBERGEN

Great Thinkers in Economics
Series Standing Order ISBN 978–14039–8555-2 (Hardback) 978–14039–8556–9
(Paperback)
(outside North America only)

You can receive future titles in this series as they are published by placing a standing order. Please contact your bookseller or, in case of difficulty, write to us at the address below with your name and address, the title of the series and one of the ISBNs quoted above.

Customer Services Department, Macmillan Distribution Ltd, Houndmills, Basingstoke, Hampshire RG21 6XS, England

Sir Arthur Lewis

A Biography

Barbara Ingham
Honorary Research Associate, School of African and Oriental Studies,
University of London, UK

and

Paul Mosley
Professor of Economics, University of Sheffield, UK

First published 2013 by
PALGRAVE MACMILLAN

Palgrave Macmillan in the UK is an imprint of Macmillan Publishers Limited, registered in England, company number 785998, of Houndmills, Basingstoke, Hampshire RG21 6XS.

Palgrave Macmillan in the US is a division of St Martin's Press LLC, 175 Fifth Avenue, New York, NY 10010.

Palgrave Macmillan is the global academic imprint of the above companies and has companies and representatives throughout the world.

Palgrave® and Macmillan® are registered trademarks in the United States, the United Kingdom, Europe and other countries.

ISBN 978–0–230–55358–3

This book is printed on paper suitable for recycling and made from fully managed and sustained forest sources. Logging, pulping and manufacturing processes are expected to conform to the environmental regulations of the country of origin.

A catalogue record for this book is available from the British Library.

A catalog record for this book is available from the Library of Congress.

The publisher gratefully acknowledges permission to reproduce copyright material in this book. Every effort has been made to trace and contact copyright holders. If there are any inadvertent omissions we apologize to those concerned and undertake to include suitable acknowledgements in all future editions. In the event that permission has not been rightfully acknowledged please contact Ania Wronski, Editorial Assistant, Scholarly and Reference, Economics, at Ania.Wronski@palgrave.com.

Contents

List of Illustrative Material

Preface and Acknowledgements

Since we became students of economics and economic history in the 1960s, we have both been fascinated by Lewis's work. In its wide sweep, its storytelling style, and most of all its passionate commitment to design a better and fairer world and then put that design into practice, it differed greatly from most of the economics we had encountered previously. From the 1970s onwards, Lewis's writings have inspired much of our research and thinking, and we have been aware of the great debt we owe him, as both writers and practitioners.

It has taken until now, forty years later, to start paying back that debt. The first steps along this road were taken in July 2004, when we both attended a conference sponsored by Manchester University to celebrate the 50th anniversary of the publication of Lewis's *Unlimited Supplies of Labour* article, at which we both presented papers. Present at that conference were, in particular, Colin Kirkpatrick, the conference organiser and economics professor at Manchester; Robert Tignor, professor of history at Princeton University, USA; Mark Figueroa, professor of economics at the University of the West Indies (UWI), Jamaica; Andrew Downes, professor of economics at the University of the West Indies, Barbados; and John Toye, professor of economics at Oxford University, and at the time acting as the head of the Centre for the Study of African Economies at Oxford. The Nuffield Foundation, through their administrator Louie Burghes, shortly afterwards awarded us a grant of some £6,000, which enabled us to undertake initial visits to Princeton, Ghana and the West Indies. These individuals constitute the nucleus of the group to whom our warmest thanks are due for initially setting us on the road. Within this group, a special mention is owed to Robert Tignor, who published the first biography of Lewis in late 2005, and who might be forgiven for looking askance at our attempts to dig in the same quarry. In fact, he has been the soul of generosity, encouraging us and setting us right in innumerable ways. Equally indispensable has been the help of John Toye, a long-standing friend of both of us, who read through the entire first draft and made very detailed comments. The general editor of the Great Thinkers in Economics Series, Tony Thirlwall, made valuable comments on our final draft.

We made use of a good number of archives, as recorded in the Bibliography, and we are grateful to all the archivists and librarians listed there, who went out of their way to help. We must, however, single out Adriane Hanson, keeper of the Lewis archive at the Mudd Library at Princeton University, for not only putting up with a quite exceptional amount of enquiries from us, but doing so in a creative way that enabled us to follow up many leads which would otherwise have run dead; and to Ruth Tait, administrator of the Ahmed Iqbal Ullah Race Relations Resource Centre at Manchester University, a special thank you for putting us into contact with the community of Moss Side and with many West Indians, Africans and white Mancunians who remembered the city as it was in the 1950s. Some of these even remembered Lewis, and could therefore speak of him with special authority; and in this regard our special thanks to Barrington Young, Elouise Edwards, Ina Spence and Victor Lawrence of the West Indian Sports and Social Club. This is also the place to thank the other people we interviewed in person: in Britain, Phyllis Deane, Gisela Eisner and Robert Lalljie; and in the United States, Mark Gersovitz, William Baumol, Angus Deaton, Henry Bienen and Gustav Ranis. In visits to the Caribbean we received great help and support from Professor Mark Figueroa at the University of the West Indies, Jamaica, and Professor Andrew Downes at the University of the West Indies, Barbados. Staff at the Caribbean Development Bank were generous with their time and facilities, and particular mention should be made of Sir Neville Nicholls, third president of the Bank and a close professional colleague of Lewis. The Caribbean has important archives. The guidance of Audine Wilkinson, former documentalist at the Institute of Social and Economic Research (ISER) was particularly valuable. Those who kindly granted us permission to reproduce copyright material are acknowledged under the relevant photographs and figures, and we ask forgiveness of those owners of copyright material whom we have tried and failed to trace. Without the generous help of all these people, who, like us, were keen to see Lewis's contribution to knowledge more widely recognised, our efforts would have come to nothing.

Most biographies are sole-authored rather than being the work of a team or, as in this case, a partnership, and it did not take us long to discover why. Any judgements one makes about an individual's personality, character and achievements inevitably contain much that is subjective and emotion-driven, and it would be miraculous if any two such judgements by two people were to concur, even if they knew the person under consideration intimately; and we did not – we have had to extract Lewis's story from the documentary record and from interviews (listed in the References) with those who did know him well. It is therefore with great relief that we can report that these difficulties were (at least to our satisfaction) overcome. This is not at all because our approaches to historiography, or to economics, are the same, but rather because they are complementary, and because, if we disagreed, we were always able to find a form of words we felt did justice to Lewis. Readers might wish to know which parts of the book to attribute to which author. Paul Mosley took responsibility primarily for the archives and interviews at Princeton (Chapter 8). He was also responsible for discovering and researching Lewis's little-known but critical venture into social development among the Caribbean community in Manchester in the 1950s (Chapter 5) and Lewis's Ghana adventures (Chapter 6). Barbara Ingham was responsible primarily for documenting Lewis's career at the London School of Economics (LSE) (Chapter 2) and his Caribbean connections (Chapter 7). Both authors have a long-standing research interest in Lewis's career at the Colonial Office (Chapter 3), and worked for significant periods at the University of Manchester (Chapter 4). From the beginning, however, we set out to produce a seamless biography in the sense that every chapter was discussed, read and discussed again at length by both authors. Changes were made and new material inserted by both authors. We hope that the joins are not too apparent!

As with any research project, there have also been many humps and bumps along the road, arising not from the difficulties of collaboration but simply from competing commitments and sometimes from lack of stamina. Occasionally, like Robert Skidelsky in his great life of John Maynard Keynes, we contemplated throwing in the towel. But like Skidelsky, 'at such times, [we] would start reading [Lewis] – anything, anywhere – and [our] resolve to press on would be revived.'[1] It was Lewis himself who removed many of the difficulties from our path.

Finally, our thanks to our families, who we know will be as relieved as we are to see this long research project come to fruition. In the Mosley family, Helena, Francesca and Nicholas are all 'arts-side' rather than 'science-side', and were therefore relieved to discover that what their partner/parent was writing this time was a biography, moreover the biography of someone who at the end of his life wrote 'In the end, economics is not enough.'

Barbara Ingham
Paul Mosley

1
The Caribbean in Turmoil: Prologue to a Biography

1.1 Lewis's trajectory

Sir Arthur Lewis is known to many as the first black (Afro-Caribbean) person to hold a professorial chair in a UK university, and as a winner of the first Nobel Prize to be awarded in Development Economics. His achievement, in fact, was very broad, and he made important contributions not only to economics, but also to political science, history and education. He aimed not only to understand the world but also to change it (as he was later to put it, 'half my interest was in policy questions'[1]) and his attempts, from the 1940s to the early 1960s, to achieve a better and fairer world through social and economic reform rank equally with, even if they were much less influential than, the writings that made him famous.

All Lewis's great work in economic analysis was produced (as we relate in Chapter 4) during a brief period between 1952 and 1955, while Lewis was working at Manchester University. His inspirational work in policy advocacy began earlier, in the mid-1940s during his time at the Colonial Office, and ended later, in 1962, after his failed attempt to hold together the East Caribbean Federation. But after the pointed summit of his pioneering development economics research and the flatter hills of his work in economic and social reform, his output became, with one or two exceptions, mundane. During his fifties and sixties, a period of peak earnings and reputation, when he won the Nobel Prize and became world famous, the creative excitement drained out of his work.

Our aim in this biography is to focus on those periods during which Lewis was producing work that was astonishing and out of the ordinary – the type of work that persuaded us that development economics was a career worth pursuing. However, the period of Lewis's exceptional research creativity between 1952 and 1955 turns out to have had a rather lengthy and fascinating gestation period, and without six chance events things might never have fallen into place to make it possible. First, there was the invitation to Lewis from the Colonial Office to do a number of consultancies on colonial development from 1941 onwards. Second, there was the moral and intellectual support that Lewis received from the Fabian Society and the Fabian Colonial Bureau. Third, there was the invitation from Friedrich von Hayek in 1943 to write a set of lectures for LSE students which evolved into Lewis's lifelong commitment to a global economic history project. Fourth, there was Lewis's own fascination with economic history and with classical models of economic growth, which provided the germ-cell of his 1954 essay, *Economic Development with Unlimited Supplies of Labour*. Fifth, there was the invitation from the United Nations in 1950 to generalize the lessons from his Colonial Office experiences to the rest of the developing world. And finally there was Lewis's own decision in late 1952 to explore Asia and thereby complement his knowledge of the African and Caribbean colonies with data on a region of the developing world he knew much less well. Without these six elements it is doubtful whether those great insights that came to fruition between 1952 and 1955 would have emerged. Additionally, though most of the time Lewis worked alone rather than as one of a team, his achievements were very much part of a social process, the roots of which lay in 1940s London, as we relate in Chapter 2, and in his birthplace in the Caribbean.

1.2   Early life in the Caribbean, 1915–33

William Arthur Lewis was born on the island of St Lucia on 23 January 1915, the fourth of five sons of George and Ida Lewis, both of them school teachers, who had migrated from Antigua in the early years of the twentieth century. St Lucia is one of the smallest of the West Indian islands (see Map 1.1), which until emancipation in 1838 were based on sugar plantations worked by slaves. Even after the slaves had been freed, a huge inequality remained between the large landowners, nearly all of them white, and the workers and cultivators of smallholdings, mainly black. In the 1920s, when the young Arthur Lewis was growing up, this inequality pervaded the structure of power, and ambitious black people were subjected to an informal colour bar. As Lewis was later to put it:

> This tiny white element dominates every element of West Indian life. Economically and politically the white man is supreme: he owns

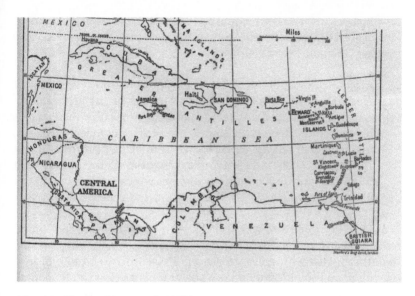

Map 1.1   The Caribbean in the 1930s
Source: W. M. Macmillan, *Warning from the West Indies: A Tract for Africa and the Empire*, Faber & Faber, 1936.

the biggest plantations, stores and banks. It is he whom the Governor most often nominates to his councils and for his sons that the best Government jobs are reserved.[2]

Within the black population there were gradations, some related to education and some related to skin colour, since the children of those black people who had interbred with white people enjoyed a status advantage. Lewis was later to describe how this operated:

> Many West Indians react by trying to identify themselves with the ruling classes. They try to marry white, or to marry some fair person, and thus great importance is attached to lightness of complexion, the 'high yaller' despising the brown, and the brown despising the black. Such persons do their best to cut themselves off from all contact with the masses; become more reactionary than the whites; and in positions of authority often act with a harshness which makes many West Indians prefer a white master to a black.[3]

In the uneducated group, definitely the worst off were to be found among the half of the black population who worked in agriculture, most of whom (as well as a high proportion of those doing other jobs) experienced great deprivation, especially if they were casually employed. 'Any teacher,' to quote Lewis again,

> can give cases of children coming into school on a breakfast of sugar and water, with no prospect of lunch. But far greater numbers eat enough and are yet malnourished because their diet is unbalanced ... There is an abundance of starchy foods, but meat, milk and other fats are so expensive as to be beyond the reach of the working classes, except as Sunday luxuries. Consequently West Indians are prey to a number of diseases which weaken but do not kill, especially malaria, yaws, hookworm and venereal diseases.[4]

Vulnerability to disease was also caused by poor housing conditions, which on plantations consisted for the most part 'of a long wooden building roofed with galvanized iron, divided from end to end by a partition, and subdivided on both sides into a series of single rooms – each of which would be occupied by a labourer and his family'[5] (see Figure 1.1(b)).

(a) Family slum housing 'Not one of the worst examples'

A slum tenement, Bridgetown, Barbados. Not one of the worst examples.

(b) Plantation housing

A range of poor barrack tenements, Georgetown, British Guiana. Many worse are to be found, both in towns and on estates.

(c) A school building, for an enrolment of 346

A poor one-room school building, Windward Islands. Enrolment 346.

Figure 1.1 Living and working conditions in the West Indies in the 1930s

Source: West Indies Royal Commission (see Moyne 1945); photos taken for and on behalf of Lord Moyne's Commission to investigate social and economic conditions in the West Indies. Reproduced by kind permission of The Stationery Office.

The island of St Lucia is small and mountainous, with a population in 1914 of almost exactly 50,000, growing to 54,000 by 1930. The only sources of livelihood at that time were the white-owned sugar estates, smallholdings producing cocoa, citrus and bananas, and the civil service and professions. The years before the First World War had been prosperous for St Lucia's trading economy, as the growing steamship trade had taken advantage of the safe harbour of Castries as an entrepôt port for coal, but the bottom fell out of this market in 1920 with the opening of the Panama Canal, and with the phasing out of coal as a fuel for steamships.[6] The inter-war economy of St Lucia never recovered from these shocks.

Within the social structure of St Lucia, black professionals were placed immediately after the few hundred white planters and government officials, and within this group, George and Ida Lewis, as primary school teachers, enjoyed an exceptional status, putting them definitely within the top 5 per cent of income earners on the island at the time.[7] There was only one secondary school, St Mary's College in the capital, Castries. In Lewis's day, primary and secondary education in St Lucia was dominated by the Roman Catholic French mission, the *Fratres Mariae Immaculatae*. The island's prevailing language was an Anglo-French patois, which in the view of an English inspector of the time held back the island's entire educational system.[8] Derek Walcott, born 15 years after Lewis, in 1930, and the other St Lucian apart from Lewis to win a Nobel Prize, vividly represents the social stratification of the island, with, at the top, 'bright row after row of orange stamps repeat[ing] the villas of promoted Civil Servants', and at the bottom, the majority living in 'two hundred shacks, on wooden stilts/one bushy path to the night-soil pits' (Walcott, 1973, pp. 9, 37–39).

In this environment, the only way forward for ambitious young black people, including the Lewis family, was education, leading to a civil service job, and/or to get off the island.

In January 1922, the young Arthur Lewis suffered an illness that forced him to miss school. His father, not wanting him to fall behind with his schoolwork, and realizing that the St Lucia primary school system was already holding him back, decided to tutor him at home, whereupon his progress, for a brief time, was extraordinary. As Lewis was later to relate: 'He taught me in three months as much as the school taught in three years, so that on returning to school I was shifted from grade four to grade six. So the rest of my school life and early working life, up to the age of eighteen, was spent with fellow students or workers two or three years older than I'.[9] (See the comic strip reproduced in Figure 1.2, published in the late 1980s by the St Lucia Schools Service in a programme to raise educational aspirations at the primary school level.)

Figure 1.2 Lewis's early years as depicted in a 1987 comic strip

Source: Ellis and Bhajan (1987). Reproduced by kind permission of Lewis Archive, Mudd Library, Princeton University, NJ.

Not only did Lewis's father educate him academically but also politically: he 'took him to a meeting of the local Marcus Garvey association' (formally the Universal Negro Improvement Association and African Communities League)[10] 'when I was seven years old' (Breit and Spencer, 1987, p. 13). As Lewis was later to insist, 'My interest in development was a product of my anti-imperialism'; and his anti-imperialism was born at an early age.

Only six months into this crash course, however, George Lewis died, in May 1922, when Arthur was only seven years old. Ida Lewis then single-handedly undertook the education of her five children, and to pay for it took on the lease of a grocer's shop (depicted in Figure 1.2), hiring a manager to run the shop during the day while she continued to teach. In his later writings, Lewis took particular trouble, especially in his *Report on the Industrialisation of the Gold Coast* and in *Economic Development with Unlimited Supplies of Labour*, to highlight women's role in development, well before the publication of Ester Boserup's famous book of 1965, *Woman's Role in Economic Development,* and indeed, in his autobiographical account, paying tribute to his mother, he wrote, 'As a youngster in school I would hear other boys talking about the superiority of men over women; I used to think they must be crazy.'[11]

Apart from her extraordinary resilience, Ida Lewis had other exceptional gifts, notably musicality. Lalljie relates that 'as she did with all his brothers, his mother made sure that he was also tutored in music. She herself played the harp, and would often play for all her sons.'[12] A love of music, and specifically Western classical music, was thus inculcated in Lewis from an early age. He became an enthusiastic amateur pianist and concert-goer, and subsequently, any opportunity to express an opinion on music – from the programming of the BBC's new Third Programme in 1952[13] to the curriculum of the Jamaica School of Music in 1961 – was eagerly grasped.

Lewis's progress through primary and secondary school was rapid: he won a government scholarship to the Jesuit foundation of St Mary's College at the age of ten, completed his Cambridge School Certificate at thirteen and his advanced certificate of secondary education (the equivalent of today's A-level) at fourteen. Anecdotal evidence from this period records Lewis as being determined, unsociable and untrusting, keeping his thoughts and his possessions to himself, behaviour that was certainly encouraged by the fact that his schoolmates were older, bigger and stronger than he was.[14] Among his fellow-students at school he became notorious for keeping his sweets to himself and not sharing them out.[15] He was capable of great spontaneous generosity and gentleness towards others, but the evidence is that this side of his nature developed in later years. His graduate students with serious financial problems are known to have received advice and immediate practical assistance, in confidence, out of Lewis's own pocket.

During all this time, the agricultural estates, the former mainstay of the economy, were crumbling, and all rural livelihoods were under pressure as a consequence of the global depression.[16] The only hope was to capture one of the rare civil service jobs. At this point, at the bottom of the inter-war depression, the young Lewis had to mark time because he was too young to compete for a scholarship to study overseas, and so he took a minor job in the St Lucia Department of Agriculture.

So, outside work, Lewis prepared for what another West Indian boy brought up by a very poor but ambitious widowed mother was to call

> this overseas examination, the most important event in our lives. It could determine whether we were going to be sanitary inspectors for the rest of our lives or were going to get into the Civil Service ... This examination determined whether we would qualify and go up to England by boat, third class, tourist class, with a borrowed winter coat, and enter a British university. It could mean life and it could mean death. If you were not lucky and careful and had failed, it meant that for generations afterwards people would whisper when you passed, and say that you had wasted your mother's money and had not got your Senior Cambridge.
>
> And because it meant all of this, we buckled ourselves down in strange and superstitious ways in order to pass the examination. The password was study: study your brains out. We sucked raw eggs to fertilise the brain, to sharpen the retentive capacities. Everything had to be learned by heart. Some of us starved ourselves because superstition told us that to be intelligent, to be a learning fool, you couldn't eat the heavy food, 'dry food', boiled yams, potatoes, eddoes and hard dumplings, which we had been eating all our lives ... We were reprieved from carrying the three-tier white enamel carrier with the policeman's lunch and dinner, and from doing all the chores around the house, because our mothers knew that the examination was important. (Clarke, 2003, pp. 179–81)[17]

Carrying much weight on his shoulders, Lewis none the less triumphed. He sat the London Matriculation Examination in 1932 and was awarded a scholarship to cover the fees of an undergraduate degree provided by any UK university. He elected to go to the London School of

Economics (LSE), to read for a Bachelor of Commerce (B.Com.) degree, of which economics was a component. In the 'personal history' that Lewis drafted much later in his life, just after the award of his Nobel Prize, he described his choice as follows:

> At this point I did not know what to do with my life. The British government imposed a colour bar in its colonies, so young blacks went in only for law or medicine, where they could make a living without government support. I did not want to be a doctor or lawyer. I wanted to be an engineer, but this seemed pointless since neither the government or the white firms would employ a black engineer. Eventually I decided to study business administration, planning to return to St Lucia for a job in the municipal service or in private trade. I would simultaneously study law, to fall back on if nothing administrative turned up. So I went to the London School of Economics (L.S.E.) to do a Bachelor of Commerce degree, which offered accounting, business management, commercial law and a little economics and statistics. This training has been very helpful in the various administrative jobs I have had to do; its weakness from the standpoint of my subsequent career (which was then inconceivable) was that it lacked mathematics.[18]

The world from which Lewis was escaping was one in which living standards, across the entire West Indies and most of the colonial empire, were continuing to fall. The first outbreak of violent protest against this occurred in St Kitts in 1935. The Governor of the Leeward Islands, instructed to report on the disturbances, gave the following analysis of the events that followed:

> I arrived in the island on 23 January and found conditions apparently quiet. The beginning of the sugar-cane reaping season was set for 28 January … On the following day the Secretary of the St Kitts-Nevis Universal Benevolent Association Ltd. wrote to the newspaper *The Union Messenger* that the labourers ought to receive a 12.5 per cent increase. The labourers are on the whole very credulous and this statement passed round by word of mouth might quickly come to mean that the wages *had* been increased by 12.5%.Basseterre, St Kitts, has always been the port where labourers from other islands are collected to be transhipped in the labour schooners to Santo Domingo and other 'Spanish' sugar islands. Many of them either remain in Basseterre for weeks waiting for ships or even take up permanent

residence there. Thus there is always a bad crowd of 'loafers' in that town. The 'strike' was started by a small number of Basseterre men, probably not more than a dozen or so, who decided to 'march' around the island, calling at every estate and ordering the peaceful labourers to 'down tools'. A gang like this marching along a road, especially if a man at the head of them beats a drum, as was done in this case, will in the West Indies quickly attract hundreds of followers.

Threats of bodily violence were offered to the working labourers in the event of their refusal, and the result was that many of them joined the 'march', and the crowd grew to great numbers. Early in the afternoon the main gang reached the 'Lodge' estate, owned by Mr Philip Todd, a highly respected elderly white planter who for many years was on the Executive and Legislative Councils ... He met the intruders, and informed them that they were trespassing and must go ... They assumed a threatening attitude and finally struck him ... In self-protection he sent for his servant to fetch his shotgun. The gun was unloaded. They thereupon set on him, knocked him down and severely belaboured him with cudgels. They then proceeded towards Estridges estate [where the workers had not supported the strike] but were overtaken by a small number of armed police under Major Duke and were turned back to town.

[The next morning] there was serious trouble at West Farm where (after the Magistrate had twice read the necessary part of the Riot Act) it had been necessary to fire three shots, but without inflicting damage. Stone-throwing had been continuous on the part of the mob.

From about 6:15 to 7pm the forces appear to have found it impossible to control the very large mob and, again after repeated warnings, it was necessary to fire, and during this period three men were killed and eight wounded ... It was several days before really normal conditions again prevailed. (House of Commons (1935), pp. 3–6. Reproduced by kind permission of The Stationery Office)

It occurred to Lewis in London that this might be the beginning of something important. By now he had joined the Fabian Society, and he had suggested to them, despite having no formal contract at this stage, that they might be interested in a contribution about labour problems in the West Indies. In July 1935, therefore, when he returned home at the end of his second year at the LSE, he made a detour via Trinidad and St Kitts to gather material. Four years later, by which time the problem had escalated and was to be described by Lewis as a 'revolution', these field notes were to form the basis of his first publication.

1.3   The approach of this book

The aim of this book is to produce an *intellectual* biography of Arthur Lewis, to explore and evaluate his contribution to development economics from the perspective of the history of ideas, searching for a logical progression in these ideas, and identifying the social and cultural context in which his ideas emerged. At the outset we point out to the reader that constructing such a biography of Arthur Lewis faces particular problems. Lewis rarely co-authored books or papers with colleagues, which makes it difficult to trace the immediate influences on his thinking. Then, on a wider front, there is the hostility of Lewis himself to 'intellectual' history, particularly his own. Throughout his life he was unwilling to provide autobiographical information, his 'Autobiographical Account' as a Nobel Laureate being an unavoidable exception. He refused to co-operate with anyone who attempted during his lifetime to write his intellectual biography. He wrote to one of his aspiring biographers, a young researcher at the University of the West Indies: 'I am not used to the form of argument which is *ad personam* rather than *ad rem*, requiring assessment of a writer's social origins, intellectual history, motivation and degree of expatriateness in order to establish the validity or otherwise of a scientific proposition.'[19] Lewis clearly identified with those economists who are anxious to stress that they are involved in a 'scientific' activity, engaging with a discipline which they believe is independent of the personalities and experiences of those investigating it. As George Stigler famously asserted, 'when we are told we must understand a man's life to understand what he really meant, we are being invited to abandon science'.

Here we meet just one of the many paradoxes and inconsistencies that characterized Lewis. He was always reluctant to contemplate the social and cultural influences on his own intellectual journey. Yet he is renowned as a development economist who was engaged personally with development issues over a long period, and was prepared to grapple with a wide variety of social and political environments. Indeed, it is difficult to find a development economist who would claim that their work is a 'hard' science, and Lewis was no exception. He was most comfortable with changing environments, going further than this to acknowledge the contribution of other social scientists in constructing models of human behaviour. As a consequence, both as a subject and an object of life-writing, one would have expected Lewis to be *more* likely than economists in general to acknowledge the influence of a multiplicity of social and cultural factors on his own intellectual history. Yet this is not the case: just one example of many puzzles to be related in this book that confound the assumptions of his biographers.

Our book is the second full-length biography of Lewis. The first, by Lewis's friend, the Princeton historian Robert Tignor (Tignor, 2005), has been justly praised for its thorough and insightful treatment of Lewis's life. A reader is entitled to ask, then, why produce another biography? Part of the answer is provided by Tignor himself, who relates in his book how difficult he found it to write the biography of such an intensely private person, and concluded that gaps in his account remained; we have tried to fill some of these gaps. It may also be that, as economists, and more particularly as development economists from the academic community in Britain who have both been Manchester-based for significant parts of our lives, we can offer some insights on Lewis's early life and career that were not immediately apparent to Robert Tignor, who approached his task primarily from the standpoint of an economic historian at Princeton. Many of the gaps we have identified in Tignor's account concern Lewis's early years in London and Manchester, a period of his life about which he was particularly reticent in conversations with his US colleagues in later years. For example, few if any of Lewis's colleagues at Princeton would have been aware of his extensive personal engagement in social projects in Manchester in the 1950s (as related in Chapter 5), or have appreciated his significance as a policy adviser to Labour leader Hugh Gaitskell on domestic policies for the redistribution of wealth in Britain. Indeed, Lewis's early involvement in politics in Britain and the Caribbean, at a time when the British West Indies was a British dependent colony, has not been widely acknowledged. Tignor pointed out, in conversation with the authors, that pressure of time had prevented him from visiting the West Indies, and though he had interviewed academics from the Caribbean who knew Lewis personally, he had been unable to make contact with many other significant West Indian personalities and institutions which we believe played an important a role in shaping Lewis, as related in Chapter 7, as a specifically *West Indian* economist.

As biographers we have had to grapple with the strange trajectory of Lewis's career: namely, the sudden emergence of his creativity, both as a writer and a practitioner, followed by its gradual decline. The sequence of chapters follows this path, moving geographically and chronologically from St Lucia to London, to Manchester, to Ghana, then back to the Caribbean, and finally to Princeton for the three closing decades.

Chapter 2 is concerned with Lewis's time at the London School of Economics. This decade took Lewis from being a raw undergraduate arriving at the LSE from one of Britain's smallest colonies, to his final appointment there as Reader in Colonial Economics, a senior appointment in one of Britain's foremost social science institutions. This was a period full of incident, including four years at Cambridge, where the young Lewis took on a huge teaching and research role in the absence of senior colleagues undertaking war work. It was also the period in which he strengthened his links with the Fabian Colonial Bureau and the Labour Party, and met a wide variety of 'anti-imperialists' from the Colonies who had turned up in wartime London.

Chapter 3 is devoted to Lewis's engagement in a research and policy-making capacity with the Colonial Office, which began in the 1940s during his London days but ended unhappily with his failure to be re-appointed to the Board of the Colonial Development Corporation. The chapter covers his turbulent role as Secretary on the wartime Colonial Economic Advisory Committee (CEAC); his post-war membership of the Colonial Economic Development Council (CEDC); and his final engagement, and its unhappy outcome, with the Colonial Development Corporation (CDC). This is a critical chapter from the standpoint of Lewis's intellectual progress, because it marks the beginnings of his distinctive approach to the problems of developing countries – outspoken, critical and always controversial, but truly the genesis of what came later to be understood as development economics.

Chapter 4 describes Lewis's work at the University of Manchester, where he occupied the Chair of Political Economy from 1948 to 1957. This decade was Lewis's most inspirational period as a researcher. His ideas did not, however, develop in an intellectual vacuum. As we relate, there had been highly significant developments in the social sciences in Manchester during the 1930s and 1940s with the arrival of a number of 'displaced scholars' from continental Europe, many of these being social scientists who were known to Lewis. Some, such as Michael Polanyi, were close friends, and had liberal, integrative world views which were harmonious with Lewis's own.

Chapter 5 explores two significant but little-known aspects of Lewis's character and values, namely his involvement during his Manchester years in improving the welfare of disadvantaged communities in Britain, both at a practical, local level in Manchester, and as adviser to the Labour Party. He was a close friend of Labour leader Hugh Gaitskell. As we relate, Lewis allowed his social commitments to grow during the Manchester years in spite of the requirement to maintain his research output, numerous overseas visits, and the demands of his growing family. In Manchester, Lewis worked tirelessly for the Caribbean community, raising funds, lobbying prominent individuals, and eventually establishing educational centres in Hulme and Moss Side to create social networks, and deliver basic employment skills, to the black immigrant community. His socialist principles were also brought to the fore at this time in his role as policy adviser to Gaitskell. The radical policies he advocated for the redistribution of wealth in Britain remain highly relevant.

Chapter 6 assesses Lewis's work as a development practitioner. In relation to the literature on 'why visiting economists fail', it asks why Lewis's brilliant and practically-conceived policy ideas were so often unsuccessful when translated into practice. For all his deep awareness of the significance of political interests in determining the pattern of development, Lewis was taken by surprise when confronted by the intransigence of Ghana's president, Kwame Nkrumah. We argue that, in many ways, this was a failure of social networking as well as of policy advice: the crucial intermediaries upon whom Lewis had depended to impart rationality and a sense of social responsibility to Nkrumah increasingly failed to get the message across, and Lewis departed in frustration before the end of his contract.

Chapter 7 describes the events surrounding Lewis's problematic return to the Caribbean, as Principal of the University College of the West Indies, Mona, Jamaica from 1960 to 1963. This was an appointment he took up after resigning from the University of Manchester in 1958. This short period before his departure for Princeton University in 1963 marked the beginning of the end of Lewis's professional involvement with the Caribbean. There were difficulties for him at Mona: personality clashes, intransigent committees, disputes with administrators – the sorts of problems Lewis dreaded in his everyday life and which he could never resolve. Faced with situations of this type, his response was always to walk. The West Indies Federation, an issue that had long been close to his heart and on which he had staked his reputation as a consultant, also failed in 1963, though it is clear that he had already made up his mind to leave Jamaica for Princeton before the Federation collapsed. Subsequently, on leave of absence from Princeton, he enjoyed a distinguished three-year appointment as President of the Caribbean Development Bank, but rejected a number of other approaches to involve himself more directly in Caribbean matters.

Lewis's response to these reverses, as related in Chapter 8, was to retreat from the slings and arrows associated with trying to make a difference in turbulent developing countries, or even turbulent inner cities in Britain and America, and to become for the first time a full-time academic with no distractions. In this tranquil environment he was able to engage with his graduate students more than ever before, and to complete his cherished project of writing a global economic history of the late nineteenth century. But much of the vitality and joy had now gone from his mood, as well as from his creative work, and he experienced intermittent spells of depression and writer's block. When he was awarded the Nobel Prize in 1979, he was not only delighted, but amazed.

On Arthur Lewis's memorial on St Lucia is this quotation from him: 'The Fundamental Cure for Poverty is not Money but Knowledge'. The quotation encapsulates Lewis's enduring legacy, and is the subject of our concluding chapter: a commitment to development that focuses on the human condition. In this final chapter we attempt to assess the contribution of this most complex individual, as a development economist, as a practitioner and as a man. Does his legacy endure, and what relevance does it have in the world of the twenty-first century?

2
'Marvellous intellectual feasts': The LSE Years, 1933–48*

2.1 Introduction

Arthur Lewis spent a decade and a half at the London School of Economics (LSE), as a student, lecturer and researcher; and yet the record of the time he spent there is sparse. There are no personal diaries, no contemporary interviews on which to build up a picture of life at the LSE in the 1930s and 1940s from Lewis's own perspective. As his Princeton colleague and biographer Robert Tignor observed, Lewis throughout his life was an intensely private person who allowed few people access to his innermost feelings.[1] But even more than was usually the case with Lewis, he appears to have been reluctant to write about or speak of personal events and encounters in this period of his life. This is not to say that Lewis underestimated the intellectual debt that he owed to the LSE. On the contrary, over half of his short autobiographical contribution to Breit and Spencer's *Lives of the Laureates* (1986) was devoted to the intellectual legacy of the LSE, where what he described as 'marvellous intellectual feasts' were served up by teachers such as Arnold Plant, Lionel Robbins, Friedrich Hayek and John Hicks.[2] He also generously acknowledged the stimulus he had received from the company of bright and high-achieving LSE students. While Lewis mentioned no names, his distinguished contemporaries at the LSE included two trade and development economists, F. V. Meyer and Alfred Maizels. Another contemporary, born in Germany in 1915, the same year as Lewis, was the development economist H. W. Arndt, later to be a Leverhulme scholar at the LSE.[3]

What is lacking for this formative period of Lewis's life, however, is the personal and anecdotal. Having arrived at the LSE in September 1933 as a raw undergraduate from St Lucia, he left at the age of thirty-three, already holding an appointment as Reader in Colonial Economics there from 1946, to take up a full professorship in 1948 at the University of Manchester. It must have been an extraordinary 15 years for the young man from the Caribbean in terms of his personal development, his rapid academic progression, and his encounters with intellectuals from a wide social and political spectrum. He also got married in 1948, to Gladys Jacobs, a teacher and schools inspector from Grenada. Those 15 years in Britain also encompassed great world events: the inter-war depression, the rise of fascism, the Second World War, planning and post-war reconstruction, Bretton Woods, Indian independence, and the growing strength of the decolonization movements in Africa and the Caribbean. Yet, as his biographer Robert Tignor observed, this was a period about which Lewis offered little subsequently in the way of comment or recollections even to his closest friends. We learn from Lewis's short autobiography supplied to *Lives of the Laureates* that when he was in London he met many of those whom he later described as being, like himself, 'anti-imperialists', but as to the who, where and when of these encounters Lewis himself is less than forthcoming. The information such as it is has to be teased out from a variety of contemporary documents, records and pamphlets.

What is very clear is that Lewis received a great deal of support from academic colleagues during his time at the LSE, in contrast with his later experiences at the University of Manchester (see Chapter 4). At the LSE he was evidently very well regarded by a number of key academics. It is easy to underestimate the sheer hard work that would have been required of Lewis to shine at the LSE in the 1930s and 1940s. His academic record there included a first-class honours degree gained in 1937 and a doctorate in 1940. His first appointment at the LSE was as an assistant lecturer in 1940. During his time at the School, in addition to a heavy wartime teaching load in Cambridge – where the LSE had been evacuated during the war– Lewis published one book and nine papers, prepared three more books for publication, and authored significant official reports and memoranda for the Colonial Office, containing proposals that foreshadowed many of those radical ideas which later in his career would come to be characterized as the 'Lewis Model'.

Throughout his life Lewis was characterized by exceptional diligence and attention to detail, which first became apparent at the LSE. There is an interesting comparison here with Harold Wilson, born in 1916 and therefore Lewis's contemporary. Like Lewis, Harold Wilson was a student of economics, in Wilson's case at Jesus College, Oxford. Both

Wilson and Lewis were Fabian socialists as students. Both had mothers who were school teachers, and both were steeped in the Protestant work ethic. As students, neither of them had the money nor the leisure to support a lavish lifestyle. Wilson's biographer Ben Pimlott (1992, p. 52) noted that, for Wilson, 'work became a compulsion, of which he was never able to rid himself ... [At Jesus College] he worked with a ferocious determination' to gain his first-class degree. Both Lewis and Wilson were employed as economists at the Board of Trade in the 1940s but their career paths diverged significantly. Lewis went on to an academic career and a Nobel Prize for economics. In the civil service at the Board of Trade, Lewis never rose above the rank of wartime temporary principal. Wilson, on the other hand, held a senior position at the Board of Trade from the start and went on to succeed Sir Stafford Cripps as President of the Board of Trade in the Attlee administration. Thereafter, Wilson took the route of politics, going on to become leader of the Labour Party and prime minister.

2.2   The London School of Economics, 1933–45

What sort of institution was the LSE when Lewis enrolled for the B.Com. in 1933? One of the first points to note is that when Lewis joined as an undergraduate the School was still developing as a higher education institution, having first opened its doors to students some 40 years earlier, in 1895. In the beginning it had focused exclusively on 'professional studies', examining students who were generally part-time, in papers for the civil service, chambers of commerce, banking and insurance (Hayek, 1946). In 1901, the School established the first undergraduate degree and it is notable that this was not in commerce but in economics. The B.Sc. (Econ) was the first university degree in Britain devoted exclusively to the social sciences. Its establishment had not been supported by the School as a whole but was the brainchild of an inner LSE group. It took the then Director by surprise (Hayek, 1946, p. 13). The focus on commerce re-emerged when William Beveridge took over as Director of the LSE in 1919, marking a period of rapid change and expansion. It was under his directorship that the degree of B.Com. was finally established. Discussions about the need for a degree in commercial subjects at the LSE had been protracted, and the degree finally came to fruition through an educational trust established by Ernest Cassel, on the advice of Sidney Webb. Chairs and Readerships were established in Accounting, Business Methods, Commercial and Industrial Law, Banking and Currency. Hugh Dalton was appointed as the first Reader in Commerce.

The history of the long-defunct commerce degree at the LSE is interesting in the sense that when Lewis applied for a place it was a relatively new but already well-defined area of study. It had many applicants and good funding. The commerce degree was by no means a poor relation of the economics programme. As discussed in the previous chapter, Lewis had said that he had wanted to be an engineer, but neither the colonial government nor the sugar plantations in the Caribbean would employ a black engineer. As he leafed through the University of London prospectus his eye was caught by the new B. Com. degree. It offered accounting, statistics, business law, business management, languages, and two subjects called economics and economic history. Neither he nor anyone else in St Lucia knew what economics was: 'No matter. The rest of the degree was very practical and would give me the basis for a job in business or some kind of administrative work'[4] At the age of 18, Lewis was already quite pragmatic about his likely employment prospects in the Caribbean, and unusually discerning for one so young in his choice of degree. He was mature for his age and very dedicated to his studies. As he remarked in his short autobiography, he was initially apprehensive that English students would be better able to handle the degree than he could; but this proved not to be the case.

There were brilliant economists at the London School of Economics in the 1930s and 1940s, some of whom had a lasting influence on Lewis's intellectual development. In his autobiographical account for the Nobel Laureate, Lewis recalled John Hicks, Roy Allen, Nicholas Kaldor, Friedrich Hayek and Lionel Robbins. He also said, however, that his greatest personal debt was to the lesser-known Arnold Plant. The Nobel Prize winner Ronald Coase was also one of Plant's distinguished students in the 1930s, as was Arthur Seldon, the joint founder of the right-wing think tank, the Institute of Economic Affairs. His former students all speak well of Plant.

Plant, together with Lionel Robbins, was a strong exponent of the classical liberal tradition in economics at the School. He had a great breadth of scholarship, however, which clearly appealed to Lewis. Ronald Coase reports that Plant was an inspiring and generous teacher.[5] Plant had an interesting career, with aspects that would have resonated with the young Lewis.[6] In the first place, he had trained and worked very successfully as a mechanical engineer before entering the LSE. Engineering would, as noted earlier, have been Lewis's own choice of career had it not been for the colour bar in the West Indies. By the early age of 21, Plant had been appointed to a senior managerial position in an engineering firm. Then he enrolled as a student at the LSE on the advice of the businessman

William (later Lord) Piercy. He studied for the newly-established B. Com. as an external student, and graduated in 1922. Simultaneously, he was registered for the BSc (Econ), and graduated from this programme in 1923 with first-class honours. Interestingly, in the economics degree, Plant specialized in economic history, which later came to be a highly important feature of Arthur Lewis's own researches.

In 1924, Plant was appointed to the John Garlick Chair of Commerce in the Faculty of Commerce at the University of Cape Town, South Africa, where he drew up the curriculum for a new Bachelor of Commerce degree. Though he could not be described as an early 'development economist', he had observed at first-hand the problems arising out of the South African racial laws. In early papers written in South Africa, he compared the restrictions placed on black South Africans to 'those commonly employed to impede competition'. He went on to argue that

> the colour of [their] skin as a basis for privileged treatment is but one particular phase of the universal habit among the lazy or inefficient of seizing hold of an entirely irrelevant characteristic of their competitors and endeavouring to persuade the general public that it constitutes a sufficient ground for legislation against that particular class as a whole'[7]

Though Plant did not publish prolifically he maintained his interest in the economics of race and racial discrimination into the 1960s, as demonstrated in the review he wrote in 1965 of the book *The Economics of the Colour Bar* by his old University of Cape Town colleague, William Hutt.[8] Plant's work on the economics of racial discrimination foreshadowed many later analyses. Arthur Lewis himself addressed this theme in his penultimate writings (Lewis, 1985b). Lewis, true to the neoclassical principles he absorbed at the LSE, identified the circumstances in which the labour market supported discriminatory hiring practices. In an analysis that echoed Plant, he pointed out that racial differences tend to facilitate segmented markets. Group solidarity comes to the fore and minorities are kept out of the network:

> Economists see the losses imposed by discrimination as deprivation of the opportunity to contribute one's talents and skills to the making of national income. They do not appreciate the picture in which the big creatures are gathered around the feeding place while the little ones are trying, with minimal success, to push their way in. (Lewis, 1985a, ch. 2)

Lewis came under fire from some of his more radical black colleagues in his Princeton years for his conservatism on racial issues. In this context it needs to be stressed that even though his writing is very measured in tone, it is nevertheless a strong and unequivocal rejection of a labour market in which, as Lewis says, 'competition is not enough'. He is especially dismissive of those who complain that they are being displaced by minorities from the jobs or training they expected: 'Such displacement is not by accident. The expectation of the job was based on discrimination, monopoly, or market failure, and should not have existed in the first place'(ibid.).

In spite of his lasting interest in the subject, race relations was not Arnold Plant's recognized area of expertise. His appointments in South Africa and at the LSE were in the area of industrial organization, and this is where Lewis fitted in. Following the approval of his PhD and the publication of the *Economica* articles resulting from it, Lewis's research was published in book form in 1949 as *Overhead Costs: Some Essays in Economic Analysis* (Lewis, 1949b), after he had left London for Manchester. Lewis later described Arnold Plant as a 'laissez-faire' economist, and though they had what Lewis described as 'intellectual difficulties', he makes clear that this did not stand in the way of their friendship. This was often the case with Lewis. He could get along with colleagues with whom he disagreed fundamentally on an intellectual level provided he respected them as people. The big-name economists at the LSE in the 1930s were mainly in the classical liberal or neo-classical tradition, which might not have been altogether to Lewis's liking. However, at the LSE he also came into contact with political scientists. Harold Laski, for example, who held the Chair in Political Science, was also chairman of the Labour Party in 1945–6 and had a strong following at the LSE among the student body and younger academics. It was Laski who recommended Lewis as a possible correspondent and reviewer for *The Manchester Guardian*.

Lewis was particularly grateful to Robbins for introducing him to the classical economists, and in particular to the work of John Stuart Mill. Lewis, as we shall see, was not partial to either biography or autobiography, but if he had been willing to follow Keynes' precedent of writing essays in biography, then surely Mill, much closer to an alter ego than to any person in Lewis' lifetime,[9] would have been the first on his list. Lewis shared many characteristics with Mill, including intellectual precocity in childhood and adolescence, a preoccupation with technical progress as the means of staving off a zero-growth 'stationary state', a tendency to be socially redistributive while supporting free-market solutions to economic problems whenever possible, and a concern for the rights and economic advancement of women. Mill's dictum, in his *Principles of Political Economy*, that with 'universal education [and] a due limitation of the numbers of the community ... there could be no poverty, even under the present social institutions'[10] could serve also as an epigraph to many of Lewis's writings on development. Lewis did pay a small biographical tribute to the classical economists – not only to Mill but also to Ricardo, Malthus and Marx – in his famous essay on 'Economic Development with Unlimited Supplies of Labour' (Lewis, 1954), to be discussed in Chapter 4.

In summary, Lewis came under a wide range of intellectual influences during his time at the London School of Economics. They encompassed all traditions in economics, from the classical and neo-liberal wing through to Keynesian and neo-Marxist theorists. The influences came not only from economists. Among the LSE community there were distinguished sociologists and anthropologists, political scientists and political activists, people of all colours and persuasions, white conservatives and liberals, refugees from Nazi Germany, and revolutionary nationalists from Africa. Some of their beliefs stayed with Lewis throughout his life, while others he confidently and precipitously rejected out of hand. Coming from a modest academic background where no one had ever heard of 'economics', Lewis could easily have been bewildered or even disaffected by exposure to so much conflicting theorizing at an early stage in his career. Instead, he gained enormously from the breadth of scholarship at the LSE. Throughout his life, his writings were to reflect what he himself called the 'intellectual feast' he had experienced in his decade and a half at the LSE.

In his Manchester years, from 1948 onwards (see Chapter 4), Lewis began to take an interest in anthropology, and became a close colleague of Max Gluckman, the South African anthropologist. However, the role that economic anthropology played in early development economics has still to be fully documented. Certainly, it appears to have been a controversial discipline at the LSE in the 1940s and 1950s. Lewis's teacher and mentor Arnold Plant was numbered among the sceptics. When Plant was appointed chairman of the Colonial Social Science Research Council (CSSRC) he articulated official hostility to social research in the Colonies by bringing to an end its funding. In 1956, Plant was to write to Audrey Richards that colonial funding of social research did not 'meet the mood of the times'. Dependencies that were on the road to independence were suspicious of social research funded by colonial governments, believing that it could constitute covert political interference. Despite valiant efforts by Audrey Richards to counter official arguments, the CSSRC was wound up finally in 1963.[11] It is highly likely that Lewis shared or even influenced his mentor in this scepticism about the role of social research in the Colonies. Lewis always had a great deal of personal respect for anthropologists such as Gluckman and Raymond Firth, but this did not always extend to the discipline itself. Social research had been given a major role in the institutes of social and economic research that were founded in the 1940s under the Colonial Development and Welfare grants. In the Institute of Social and Economic Research (ISER) in Jamaica, for example, founded in 1948, the early focus was on models of social stratification, with research led by radical sociologists such as Lloyd Braithwaite. However, when Arthur Lewis returned to the Caribbean in the early 1960s, and set up the ISER of the Eastern Caribbean in Barbados, funded by the Ford Foundation, he placed the emphasis firmly on development economics. Under Lewis it concentrated on economic analysis supported by statistical evidence. It undertook the collection of basic statistical information on national income and foreign trade, together with feasibility studies for agriculture, industry and tourism, in order to provide a basis for development planning. 'Social' research as Lewis interpreted it was to be restricted to statistical surveys of health, housing and educational needs (Progress Report of the Institute of Social and Economic Research (Eastern Caribbean) 1963–1965).

2.3   From undergraduate student to assistant lecturer

Arnold Plant, who returned to the School from his Chair at the University of Cape Town, came to be a very strong supporter of the young black student from the Caribbean. Plant was responsible for the applied economics course that Lewis attended in the final year of his undergraduate programme. It was Plant who recommended Lewis for doctoral research in 1937 and offered him his first appointment as temporary assistant in the commerce department at the LSE, supported by a postgraduate scholarship to study for a doctorate under his supervision. The topic for the doctoral research was pricing, in circumstances where average cost exceeds marginal cost. The research set out to demonstrate how firms could cover fixed costs in such situations. Lewis was always generous in his acknowledgement of the debt he owed to Arnold Plant: 'He was my mentor and without his word at crucial points I would have received neither the scholarship nor the assistant lectureship. This was the school's first black appointment and there was a little resistance.'[12]

Frederic Benham was another key academic who had returned to the School in 1930 after six years at the University of Sydney. Lewis was not generously disposed towards Benham in later years and was heavily critical, as we relate below, of the report Benham produced in the early 1940s on Jamaica. Another key appointment made at the LSE in 1929 was that of Lionel Robbins, who returned to the School following a period as Fellow of New College, Oxford. Robbins taught the principles of economics course, which contributed one-third to Lewis's final exams for the undergraduate degree. Lionel Robbins, Friedrich Hayek, Roy Allen and John Hicks were the established 'big names' at the LSE. Lewis later described them as being in the vanguard of neo-classical economics and vociferous in their attacks on the new Keynesian doctrines that were espoused by the younger lecturers (Lewis, in Breit and Spencer (1986), p. 4).

Lewis was awarded his PhD from the University of London in 1940, for the dissertation eventually called *The Economics of Loyalty Contracts,* for which Plant had recommended and supported him. The thesis (Lewis, 1940a) discusses firms' practice of offering a discount to customers who stay loyal to the supplier, a practice that is now universal in the shape of devices such as the 'Tesco card' or 'Boots card', but was relatively rare in wartime Britain, and both the choice of topic and Lewis's treatment of the theme can be seen as very forward-looking. He analyses loyalty contracts as ways by which firms try to cope with fluctuations in demand in the face of inescapable regular overhead costs, and warns (Lewis, 1940a, ch. 4) that while, in a state of active competition, loyalty contracts enable the public to derive dividends from the stabilization of the market, the opposite is the case if conditions are monopolistic. He gives the Lancashire cotton industry, the steel industry and tied breweries (Lewis, 1940a, pp. 127, 128, 158) as examples of the latter case, where the firm's competitiveness and the consumers' welfare have both suffered through the imposition of loyalty contracts. He is alert to the possibility that bulk discounts may be regressive (Lewis, 1940a, Appendix A), as in the case of the low-income commuter who cannot afford an annual season ticket and has to buy a monthly one even though the annual one would cost him less. The thesis is the foundation of Lewis's reputation in industrial economics, and of his own self-confidence as an analytical economist.

In 1941, Lewis, his thesis now approved and starting to appear as a series of articles in *Economica,* was recognized formally by the University of London Senate as a teacher of economics at the LSE. In 1942, he was appointed external examiner in applied economics, to replace Frederic Benham, who had travelled to the West Indies as economic adviser to the Comptroller for Development and Welfare. The University of London needed to make stringent efforts at this time to have the teaching staff of its constituent colleges released from war service. The LSE had already relocated to Cambridge, where it was accommodated in 'The Hostel', a new building at Peterhouse. Lewis was one of a relatively small number of academics from the LSE not recruited to the civil service or armed services and therefore he was free to teach the undergraduates who had been relocated to Cambridge.

Teaching at Cambridge was onerous. The numbers of LSE students did not fall proportionately with the numbers of staff available. The average age of students fell, and the proportion of women students rose.[13] Kari Polanyi Levitt, the daughter of Karl Polanyi, was an LSE undergraduate in the 1940s and was taught economics by Lewis at Cambridge. Her recollection is that the economics classes were very large. She recalls that they comprised both Cambridge and LSE undergraduates. Ralf Dahrendorf, in his history of the School, claims that during the Cambridge sojourn LSE lectures and classes in economics and Cambridge teaching in economics became 'increasingly intertwined' (Dahrendorf, 1995, p. 345). Kari Polanyi has strong recollections of Lewis's teaching at Cambridge. She remembers him drawing the marginal product of labour curve for students pointing out the relationship between the demand for labour and the wage rate, and true to his neo-classical training stressed that a lower wage rate must lead to an increase in employment. After the lecture was finished, Kari approached Lewis and disagreed. She referred to the Keynesian case and the unemployment of the 1930s that could not be resolved by wage cuts. In an interview in 2006, she recounted with humour her teacher's somewhat pompous reply: 'Miss Polanyi, I assume that you have come to [the] LSE to study economic science. When you have studied it, come back and I will answer your question.'[14] Kari Levitt's memories of the large numbers of students in the School's economics lectures in Cambridge is borne out by the records of the time. The economics lectures were held in the University's Biochemical Laboratory or, failing that, in rooms in Mill Lane. When the LSE asked for more lecture rooms it was told that the University needed the accommodation for its own students. Nevertheless, the LSE seems to have been privileged in comparison with the other London colleges. The Principal of King's College, University of London, was refused accommodation for 500 students in Cambridge, on the grounds that the lecture theatres were 'already fully occupied from 9.00 in the morning until 5.00 in the evening' with evacuated students from the LSE and Bedford College for Women.[15]

The LSE Calendar for 1942–3, issued from the School's wartime address at Peterhouse, Cambridge, gives details of the lectures Lewis delivered at Cambridge. On Tuesday mornings, during the Michaelmas and Lent Terms, he was responsible for a total of 24 lectures on the economics of transport. (On Tuesday afternoons, Rosenstein-Rodan lectured the students on the theory of production). In the Summer Term at Cambridge, Lewis conducted a Friday afternoon class on the Economics of Transport. Additionally, in the Michaelmas and Lent Terms, Lewis provided 18 lectures on the organization of business enterprises and problems of business policy, and 24 classes in elements of economics, covering topics in money, banking and international trade. By any standards this was a substantial teaching load for a young and inexperienced academic who was heavily involved in research, and it took its toll on Lewis's health. In Dahrendorf's history of the LSE there is a photograph of the young Lewis, with Hayek and their students, at Cambridge in 1942. Lewis, always a serious figure, looks much older than his 27 years.

It was while teaching in Cambridge that the 'Colonial Office connection' and thus Lewis's work on development economics, began. Despite substantial teaching duties in the new environment of Cambridge, at this point in his career Lewis was already involved in his first serious piece of research for the Colonial Office under the auspices of the LSE. In August 1941, Lord Hailey, by then at the Colonial Office, notified Carr-Saunders, the Director of LSE, that William Beveridge (Under-Secretary at the Ministry of Labour), needed a Memorandum to be prepared on the financing of mining and industrial development in the Colonies. It would seem from the surviving correspondence that Lewis was the one who followed up the approach from Beveridge with a visit to the Colonial Office in London. The tone Lewis adopted during this visit can perhaps be gauged from the letter Hailey subsequently sent to him. It stressed that 'plantation enterprises [were] not to be considered'; 'LSE [should] prepare a factual Statement', and that 'the work should be confined to ascertaining the facts and making a precise survey of the issues involved'.[16] It seems that Lewis had pressed the case with Hailey to include plantation agriculture in the survey. After all, Lewis was from a plantation economy in the Caribbean and presumably had a special interest in the topic. It would also seem that Lewis was hoping to embark on a much wider brief than a straightforward statement of the 'facts'. Carr-Saunders then wrote to Hailey saying that it had been agreed by his colleagues in the School, after discussion, that 'Dr W. A. Lewis would be the most suitable member of staff' to carry out the required research.[17] However, Hailey needed to be convinced. He had asked for the co-operation of the School rather than any one member of staff. Lewis, moreover, still persisted in his view that a wider brief was needed and had written to Lord Hailey querying what the Colonial Office meant by 'factual statements' and enclosing a synopsis of his own proposals for the research. Hailey was clearly put out and told the young researcher that 'it appears from your synopsis that you are contemplating going beyond an objective factual statement to suggestions as to what should be done in the future'; Lewis should 'keep objective factual statements and your own proposals separated one from another'.[18]

What is fascinating in this exchange is the confidence of Lewis, then a very junior lecturer, which encouraged him to question the ideas of Lord Hailey in this way. Hailey, a former Governor of the United Provinces, was a man very much senior to Lewis in age as well as status. Though his influence at the Colonial Office was beginning to wane, Hailey remained a prominent adviser on colonial issues and a recognized authority on African issues well into the 1950s. Characteristically, Lewis went his own way on his first research project. His *Memorandum on the Flow of Capital into the British Colonies* when it appeared in April 1942 (Lewis, 1942b) contained far more than simple factual statements: it was his first venture into the previously undiscovered world of development economics. He had extended his brief to cover plantations. He had made contact with and was given the co-operation of the Cadbury family soon after the project started, and visited Birmingham on a number of occasions to discuss the operation of the Cadbury cocoa plantations in West Africa.[19]

Lewis was teaching in Cambridge when he was carrying out this research, and it is clear from correspondence with LSE Director Carr-Saunders that he found the combination of teaching and research very demanding. 'The bulk of my work on the subject will have to be postponed to the Xmas vacation when I shall be able to spend two or three weeks in the CO [Colonial Office] library' (LSE Archives: Lewis to Carr-Saunders, November 1941). Lewis had already asked Carr-Saunders for the help of a part-time research assistant but it does not appear that his request was granted. There was in any case only a handful of research students and research assistants remaining at the LSE during wartime. There were also financial difficulties. Lewis was always short of money and needed travelling expenses to visit London from Cambridge. When away from Cambridge he still had to pay his landlady, Mrs Beales, a guinea a week to retain his room. He asked if these expenses could be charged to the project.[20] Mrs Beales was the wife of the LSE economic historian Lance Beales, who owned a large house in Cambridge, and other LSE faculty also lodged there. Lionel Robbins was one of several who recalled his stay with the Beales', where 'the old atmosphere of good talk and stimulating contacts persisted' (quoted in Dahrendorf, 1995, p. 347).

Lewis had decided to conduct the bulk of his research in London, in the Colonial Office library. We know that in Cambridge he would have had access to the University and Marshall libraries, but resources there were unsuited to research on contemporary colonial issues. It may also have been the case that, as a young researcher from the LSE, Lewis could not count on much support from the Cambridge economics establishment. Piero Sraffa, who was the acting Librarian in Cambridge at the time, and who had only recently returned from internment, had already written to Carr-Saunders asking that the LSE recompense the University Library for books missing from the Marshall Library, books that were 'not of the type that Cambridge men are in the habit of using' (LSE Archives: Correspondence between Sraffa and Carr–Saunders, 1941). Sraffa also held the London visitors responsible for extra wear and tear on books and furnishings, for increased overtime for the domestic staff and, in a dramatic finale, for the disappearance of a *Facit* calculating machine from the Statistical Room of the Marshall Library. It was hardly a warm welcome from the Librarian for the evacuees from the LSE.

For whatever reason, Lewis seems to have preferred to carry out his research in London, though there were meetings in Cambridge to discuss the progress of the work. One meeting at Peterhouse in November 1941 involved Lord Hailey and the senior LSE academics, R. W. Firth, Frederic Benham, Vera Anstey and Dudley Stamp. However, the growing involvement of the LSE in Colonial Office research had already provoked a response from the Colonial Research Group at Oxford's Nuffield College. Lord Hailey had been instrumental in the setting up of that group. It was led by the redoubtable Margery Perham, the respected and well-connected Africanist at Nuffield College. She and her colleagues in the Oxford Research Group (Radcliffe-Brown, G. D. H. Cole, R. Coupland, A. G. B. Fisher and Sir Allan Pym) had long enjoyed the support of Hailey and were clearly disappointed by the switch of allegiance to the LSE by the Colonial Office. Relations between the LSE academics and the Oxford Group could not have been helped by the bitter and damning review of Margery Perham's book *Africans and British Rule* that Lewis had written for the *Newsletter of the League of Coloured Peoples* earlier in the year.[21]

The brusque letter Carr-Saunders received from the Nuffield Group no doubt reflected a measure of hurt feelings following the review, as well as changing fortunes at the Colonial Office, where the influence of Lord Hailey and the traditionalists was on the wane. The Colonial Research Group in Oxford reminded Carr-Saunders that it was 'in constant touch with Lord Hailey' and expected to be kept fully informed of the progress of the research on capital flows.[22]

Lewis completed his research on the flow of capital into the Colonies by the spring of 1942. He had researched and drafted the Memorandum, 'Some Aspects of the Flow of Capital into the British Colonies' (Lewis, 1942b) in less than six months. He wrote to Carr-Saunders, 'Herewith draft memorandum for Lord Hailey. I am sorry it is so long delayed but it proved quite impossible to do any work in term time. It is about 16,000 words' (LSE archives: Letter from Lewis to Carr-Saunders, 31 March 1942). The paper is a milestone. Without any precedents to guide him, Lewis went beyond the requested 'factual statement' mapping out the flow of capital into the British African and Caribbean colonies, and proposed the bare bones of an explanatory model of the driving forces which explain that flow. This model contains the propositions: (1) the ratio of saving to income is key for economic development (p. 13); (2) the surpluses built up by businesses operating in the developing world are key for determining the savings ratio (pp. 4, 12–13); and, most important, (3) the flow of capital into and through the colonial economies is characterized by severe risks and market imperfections which are also key to determining the pace and character of development, and which need to be remedied by government policy (pp. 3, 10, 15). All of these, of course, were propositions that would play a key role in Lewis's creative 'purple patch' of 1950–4. Under the last of these headings were political economy issues that would also play a major role in Lewis's later work, such as the reluctance of banks and merchant houses to invest in business propositions in the Colonies, the 'drain' of colonial surpluses from the Colonies back to Europe, and the difficulties that small businesses in least developed countries (LDCs) experience in raising capital, are also explored (pp. 6–7, 14, 15).[23] Mineral development in Africa is exposed as basically a giant oligopoly with interlocking directorships everywhere (p. 27) and possible fiscal responses to this by government, including nationalization and planning, are considered (pp. 24–5, 28, 31). Lewis explicitly questions here whether much of the capital that had flowed into the Colonies had maximized the welfare of colonial peoples (Ingham, 1992, p. 704). At this point, the tone becomes personal in a way that is quite alien to Lewis's work on industrial economics, and which readers of Lewis's subsequent work will readily recognize:

> [Development through multinational companies] is unlikely to pro-vide all the capital that is required by the small miner, the factory, and the farmer. In these days, when there is so much talk of develop-ing secondary industries in the Colonies, this fact cannot easily be over-emphasised. Suppose that a man wishes [to borrow] £10,000 to start a shoe factory in Jamaica or the Gold Coast. Where can he get it? Not in the London market: not from the banks ... Unless the small man can be given access to the capital market, the development of secondary industry must be handicapped, and cannot hope to be independent of producers elsewhere.[24]

This paper's insights on the imperfection of developing-country cap-ital markets pave the way for Rosenstein-Rodan's 1943 paper on the economic problems of Eastern and South-Eastern Europe (which also applied the idea of external economies to developing countries, and, by a delightful coincidence, used the illustration of an incipient shoe factory to make its point), as well as for Lewis's paper with Durbin, of the same year, on colonial economic policy: the two papers that, as we argue in our next chapter, mark the beginnings of development eco-nomics as a discipline.

The heavy load of teaching and research in two quite separate areas, however, took its toll on Lewis's health. In April 1942 he was admitted to hospital in London where he was operated on for the removal of his appendix. It seems that this operation was not wholly successful in treating his symptoms. Two years later, Lewis was back in the Woolwich Memorial Hospital, where he was diagnosed with a duodenal ulcer.

2.4   Publications

Lewis published three papers in *Economica* between 1941 and 1946 that were based on the material in his doctoral thesis, later to be published in the book *Overhead Costs*.[25] In each of these papers the reader can find something that reinforces or challenges current concerns about the behaviour of firms. In the paper 'The Two-part Tariff', Lewis examined the incentives to two-part charging. He clearly distinguished five sets of circumstances in which a business would seek to make a fixed charge as well as a charge related to units consumed. The first circumstance, as in electricity supply, is where equipment is left idle for periods of time in consequence of periodic *fluctuations* in demand. Second, a business might choose a two-part tariff to escape *risks* of unforeseeable changes in demand. A third set of circumstances is when a business tries to extract some of the *consumer's surplus*. Fourth, the two-part tariff could be a form of *price discrimination*. Finally, two-part charging could be based on the existence of differential *customer costs*, which do not vary with consumption. Much of Lewis's analysis of differential customer costs remains relevant today. One has only to think of current debates about the higher charges made to consumers of gas and electricity who use pre-payment meters. The paper goes on to explore, developing the final chapter of Lewis's PhD, whether two-part tariffs are in consumers' interest. Again, the debate is very up-to-date in tone, with Lewis arguing that 'the public's principal safeguard against the abuses of tariff making is competition, which makes exploitation impossible' (Lewis, 1941).

The paper 'The Effects of Loyalty' takes on an interesting and related question, namely the reasons why a firm may differentiate between loyal and disloyal customers. Again, it is a question with modern resonances in an era of widespread use of loyalty cards and loyalty discounts. Lewis argues that discounts may emerge even in highly competitive industries if they are related to costs of supply. For example, if the sales are made on a credit basis only one account will be necessary for the loyal customer who offers repeat business. There can be real economies in quantity selling, and quantity discounts can often be justified on the grounds of lower costs. But loyalty discounts may have a more sinister purpose if they are used to maintain or extend a monopoly position. One of the examples Lewis gave, as we saw from his doctoral thesis, was of the 'tied' public house, which has been outlawed only in more recent times. In Lewis's analysis, the brewers who imposed 'loyalty' on their tenants by insisting that they should purchase only that brewer's beers, wines and spirits were exploiting both tenant and public.

Finally, the third of the papers in *Economica*, 'Fixed Costs' (1946) is a significant analysis of the co-ordination of investment decisions in industries with a high ratio of fixed to variable costs, and where similar services are supplied. The examples given are gas and electricity, and road and rail transport. Lewis goes on to explore the implications of investment decisions in these circumstances. For example, if a rail company is contemplating laying a new track, its decision whether to go ahead or not might depend on whether a road authority decides to build a feeder or parallel road. Can price competition secure proper co-ordination of investment decisions in these circumstances? Lewis believed that the answer, on balance, was 'Yes'. Nationalizing these enterprises to co-ordinate investment decisions was therefore unnecessary and would lead to bureaucratic inefficiencies. It was not necessary to nationalize the railways and road transport to co-ordinate investment decisions. The market could be relied on to carry out this function. The case for nationalizing the railways could only be based on scale economies, and this would lead to the concentration of economic power. Even so, scale economies applied only to the tracks and not the trains ... possibly anticipating more recent debates about the splitting of 'tracks' and 'trains' when the railways were later denationalized in the UK.

In the 'Fixed Costs' article, Lewis came down in favour of competitive market solutions wherever possible, to resolve issues of co-ordination for infrastructural investments. This argument was taken an important stage further in the book *The Principles of Economic Planning*. This book first saw the light of day in the summer of 1948 as a Fabian Society pamphlet. As Lewis makes clear in his Preface to the new edition in 1950, its reception as a Fabian pamphlet had been rather mixed. Some colleagues complained that it was an anti-planning book, while others criticized the author for his excessive fondness for government intervention. Not for the first time, Lewis occupied the rather uncomfortable middle-ground position, attacked from both the right and the left. In the planning debate, Lewis, as he said, had little sympathy 'for those who wish to proceed mainly by surrounding people by licences, quotas, and other orders specifying where they may work, what they may make, where and what they may buy, and to whom they may sell'. What he called 'planning by direction' was costly, inefficient, and had a stifling effect on enterprise. Instead, he envisaged a market economy 'modified by state action at many crucial points'. This was to be the hallmark of Lewis's economics throughout his long academic career. A great deal in his book has stood the test of time; for example, the emphasis throughout on the need for governments to encourage greater mobility of factors of production because 'the smoothness with which the market economy functions depends on the extent to which resources are mobile; it is immobility that necessitates planning by direction' (Lewis, 1949c, p. 86). There was also a chapter entitled 'Fair Shares for All', a hallmark of Lewis's socialist credentials, placed firmly at the beginning of the book and not as an afterthought towards the end, as distribution issues so often are in economics texts. In this chapter, Lewis claimed that progressive income taxes had probably gone as far as they could in the UK in redistributing income. Instead, the emphasis needed to

be placed on the redistribution of assets through death duties and lev-
ies on capital. More than this, the state should actively seek to reduce
inequality of opportunity in education and employment. There is nothing
remotely dated about the emphasis Lewis placed on equality of opportunity, nor on the role he envisaged for the development of human
capital, both as a means of increasing opportunities and as a way of
enhancing labour mobility in a mixed economy.

Lewis also wrote four other books during his London years. There
was *Economic Problems of Today*, written and published in 1940 (Lewis,
1940b), just after he had finished his doctorate; plus three books that
were written in London but not published until after he had left the
LSE. These three were *Overhead Costs: Some Essays in Economic Analysis*
(1949); *Economic Survey, 1919–1939* (1949); and *The Principles of Economic
Planning* (1949). The first book tends to be overlooked and regarded as
'lightweight', which is unfortunate. The book was written, as Lewis
says in the Preface, not for the specialist economist but for the general
reader, and he acknowledged the important role of 'intelligent layman'
played by his friend L. A. H. McShine, who had caused Lewis to clar-
ify the exposition.[26] There is a tendency to underestimate economics
when it is written in a simple style. This book is no exception but its
simplicity is deceptive. As an example, the chapter entitled 'Property'
raises a number of difficult ethical and philosophical questions for the
economist. The arguments developed for reforming inheritance tax to
achieve a wider distribution of property in a 'mixed' economy have not
dated at all. It is worth quoting from the Preface to Lewis's book as it
encapsulates what he believed about the role of economics in everyday
life, and his role as a teacher of economics:

> Sooner or later, at work or at the polls, every one of us is called upon
> to pass judgement on these issues, so as to shape and reshape the
> social conditions in which we live. To fail to understand them is
> to pass the initiative into the hands of groups whose actions may
> change the whole pattern of our lives ... let the fate of Germany be
> a warning to any who would leave it to 'politicians' to settle these
> matters for him. (Lewis, 1940b, p. v)

The remaining three books Lewis completed while at the LSE are
better known. *Overhead Costs*, mentioned above, was based on the
research in industrial organization that Lewis carried out for his doctoral thesis. *The Principles of Economic Planning*, based on a Fabian
pamphlet, was written, as Lewis wryly pointed out in his Nobel

Autobiographical Account, in what passed for his 'spare time' in his London days. It deals with aspects of planning in a 'mixed' economy. The third book, *Economic Survey, 1919–1939*, was a study of the inter-war depression based on the lectures Lewis gave at the LSE between 1944 and 1948, and is Lewis' first foray into global economic history. Both its origins and its long-term consequences are fascinating. The book originated because one day in 1945 Friedrich von Hayek, the LSE's head of the Economics Department at that time, asked Lewis to do a set of lectures on the economic history of the inter-war period. Lewis, so the story goes (Lewis, 1986), protested that he knew nothing about this subject, only to receive from Hayek the riposte that 'the best way to learn a subject is to teach it'.[27] So teach it he did, and *Economic Survey*, which emerged from this, reviews separately the macro-economic experience of both trends and cycles in Britain, Germany, France, the USA, Japan and Russia between the wars, before combining the separate stories into a global perspective and considering the implications for future trade and investment policies. Lewis insisted that the book 'is not intended for professional economists at all [but rather] for students at about second year level',[28] but in spite of his disclaimers it has a claim to be considered one of the first works of global economic history; at that stage, national accounts for the world economy, not to mention for developing countries as a whole, did not exist, and so all Lewis could do was to combine the rather skeletal macro data that existed at the time for the six countries mentioned with trade data for the rest of the world. Though Lewis had much else on his plate at this time and did not follow up on this lead until he left the LSE, a seed was sown at this time which was to bear fruit for the rest of his working life.

At Manchester, as we shall explore in Chapter 4, he made several attempts to model global production, prices and trade, and later became concerned with understanding the developing-country part of the picture – why positive shocks are converted into sustained growth in some developing countries but not in others, a research programme which sustained him for most of his Princeton period during the 1960s and 1970s. Being asked to teach something one knows nothing about may, as in this case, have a remarkable research payoff.

Taken together, what is so astonishing about these three books is the sheer breadth of the subject matter. They range over price theory and its applications, political economy and global economic history. The insights are all the more remarkable when it is recalled that Lewis was then at the very beginning of his career in economics.

2.5   Communicating with the public

Unusually for LSE economists of his generation, Lewis was a pioneer in the art of public relations. In his LSE days he was seldom out of the newspapers, reviewing books, and even films, for *The Keys* (the journal of the League of Coloured Peoples), and offering serious comment on a variety of economic issues. He was outspoken and uncompromising in his views.

The problems he presented for editors surfaced in his dealings with *The Manchester Guardian*. Lewis wrote articles and reviews for the paper from 1945 to 1955, a period when it was under the famous editorship of A. P. Wadsworth. Under Wadsworth, the paper maintained its radical and critical credentials, but moved more to the centre-left. In Labour Party shorthand, it was Ernest Bevin, rather than Aneurin Bevan. Wadsworth first wrote to Lewis at Peterhouse in June 1945, a month before the General Election that to put the Attlee government into power:

> Harold Laski tells me that you have got released from Government shackles and suggests that you might like to write an article for us on Benham's report on the economic future of Jamaica. I should be extremely glad if you could, and would suggest a length of about 950 words. (*Manchester Guardian* Archives: Letter from A. P. Wadsworth to W. A. Lewis Esq., June 1945)

Harold Laski, who had recommended Lewis to Wadsworth on his release from the Board of Trade, was a prominent Fabian, as was Harold Wilson.[29] (Wilson remained a member of the Fabian Society executive until 1945.) Lewis accepted Wadsworth's invitation, and sent the review to Wadsworth just days ahead of the 1945 election: 'herewith the promised article on Benham's Report. When one disagrees so completely with an important state paper, it is Herculean to confine oneself to 950 words' (*Manchester Guardian* Archives, Letter from Arthur Lewis to Wadsworth, July 1945). This review of the Benham Report was an example of Lewis's rhetorical talent, expressed in withering critiques of books and reports with which he disagreed. There is little doubt that his review would have incurred deep displeasure in some influential circles, particularly as the principal author of the Report, Frederic Benham, was a senior colleague of Lewis at the LSE, where he held a Chair in the Commerce Department. Wadsworth, no doubt wisely, drew back from giving Lewis's article the formal blessing of *The Manchester Guardian* (whose motto is 'Comment is free, facts are sacred').[30] Wadsworth replied to Lewis:

> I am a little doubtful whether your analysis of the Benham Report is not too critical to be used as an article. I mean it would be criticised as not giving quite an adequate account of the proposals demolished. It would however, do admirably in our correspondence columns, and it would, of course, be paid for at article rates. (Wadsworth to Lewis, August 1945)

We do not have a record of the original review of the Benham Report that Lewis submitted to the newspaper. He did publish elsewhere, however, a long and highly critical article about the Benham Report.[31] In all likelihood this was substantially the one that Wadsworth rejected. The letter that Lewis substituted, which appeared in *The Manchester Guardian* in August 1945, was stinging in its criticism of the Benham Report. Lewis accused the author of the report of making 'elementary errors' in his desire to discourage 'at all costs' a policy of industrialization in Jamaica. The report was 'naïve' in suggesting that the Jamaican balance of payments could be righted simply by exhorting workers to become more productive. According to Lewis, 'twice as many people [were] trying to live on the land as it can support and this is the principal cause of the very high level of unemployment which is the island's gravest social problem'. There were 'technical errors' too, and the report 'does not even see the significance of the figures it publishes'. The report 'fails miserably'. The policy it advocates is 'most dangerous'. It would 'increase unemployment, prevent development and bankrupt the island' (Lewis, Letter to *The Manchester Guardian*, 17 August 1945). It is difficult not to detect a personal element in this review. Possibly Lewis resented the fact that it was Benham and not himself who had been appointed to conduct the enquiry into the economic future of Jamaica, though a significant factor in the appointment of Benham must have been that he had already spent three years in the West Indies, as an economic adviser. Benham had been educated in the classical liberal tradition, and as a disciple of Edwin Cannan at the LSE he was a strong opponent of tariffs and other forms of trade protection, which Lewis favoured at this point in his career. But this could not explain why Lewis produced such a damning review. After all, Arnold Plant, with whom Lewis always maintained very cordial relations, was an equally strong advocate of the benefits of an unfettered price mechanism. It is unlikely that Lewis would ever have penned such a hostile review of Plant's work.

In 1948, after Lewis had moved to the University of Manchester, he submitted another article to *The Manchester Guardian* with which the Editor disagreed. This time it was an article advocating an export tax on cotton goods from the UK. Bearing in mind the liberal free trade antecedents of the paper, this was not a happy choice. It is hardly surprising that the Editor declined the article, saying that 'the views you put are very different from ours ... we are afraid that the loss of good will, both political and commercial, caused by an export tax would be far greater than we can afford' (Acting Editor of *The Manchester Guardian* to Lewis, June 1945). Lewis was asked once more to replace the article with a letter. More congenial, however, would have been the invitation from Wadsworth for Lewis to review a recent book by the late Evan Durbin: 'I kept it back for you because it would be nice to have it treated with a little sympathy, and I am afraid that most of our academic colleagues would hardly approach it in that way' (*Manchester Guardian* Archives: Wadsworth to Lewis, November 1949). The book in question was Durbin's *Problems in Economic Planning*, published posthumously in 1949. Durbin, a Fabian socialist, had been one of the strongest supporters of Lewis on the Colonial Economic Advisory Committee and may indeed have been instrumental in getting him appointed as Secretary to the Committee. Durbin was a lecturer in economics at the LSE when Lewis arrived as an undergraduate. At the outbreak of war he had joined the economic section of the War Cabinet and was later appointed personal assistant to Clement Attlee. In 1945, he was one of the new Labour MPs, a group that included Hugh Gaitskell, Richard Crossman and Harold Wilson.

Throughout his life Lewis went on to write short articles, letters and reviews on a variety of topics for newspapers and periodicals. In this way he communicated with a wide range of people unconnected with his academic and political life. In his London days he was both editor and a regular contributor to *The Keys*. In this role he did not confine himself to economics but tackled head-on the racial discrimination and exploitation familiar in the everyday experiences of his readership. Even the popular film *Gone with the Wind* became the subject of one of his critical reviews. His conclusion was that its depiction of black people as a group whose every act was comic was unlikely to improve the image of black people.

In his London days, as was evident in his treatment of Margery Perham's and Frederic Benham's work, Lewis could write highly critical, even offensive, reviews of anything or anyone with whom he disagreed.

It is interesting that the South African-born activist and writer, Peter Abrahams, tells us that, in left-wing circles in London in the 1940s:

> the competition to be published was fierce, fiercer if anything than the competition for certain jobs. And any means to put down the competition was used. Racial prejudice, sex discrimination and sneering at each other's work were all fair game. Book reviews were means for cutting down some and promoting others. (Abrahams, 2000, p. 43)

It is highly probable that Lewis sought out book and film reviews to provide much-needed additional income at this point in his career. When the LSE was evacuated to Cambridge he had found it difficult to meet the additional costs of lodgings in London to carry out his research. He lodged in Redcliffe Gardens, Chelsea, even then a cosmopolitan and bohemian locality favoured by artists and writers. It is salutary to remember that many of Lewis's colleagues at the LSE would have been much more financially secure than he was – they were often public-school men coming from well-to-do backgrounds. Even those from modest backgrounds could usually count on support from family and friends close at hand to help them at critical points in their career. Lewis, like most of his young contemporaries from the Caribbean, had none of these advantages, and until he had become firmly established as an academic, his financial situation must have been quite precarious.

2.6 The final years: the LSE post-war

By 1945, Lewis had been 'released' from a temporary post at the Board of Trade and had returned to academic life in Cambridge. He had been employed on a part-time basis at the Board of Trade since 1943. The Minutes of the LSE Professorial Council for 1943 record that Dr Lewis had received permission to accept a part-time administrative position with the Commodities and Relief Department of the Board of Trade. The Council was assured that Lewis would be able to continue his lecturing duties at Cambridge. It is noteworthy that his initial appointment was not at a high level. Lewis was appointed as an Administrative Officer Grade 1, though it appears that on leaving the Board of Trade his status had risen to that of Principal. The comparison with Harold Wilson, who was on a very different trajectory at the Board of Trade, is interesting. Wilson, previously research assistant to Beveridge, had been appointed to a senior position in the Mines Department at the Board of

Trade in 1942, having been strongly supported in this appointment by Hugh Dalton, the president of the Board of Trade. In 1943, when Lewis was offered the appointment of Administrative Officer Grade 1, Wilson was already in the US as a representative of the Board of Trade on the Committee of the Anglo-American Combined Chief of Staffs.

It is tempting to speculate on whether 'colour' played any role in Lewis's early release from the Board of Trade, since the best temporaries were usually asked (and expected) to stay on in the civil service. Lewis was never offered a permanent post, unlike Harold Wilson who, when he wanted to stand for election to the House of Commons in the 1945 election, had to engineer his early release from the Board of Trade. Wilson left the civil service with an OBE in the 1945 honours list.

Lewis returned to being a full-time economics teacher at the LSE, but his work there now bore the impress of his Colonial Office experiences. Robert Tignor's biography of Lewis stresses the high regard for Lewis's teaching, as revealed in the LSE staff files. Indeed, no lesser a person than Hayek had described Lewis as 'one of our best teachers'. The range of his teaching at the LSE was unusually wide, from economic theory, business economics and transport economics to economic history and the inter-war economy of Europe and North America. From 1944, he also offered a course in colonial economics in London, and when he was appointed Reader at the LSE in 1947 it was designated in the area of colonial economics.

Lewis's role in London's colonial studies activities is worth closer scrutiny. Colonial studies and colonial economics saw important changes during the 1940s. In the late 1930s, under pressure from the Colonial Office, colonial studies had been the subject of review at the places where it was taught, principally Oxford, Cambridge and London University. In response to questions from the Colonial Office, the University of London Senate had set up a special advisory board on colonial studies in 1942, recognizing that 'in the post-war period a new era in colonial development is bound to open and measures of reorganization and development are already being planned at the Colonial Office'.[32] A survey of what was on offer at Oxford and Cambridge had been requested by the Colonial Office in 1938. At Oxbridge, the courses had scarcely changed since they were introduced a decade earlier, with the aim at that time of preparing cadets for the Colonial Service. At all three institutions, London, Oxford and Cambridge, the courses in colonial studies ran for a single academic year. Economics was only one of the disciplines covered. The focus in economics was on economic theory, and currency and banking. Other subjects covered were law, anthropology, languages, history, geography and colonial administration. Margery Perham was the examiner in colonial administration for all these courses.

Lewis always claimed that the economics taught on the one-year vocational courses in colonial studies was not what we understand now as development economics. Lewis made this clear in his Laureate autobiographical note, claiming that he did not teach development economics as such until he arrived at Manchester. Rather, on the colonial economics course in London Lewis said he taught what he called 'elementary economics' with an emphasis on economic policy. Closer scrutiny reveals that this was not strictly true. The colonial economics course Lewis taught at the LSE was in two parts. True, the first part was a conventional introduction to microeconomics: the price system, and exchange and specialization, though possibly with a greater emphasis on the functional distribution of income than would be expected in a standard course in economics. However, the second part of the course, entitled 'Applied Economics for Colonial Students' was very much in the development economics mould. The LSE Calendar for 1947 lists its components as 'agricultural economics; population density; land tenure; marketing, credit, and co-operation; international commodity arrangements; seasonal fluctuations; secondary industries including handicrafts; the role of the state in development; and imperial preference. The course was delivered by Lewis. It is difficult to imagine anything closer to 'development economics' in British universities and university colleges in 1947. It is possible, however, that Lewis had left the LSE for Manchester by the time Part II was due to be delivered.

Until 1945, the scholars selected for training on courses for officers in the colonial service were exclusively from Britain, were male, white, and overwhelmingly graduates of either Oxford or Cambridge. Their fees on the colonial studies courses were paid by the Crown Agents. It was not until 1947 that the Colonial Office made it known that it would welcome a few locally recruited officers on colonial studies courses as well as some ex-servicemen who had missed out on a University education. This is a point worth stressing, because it places in context the rejection Lewis himself received when he applied for a post in the colonial service as an administrator in Port of Spain, Trinidad, after he had graduated with first-class honours from the LSE in 1937. The rejection Lewis received could not have been wholly unexpected by him, given the norms of the time. Tignor recalls that, in later years, Lewis referred to this experience only in the presence of individuals with whom he had a personal friendship, whom he knew to be sympathetic, and that this rejection by the civil service in Trinidad had left its mark on him.

By the date of Lewis's promotion in 1947 to Reader in Colonial Economics at the LSE, Arnold Plant had returned from wartime service to take on the Business Administration course previously delivered by Lewis. Similarly, Lewis's connection with Transport at the LSE ended with the appointment of Gilbert Ponsonby (later Reader in Transport), who delivered the Economics of Transport course. Lewis's designation as lecturer at the LSE had been 'with special reference to Transport'. We do not know how Lewis responded to these changes, which removed his teaching responsibilities for both business and transport. Though he had been promoted to Reader, it was in the area designated as Colonial Economics, at a time when the specialism had a relatively low status and was not part of the LSE undergraduate degree programme. Whether this was a factor encouraging Lewis to look elsewhere for promotion to a Chair one can only speculate. In December 1947, the Minutes of the Professorial Council recorded that Lewis, 'recently appointed to the Readership in Colonial Economics is resigning to take up a Chair in Economics at the University of Manchester'. The relationship of a decade and a half between Lewis and the LSE had come to an end.

3
The Colonial Office and the Genesis of Development Economics

3.1 Lewis's hinterland: 'anti-imperialists' and the Fabian Colonial Bureau

When he first went to London, Lewis was lonely, shunned by many because he was black, and intellectually isolated. Since the beginning, as we have seen, he had been shy and reticent in nature. This made it still harder for him to form friendships and social networks. But, as he relates, 'some doors that were supposed to be closed opened as I approached them. I have got used to being the first black to do this or that'. On the other hand, he was 'subjected to all the usual disabilities – refusal of accommodation, denial of jobs for which [he] had been recommended, generalized discourtesy and the rest' (Breit and Spencer, 1986). Throughout his life, Lewis was reluctant to speak or write about his very personal experiences of racial discrimination. However, especially after the completion of his PhD in his mid-twenties, the growing support of Plant and others at the LSE gave him confidence, contacts began to be developed, and provided Lewis with a hinterland that could support him in case of need. In the field of development and left-wing politics, these contacts were of two kinds: London's floating population of 'anti-imperialists', and the Fabian Society.

Among the former group, a friend of Lewis in his early London days was the writer Peter Abrahams, a black South African newly arrived in London in October 1940 at the age of twenty-one. In his biography, *The Coyoba Chronicles*, Peter Abrahams recalls that

> there had not been many black faces on the streets of London in those days. The great influx from Africa, the Caribbean and the

Indian sub-continent was still in the future. Most of the blacks seen in London were in uniform, part of the country's fighting forces, 'our boys', there to defend the 'mother country'; the empire in solidarity against the Nazis who would enslave the world. The racism of the Nazis threatened to make whatever we had experienced look like child's play. If they could be so brutal to the Jews, what would they do to the blacks? (Abrahams, 2000, p. 45)

Peter Abrahams was a member of the circle of left-wing anti-imperialists with whom Lewis associated in his London days. London was where anti-imperialism, pan-Africanism and socialism came together, supported by groups of West Indian and West African students, lecturers, teachers, doctors and lawyers. There were very few black females in these circles, neither women students nor professionals, but there was a small cohort of influential and committed white women with political or trade union connections. The anti-imperialists were by definition of the left, but the spectrum was wide and represented all shades of socialist, communist and Marxist ideology. Lewis's sympathies were with the Fabian socialists, who had long since shed the conservative imperialism of the Webbs to embrace a reformist agenda. What surprised Lewis's contemporary Peter Abrahams was the degree of colour prejudice he found in London among white radicals. Without a union card or party membership it was extremely difficult for a black person to get a job in white-dominated political and union circles. Accommodation was also very difficult to obtain:

What came across clearly to me was that communists, leading communists no less than the members of the Working Men's Clubs, saw a difference between black and white, because they were black and white. The brave new communist world of the future, if it ever came, would not necessarily be a world free of race or colour. This was the first of many encounters with colour consciousness among communists, socialists and other left-wing radicals. (Abrahams, 2000, p. 45)

In wartime London, the leading black radical anti-imperialists were C.L.R. James, George Padmore and Jomo Kenyatta. They were joined in 1947 by Kwame (then Francis) Nkrumah, who travelled to England and registered for a doctorate at the LSE. Nkrumah never finished his studies at the School but returned to the Gold Coast where, after the customary period of imprisonment by the colonial administration in 1950, he led his Convention People's Party to independence in 1957.

George Padmore from Trinidad was a man of the hard left, a card-carrying Communist Party member who had occupied a senior position in the Communist International. Peter Abrahams recalled Padmore as an austere and unyielding individual, 'the man we never argued with, never crossed. It was the "Comintern man' who was contemptuous when Jomo had too much to drink. Or when Kwame was late for a meeting because of some woman'.[1]

Though Lewis was acquainted with all these individuals in his London days, it is not easy to assess how he related to them. Yoichi Mine, in his paper devoted to Lewis's work for the Fabian Colonial Bureau (Mine, 2004), tells a thought-provoking story that illustrates Lewis's ambiguous attitude towards his radical nationalist colleagues. Rita Hinden, the South African-born economist who had taken the initiative in establishing the Fabian Colonial Bureau in 1940,[2] and for some time was its only staff member, was organizing a conference on the future of British colonialism. She consulted Lewis about possible speakers, and Lewis replied that 'they should not invite Peter Abrahams because it was not Labour's friend but its enemy who should be called in'. But they were not to invite George Padmore either, 'because his widely published writings are a possible source of trouble'. In the end, Rita Hinden made up her own mind and invited Nkrumah as the main speaker, with Lewis to follow. Characteristically, Lewis denounced both the right and the left. On the right, he castigated the Colonial Office for its racism. But he also condemned the militant anti-imperialists of the left for their neglect of practicalities, and their endless debates about 'general principles of the rights and wrongs of mankind'.[3]

Hinden, valuably from the point of view of the Fabian Society, which was weak on Africa, had become an Africanist after completing her Ph.D. on economic development in Palestine. In her book *Plan for Africa*, written at the request of the Fabian Society and published in 1941, Hinden reported on her several years of research, focused on Northern Rhodesia (Zambia) and the Gold Coast (Ghana) whose aim, she wrote, was 'to analyse the economic development in the Colonies during the years of conflict which have passed, in order to learn lessons for the years of peace which are to come'.[4] But some element in her interpersonal chemistry with Lewis certainly did not gel, and, especially after the 1945 election, their relationship was to go from cordial to something on the wrong side of prickly. After completing the 1948 version of *Colonial Economic Development* – a much-revised version of the paper with the same title that Durbin and Lewis were to pilot with the Colonial Economic Advisory Committee in 1943 (National Archives,

1944) – Lewis sent her a copy accompanied by one of his barbed cover-ing letters. This one read:

> Dear Rita,
> This is the paper I shall read to the Manchester Statistical Society on January 12th. Printed copies will be available shortly after.
>   The viewpoint and conclusions are the exact opposite of your own, so you may find it helpful in revising your pamphlet, at least to know what it is you have to attack.[5]

What can Rita Hinden have wanted to attack? We can only speculate.[6] But the letter is certainly a warning against any cosy vision of the Fabian Colonial Bureau as an affectionate band of brothers, important though it was in providing much-needed support to Lewis and his view of the world.

Even before he became a member of the Bureau's board in 1941, Lewis had involved himself in anti-imperialist activities on behalf of the Bureau's parent body, the Fabian Society. Sensing that the strikes in St Kitts in 1935 might be the start of something big, he had already, at the age of 20, made a research trip there on his way home to St Lucia in July of that year. He did so again in 1938. In his autobiographical account, Lewis tells us that *Labour in the West Indies* was based on news-paper accounts and conversations with some of the trade union leaders. He does not specify where these conversations took place.

Labour in the West Indies is no ordinary pamphlet. It begins with a vision of paradise lost:

> Nearly four thousand miles across the Atlantic lies a beautiful chain of islands forming a crescent from Florida in the United States to Venezuela in South America, and enclosing the blue waters of the Caribbean Sea. Though the British public seldom hear of them, the British West Indies are among the oldest and were once the most highly prized of British domains ... For two centuries the islands were a scene of great prosperity, but in the nineteenth century that prosperity vanished ... Once more they are in the public eye; but now on account of their poverty. (Lewis, 1939, p. 6)

There follows Lewis's description of the political environment and living conditions in the West Indies – on which we drew in Chapter 1 – and of the protests against those conditions that began in St Kitts in 1935 and then spread to Trinidad in 1937, to a general strike in Jamaica in 1938, and eventually to most of the islands, a process which he described collectively as a 'revolution'. The paper contains an early exposition of the idea of the 'vicious circle of poverty', in which low productivity is caused by poor health, which is caused by low government spending on health, drainage and nutrition, which is caused in turn by low productivity and income, which is then used as an excuse to justify low government spending, and so on. But Lewis then adds defiantly, 'there is no vicious circle for men of determination'.[7]

There is also a detailed account of the advances in collective bargaining, and in black politics, which flowed from those protests. But then the argument bursts its banks, and Lewis's final section is nothing less than a manifesto for the evolution of a democratic and developmental West Indies. He writes:

> The real significance of the revolution of 1935–38 is that such narrow political thought [Lewis is referring to the Dominica conference of 1932, which resisted the idea of a universal adult suffrage] has faded into insignificance. The major issues discussed today no longer revolve around the aspirations of the middle classes but are set by working class demands. Initiative has passed into the hands of trade union leaders and new working class bodies like the Progressive League of Barbados, the Working Men's Association of St Vincent, and the People's National Party of Jamaica. These also have much middle class support, and many have strong middle class leadership, but their programmes are much wider than their predecessors. (Lewis, 1939, p. 33)

But to meet the demands of both the working class and the middle class, economic development is needed; and to achieve economic development, there needs to be growth and redistribution out of that growth to offset the extreme inequity and injustice of the pre-war West Indies. To achieve this, Lewis wrote:

> new sources of revenue must be found to replace the existing staples. The tourist trade offers some prospects but seems unlikely ever to become a principal source of revenue. The policy which seems to offer most hope of permanent success is for these islands to follow in the footsteps of other agricultural countries in industrialisation. There is scope for factories for refining sugar, making chocolate, utilising copra, making dairy products etc. Such enterprises would need to be subsidised at the start while local labour was trained and the

local market won, but after the initial period should be able to stand on their own legs. No other policy seems to offer such permanent prospects as the development of local industries.[8]

In addition to industrialization, Lewis advocated imperial prefer- ences for sugar exports, and spending on social welfare also needed to increase. The poverty he saw around him, the 'ragged clothing, dilapi- dated housing and undernourished condition of the masses and their children' could be alleviated by redistributive taxation and social wel- fare measures. In the political sphere, he put his faith in the emergence of responsible trade unionism as opposed to militant political action to remedy the deficiencies of colonialism.

At this same time, on the eve of the Second World War, a Royal Commission, under the chairmanship of Lord Moyne, was sailing for the West Indies to make its own investigation of the political distur- bances in the islands, which it did not describe as a revolution, and to make recommendations. The recommendations of the Moyne com- mission also did not follow Lewis's route, and, while conceding that both reform and new money (provided in 1940 under the Colonial Development and Welfare Act) were urgently needed, insisted that 'a new economic policy for the West Indies must ... be an agricul- tural policy ... Some small increase of industrial employment may be afforded by the development of secondary industries; but these will at best be of relatively unimportant proportions, and would be dependent for their prosperity (on) agriculture'.[9] Lewis did not agree. Of course, there was very little industrial activity in the West Indies at that time, which could provide him with empirical material to support his case, and so much of his writing about the possibilities for indus- trial development was based on hope rather than experience. But there was already one exception to this rule, which in that same year Lewis duly made into an excuse for one of his West Indian detours. Even in the 1930s, as Lewis noted, Puerto Rico, one of America's few colo- nies, was developing export-based industries, essentially on what was to become known as the *maquiladora* model of assembling products for US-based corporations at much lower labour cost than in the conti- nental USA. Lewis embarked on a love–hate affair with Puerto Rico, 'its lovely airy houses, its big, hideously grinning American cars, its little skyscrapers', but did not neglect to observe that 'as the splendid façade of the capital city gives way to the poverty of the countryside ... the secret of good living has not been widely shared'.[10] Lewis's *Puerto Rican Notebook* was published in *The Observer* in June 1940, and the Puerto

Rican example of competitive export-based industrialization in a small island economy was to serve as an example for Lewis throughout the 1950s and 1960s; for example, in his *Report on the Industrialisation of the Gold Coast* in 1953 and in his mission to Nigeria for the OECD in 1962. Long before any of this, however, he sent written evidence to the Moyne Commission, in essence recapitulating the manifesto for the advancement of the West Indies which forms the peroration of *Labour in the West Indies*, and in particular repeating his proposition that industrialization was an important part of the way forward for the West Indies.[11]

The Fabian Society, which had published *Labour in the West Indies*, was to become a critical element in Lewis's hinterland: it was among Fabians such as Arthur Creech Jones, Evan Durbin, Rita Hinden and Harold Laski that Lewis found his intellectual home in his London days. The Fabian Colonial Bureau was created in 1940 by Arthur Creech Jones, at the time MP for Shipley, Yorkshire. Creech Jones (1891–1964) was a Labour MP a generation older than Lewis who, since entering Parliament in 1935, had taken a special interest in colonial matters, and within this, in educational policy; since 1937 he had been a member of the Colonial Office advisory committee on education in the Colonies. He left school at thirteen and, having gained much of his own education at night school through the Workers' Educational Association (WEA), became in due course an impassioned supporter not only of the WEA but also of the cause of adult education as a particularly high-priority part of what he was to call 'mass education',[12] as an instrument for promoting equality of opportunity everywhere, and most particularly in developing countries, which were becoming his area of specialism. The problem was certainly an urgent one: across the whole of British colonial Africa, it was estimated in 1939 that only 12 per cent of children of school age received any sort of education.[13] Creech Jones was sensitive to the criticism that, as the veteran socialist Norman Leys put it, the previous Labour administration of the early 1930s ' had left no mark on colonial policy',[14] and felt that, at a time of political opportunity, it was important for that mistake not to be repeated for lack of a proper knowledge base, and thought-through policy packages, on which the Labour Party could draw. Within the wartime coalition government, Creech Jones, not yet a minister, was none the less able to capture a good deal of the responsibility for policy formulation in the Colonial Office – a territory avoided by the majority of ambitious politicians even after it was relabelled as 'development policy'. It was Creech Jones who persuaded the Colonial Office education advisory committee in 1941 to convene an Adult and Mass Education sub-committee, whose report on *Mass Education in African Society*, presented in June 1943,[15] was influential in crystallizing the development policy of the wartime coalition government, and later of the Labour Party in government. The report eloquently advanced the idea that mass education could overcome 'a narrow sectionalism, operating behind barriers which divide (people) from their fellows'[16] and by implication that mass education could help build stronger and more accountable states which were less vulnerable to fragmentation and internecine conflict. This idea was to be formalized as part of the 'new economics of conflict',[17] and picked up enthusiastically by aid donors 60 years later.

In searching for suitable institutions through which mass education could be achieved in the developing world, the sub-committee picked out trade unions and co-operatives as being particularly promising:

> We have only to look at the last two hundred years in English history to see how powerful an incentive to mass education both the cooperatives and the trade unions have turned out to be. English experience shows too how wide a view they took of education, regarding it not only as literacy and improved technical skill but as involving a new outlook in both local and central government and on citizenship.[18]

The Creech Jones committee already knew, however, that institutional transfer was not a straightforward thing, and acknowledged that this approach, redolent of the traditions of the British labour movement, could not simply be transplanted on to African soil. It therefore embarked on a remarkably broad-ranging review of experiences in other, mainly developing, countries, including Russia, China, Turkey, Indonesia and the southern states of the USA. The committee was aware of the possibilities of radio and film as media for reaching remote populations, and particularly commended

> the Desa [village] schools system of the Netherlands East Indies [now Indonesia] ... where the aim is to teach the three R's within a short period of three or four years to all children ... If universal schooling for children could be introduced everywhere immediately, accompanied as in the Netherlands East Indies by the provision of cheap literature, illiteracy might be abolished within a generation, and the second aspect of mass education, that of adult literacy, would be less urgent.[19]

While some of the Committee's examples are from totalitarian countries, the document evinces not only support for a democratic model of development but also a very modern emphasis on 'the planning of mass education of the community as a movement of the community itself, involving the active support of the local community from the start' – what we would now call development from below.[20] There were no numbers in this paper; this was not a plan, but rather a document designed to spread ideas and stir up enthusiasm for a principle. In this, it was extraordinarily successful; not least with Lewis, who had joined the board of the Fabian Colonial Bureau in 1941.[21] The idea of mass education crystallized one of the key policy principles for which he had been searching, and the worldwide empirical illustrations in the Committee's report found their way into a number of his publications, including his *Theory of Economic Growth* (1955). As we know from his *Labour in the West Indies* paper (1939) he also took an initially favourable view of what co-operatives and, in particular, trade unions could do to achieve mass education. Though his view of trade unions was to become progressively more jaundiced, he remained, both as an educator and a policy adviser, loyal to the mass education approach to development throughout his life.

Another new arrival on the board of the Fabian Colonial Bureau in 1941 was Evan Durbin, like Lewis an economics academic at the LSE. Durbin was to become a true friend to Lewis and possibly the only person apart from Arnold Plant to whom he was willing to defer. They made a perfectly complementary partnership: Durbin being UK-focused[22] and an activist with a tendency to intellectualize (he eventually became a junior minister in the Attlee government, alongside Hugh Gaitskell, who had read PPE at Oxford around the same time), and Lewis already developing-country-focused and an academic anxious to have his ideas applied in practice. Lewis's working habits being somewhat solitary, it was only rarely that he achieved a creative partnership with another individual: this was certainly one of the times. Even their interpretations of Fabian socialism were from the same stable, both being 'Hayekian socialists' who emphasized the role of saving as a long-period virtue that stimulated growth, rather than, as Keynes portrayed it, a short-period vice which depressed effective demand.[23] (Durbin wrote a pamphlet and a book on this theme in the 1930s (Durbin, 1933, 1935) in advance of the publication of Keynes' *General Theory*. Lewis never ventured so far into Keynesian macro-economics, but the idea of savings as being the key to economic growth was to take shape in 1955 as his most famous aphorism: 'The central problem in the theory of economic growth is to understand the process by which a community is converted from being a 5 per cent to a 12 per cent saver'.)[24]

Both Lewis and Durbin were committed both to planning and to the market, and were fascinated by the possibilities and contradictions embodied in the notion of democratic socialist planning; both, indeed, were to publish books on this theme with almost identical titles in 1949, which were reviewed in the same issue of the *Economic Journal* by the fellow Fabian (and also future Nobel Prize winner), James Meade.[25] Lewis was deeply shocked when, in September 1948, Durbin was drowned off the coast of north Cornwall rescuing one of his daughters from the sea, and more than 30 years later was moved to tears when, at Princeton, that daughter brought him a blurred photo of the two of them together at a Fabian Society gathering.

It is much to the credit of the Fabians – especially Durbin, the member of the Society whom Lewis took most seriously as an economist – that they offered the young black economist a great deal of support and were to have a significant influence on his subsequent career. The Fabian Colonial Bureau, as we have seen, was a relatively new arrival on the socialist scene in wartime London. Importantly, because it was a separate organization from the Fabian Society, receiving funding from the Fabian Society, and later from the Trades Union Congress (TUC) and Labour Party, but without any formal affiliation to these bodies, it could boast that it was free to develop its own ideas on colonial affairs, and to support its own research and lobbying on colonial issues. In his LSE days, Lewis was frequently called on to author pamphlets or address conferences sponsored by the Bureau. He was a speaker at the Peace Aims Conference of the National Peace Council held in Oxford in January 1942. Arthur Creech Jones, Labour Member of Parliament and chairman of the Fabian Colonial Bureau, was the main speaker; Rita Hinden was another. Not every anti-imperialist in the developing world, however, would be impressed by the Fabians. As we relate in Chapter 7, the radical Tobago-born sociologist, Susan Craig, was to strongly condemn Lewis, and Fabian socialism in general, in the 1970s as an insidious influence on the post-independence fortunes of the Caribbean.[26] Her case was that the later leaders of the Caribbean labour movement such as Grantley Adams and Norman Manley were too ready to fall in with the plans of the British Labour Party, the British trade union movement, and the philosophies of Fabian-inspired intellectuals such as Lewis. It was the Fabians, with their support for 'responsible' trade unionism in the Caribbean, in her view, that had betrayed and out-manoeuvred the radical and nationalist elements in the Caribbean labour movement. Echoing issues that later emerged around US Central Intelligence Agency (CIA) finance for liberal intellectuals in Britain in the 1950s, Susan Craig blamed the substantial US finance provided for 'responsible' unions in Guyana, Barbados, Jamaica, Trinidad and Tobago for perpetuating neo-colonial relationships in the Caribbean. US finance strengthened US control over local labour in the bauxite industries. Influence was exercised through the selection of personnel, through specific training programmes and the targeting of funds, to ensure that the labour movement in key export sectors of the Caribbean remained 'anti-communist'. Susan Craig (1977) indicts Lewis in his 1939 pamphlet for his support of what he termed the 'sober, responsible men' who were seeking to replace 'irresponsible extremists' in the labour movement. Lewis, of course, believed that the West Indies needed to attract foreign capital and that this would not happen if there was serious labour unrest. Whether Lewis's support for the moderate elements in the Caribbean labour movement went any deeper than this, and indeed the extent to which he was tied ideologically at this stage in his career to his colleagues in the Fabian movement, is very difficult to say.

3.2   The Colonial Economic Advisory Committee, 1943–4

The paper on the flow of capital into the British colonies, which Lord Hailey commissioned from Lewis in 1941 (Lewis, 1942b) was a one-off: an isolated paper commissioned to meet the specific need of defining the terms on which the Colonies could access capital. However, this one-off gradually turned into a long-term relationship between Lewis and the Colonial Office, and as it did so, Lewis's perception of himself and his role also changed. In October 1942, Lewis was asked to take on a second research project for the Colonial Office, together with F. V. Meyer, with whom Lewis was later (1946) to publish a paper, one of very few of Lewis's published papers under joint authorship. On this occasion, the Colonial Office agreed to pay for the research, though the surviving correspondence suggests that the LSE had great difficulty in getting the Colonial Office to pay up. There were three aspects to the research: imperial preferences; textile quotas; and government expenditure on public works. Lewis arranged for the final reports to be typed up and submitted, and early in 1945 he wrote to Carr-Saunders specifically about the research on public expenditure:

> it is a purely historical and statistical document, without direct relevance to policy and publication is not urgent. After the war I think

> we might try to get a grant out of the CO [Colonial Office] for it,
> since it will have a propaganda value for them, in showing that the
> development expenditures of colonial governments have been much
> greater than their detractors suggest. (LSE Archives: Letter from
> Lewis to Carr-Saunders, January 1945)

The following year, Lewis's relationship with the Colonial Office
became more long-term and institutionalized. As the war began to go
better for the Allies in 1943, so the work of the UK Colonial Office
began to turn, for the first time, from care and maintenance of the
assets the Colonies represented to their development and preparation for eventual independence.[27] This huge and exciting step, which
would give Lewis his first important experience as a development practitioner, was taken through the medium of a new body to be known
as the Colonial Economic Advisory Committee (CEAC), established in
October of that year with the purpose of providing expert advice on
colonial development policy. Chaired within the Colonial Office by the
Duke of Devonshire, it included ten external members, of whom two
(Henderson and Durbin) were working as academic economists, and
most of the rest being professionals or business people with colonial
experience.[28] Subsequently, another senior academic, Lionel Robbins,
was appointed to the Committee. There were two senior civil service
staff, Sydney Caine and Gerald Clauson, both of them with significant
skills in microeconomics.[29] The Committee was to have specialist working groups, or sub-committees, on the themes of agriculture, mining,
industrial policy, finance, marketing and research, and an additional
sub-committee to set the agenda.

   After casting around, mainly in the LSE, for a 'really competent'
Secretary to the committee,[30] the Colonial Office selected Lewis for this
post, and Lewis, with positive encouragement from the Director of the
LSE , took a year's secondment for this purpose. Lewis's publications
to this point, as related above, were mainly in industrial economics,
and he had spent most of 1941 and 1942 writing up materials from his
Ph.D. for publication. He was, however, an experienced consultant, who
since 1938 had done a number of assignments for the (UK) Ministry of
Information, Board of Trade, the two assignments for Lord Hailey, and
other government bodies, to the point of repeatedly triggering struggles with the Secretary and senior staff of the LSE about the number
of hours of consultancy he was doing, the proportion of his earnings
he was allowed to keep, or both.[31] Most of his knowledge of developing countries, however, at this stage, related to the Caribbean, with

the exception of the crucial first report for Lord Hailey entitled 'Some Aspects of the Flow of Capital into the British Colonies' (1942b), which had given him a bird's eye view of all the Colonies, which had been commended by Hailey and several members of the Colonial Office.

Once selected for the post of Secretary of the CEAC, Lewis, despite his lack of managerial experience and access to empirical material on developing countries, threw himself into the job; indeed the word 'Secretary' does not properly describe the role the 28-year-old Lewis chose for himself, which was nothing less than to determine, co-ordinate, and where necessary research, a programme for the economic development of the British colonies. Within two months of taking on the job of secretary, in November/December 1943, Lewis had picked and won a fight with Caine on the question of whether the Committee's agenda for action should be reactive, responding ad hoc to requests from other departments, or proactive, making explicit recommendations for what the development strategy for the Colonies should be. The matter was referred to a no doubt surprised Secretary of State, who opined in favour of the strategic role.[32] In support of this strategic role, Lewis, between the end of 1943 and September 1944, personally wrote or co-authored strategy papers on mining policy, industrial policy, marketing policy, planning machinery, and colonial economic development as a whole, and commissioned much other research on developing countries from both inside and outside the Colonial Office: he had been handed the opportunity to construct, for the first time, a database and research portfolio on the then embryonic subject of development policy, or 'colonial economics' as it was then known. Meanwhile, Caine retreated into the role of Sir Humphrey,[33] to scheme in favour of the more minimalist, or reactive, role which he favoured for the office.

Before we discuss in detail how the contest played itself out, we need to examine in a little more detail how the Committee gathered information on colonial economies and colonial policy, given that in those days no national income statistics, country economic reports, policy reviews or project appraisals – such as the international financial international institutions and aid donors now have to hand for all developing countries in which they are interested – were available for any developing country, nor did any think tanks exist from whom the Colonial Office could commission policy research. The inspired title of Wolfgang Stolper's (1966) book about Nigeria in the 1950s, *Planning Without Facts*, even more accurately describes the kind of policy-making that Lewis and his colleagues were doing in the 1940s. In the main, what the Colonial Office did in 1943–4 was to commission reports on particular regions or sectors of the colonial empire, which frequently entailed field visits of several months, as in the case of Sir Alan Pim's report on the development of colonial agriculture[34] and Noel Hall's report on the economic development of West Africa.[35] These enquiries themselves were forced, of course, to plan without facts, even on matters as basic as national income and expenditure; typically, all that was available were trade statistics and government expenditure data, both of which were full of gaps and inconsistencies. And in the absence of facts, all that was left was to use these threadbare data, to conduct interviews with key informants, or to fall back on inspired guesses.

However, the Colonial Office was at the very least aware of the problem. There was a Colonial Economic Research Committee, which predated CEAC. On it were a number of well-known economists under the chairmanship of Lewis's supervisor and mentor at the LSE, Arnold Plant. The economists on the Committee included Professor G. C. Allen, A. G. B. Fisher, A. J. Brown and E. A. G. Robinson. Arthur Lewis and Evan Durbin were added to the membership when the Research Sub-Committee became a sub-committee of CEAC. Its main Report was published after the resignation of Lewis, but he would most certainly have been in sympathy with the recommendations. The Report drew attention to the need for colonial statistics on production, incomes, occupations and land use. A large number of subjects for study and research were listed in the Report: the standard of living; cost of living; national income; land use; supply of capital; migration; export prices; and the balance of payments. It was stressed that work on colonial economic problems should be carried out as systematically, and 'at the same level of competence' as work on comparable economic problems in Britain.[36]

Other gap-filling expedients were also available. For example, even by the mid-1930s a literature was beginning to emerge on problems associated with the inter-war depression that had been known to cause distress in developing countries – in particular, the collapse of primary commodity prices (and to a lesser extent export volumes). Studies on this issue had already been conducted by Lamartine Yates, Leubuscher and, as mentioned earlier, Sydney Caine: Lewis had also referred to them in passing in his LSE lectures on the inter-war depression, which later became *Economic Survey 1919–1939* (Lewis, 1949a). Colonial monetary systems had been studied by Gerald Clausen, also now on the Colonial Office staff. More innovative than any of these was the inspiring leap in the dark taken by Paul Rosenstein-Rodan,[37] like Lewis, an academic, working at University College London since 1931 in the field of industrial development. Rosenstein-Rodan later claimed that 'eastern and south-eastern Europe were selected as a model not because of any special interest in those countries, but because their governments in exile were in London and because eastern and south-eastern Europe (like Latin America) constitute a group of similar but not identical models'[38] (he was born in Kraków, which may or may not be relevant). Rosenstein-Rodan's paper took a Keynesian approach to the development of industry in low-income (and specifically poor eastern European) countries, arguing that it was constrained by lack of effective demand, without which no factory could operate on an economic scale. To overcome this constraint, Rosenstein-Rodan recommended a 'big push' in which multiple complementary factories would be created with state subsidies; the employees of each of these newly created factories would, by spending their wages, create the demand for the production of the other newly created factories and thereby make all of them viable. The paper was published in the *Economic Journal* for 1943, to coincide perfectly with the big push that Lewis himself was making to establish a comprehensive policy agenda for the CEAC.

With the support of the Fabian Colonial Bureau, and in particular with Durbin at his side on the CEAC, Lewis ventured into battle. Except that there was no battle, in the sense of harsh words. The two meetings following Lewis's tactical victory – on 9 December 1943 and 15 February 1944 – had the appearance of complete normality, and to the next, on 27 March 1944, Lewis sent his apologies, having been forced to take a month's leave on account of a severe stomach complaint that was eventually diagnosed as a duodenal ulcer.[39] What was important, however, was what was *not* happening. With the sole exception of the mining subcommittee, nobody was producing any strategy papers on 'questions of principle' as required, nor were committee members referring any policy issues to the main committee for discussion. To Lewis, though there was no formal evidence of this, it was clear that his activist strategy was being undermined by Caine instructing committee members to treat all issues of development policy as, by definition, 'political' and therefore off-limits. To foil these delaying tactics, Lewis persuaded the Agenda sub-committee to instruct him and Durbin to present a paper on strategy. This document, entitled 'Colonial Economic Development', emphasizing the need for urgency and designed as an agenda 'to promote the most rapid economic development that is practicable',[40] was presented on 23 June 1944. The paper attempted to summarize and connect the findings of the Advisory Committee's thematic working groups, and to convert them into an agenda for action. It was the first development policy manifesto ever produced.

The Lewis–Durbin agenda contains four building blocks of central importance: between them, the acorn which over the following ten years was to grow into the core of Lewis's thinking on development policy. These are:

(i)   Key markets work badly in developing countries

Poor countries are poor because the markets for the crucial factors of production – labour, capital, agricultural inputs, and often also land – are defective or simply absent, requiring the state to step in if any kind of development is to occur from a subsistence level. In Durbin and Lewis's words:

> It seems to be thought that because industry developed in Britain or in the USA without much government planning, therefore *laissez-faire* is also the appropriate policy for the Colonies ... [But Britain's] successors have established themselves only with the help of much government intervention and protection; industrialisation cannot grow slowly and 'naturally' in these days; either it reaches rapidly a scale on which it is large enough to compete economically, or it never gets started. And it ignores the need for securing a proper balance of industries. Whatever the merits of *laissez-faire* in Britain or the USA, it is quite out of place in trying to develop backward regions today ... Britain and the USA in the 18th century were countries with a long commercial tradition behind them, and with much entrepreneurial skill. In the British colonies there is no such parallel, except to a limited extent in the Far East and the West Indies. There are no 'natural economic forces' that we can rely on to produce industrial development in Africa at the necessary rate; either the government must take an active part in planning development, or there will be little or none.[41]

The idea that capital markets worked badly in developing countries had already, of course, been sketched out in Lewis's report of 1941–2 for Lord Hailey (Lewis, 1942b); this idea is now generalized to other key markets supporting the livelihoods of people in developing countries. The wording of the quotation is specifically targeted at Caine, who, in spite of paying lip service to the idea of planning, was an enthusiast for the role of private enterprise in the environment of developing countries (Ingham, 1992, p. 702).

(ii) Selective industrialization

Five years previously, in his study *Labour in the West Indies*, Lewis had made a case for the development of secondary industries as an instrument to lift poor countries out of the poverty trap (Lewis, 1939, p. 36). This was necessary, he argued, because of unfavourable trends in the factoral terms of trade for primary products (Ingham, 1992, p. 698), and because 'the incomes of agricultural countries fluctuate more widely than the incomes of industrial countries'.[42] Lewis and Durbin now stressed that such measures to transform the industrial structure, which initially will be uneconomic and therefore need to be protected in some way, must be selective, in relation to both the products supported and possibly the regions and countries where industry is promoted, to optimize the allocation of scarce resources. Lewis and Durbin spelt this out as follows:

> We must think not in terms of 'industrialising the Colonies', meaning each and every colony, but in terms of creating a *limited number of industrial centres,* into each of which shall be concentrated the factories serving all the Colonies within its geographical region. This point requires some emphasis. To attempt to create factory industries in every single colony, whether by tariff protection, licensing, subsidy or the other devices we are asked to support, is the surest way to waste the monies provided for development.[43]

In face of a radical orthodoxy (now supported by the Rosenstein-Rodan model) which was already advocating industrialization in the form of a 'big push' on all fronts without regard to country size, this emphasis on restraint and specialization was innovative and crucial. Through his small-island spectacles, Lewis had seen what other advocates of radical development solutions had been unable to see.

*(iii) Raising agricultural productivity, including
smallholder productivity*

This is a primary development policy objective, directly as a means of providing better nutrition for poor and often malnourished people, and indirectly as a means of providing vital inputs (of food, labour and foreign exchange) to the rest of the economy, including the emergent industrial sector. As Lewis and Durbin put it,

> one of the most striking features of the Colonies is undernourishment and malnutrition, due to the fact that the people have not enough to eat ... and also to the fact that diets are not sufficiently

varied. The principal cause of this is low agricultural output, and an increased output of foodstuffs should be one of the principal objects of economic policy.[44]

In a note Lewis sent to Caine on topics which the CEAC subcommittees might investigate, Lewis put an 'agricultural revolution' at the top of the agenda (Ingham, 1992, p. 698). In some cases the revolution could be achieved by providing modern inputs to existing small-scale plots, but in others reorganization would be needed, either through schemes to settle smallholders on new lands, or by consolidation of existing micro-holdings up to an economic size. At this stage, it was the last of these options that Lewis and Durbin tended to favour.

Lewis now broke new ground by linking the agricultural revolution and mass education agendas.

(iv)   'Mass education' as a means of raising the productivity of both the agricultural and non-agricultural sectors

The mass training of the populations of developing countries, which, as discussed above, had for some years been under consideration by Creech Jones' Adult and Mass Education Sub-Committee,[45] was now declared by Lewis and Durbin to be a 'sine qua non of rapid progress'. 'A large number of agricultural schools,' they declared, must be established for mass training of village leaders',[46] where 'very large numbers of men, a few for each village, may learn, in a fairly short stay (and at the same time as they learn the alphabet) the elements of agricultural science and the basic principles of agricultural reorganisation'.[47]

The crucial contribution of Lewis and Durbin was to link the rather woolly idea of mass education, which had been in circulation for a number of years, to the fundamental problems of underdevelopment – market failure and the stagnation of smallholder agriculture – which determined most poor people's livelihoods. Whereas Creech Jones' Adult and Mass Education Sub-Committee, as we saw above, had leaned towards the idea that trade unions and co-operatives were the key agencies through which community mass education should be promoted, Lewis, with his instinctively more agriculture-focused approach to the developing economy, now tended to place the responsibility less on trade unions, which are mainly urban institutions, and increasingly on rural extension and training. Without ever formalizing his ideas, he had already become wedded to a view of the world in which smallholder agricultural productivity was the key to development; and since he saw mass education, in the sense of agricultural extension, as the key to smallholder productivity, it is no wonder that he returns to this theme every time he is asked to advise on development policy. It is tempting to see in Lewis and Durbin's recommendations an anticipation of the 'new growth theory' of the 1990s (Romer, 1986; Barro and Sala-i-Martin, 1995) in which education creates knowledge, which in turn drives technical progress, which goes on to drive all economic growth. Certainly, Lewis's insights of 1943 are intuitive and formulate a commonsense rather than an axiomatic body of knowledge. None the less, they mark the beginning of the modern theory of development. They bring together Lewis's nascent thoughts about trade and protection, already given a preliminary airing in *Labour in the West Indies* (Lewis, 1939), together with Durbin's ideas about planning and the market, and an emerging Labour Party consensus on mass education.[48]

Apart from these very overt bullet-points – the first of them, of course, aimed directly at Sydney Caine – there are many other more discreetly coded messages of encouragement, acknowledgement or outright defiance for individuals who had supported, influenced or obstructed Lewis or Durbin. There was a message of support, of course, for Creech Jones and his adult and mass education sub-committee, but also for those who in the Fabian Society and elsewhere had dared to speak up for selective protectionism, such as the Colonial Office's own adviser, Noel Hall, who had produced a report on Africa whose first few pages Lewis had decorated with red ink, until he saw the radicalism of the policy message Hall was trying to convey.[49] The remarks on the dangers of laissez-faire and on selective industrialization (in order to reach an economic scale of production as quickly as possible) bear the hallmarks of the Rosenstein–Rodan paper, which it would have been proper to acknowledge, in a footnote at least.

But there were others who also needed to be convinced. It is hard, now that development has become established as a guiding star for policy-makers everywhere, to recall that in the 1940s there were many influential people who believed, not only that the economy should be left to market forces, but that development was not necessarily a good or useful thing. They included, as we have seen, members of the CEAC, such as the backwoodsman, Sir John Hay, who 'was sceptical about whether progress was really needed'.[50] There were others who argued 'that the growth of factory industry in the Colonies will react unfavourably on the British standard of living'.[51] To counter this kind of belief, Lewis and Durbin found it necessary to go back to their document and draft an Introduction explaining that development of poor countries would hurt nobody, and actually was advisable – not only to make people healthier and happier, but even more because 'a slow economic development was hardly practical politics ... The articulate leaders of [colonial peoples], a growing number, clamour for self-government, which can only be real if it is given solid economic foundations'.[52] Without development, there would be turbulence, possibly civil war. The message needed to be given in this alarmist way simply to instil a sense of urgency among the committee.

This never-published document, a mere twelve pages long, lays the foundations of development economics, in conjunction with Rosenstein–Rodan's *Economic Journal* paper of 1943. Before these two papers were written, analysis of developing countries was largely descriptive, and said nothing about how to achieve development. Now, at last, a story at least existed which wrestled with the fundamental problems of development, and did so in a way that was joined-up rather than consisting of *ad hoc* recommendations on individual components of development policy, such as commodity prices or mineral taxation. The great new idea is not just the four building blocks mentioned above, but rather the message that they needed to be assembled into an integrated strategy for development from a subsistence level to take place. That strategy was then further combined with the new concept of the Colonial Office as an economic development agency for the Colonies, transferring a blend of expertise and ideas alongside Colonial Development and Welfare Fund (aid) money, exactly as the World Bank and other development agencies still attempt to do at the time of writing.[53] Being so innovative, the concept, of course, encountered opposition: none of the other members of the CEAC properly understood Lewis's ideas or accepted the need for an integrated development strategy. Even Durbin, knowing little of the atmosphere of developing countries, could only take Lewis's ideas on trust and intuition, and give him political support, which he did loyally. Lewis and Durbin's only other supporter on the CEAC was Sir Bernard Bourdillon, a former governor of Nigeria, and his support again was largely based on instinct rather than logical argument. When these three took on the might of the Colonial Office with a totally new idea, a war of attrition was bound to result.

The document none the less succeeded; in the sense of being submitted, in the form of a watered-down version for which the entire sub-committee, including Caine and Clauson, took responsibility,[54] to the Colonial Secretary, Oliver Stanley in the form of a set of questions which the minister was requested to answer. But by the time the replies were received,[55] Lewis had resigned. Why? It is not correct to say, as

Tignor does, that Lewis 'had to go'.[56] He was not asked to go, and several members of the committee very much wanted him to stay. Moreover, it is clear that Lewis was not alone in having problems with the CEAC. Though its sub-committees struggled on until 1946, when the Colonial Economic Development Council (CEDC) was inaugurated, the CEAC itself was in disarray from 1944. Late in that year, Evan Durbin had considered resigning, but was persuaded to stay on by the Secretary of State. Arthur Lewis resigned as Secretary in November 1944. Lionel Robbins stayed on, though he had never been a regular attender at meetings. Hubert Henderson resigned early in 1946. In the letter that Durbin sent to Oliver Stanley offering his own resignation, he said that he was out of sympathy with the assumptions on which the Committee was expected to base its work. In this letter, Durbin pointed out that there were few, if any, professional economists who knew as much about colonial economic policy as did Lewis. Indeed, there would be 'no better way of reinforcing the Committee itself than by appointing Dr Arthur Lewis to it'. The Secretary of State, though unwilling to accept Durbin's resignation, did not feel that Lewis's name should be added to the membership of the CEAC. While he had the greatest respect for Lewis's intellectual ability, now was not the time to add to the membership of the Colonial Economic Advisory Committee.[57]

Lewis's resignation letter took the form of a long and bitter Memorandum (CO/852/586/9) which described his Secretaryship as 'largely a waste of time'. He complained that 'the Committee was confined to discussing small matters, and that with some exceptions it was not allowed to deal with the more important ones'.[58] Indeed, he provided a list of themes which he had asked to be referred to subcommittees for review, three of which had been referred for study as requested, seven had been rejected, and eleven had not been determined. Three of the eleven undetermined issues, however, were the core matters of agricultural policy, industrial strategy and planning machinery, identified above as fundamental, and referred to the Secretary of State precisely because they were 'political' – that is, in Lewis's interpretation, too important for the sub-committee members to wish to put their heads above the parapet and design a plan of action.

Lewis's resignation Memorandum also made clear that in his view what he described as 'the attitude of the Office' was partly to blame for the difficulties of CEAC, what he described as a 'touchy and uncooperative atmosphere' in which there was resentment if discussions impinged on the policies of other Departments, or appeared to involve overturning the Colonial Office's administrative arrangements in the

Colonies. Sydney Caine did not make a detailed response to the resignation Memorandum, but in his comments on it to the Permanent Under-Secretary George Gater, was very critical of Lewis.[59]

Relations between Sydney Caine and Arthur Lewis were never going to be easy. Like the civil servants he complained about, Lewis himself could be touchy and uncooperative. He often found it difficult to see any merit in alternative approaches, or appreciate other points of view, despite the fact that they might be competently researched and sincerely held. When one of the authors of this book interviewed Sir Sydney Caine in London in 1990, he said of his relations with Lewis 'We agreed entirely on the end result which we were trying to achieve, but differed greatly on the means.' There is sufficient evidence in the personality of the young Lewis to explain why he would quit a month before the Secretary of State was due to reply – a Secretary of State who, moreover, had shown willingness the previous year to back the 28-year-old Lewis's version of the committee's vision rather than that of the far more suave and experienced Caine. Lewis's judgement could be premature and his actions impetuous. (Later, we shall again observe Lewis, in the West Indies, employing the risky tool of an ultimatum, but this time with more success.) He even enjoyed, in the 1940s, an asset he had to make do without in many of his later battles, namely trusted and expert allies – not only Durbin, but also Sir Bernard Bourdillon, a colonial administrator recently retired from the governorship of Nigeria, who appears to have been thoroughly convinced by Lewis's advocacy of a strategic role for the committee.

However, the wrangling which characterized the relationship between CEAC and the Colonial Office went far beyond the impatience of its young Secretary. There were great differences in economic philosophy between Durbin, Lewis and Bourdillon, and their counterparts in the Economic Division of the Colonial Office.[60] Colonial Office thinking was still highly orthodox. At its heart was Sydney Caine's very strong presumption in favour of private initiatives to promote industrialization. In a Memorandum in 1943 he had argued that it was 'nonsense' to suggest that development could not take place unless it was planned by the government: 'Nothing is more demonstrably untrue for the Colonial Empire, where tremendous developments have been produced by the planning of private enterprise.'[61] The role he envisaged for the state centred on the provision of finance in situations where private capital was unwilling to underwrite the risks. In this 1943 Memorandum, Caine advocated a special role for government-sponsored companies operating along commercial lines. He gave as an example the Belgian Congo.

Ironically, it was the fear of a Congo-like political disaster that encouraged Lewis in the late 1950s to favour federation for the West Indies.

There is evidence to suggest that even in March, when he was ill, Lewis was planning to be back teaching at the LSE by September, which at a minimum would have required him to renegotiate a part-time contract in place of his secondment.[62] In any event, Lewis did resign outright, leaving Durbin and Bourdillon to fight on, for the moment, alone. At this point, at the age of 29, something was lost to Lewis which never reappeared – the ability to influence policy and welfare across a whole mass of poor developing countries. From this point on, his contributions were to be less ambitious, and often more academic in nature. But the vision born in the late spring of 1943 continued to inspire him, and to blossom in increasingly sophisticated forms into his mature work. And, of course, he now had, as a result of his Colonial Office experiences, an astonishingly wide laboratory of case-study materials that he could feed into his teaching and research. While he was to describe his work with CEAC disparagingly as a 'waste of time' to his boss Carr-Saunders,[63] it had in fact been anything but that: it had been the making of him and his research career.

In January 1945, in response to an earlier request from Lewis, the Colonial Office produced an account of the action taken on CEAC reports submitted to it before the end of 1944.[64] There was not much to say. The report entitled *'Machinery for Economic Planning'* was stated to be 'under consideration', with no final decisions having been taken. The report called *'Manufacturing Industry'* which Lewis had claimed in its final form to be of little value, was being circulated to colonial governments in the form of a Memorandum. No decision had been reached on the *'Report of the Minerals Sub-Committee'* which Lewis felt, alone among the sub-committees, had done an 'excellent job'. Action had been taken on other matters such as economic research, marketing and communications, but this was, on the whole, very minor action in uncontroversial areas. Thus the immediate impact of the CEAC on development policy was very limited. *Colonial Economic Development,* that remarkably shrewd initiative that originated with Lewis, appeared to have sunk without trace.

In June 1946, Secretary of State George Hall announced his intention of winding up the CEAC and replacing it with the Colonial Economic and Development Council (CEDC). The new body was soon to encounter many of the problems that had brought down the CEAC. Of the original members of the CEAC, only two – Bourdillon and Sir William Goodenough (of Barclays DCO and chairman of the marketing sub-committee) were invited to serve on it. Lewis had to wait until the CEDC was reconstituted by Creech Jones, before he could serve on it. However, there was nothing untoward about this. Academic economists initially did not feature at all on the new CEDC. In 1945, there was a deliberate scaling down of external economic advisers recruited into academia from Whitehall. Ministers in the incoming Labour government tended to favour instead their own personal advisers, drawing them from a specific circle of trusted colleagues and experts who shared to a great extent their own world view. The situation in the Colonial Office was no different. In 1945 the stated preference was for 'practical people' rather than academics.

3.3   Lewis and development policy after the war

Within less than a year, the 1945 election had been won by the Labour Party. The following five years, to borrow from the title of a volume of Winston Churchill's war history, were a period of 'triumph and tragedy'. Never in recent memory had hopes been so high – not only had the war been won, but unemployment and poverty in Britain and across the industrialized world were in the course of being reduced to levels never previously seen. But Britain's economic supremacy had been irretrievably lost, and her empire was about to disappear. This was the part of the process over which Creech Jones, now installed initially as Minister of State in the Colonial Office, and shortly afterwards as Colonial Secretary, was asked to preside with as brave a face as possible.

The office of Colonial Secretary is not high in the Cabinet pecking-order, and from the start Creech Jones knew that his best chances of pushing through the more compassionate and idealistic parts of his agenda depended on his being able to gain the support of his more powerful colleagues – such as Ernest Bevin, the Foreign Secretary, and Hugh Dalton (later succeeded by Stafford Cripps), the Chancellor of the Exchequer. Therefore, his reforms of the Colonial Development and Welfare Act in 1945, his actions in support of human rights in the Colonies, his funding of the Owen Falls complex in Uganda – intended to serve as power-plus-secondary industry hub for East Africa and bearing the impress of Durbin and Lewis's 'selective industrialization' thinking – and dearest to his heart his initiatives on mass education, were all now able to be given legislative backing. All these initiatives needed at the same time to be tempered, however, by actions that would bring in foreign exchange or protect Britain's interests in a global, rather than simply a colonial or developing-country context. On these grounds, he also caused the Overseas Food Corporation, with the remit of augmenting food supplies from the Colonies, and the Colonial Development Corporation, with the remit of levering private capital into the operations of the Colonial Office, to be created. The purpose of these operations was to endear himself to the Chancellor of the Exchequer by securing foreign exchange – and to the Foreign Secretary by enabling him to negotiate matters such as Marshall Aid from a slightly less weak and dependent position.[65]

With the arrival of a Labour Government in 1945, Creech Jones had become first a junior Colonial Office minister and then Colonial Secretary, and on his promotion he moved rapidly to involve Lewis, whom he respected not only intellectually but also as someone who himself had had to struggle to be heard in the making of development policy.[66] In 1947, Creech Jones restored Lewis to a position of influence within the Colonial Office, by inviting him to become a member of the CEDC. The CEDC did not have such exalted powers as Lewis had wished the CEAC to have – it was in essence an evaluative body with the purpose of reviewing the development plans of the Colonies, rather than an ideas factory for framing and accelerating their overall development.

Readers will recall that no professional economists or academics were appointed initially to the CEDC. Addressing the first meeting of the new council, Creech Jones gave an explanation for this: 'existing machinery for dealing with development needs strengthening ... the Secretary of State needs the advice of practical people with experience not only of the Colonies but of the world outside ... people who are familiar with finance and industry and economic problems'.

However, from the beginning, selected academics were appointed to the sub-committees of the CEDC, where most of the important policy discussions were taking place. The delegation of all the important advisory work on the CEDC to sub-committees was a shrewd and deliberate ploy on the part of the Secretary of State, Creech Jones. Of the sub-committees the most influential was the Colonial Economic Research Committee (CERC), which was widely regarded as the true successor to CEAC. It was the most influential in terms of policy. Hubert Henderson was the first chairman, but he was quickly replaced by the ubiquitous Arnold Plant. As might be expected, Arthur Lewis served on this sub-committee, together with prominent economists G. C. Allen, A. J. Brown, Herbert Frankel, E. A. G. Robinson, Ronald Tress and Richard Stone. Ida Greaves was Secretary for some period of time, as also was Phyllis Deane. Phyllis Deane came to the Colonial Office from the National Institute of Economic and Social Research (NIESR),

where her special project had been to apply national income accounting techniques to colonial economies.[67] In the early 1950s she worked
on a project in Jamaica, collecting national income statistics under the
direction of Arthur Lewis.

By 1947, Arthur Lewis and Rita Hinden were on the main Council of
the CEDC. Both were Fabians and long-term allies of Creech Jones. As
members of the Fabian Colonial Bureau, Lewis and Hinden had spoken
and written extensively on colonial issues alongside Creech Jones.[68] As
his appointees to the CEDC they were very much in the mould of personal advisers to the minister, sharing his approach to colonial policy
and driving forward a specific agenda for colonial development. Given
their backgrounds, both also had personal experience of colonial rule
to add to their academic credentials. Rita Hinden also went some small
way towards addressing the male bias of the CEDC and its predecessor
CEAC. Creech Jones, it should be added, was a well-known supporter of
an enhanced role for women in public life.

Within a year of the invitation to serve on the CEDC, Lewis's academic career had taken off, with his appointment to a chair at
Manchester, as discussed in Chapter 4; and he failed to appear at more
than half of the meetings of the CEDC. He no longer had the pleasure
of Durbin's company, whose engagement with development issues was
basically confined to his time on the CEAC, and who was now in the
new administration as a junior minister.[69] But Creech Jones insisted
on having his opinion on a wide range of issues, including pricing
and investment policies for infrastructural investments.[70] Lewis's most
influential re-entry into Colonial Office affairs consisted, however, of
a paper entitled *Principles of Development Planning* – 'planning' being
at that time an adjective used by many to make a political argument
seem more rigorous,[71] but here used to mean manpower planning. The
context was that Lewis, having been relegated to the role of examining
the Colonial Office's published development plans, did not liked what
he saw, and indeed pronounced them 'a grave waste of money'.[72] The
reasoning behind his approach, extracting a powerful argument from a
single back-of-the-envelope approximation, is illustrated by his critique
of the largest of the plans, that for Nigeria:

> I take the published Nigerian plan, which is the largest, and relates
> to more than one-third of the colonial peoples. The distribution of
> expenditure is follows:
>
> [a table follows illustrating that 10 per cent of public expenditure
> is devoted to education].

Detailed examination of the plan shows how little it is conceived in terms of education. Of the £8,500,000 [committed to] the general medical scheme, 39% is for buildings, 32% for hospital and specialist staff; even ordinary public health, as generally conceived elsewhere, is barely [provided for], let alone plans for mass extension work. Similarly, of the £2,300,000 to be spent on agriculture, 21% is to be spent on buildings, and 26% on the salaries and passages of European staffs. There is provision for 'up to 640 African agricultural assistants', but what is 640 among 22 million? There is no provision for agricultural credit, or for the cooperative movement. But how could there be, when only 7% of the money is allocated for agriculture, forestry, fishery and industry services together? But the education plan is the most curious of all, for while it provides for secondary schools and teacher training, there are only token sums for mass education and for primary education, the cost of the latter being left mainly to the small resources of the missionary societies.[73]

Lewis uses arguments of this sort for several colonial countries, and concludes, as illustrated above, that development planning across the entire Colonial Office is not a new dawn, but rather a jumble of unrealistic numbers that do not correspond to real needs.

But from this wreckage he now plucks out one of the four principles that had served as building blocks for his *Colonial Economic Development* paper with Durbin in 1944. Not surprisingly, this turns out to be Colonial Secretary Creech Jones' pride and joy – mass education. By then the Colonial Office's Mass Education sub-committee had been converted into a Mass Education and Community Development sub-committee, making it sound more Southern-oriented and, as it would be called these days, 'touchy-feely'. Lewis proposed the elevation of mass education to the status of not just one of four principles, but of the prime mover in development:

The key to rapid and effective colonial development is mass adult education: education not just in literacy, or even primarily in literacy, but in life – in agriculture, in hygiene, in domestic living, in cultural values, in democratic organisation, in self-help, and so on.

It is to the credit of British administrators that they have kept their standards high, insisting on high technical qualifications for appointment to medical, agricultural, and similar posts. But fully qualified technicians are few and costly: they cannot be employed in large numbers, and even if they could be, the gap between them and the people is so large as to diminish their effectiveness. If a mass attack is to be made on colonial conditions, it must be by mass employment of the partially qualified.[74]

As is implicit in this quotation, Lewis's conception of mass education has broadened from what it was in 1944. Then, it had a clear bias towards agriculture and rural development. Now, it is concerned with other sectors of the economy, in particular health (notably public health and the control of epidemic disease), manufacturing and construction, and the training required for those activities. In his report he asks the Colonial Office, as his primary negative recommendation, to cut its expenditure on activities not of primary developmental importance, notably infrastructure and lavish buildings, in order to focus on mass education. At this point Lewis's vision takes on a pastoral tone, some might say bordering on the impractical:

> The money spent building a fine school for 500 children could be much better spent on training the teachers who will gather thousands of children round them in the open air under trees for their first entry into the new world of reading.[75]

What happens when it rains?, one would love to ask.

Lewis's positive recommendation is that colonial administrations should refocus their expenditure on relieving 'bottlenecks', primary among which is 'training the local staff and multiplying the agricultural assistants, the sanitary workers, the medical assistants and teachers who are the spearhead of development'. Therefore, he proposes that 'the first priority should be the multiplication of partly trained assistants to work in mass education campaigns'.[76]

Though the Colonial Office bureaucracy, understandably, did not like being told that their development plans were a waste of resources, they were content to go along, rather huffily, with Lewis's reformulation of Creech Jones' mass education proposals,[77] often insisting that they were just 'an intensification of district administration',[78] in other words, of the decentralization of power to the regions with an emphasis on the more backward districts. In May 1948, the Colonial Office was asked to reflect, in each of its territories, on what might be needed to get the idea of 'mass education and community development' understood and implemented, and once that was done, to set up training centres in each territory, or, in Nigeria, in each region. It was emphasized that mass education did not mean just the expansion of government facilities, and that 'the maximum encouragement should be given to spontaneous movements organised by missions and other voluntary agencies',[79] with co-operatives having an especially privileged place among these. A flurry of global paperwork flew back and forth all through the summer and autumn of 1948 as each territory laboured to produce its statutory mass education strategy, just as today's aid-recipient countries now labour to produce their Poverty Reduction Strategies. In the process, Lewis's recommendation that the budget for mass education should be increased at the expense of central services, such as higher education and infrastructure, was watered down, and individual colonies' mass education strategies were represented as an evolution rather than a revolution.[80] Nor did the Colonial Office pick up on the idea of mass education as being driven by 'the community' – that is, native Africans and West Indians, even though at that very time riots in the Gold Coast (and elsewhere) were trying to emphasize that the distribution of power, and not just resources, needed to change.[81] Lewis had certainly achieved much a more harmonious relationship over development policy this time than he had four years previously; but whether it brought more leverage is debatable. His mass education initiative was brilliantly conceived and widely circulated, but in spite of the misleading title given to the document, *Principles of Economic Planning*, which sounds comprehensive enough, it did not cover the whole field of economic policy as in 1943–4, and in fact shone its spotlight simply on mass education, which is only one of the many problems of development.

Lewis's interventions in colonial development policy in 1944 and 1948 indeed make a fascinating comparison, the former a comprehensive strategy which, for all its innovative brilliance got nowhere, and the latter a single-issue campaign that was successfully embodied into policy. One's judgement on the achievements of the 'year of mass education' is inevitably subjective. If a sympathetic approach is taken, Lewis successfully caught a political tide, and furthermore did so by applying conscientiously the economist's approach of 'going for the cancer', concentrating scarce public resources where they could do the most good. But a less charitable observer might say that the quality most evident in the 1944 document, its comprehensiveness and integration, has been lost.

The mass education wave eventually receded, even before the end of the Attlee administration and its replacement by a less egalitarian government; but the guiding idea remained, and indeed is an approach which has never, except in the dark days of the 1980s, lost its political salience, both in Britain and globally. Indeed, even within the life of the Creech Jones initiative, the Mass Education sub-committee had been renamed the Mass Education and Community Development sub-committee – thereby prefiguring the multiple uses to which the idea of community development was to be put during the McNamara pro-poor initiatives of the 1970s, as well as the focus put on primary health and education during the much more extensive period of 'poverty focus' 20 years later, leading to the establishment of the Millennium Development Goals.[82] Not only this, but 'new growth theory', which elevates knowledge to the status of a factor of production more powerful than any other in promoting economic growth, has now risen, without any acknowledgement whatever to Lewis, to dominate modern thinking on growth (Romer, 1986; Barro and Sala-i-Martin, 1992; Sala-i-Martin, 1997; Hendry and Krolzig, 2004). And while the idea of mass education was not Lewis's but simply a wave that he rode, it was he who first researched its economic implications, and exposed the disconnect between mass education as an idea and the material resources which colonial governments were making available for its implementation. The exercise had been a useful one for him, and he remembered his Colonial Office datasets when writing *The Theory of Economic Growth* in 1954 – and even more when writing *Development Planning* almost 20 years later.

Apart from mass education, there is another important strand of policy in which Lewis's influence can be traced, relating to rural credit and indebtedness. Arthur Lewis was the economist with first-hand experience of colonial agriculture. Among his circle of radical friends and colleagues in London, peasant agriculture, rural labour and the plantation system were at the forefront in debates on decolonization. He made a strong personal contribution to deliberations in the CEDC about the role of agriculture and, in particular, rural credit and cooperatives. Often in his writings in the 1940s he championed the development of peasant agriculture: the urgent need for rural water supplies; the need to promote improved tools, fertilizers and soil conservation; the value of agricultural extension schemes; and the importance of village-level savings and crop insurance schemes. None of these policies would be out of place in today's rural development agenda. They do not seem at all 'radical' or 'revolutionary'. But in Lewis's time at the Colonial Office this is how they were regarded. Speaking at the Manchester Statistical Society in 1949 about the lack of progress in peasant agriculture Lewis said:

> we have not got past the stage of thinking in terms of new highly mechanised plantations, and begun to put the emphasis on increasing the yield of native production. In consequence the provision for

agricultural education is meagre, the capital needed to expend production has not been set aside, and the necessary institutions are not being established ... until it is accomplished a potential source of wealth remains relatively underdeveloped. [83]

In 1946, a UN/FAO Conference called on colonial governments who were interested in rural development to halt the progress of rural indebtedness. The Colonial Office reported on this and proposed that enquiries should be set up to look into the debt position of rural communities in the British colonies.[84] Lewis proposed that this be considered in the Research sub-committee of the CEDC, and with the support of Lewis and probably also at his direction, a Memorandum was drawn up by the Secretary to the sub-committee, Phyllis Deane, criticizing the Colonial Office's neglect of the problem of rural indebtedness. The subject had 'so nearly perished of old age and lack of nourishment'.[85]

The Colonial Office had neglected the problem, and in consequence there were large gaps in the information on indebtedness. The Memorandum turned out to be a masterpiece of special pleading on behalf of the academic community, not surprisingly, bearing in mind the membership of the Research sub-committee. It went on to recommend that

> honest and thorough research by private researchers with no aim but the advancement of knowledge may in the long run provide the best foundation for public policy. If such work can be sponsored and financed by universities, trusts or private institutions, it should be given a full measure of official support.

The Colonial Office accepted the recommendations in the Memorandum, but there is no evidence of any subsequent action being taken in the way of official support. Rural credit provides one post-war example of Lewis lobbying in a practical way for agricultural development. While he was still in situ on the CEAC, its Finance sub-committee had submitted a report on agricultural credit in the Colonies, which was not published until 1946. The striking feature of the report is how it articulates many of the problems that have now come to be identified with micro-finance. Existing short-term credit facilities for small farmers are inadequate. Loans are needed to meet expenses in the interval between sowing and harvesting. Banks are not interested in handling rural credit, as repayments are uncertain and recovery of debt difficult. Moneylenders with local knowledge thrive in these situations.

The preference in the CEAC report was for co-operative credit societies, a proposal that was to please Creech Jones and his colleagues in the Fabian Society:

> members are usually well-known to each other, and loans, which are issued on personal security, are backed by the unlimited liability of the whole membership. There are few formalities, operating expenses are low, and the rate of interest charged for loans is moderate ... to succeed it demands punctual dealings, thrift, honesty, and an appreciation of the value of self-help and mutual aid.[86]

Lewis, as we have already noted, was a firm advocate of thrift. An increase in personal saving was always high on his list of desirable changes in poor societies. He was less convinced, we would suggest, by the supposed strength of the co-operative ethos in delivering the desired results. As in farming, for example, he would never concede that larger units organized on *collective* principles might raise productivity levels in agriculture significantly. His own solution to credit shortages, however, was certainly innovative. In a later note to Creech Jones on the Colonial Development Corporation, Lewis took the opportunity to stress the importance of rural credit to the Colonies. He pointed out that this was not a policy that could be put into effect at a distance. It was 'a job for agencies on the spot, with very careful supervision'. He went on to suggest that the CDC had been willing to lend money to local institutions for the expansion of rural credit, and that he himself had tried to encourage the government in Jamaica to borrow from the Corporation for this very purpose but without success. In fact, he said, there had been no enthusiasm among colonial governments for promoting rural savings and credit institutions with funds from the CDC. Of course, the Corporation was not permitted to lend directly to governments, but it was allowed to support public corporations, and from there it could have channelled funds, under supervision, to local savings and credit institutions. However, for this it needed the support of the colonial governments, and it appears that this was not forthcoming.

Like the CEAC, the CEDC was never regarded as a success in official circles. The incoming Conservative Secretary of State, Lennox Boyd, wound it up with few regrets in 1951. The CEDC membership had comprised the great and the good: ex-colonial governors, Members of Parliament, directors of companies with overseas operations, senior members of the TUC and the co-operative movement, plus a sprinkling of academics. When the CEDC was wound up in 1951, the Colonial Office stressed its lack of achievements, though in truth it had never been encouraged to achieve anything. It was rare for the number of members attending the full Council meetings to rise above six, out of a dozen or so who were eligible. The usual number of attendees at such meetings was two or three. One does not have to search far for the reasons for this. All the important advisory work took place in the sub-committees. This was how Creech Jones wanted matters settled, and much took place behind closed doors. Understandably, the Council had misgivings about its role from the start. After the Secretary of State had departed at its first meeting, the chairman expressed the view that, 'if these Committees with outside membership did all the detailed work and submitted conclusions to the Council, the latter might find itself with little more to do than formally endorse the Committee's recommendations'.[87] Which is, of course, what happened, though few of the recommendations of the sub-committees ever found their way into colonial policy.

3.4   Lewis and the Colonial Development Corporation

In August 1943, Sydney Caine produced a Memorandum for the CEAC. It was drawn up at the point during the Second World War when the tide was beginning to flow towards an Allied victory, though there was still a long way to go. Caine's Memorandum arose from his perception that there was 'not enough original and coherent thinking about the possibilities of development.' Machinery for that kind of thinking was virtually non-existent, in fact, and as a result not enough schemes were being produced: Caine commented, 'When the war is over, we shall be asked where our plans are, and the answer is likely to be somewhat embarrassing'.

It was these considerations which led Caine to the conclusion that it would be 'necessary to set up a body independent of existing authorities ... in order to conceive and carry out the major projects'. Caine went on to say 'I think a strong organisation in or attached to the Colonial Office, with considerably more powers or at any rate habit of initiation than exists at present, is really essential ... This is perhaps getting dangerously near the idea of a Colonial Development Board.' Caine's proposal for 'a company clothed in commercial form but in fact working as the agent of Government' came as close as his Memorandum got to proposing a structure recognizably similar to that eventually accorded to the CDC.

To understand why Lewis might have had misgivings about this project from the start, it is important to place the initiative in context. Towards the end of the Second World War, the problem of war finance was being overtaken by the massive anticipated costs of reconstruction both at home and abroad. After brief discussions in the Treasury, in the final phase of lend-lease, Keynes circulated a Memorandum to the War Cabinet on overseas financial policy. Taking stock of the situation, with an annual deficit running in current prices at about £1,400 million per annum, Keynes warned of 'an indefinite postponement of colonial development' unless further financial aid was forthcoming from the USA.[88] What is important to note here is that the USA was to provide aid to Britain to enable it to support colonial development. Caine had made it absolutely clear in reply to a question put to him by the CEAC in 1944, that neither foreign countries (that is, the USA) nor international development banks would be approached for direct assistance to the Colonies: 'H.M.G. will *not* approach any foreign countries or international investment fund which may be established, specifically for loans for colonial development.'[89]

At this stage in the planning for the CDC, the Colonial Office was mindful of the pressures in the Conservative Party, and the strong opposition to the Bretton Woods agreement from Beaverbrook and others close to Churchill.

Lewis, it should be remembered, had already questioned whether much of the British private capital that had flowed into the Colonies had raised the welfare of their populations in any way. More important, perhaps, he questioned whether investment in the Colonies from countries other than Britain should have been resisted so heavily.[90] Lewis was critical of the way in which US investment in Britain's colonies had been discouraged by successive British governments after 1918. In Trinidad, of foremost interest to Lewis, only British companies could lease oil lands. As for exports, discriminatory duties discouraged the export of tin ore from Malaya and Nigeria to the USA. Finally, colonial government loans could only be raised in London. There were also misgivings surrounding the new Bretton Woods arrangements, especially funding from the International Bank for Reconstruction and Development (IBRD) (The World Bank), an institution for which Lewis's former teacher at the LSE, Lionel Robbins, had taken a leading role in support of in negotiations. Lewis was later (1949) to criticize strongly the failure of the Colonial Office to engage with the World Bank.[91] It is not hard to see that Lewis would have had difficulty from the outset with proposals for the new public corporation, seeing them as yet another manifestation of imperial exploitation.

We have reported in this chapter that Arthur Lewis had resigned the CEAC Secretaryship in November 1944 and was not initially included in the CEDC when that was set up in 1946, with a 'Development Division' under Sydney Caine. One of the first matters the CEDC was asked to discuss was the response from colonial governors to the possibility of establishing development corporations, a Memorandum (which drew heavily on the earlier Caine Memorandum) having been dispatched to colonial governments in 1945. At its meeting in December 1946, the CEDC noted a certain 'inertia and opposition' on the part of colonial governments, and it was further remarked that large sums of money would be needed to finance the proposed development corporations.

Caine nevertheless persisted, though the attitude of colonial governors might have influenced the decision of the CEDC in early 1947 to recommend the setting up not of many corporations, but of a single one. A second Memorandum, entitled 'Proposed Formation of a Colonial Development Corporation' was prepared by Caine in April 1947. The Corporation's 'primary jobs' would be the preliminary investigation, promotion and launch of new enterprises of a productive kind. The Act of Parliament establishing CDC was passed in 1948. The remit of the corporation was: 'to promote increased colonial production on an economic and self-supporting basis with an eye particularly to the production of foodstuffs and raw materials, where supply to the United Kingdom or sale overseas will assist in (improving) the balance of payments'.[92]

At the same time, the corporation was required by its terms of reference to avoid projects that ordinary private enterprise was willing to handle. In essence, its function was, and still is, to lever private capital into the UK government development effort. This gives it an inevitable bias towards middle-income beneficiaries, since private capital is not interested in projects whose private yields are low or risky, irrespective of what their social yield might be. Indeed, the CDC was (and in its modern incarnation as the Commonwealth Development Corporation, still is) in intention the most commercially advantageous, and least idealistic, element in the aid programme. At the outset, in 1948, there was broad support for the idea of the CDC (Creech Jones, as we have seen, was particularly keen on any instrument that would give him leverage within the Cabinet, and CDC achieved this, because it delivered – or was expected to deliver – scarce foreign exchange).

But there was much debate about the micro-strategies it should follow, and in particular about whether it should target large-scale or small-scale firms. Surprisingly, it was the Labour Party, the advocate of mass education and of vulnerable Third World people, who were the main proponents in Parliament of 'big push' mechanized agriculture, and the Conservative Party, the party of capital, which spoke up most for peasant production. It was Lord Swinton, a former Conservative Colonial Secretary in the Lords, who insisted, 'Development cannot all be large-scale ... indeed the greater part of production in the Colonial Empire will continue in the future, as it has been in the past, to be the work of millions of small producers,'[93] Lewis was invited by Creech Jones to join the board of the CDC in 1948, at the same time as the CEDC, but he declined the invitation, under the stress of the many additional commitments attached to his new professorial post in Manchester.

As we have seen, Lewis's growing professional commitments probably masked his fundamental unease with the CDC. Nevertheless, three years later, in 1951, the invitation was renewed, and this time Lewis accepted. But by now the Labour government was on the verge of being replaced by a Conservative administration, and in this environment the socialist Lewis was to find it even harder to gain support for his ideas within the CDC. The experience of developing countries that Lewis gained within the Colonial Office percolated into his research through a number of channels. At this exciting moment, however, at the end of the 1940s and beginning of the 1950s, he did not write his development policy ideas up for publication: they remained buried in the archives of the Colonial Office. What he longed to do at this time, rather, was to return home to the West Indies with the help of his new 'colonial economics' perspective, and to blend that perspective with the long-period historical approach of which he had become so fond at the LSE. His feelings are expressed in a letter written to the Director of the LSE at this time:

For some years I have been hoping one day to write a social and economic history of the West Indies since the emancipation of slavery in 1838. The field is practically untouched although the period is fascinating. I have been reading through the literature off and on, and am actually giving a course on it to the welfare students. But it cannot be mastered without time, and in particular it will be necessary to work in local records, especially in Jamaica, for a good deal of material which is not available in London. My only hope of being able to complete such a study on a really scholarly basis is something like one of these Leverhulmes, for a year.[94]

Lewis's wish to write a history of the Caribbean, with funding from Leverhulme, did have a very positive outcome. As related in an interview with Gisela Eisner, Lewis's doctoral student at University of Manchester, it funded two researchers, of whom Gisela Eisner was the second, to travel to Jamaica to carry out research under the direction of Arthur Lewis. In Dr Eisner's case, the result was her impressive book, *Jamaica 1830–1930: A Study in Economic Growth* (1961) to which Lewis wrote a generous and substantial Foreword from his office as Principal of the University College of the West Indies in Mona, Jamaica, in 1959.

Lewis's work for the Colonial Office on planning for developing countries served to rebuild his morale substantially after the rebuffs of 1943. At the same time, it served as a window that opened up new ways of looking at the experience of developing countries, both historical and analytic, and connected Lewis to a new range of intellectual contacts around the world, who then enabled him to generalize his ideas and thereby to launch himself into more ambitious work. By early 1950, indeed, instead of having to volunteer to produce a development plan for the British colonies, Lewis was being invited to produce one for the entire developing world.

Lewis, as discussed above, did not accept the seat on the CDC that he was initially offered while still at the LSE, in early 1947. Between 1947 and 1950, under its first chairman, Lord Trefgarne, the CDC lost a great deal of (public) money on its initial investments, and became an embarrassment to the government rather than the jewel in the financial crown that Creech Jones had fondly wished it to be. By 1951, when the Corporation was reporting a loss of almost £3 million for the previous year,[95] there was a chorus in the press castigating the CDC as a white elephant, and clamouring for it to be reformed or shut down.[96] The former course was chosen, and at the end of Trefgarne's term, Lord Reith, the austere Scottish chairman of the BBC, was asked to take over. Shortly after this, in May 1951, the invitation to Lewis to become a member of the board was renewed, and this time he accepted.

By now, Lewis could no longer be characterized merely as a bumptious young man in a hurry, as many of his adversaries on the CEAC had labelled him. In 1951, as we shall discuss in Chapter 4, he was to play a leading role in the preparation of the UN's *Measures for the Economic Development of Underdeveloped Countries*. He was no longer a lecturer doubling as Secretary of a working group on the Colonies, but a professor of development economics with global experience.

However, in this new role, Lewis was constrained five times over:

(1) There was a mess to clear up. CDC had lost so much money in its early, experimental phase that there was no more scope for exciting experiments but only for the grey and unromantic work of consolidation.

(2) Lewis's raw material was not, as on the CEAC, the exciting job of planning overall development strategy, but simply one particular, not very visionary, element within this.

(3) As an ordinary board member, Lewis did not have the freedom of manoeuvre he had had as secretary to the CEAC to set the agenda: the agenda was set for him.

(4) After 1951, the government was Conservative. Even though Lewis could still draw on intellectual and moral support from the Fabian Society, he now had less support around the table when introducing proposals that were distributionally progressive.

(5) Indeed, Lewis had less 'social capital' available to him than he had had on the CEAC: there was nobody on the board to support him if opinion were to turn against him. Durbin had died in 1948; the only economist on the CDC board was the conservative Oxford professor, S. Herbert Frankel, who did not even share Lewis's belief in the need for accelerated development.

During his time at the CDC, Lewis made one overseas trip on behalf of the Corporation, to Malaya and south-east Asia, in September 1952, and submitted one Memorandum to the board, dated 20 December 1952. Like his CEAC memoranda, it seeks to establish operating principles for the organization. Its point of departure is that CDC projects need to incentivize development around the entire local economy, a principle later made famous by A. O. Hirschman:[97]

> The most useful projects are those which start a chain reaction. That is, those the consequence of which is that other entrepreneurs are set in motion, so that the total increase in output resulting from our action is a multiplier of what we produce ourselves.[98]

Gradually, all of the four guiding principles from his 'Colonial Economic Development' document of 1943 were then brought to bear on the unpromising raw material of the reform of the CDC. He began by applying to the Corporation his third fundamental principle of development policy: small-scale agriculture is the crux, both on equity and efficiency grounds:

> The greatest of all needs in colonial development is to get more capital invested in native production, whether in agriculture, animal husbandry, fishing or workshop industry (mining is not a small-scale industry, and transport and commerce get as much capital as they need).[99]

He then brought in the fourth principle – mass education – arguing that:

> Our plantations should be planned in the way which teaches native producers most. They should preferably be small, and not highly mechanised.[100]

Innocently enough, he then invokes the economist's standard principle that enterprises, including CDC, need to operate at the least cost if they are to be competitive and avoid being a burden on the taxpayer – a proposition which, of course, was of particular relevance to the retrenchment that the CDC was being required to carry out. But then, to make his key point, he goes back to his old CEDC habit of splitting the functional allocation of expenditure into its component parts, and, by exposing what lies underneath, lights the touchpaper:

> *High overheads.* We ought to keep the European staff down to a minimum. For several reasons:
>
> (i) European staff is very expensive. In many cases our project has to face the competition of enterprises run by natives, Indians, Chinese, local whites, or foreign producers. To such people an annual income of £300 a year is a lot of money, and if we are to start off with a managerial bill running up to £10,000 (Project Manager, Accountant, Engineer and what not) our chance of competing is zero.
>
>   The corollary of this is: keep out of any industry which is already attracting many small people – road transport, rice, cotton, fishing, rubber – unless we are absolutely certain that we have some new technique which is so much superior to theirs that it can bear heavy overheads. Unless we can get our overheads down, the field in which we can hope to be successful is rather narrow.

(ii)   If we have high overheads, we are driven to have very large projects in order to carry them. This is actually bad reasoning, since, the larger an agricultural project, the more likely it is to fail [but] ... our agricultural projects are almost without exception too large.

(iii)   We should also keep the European staff down because the mission to develop is a mission to develop people, not land. To train and use local staff wherever possible. One of the aspects of 'imperialism' which is most resented, whether in commerce or in government, is its tendency to create jobs for the boys – to bring people in to do jobs that the local people can do. CDC must at all cost avoid this charge. I have the impression, based on very little evidence, that this charge can be levied on CDC in respect of some of its accounting and engineering staff on overseas projects. The local book-keeper and local mechanic, I suspect, might be used more in place of imported staff. The number of Europeans we need to run a project and the salaries we have to pay them have continually astonished me in CDC. It has been explained to me that this is partly my West Indian background: in the West Indies there is a fair amount of cheap white and coloured experience-trained staff for management, accounting and engineering, so that overheads are kept down. But I am not satisfied that this is the only explanation.[101]

In May 1953, Lewis received a letter from the Colonial Secretary, Oliver Lyttelton, informing him that his appointment to the board of the CDC was not to be renewed. In an interview with *The Manchester Guardian*, Lewis expressed his hurt and disappointment:

'I can only conclude,' Professor Lewis told a *Manchester Guardian* reporter last night, 'that Mr Lyttelton's decision is a result of a broadcast talk I made last July in which I opposed the Central African Federation scheme. Even so, I had always thought my appointment to the corporation left me free to comment on events. Certainly other members of the corporation have criticised other aspects of Government policy.[102]

The hurt was greater because Lewis had been taken by surprise. In contrast with the case in CEAC, where he had seen a collision coming and taken his own steps to avoid it, in this case he had not foreseen trouble.

However, Lewis had by that point been given some background information as to what was the root cause of the trouble. A fortnight before
his interview with *The Manchester Guardian*, he had telephoned the
chairman of the CDC board, Sir Thomas Lloyd, and had a discussion
with him. (On the front of the file that gives the record of that discussion, the words 'dismissal of' Professor Arthur Lewis have been deleted
and replaced by the words 'non-reappointment of').[103] The record of
that conversation is as follows:

[Lewis said on the telephone] that he would very much like to know
what the reason [for his dismissal] was; whether we at the CDC had
not been satisfied with him; or whether there was something political between him and the CO.

I had replied then to the effect that there was not necessarily anything of either; and it was not a 'dismissal'; the term for which he was
appointed had expired ... I said that if he would care to look in on me
on his next visit to London I would be glad to see him; this meeting
was accordingly fixed.

When I saw (the) S(ecretary) of S(tate) early in the year he had gone
over the appointments expiring in February ... And though, because
[Lewis's appointment did not expire until April] there was no discussion about himself, it was obvious to me that S of S was not minded
to reappoint him; and indeed I had gathered this some time before.

Repeating that there was no need to search for specific explanation, I said I would tell him if he liked what had occurred to me as
possibly part explanation of the attitude I had sensed. It was not anything to do, as far as I knew, with [the] Central African Federation
(which he had mentioned on the telephone): it might perhaps have
something to do with a broadcast he had made last summer. I had
not heard it [but] there was no doubt that it had been considerably
resented.

Professor Lewis said he had wondered if that were the explanation ... I said there was another small matter ... He would
remember saying when he met Dato Onn [the head of a Malaysian
Corporation in which the CDC was considering investing, whom
Lewis had visited on business in late 1952] he had found him hostile to the Corporation, regarding it as an instrument of imperial exploitation or something of that sort. In a letter to me he
(Professor Lewis) had remarked that, having agreed with him (or
words to that effect) they had got on well together. I said it was a
long letter about conditions in Malaya and the Corporation's work

there; I had copies circulated to the Directors. I knew that this remark about Dato Onn had been taken amiss by some of our own people. But I was sure that had nothing to do with the present position.[104]

There is a confusion within Sir Thomas Lloyd's remarks, since the broadcast Lewis had made in July 1952, contrary to the implication of Sir Thomas's remarks, was indeed about the Central African Federation. Lewis's message was that the Federation (of Southern Rhodesia, Northern Rhodesia and Nyasaland, which came into being in 1953) was not a thing that Britain should encourage, because it would give support to racial discrimination, which was at the time being practised in Southern Rhodesia, the dominant partner in the federation. This was something he had been saying for a long time, and in February 1953 he had written to *The Observer* newspaper that 'if this [federation] scheme is pushed through, the good name of Britain will stink throughout Africa, in Asia, in America, and throughout the United Nations'.[105] However, as the interview transcript shows, the reasons for Lewis's dismissal go much deeper than the position he had taken on Central Africa. He had accused the Colonial Office of conniving at racial discrimination by giving preference to high-cost European labour over low-cost indigenous labour – in encouraging Central African federation certainly, but also in Malaya in the case related by Sir Thomas, where he was regarded as conspiring with another non-European to be disloyal to 'the home team'; and indeed, on every one of the CDC projects mentioned in Lewis's internal memorandum of 20 December 1952. Through this discrimination, not only was hypocrisy being perpetrated, but the CDC's (that is, the taxpayer's) money, for which Lewis was a trustee, was being squandered. Given that Lewis no longer had friends at court, it was no wonder that the Colonial Office refused to tolerate such candour any longer. But the reverse to his position still hurt Lewis bitterly. In other cases, as we have already seen with the CEAC, his relationships with bodies he was advising were to end in frustration and acrimony; but in those cases he was always able to exit on something like his own terms. Only in this case was he removed against his will.

4
'It takes hard work to be accepted in the academic world': Manchester University, 1948–57

4.1 Leaving the LSE

'Dr. Lewis who was recently appointed to the Readership in Colonial Economics is resigning to take up a Chair in Economics at the University of Manchester.' This brief statement in the Minutes of the London School of Economics Professorial Council in December 1947 signalled the end of Lewis's critical decade and a half at the LSE, the phase of his life he described so graphically in his Laureate autobiographical account, as offering him such 'marvellous intellectual feasts'.

Why Lewis decided to leave the LSE in 1947, having been promoted so recently to Reader, is a difficult question to answer. Robert Tignor, Lewis's American biographer, confirms that Lewis did not discuss in later years the reasons for his move to Manchester, nor, it appears, did he provide any clues as to whether the move had fulfilled his expectations. In Lewis's own account, in the Laureate autobiography, he devotes just one sentence to the University of Manchester, which simply records his appointment there to the Stanley Jevons Chair in Political Economy. So what prompted the move to Manchester, a move that deprived him of the intellectual traditions of the LSE which he clearly valued, and took him away from his base within the broader radical community of 1940s London?

Tignor believes that Lewis was keen to leave the LSE because he could see no further promotion prospects, given the age structure of the School. This is possible, but it is unlikely to be the whole story, since Lewis was still relatively young for a Chair at the University of London – Chair appointments at the LSE were still the responsibility of the University of London at that date. Recall that Lewis was only 33 years of age when he left for the Chair at Manchester. As he had recently been promoted to a Reader at the LSE, and had the support of senior faculty such as Hayek and Plant, it seems reasonable to assume that he would also have progressed to a Chair at the LSE in due course had he remained in post. Other, more immediate factors, may have come into play and influenced his decision to leave the LSE and move to Manchester.

As noted in Chapter 2, Lewis had taken on a wide range of teaching and administrative roles at the LSE during the war years. Because he was ineligible for war service, he had been available to teach on the LSE degrees during the School's evacuation to Cambridge. He had taught extensively on courses offered in Cambridge to combined classes of Cambridge and LSE undergraduates. The LSE Calendars give details of the lectures Lewis delivered at Cambridge during the war years. He had sole responsibility (24 lectures) for the economics of transport. He provided lectures on business enterprises and business policy. In the core Elements of Economics course he covered topics in money, banking and international economics. This was a substantial and demanding teaching load, involving prestigious courses in the core economics degree programmes.

By 1946, however, Lewis appears to have 'lost' this teaching. Arnold Plant had returned from wartime service to take over the business administration courses. Gilbert Ponsonby had arrived at LSE, newly appointed to deliver the economics of transport lectures. He later became Reader, and later Professor in Transport at the LSE. Remembering that Lewis's own designation at the LSE had been as Lecturer 'with special reference to Transport' one can only speculate how Lewis might have responded to these changes, which withdrew his wider teaching responsibilities on the core undergraduate degree programmes. That was not all. In the absence of Arnold Plant and Frederic Benham on war service, Lewis had been appointed as external examiner in economics for the University of London. When faculty returned after the war, Lewis's appointment as external examiner came to an end.

There is no doubt that the colonial economics course that Lewis took on, willingly or otherwise, to replace his undergraduate teaching (the designation of his recent promotion to Reader was in colonial economics) was of a fairly low status at the LSE. It was not offered in the LSE undergraduate degree programme but was part of a one-year vocational training course provided by the University of London, with the aim of preparing young cadets and officials for the colonial service. Such courses had been offered since the early 1930s at Oxford, Cambridge and

London. Recruits were overwhelmingly male graduates of Oxford and Cambridge, who had their fees paid by the Crown Agents. Economics was only one of the components of these courses and was by no means the most important subject. The other subjects covered in the courses were law, anthropology, languages, history, geography and colonial administration. Within economics, the focus was on economic theory, currency and banking.

The colonial studies courses offered in Oxford, Cambridge and London were under increasing scrutiny from the Colonial Office during the 1940s. Times were changing and it was recognized that the ingredients in the mix also needed to change. The colonial economics course for which Lewis was responsible post-war at LSE resulted from a review in 1944, which had recommended that London courses be updated to bring them more into line with Colonial Office thinking in the decolonization era. The newly designed LSE course in colonial economics had two parts. The first part was a conventional introduction to micro-economics: the price system, exchange and specialization, and the functional distribution of income. The second part, entitled 'Applied Economics for Colonial Students' was something quite new. It came as close to development economics as one was likely to get in British universities in the 1940s. The LSE Calendar for 1947 lists its components as follows: agricultural economics; population density; land tenure; marketing, credit, and co-operation; international commodity arrangements; seasonal fluctuations; the role of the state in development; secondary industries including handicrafts; and imperial preference. The lecturer was stated to be Dr Lewis. Scrutiny of the topics on offer leads to the conclusion that he most probably designed the course as well.

Why, then, did Lewis claim in his Laureate autobiographical account that he did not teach development economics as such until he arrived at Manchester? The likely answer is that he had already left the LSE for Manchester by the time Part II was due to be delivered. The evidence for this is in the correspondence relating to Dr Ida Greaves, who took over the Colonial Economics course in 1948. This correspondence also sheds light on the low status of the colonial economics course at the LSE as well as calling into question the School's treatment of Ida Greaves, one of its more distinguished female postgraduates. In June 1948, Carr-Saunders, the LSE Director, wrote to Ida Greaves in Barbados, soliciting her help on the Colonial Economics course:

I am writing to ask you whether you can help us next session. Dr. W. A. Lewis, Reader in Colonial Economics, has resigned from the staff of the School in order to occupy a Chair at the University of Manchester. We are not proposing to fill the Readership for the moment, and in these circumstances we have to make provision for certain teaching in colonial economics next session ... we would offer an honorarium of 250 guineas.[1]

Ida Greaves was not a junior postgraduate research fellow or teaching assistant, as might be inferred from Carr -Saunders' letter and the modest remuneration on offer. She was older than Lewis by some ten years and had graduated from McGill University in Montreal in 1930 with first-class honours in Economics, followed by Resident Fellowships at Harvard and Bryn Mawr in the USA. In 1932 she had arrived at the LSE to study for a doctorate on the organization of labour in tropical agriculture, under the supervision of Arnold Plant. Her thesis, highly commended by Plant, who described her as a 'brilliant' student, was published by George Allen & Unwin in 1936. When contacted by the LSE to take on Lewis's teaching she was dealing post-war with family matters at her father's home in Barbados, following a spell working with the embryo United Nations.

Ida Greaves taught on the colonial economics course at the LSE for two years from 1948, before resigning in 1950 to take up a post in Trinidad. The LSE honorarium of 250 guineas per annum was far from generous. It covered supervisory work, plus designated lectures and weekly tutorials in colonial economics.[2] It would appear that the LSE expected (and got) value for money. The post of Reader vacated by Lewis was never filled.

The courses at LSE for cadets in the colonial service ended in 1950, and those for officers ended in 1954. Dahrendorf discusses the decline in the number of 'occasional' students at the LSE as part of a planned change in the composition of its student body after 1945. It was intended that there should be a rise in first degree and postgraduate degree students. Colonial economics was discontinued alongside the Railway Course, the Exchequer and Audit Course, and much of the provision for evening students.[3]

It is open to speculation as to how Lewis would have seen his own future and that of colonial economics in this changing academic environment. There was a further consideration: Lewis had married Gladys Jacobs in 1947 in Grenada. His financial position in London had always been precarious and now there were further responsibilities.[4] A Chair at Manchester must have seemed an attractive proposition, offering a higher salary, cheaper and more suitable family accommodation than provided by his Chelsea flat, and possibly more secure career prospects.

Figure 4.1 Lewis's house in West Didsbury, Manchester
Source: Author photograph.

Early in 1948, he moved to West Didsbury, Manchester (see Figure 4.1), where his two children, Barbara and Elizabeth, were born, and where his most celebrated works were written.

Against this, he would have needed to set the prestige of the LSE in teaching and research in economics. Earlier in 1947, Lewis had been turned down for a Chair in another provincial university, in this case, the University of Liverpool. His failure to be appointed to a Chair at Liverpool was a disgraceful episode based on quite open racial prejudice.[5] In retrospect, however, Lewis lost nothing by this setback in Liverpool. In the late 1940s the academic and business community in Manchester was significantly more diverse, more tolerant and less provincial than its Liverpool counterpart. Manchester turned out to be the place where Lewis flourished as an academic, and more widely as an economic adviser and internationally respected consultant on development.

Lewis's decade at the University of Manchester was for him one of unremitting effort. It involved the young Lewis in writing, research, teaching, travelling, broadcasting, and even in pushing forward local good causes. He put his heart and soul into his role as an academic economist during these years. In 1958, at the end of his Manchester years, Lewis's colleague from his London days, George Padmore, died in Accra. Lewis wrote a moving tribute to him, from which the quote in the heading of this chapter is taken. In it, Lewis alludes to the sheer hard work necessary for him to be accepted as an economist in the academic world of the 1940s and 1950s.

4.2   Manchester's academic community

What kind of academic community did Lewis encounter when he arrived at the University of Manchester in 1947?[6] The university had evolved very differently from the LSE. In the immediate post-war period, the Victoria University of Manchester (this was its designation until 2004) was the largest civic university in Britain, with Faculties covering arts, science, law, medicine, music, philosophy, technology and education, plus, of course, the Faculty of Economic and Social Studies, in which Lewis's Chair was located. Economics did not have the prominence it enjoyed at the LSE. Instead, the University that Lewis joined still reflected 200 years of Manchester's industrial past. Textiles had been the foundation of Manchester's industrial pre-eminence two centuries before, but newer industries such as aircraft and pharmaceuticals had arisen to take the place of the declining textile industry. There was also a flourishing commercial presence in Manchester, with a number of powerful locally-based banks. In the university, support for academic developments, for new degree programmes, for buildings and even for Chairs, was still heavily dependent on the enthusiasm, not to mention finance, coming from local business and industry. For example, there were a substantial number of prestigious postgraduate research scholarships and fellowships in applied sciences, mathematics and engineering, all funded by industry. Lewis, during his time at Manchester, needed to attract the interest of industrial leaders and heads of banks in support of various projects. In the immediate postwar period, physics, chemistry, and medicine were the recognized centres of excellence at the University of Manchester, and there were hugely important research developments in applied science, technology and mathematics. The year 1948 marked the world's first electronic digital storage computer, built in the Department of Mathematics at Manchester. Here were based the Bletchley Park code breakers led by Alan Turing. In the 1940s, Manchester University was also the home of the distinguished radio astronomer Bernard Lovell, who went on to construct the celebrated radio telescope at Jodrell Bank in Cheshire.

From what we know of Lewis, with his interest in industrial and applied economics, and even his juvenile ambitions to train as an engineer, Manchester's strong practical inclination in science and technology would not have been a deterrent to him in seeking a post at the university. He would have known, however, that economics did not have the same status as the discipline at the LSE. It was not one of Manchester University's more prominent Departments. The seven Departments that comprised the Faculty of Economic and Social Studies occupied just one wing of a grim Victorian building in Dover Street, which had previously housed the Manchester High School for Girls. Much of Victorian Manchester remained on the south side of the city in the 1940s, and parts of Dover Street were little changed from the 1840s, when No. 1 Dover Street was the first Manchester home of the novelist Elizabeth Gaskell and her husband, a Unitarian minister. When Lewis joined the Economics Department, some areas of the Faculty were still accommodated in outlying areas of south Manchester in temporary buildings.

At the University of Manchester in 1948 there were only two Chairs in the Department of Economics. There was the more senior Stanley Jevons Chair in Political Economy, which Lewis himself came to occupy from 1949, and a second Chair in Social Economics. Lewis's predecessor in the Chair of Political Economy was John Jewkes, who had succeeded John Hicks. Hicks had held the appointment between 1938 and 1945 before his return to Oxford. John Jewkes had been recruited initially as Professor of Social Economics in 1936. Ely Devons was appointed to the second Chair in 1948, and at that point the designation was changed from Social Economics to Applied Economics. The fact that the University had only two Chairs of Economics when Lewis took up his appointment is indicative of the gulf in status at that time between economics at Manchester and at the LSE. At the LSE, Arnold Plant and Lionel Robbins were back in post after the war. In addition, there were Professors Friedrich Hayek; F. W. Paish; E. H. Phelps Brown; R. S. Sayers; R. S. Edwards; Basil Yamey; and James Meade. These were the senior colleagues Lewis left behind when he moved to Manchester. It cannot have been an easy decision for him. The Department of Economics at Manchester remained a two-Chair Department through most of Lewis's time there. Towards the end of Lewis's Manchester years, in 1956, Harry Johnson was appointed to a third Chair – that of Economic Theory. After Lewis's departure in 1958, further Chairs were established, including one in Econometrics.

Though Lewis made intellectual sacrifices when he moved to Manchester, it would be wrong to infer from this that his achievements during the Manchester years emerged in some kind of intellectual vacuum. On the contrary, there had been highly significant developments in the social sciences in Manchester during the 1930s with the arrival at the University of significant numbers of 'displaced scholars' from continental Europe. Many of these social scientists had radical sympathies which harmonized with Lewis's own, and in retrospect their world views were probably more congenial to him than those of his colleagues at LSE, most of whom were wedded to liberal, and often to strict neo-classical, perspectives. Lewis seldom co-authored papers or books with colleagues, so it is difficult to trace influences on his thinking. It is unlikely, however, that he was unaffected by the intellectual influences current in social science in Manchester from the late 1930s onwards.

The complex history of Manchester's role in receiving displaced academics from Germany and Eastern Europe in the 1930s has begun to be unravelled.[7] Manchester was fourth, behind Oxford, Cambridge and the LSE, in receiving refugee scholars. Most of the academics placed in Manchester – professors, lecturers and students – came from science, technology or medical disciplines. Michael Polanyi was one of these. His career, however, was unusual in that he had arrived in Britain as a distinguished physical chemist. In 1933, he had resigned his Chair at the Kaiser-Wilhelm Institute of the University of Berlin in protest at the treatment of Jewish intellectuals. He accepted a Chair in Physical Chemistry at Manchester, in the Department made famous by the work of Ernest Rutherford, and later in the 1930s was instrumental in bringing to Britain his brother, the economist, Karl Polanyi, author of that remarkable economic history, *The Great Transformation* (1944). (Karl Polanyi's daughter is the development economist Kari Polanyi, who was a student of Lewis's at the LSE.) Dismayed by events in Europe, however, Polanyi had turned his mind increasingly towards philosophy, economics and social analysis, culminating in his book *Science, Faith and Society* (1946/1964), and he resigned from his chemistry Chair, with a view to emigrating to the USA and making a career in the social sciences there. However, this plan did not work out. Encouraged by Lewis, whose support at this crucial juncture he never forgot,[8] he applied to Manchester again, this time for a social science post; and was appointed to the Chair in Social Studies in 1948.

Gisela Eisner, herself a refugee from Nazi Germany brought to Britain at the age of eight on the *Kindertransport*, was Lewis's only doctoral student at Manchester. She recalls that, on a personal level, Lewis and Michael Polanyi were on very good terms. She remembers Polanyi as a quiet, even reclusive, academic who took refuge behind a closed office door to avoid the more robust exchanges which often took place among staff in the Faculty of Economic and Social Studies. What Polanyi shared with Lewis was a strong belief in the correctness of the Keynesian revolution. Lewis and Michael Polanyi were both to make significant though quite different contributions in the field of knowledge and innovation in economic growth.

Manchester by the late 1930s was also home to other economists of a radical persuasion who, like Michael Polanyi, were Jewish refugee scholars.[9] They were to be counted, along with Lewis, among the pioneers of development economics. Hans Singer held his first appointment at Manchester University between 1938 and 1944, having left Germany in 1933, where he had begun to prepare a dissertation on long-run development under the direction of Joseph Schumpeter. That research was later completed at Cambridge under the supervision of Colin Clark. Singer then carried out research for the Pilgrim Trust into the condition of the unemployed before taking up his Manchester appointment.[10] He had left Manchester for Glasgow University before Lewis arrived, but the tradition of research into the causes and consequences of unemployment that had been established in the Department, under the leadership of John Jewkes, continued after Singer's departure.

Between 1943 and 1946, the development economist Heinz Arndt, also a Jewish refugee scholar, worked as an assistant lecturer in the Economics Department at Manchester with John Hicks and John Jewkes. Arndt was known personally to Lewis from their LSE days, and when Lewis took up his Chair at Manchester he received a letter from Heinz Arndt asking for his support in an application Arndt intended to make for the Readership in International Trade at Manchester which was about to be advertised. In his biography, *Arndt's Story*, Coleman *et al.* (2007) recorded that Arndt did not get on with John Jewkes during his time at Manchester, a factor of which Lewis was fully aware. Lewis replied to Arndt, 'Jewkes was not popular at the end, and the fact that you and he did not get on may be counted by some in your favour'. To Arndt's surprise, and possibly Lewis's, Arndt was not invited even to appear before the selection committee. In a roundabout way, Arndt found out from friends of Lewis in London that Hicks, having moved to Oxford, had written an unfavourable referee's report about him. This hostile reference from a highly regarded economist was the end of Arndt's Manchester hopes.

The Arndt anecdote is interesting from a number of angles. Lewis was not a man who could be relied on in every circumstance to promote the career interests of those friends and colleagues who found it necessary to apply to him. This would not be the last time that someone was to feel let down by Lewis, the uncomfortable sense that perhaps he could have done more. Lewis was a very honest man. Lobbying for this or that person was certainly not his style. There is very little evidence in Lewis's various letters and papers of him ever 'going the extra mile' for a personal friend or colleague, though he was invariably helpful to his students. Letters recording exchanges between Lewis and other academics soliciting his support for career reasons sometimes make painful reading. The Arndt episode is also salutary in reinforcing the message that Manchester's Department of Economics was not the most straightforward and harmonious of places to work, as Lewis himself was to discover.

The post in International Economics that Arndt had failed to secure went instead to Kurt Martin (formerly Mandelbaum) who was appointed as Senior Lecturer in 1949 and stayed in the Department of Economics as Reader until 1967. It is a reasonable supposition that his appointment must have been acceptable to Lewis, though there are no surviving letters or other documents that would enable us to enlarge on this. Kurt Martin was one of the most significant of the early development economists, though his contribution has never been fully acknowledged. His reputation as an academic in Britain was based on his book *The Industrialization of Backward Areas* (Mandelbaum (Martin) 1945), which contained many of the themes associated with the emerging discipline of development economics, including disguised unemployment.

Kurt Martin was a refugee from Nazi Germany. His doctoral research had been supervised by Carl Grunberg – 'the first avowed Marxist to hold a Chair at a German University'.[11] The doctorate was awarded in

1926, after which he held an important research position at the newly-founded Institute of Social Research in Frankfurt, a privately-funded centre for radical social science. Martin came to Manchester via the Oxford University Institute of Statistics, where he had worked on post-war reconstruction in Germany. Born in 1904, he was a full decade older than Lewis, and was in his mid-forties when he was appointed as Senior Lecturer at Manchester. It is probable, given their divergent research interests and travels, that Lewis's and Martin's paths in the Department seldom crossed. Lewis spent a substantial part of his Manchester decade visiting the developing world, whereas Kurt Martin was still strongly focused on Central, Eastern and South Eastern Europe, travelling extensively to Poland, Hungary and the Soviet Union. However, Lewis was admiringly aware of Martin's role in shaking the market-clearing assumptions of neo-classical economics, acknowledged that contribution in *The Theory of Economic Growth*,[12] and Martin was to exchange affectionate correspondence with the Lewises a quarter of a century after leaving Manchester.[13]

Among Lewis's new economist colleagues at the University of Manchester were two academics who, with their families, would become firm friends of Arthur and Gladys Lewis. The first was Ely Devons, appointed to the Manchester's Chair of Applied Economics in 1948. He resigned from that post in 1959 to take up the Chair in Commerce at the LSE. Devons had graduated in Economics from Manchester and had subsequently been employed as an assistant researching the cotton industry alongside John Jewkes. During the Second World War he had worked on post-war planning in the economics section of the Cabinet. When he returned to the University of Manchester in 1945 it was as Reader in the Department of Economics.

Devons was a highly respected applied economist, recognized for his engagement with policy issues, backed up by sound statistical analysis. He shared, possibly to a fault, Lewis's conviction that economists should eschew grandiose claims for the discipline, clearly delineating what economics could and could not deliver to policy-makers, and Lewis appreciated Devons' clarity of mind and restraint as being complementary to his own impulsiveness.[14] A mark of Lewis's respect for Devons is that he wrote a personal letter to Devons in March 1958 informing him that he would be taking up the Chair in Economics in Jamaica, 'I have written to Cooper [Mansfield Cooper, Vice-Chancellor] today sending in my resignation ... We have one of the best departments in the world, not only in academic quality and reputation, but also in good fellowship and team spirit. I will miss our lunchtime and teatime frivolities no less than the austerity of our seminars.'[15] As recalled by Gisela Eisner, Lewis's doctoral student, Manchester in the 1950s still had an old-fashioned social programme, in which Professors Devons (Economics) and Gluckman (Social Anthropology) held formal social events for staff and postgraduates. These were the 'frivolities' to which Lewis referred. At these events, Mrs Devons normally played the piano, but occasionally Lewis himself, an enthusiastic pianist but a shy man, could also be tempted to oblige.[16] Gladys Lewis usually attended, and on more than one occasion there were visits from Arthur Lewis's brothers, including the one who was later to become Governor of St Lucia.[17]

Lewis and his wife also counted as family friends fellow academic Kenneth Lomax, a monetary and macro-economist, and his wife, Leah. A letter sent by Mrs Lomax in 1959 to Professor and Mrs Lewis in Jamaica hints by way of contrast at something less than 'good fellowship' abroad in Dover Street, outside their particular circle of friends. New appointments had already been made – not all of whom, she suspects, would have been congenial to Lewis had he stayed in Manchester. For example, the distinguished monetary economist, Harry Johnson – who, as we shall see, had already been involved in abrasive exchanges with Lewis regarding trade theory – had been appointed to a new Chair in Economic Theory in Manchester in 1956. This was followed by three more appointments to Chairs after Lewis left: in Economics, Political Economy and Econometrics. The correspondence with Leah Lomax suggests that Lewis would not have approved of the three new appointees, or of the method of selection. Mrs Lewis, who replied on behalf of her husband, made clear that Lewis himself had not been consulted on University matters after he had left Dover Street, and 'had no idea what was afoot'.[18]

Another economist with whom Lewis got off on the wrong foot, but with whom a relationship of mutual respect eventually developed, was John Mars, who came as a young lecturer to Manchester after the war. Mars registered for a PhD on dynamic economics under Devons and Lomax, whose historical chapter took him deep into Lewis's territory of the history of economic thought. When he submitted part of the draft thesis, on the historical antecedents of the subject, to *The Manchester School*, Lewis's two-and-a-half-page review began in a tone of jovial mockery:

> Your over-excitement at discovering the existence of dynamics runs away with you. To read these pages one must conclude that you think that every English economist from Jevons to Pigou was an idiot ... I have commented before that your writings on this subject appear to set up windmills for the pleasure of knocking them down.[19]

Lewis does concede that Mars' contribution 'would do well as an appendix to a book which was itself a contribution to dynamic theory'[20] but ends by rejecting the paper. However, from this low point, things improve. Mars took no offence, and continued to write long letters to Lewis, which progressed from mildly barbed to fulsome, to bounce ideas off him;[21] Lewis later returned the compliment, and asked Mars to read Lewis's own work on long-period growth; the PhD was eventually awarded and published. When Lewis' work was eventually published as *The Theory of Economic Growth,* Mars was one of the half-dozen people to whose influence Lewis paid tribute in the preface.

Gisela Eisner, however, confirms that Lewis's overall feelings about Manchester in the mid-1950s do not support the formal sentiments he expressed in his resignation letter.[22] The reasons for Lewis's dissatisfaction with Manchester are not easy to discern, because Lewis never spoke of his experiences there. Nevertheless, there is reason to believe that Lewis did not get on well with certain colleagues. One such was Dennis Coppock, later to be appointed to a Chair in International Economics at Manchester.[23] There may also have been some resentment among his colleagues at the appointment of Lewis on a number of prestigious international consultancy assignments, which kept him away from departmental duties. Furthermore Dr Eisner recalled an occasion when Lewis had not been treated appropriately by his colleagues. An important position in Uganda arose, to be filled through the Faculty. Lewis, though interested and well-qualified, was not invited to put himself forward for this appointment. Instead, Austin Robinson was approached to nominate a candidate. Lewis was upset to discover that Robinson had ignored Lewis's own candidacy and recommended instead a junior academic without any overseas experience.

In many respects, Lewis's relationships with Manchester colleagues, as he increasingly came to regard the whole of the social sciences rather than just economics as his field of enquiry, were happier outside the Economics Department than inside it. This was particularly true in the case of Max Gluckman, the Professor of Anthropology. Born and educated in South Africa, Gluckman became from 1942 to 1947 head of the Rhodes–Livingstone Institute in Lusaka, Zambia, where in addition to his research on the legal systems of the Barotse of Central Africa he supported the publication of works that would be of practical help to local administrators. When Gluckman arrived in Manchester a year after Lewis in 1949, the anthropology department to which he came as head already had a number of lively working relationships with the Colonial Office, including those that had enabled Phyllis Deane to produce the first-ever national accounts for a developing country,[24] and as Gluckman came to realize the potential for collaboration with the Economics Department he roped in Devons, as well as Lewis, to help him use statistics to analyse social structure and mobility.[25] The three men, from their separate departments, jointly supervised several Ph.D. students, including the outstanding Scarlett Epstein.[26] Unlike all of Lewis's economics colleagues, Gluckman found his main subject matter among poor households in developing countries, and unlike most of the economics department, he was driven by a strong radical urge to improve the often appalling conditions in which the people of developing countries lived at that time. Politically he was to the left of Lewis, and willingly accepted the charge of seeking to move social anthropology in a Marxist direction; however, unlike his wife, Marie, he never joined the Communist Party.[27] When, in early 1950, Patrick Gordon Walker, a Colonial Office minister of state in the Attlee government, decided to exclude Seretse Khama, a Bechuana chief and future president of Botswana, from the Bamangwato territory of Bechuanaland in order to please the South African apartheid regime, Gluckman and Lewis both published letters in *The Manchester Guardian* deploring the decision,[28] which helped to seal their friendship. Like Polanyi, Martin (Mandelbaum) and Gisela Eisner, Gluckman was a Jewish émigré. All his life, Lewis would find himself better able to get on with exiles, like himself, than with WASPs.

Gluckman's arrival therefore gave Lewis the opportunity to extend his knowledge of an area of the developing world – Southern Africa – of which he had no field experience, and a point of contact with African households and communities, rather than with the governments and international organizations with whom he and his other university contacts dealt routinely. Lewis was fascinated by Gluckman's account of the micro-politics as well as the micro-economics of many African subsistence economies, and in particular by his observation that 'even though there are no governmental institutions ... [and even if] men quarrel in terms of certain of their customary allegiances, [they] are restrained from violence through other conflicting allegiances which are also enjoined on them by custom'.[29] Gluckman, for his part, gradually became more and more interested in the anthropology and sociology of economic life, and in particular in saving and borrowing behaviour within the subsistence and smallholder economy.[30] It was, above all, from him that Lewis acquired the confidence to represent rural subsistence households not as a unit within which maximizing behaviour can be observed (as in conventional neo-classical economics) but rather as a redistributive extended family network – even if it was a family from which conflict was not absent – the vision that is conveyed in his ground-breaking publications of the 1950s.

One of the qualities that had impressed the selection board convened for Lewis's appointment to a Chair at Manchester was his ability to attract research funding from international bodies. When he arrived in Manchester, Lewis brought with him research funding from the Rockefeller Foundation for a project on Jamaica. A research assistant was appointed but he did not think that the research was worthwhile and left after two years to take up an academic post in Jerusalem. Gisela Eisner then applied for the post and was appointed by Lewis. Her doctorate, awarded in 1957, commended by Max Gluckman, was the first to be awarded from the Faculty of Economics and Social Studies for many years. By all accounts, Lewis was an excellent research supervisor, very conscientious, setting high standards for research assistants and research students. He was very critical of errors and if the criticisms were taken personally this could lead to problems. Such was the case with Charlotte Leubuscher, another refugee scholar. Lewis was very critical of her work but the criticisms were not accepted. This is understandable to a large extent, as Dr Leubuscher was a distinguished academic and not a junior researcher. Born in 1888, she had held the post of Assistant Professor of Economic Science at the University of Berlin at a time when women in German universities had suffered huge disadvantages.

4.3   Overseas assignments and explorations

A distinguishing feature of Lewis's Manchester years, in contrast to his LSE career, was the extensive foreign travel and overseas consultancies he undertook in a professional capacity. From his earliest days at Manchester there were approaches for his services from a wide range of international bodies and commissions. In part, this was a consequence of his increased visibility as the holder of a chair in economics at a premier British university. And, of course, the demand for economists like Lewis, with interests in growth and development, was increasing in the post-war period in consequence of moves towards decolonization, and various resolutions of the United Nations to increase employment and reduce poverty in the developing world. The fact that Lewis was born in the Caribbean, and had first-hand knowledge of the conditions in poor agrarian societies, was no doubt an added recommendation. The overseas assignments Lewis undertook during his Manchester years are critical to an understanding of how, from his unique and privileged position, he came to view the prospects for development at the beginning of the second half of the twentieth century. Arguably, the reports he produced, the policies he advocated, even the warnings he gave, are as important today to development economics as the formal theories associated with his name.

Until 1950, all Lewis' consultancy work had been conducted within the British Empire, and typically for the Colonial Office, which inevitably gave it an Afro-Caribbean bias. However, in April 1950, Lewis was invited by the United Nations to attend a conference in Puerto Rico on comparative development experiences, at which each delegate was expected to present a paper on development policy and strategy in areas of their own expertise;[31] Lewis's paper was on development in the British colonies. This meeting, for the first time, brought Lewis into face-to-face contact with specialists from Latin Americans, Asia and the Middle East, and enabled him to exchange ideas and data with them. The paper itself was received so well that, later in the year, Lewis was invited by the United Nations to be one of a panel of five experts whose terms of reference were 'to prepare, in the light of the current world situation and of the requirements of economic development, a report on unemployment and under-employment in under-developed countries, and the national and international measures required to reduce them'. The chairman of the panel was George Hakim (Lebanon) and the other members were Alberto Baltra Cortez (Chile), D. R. Gadgil (India) and T. W. Schultz (USA) The invitation was a major opportunity for Lewis: the World Bank, at that time, was in project mode and not equipped to deal with the problems of very poor countries,[32] which left the United Nations as the only authority able and willing to commission what was to be the first global manifesto on development policy in poor countries. Lewis sought and was granted a year's leave of absence from Manchester to serve on the panel. Through it, he was to gain for the first time credibility as a global policy adviser – before he had published anything in his own right in the field of development. After the appearance of the report, he wrote, and published, not on 'colonial economics', but on development.

The report that came out of the UN study appeared under the title *Measures for the Economic Development of Underdeveloped Countries* (United Nations, 1951). As noted by John and Richard Toye's recent intellectual history of the UN system's development work, it was much less concerned with specific recommendations concerning employment policy than with general development strategy, and in drafting this overall strategy 'the report appears to have been heavily influenced by the thinking of

Arthur Lewis'.[33] Certainly, there is an emphasis on the already familiar Lewis themes of capital accumulation and technical progress, and the report's statement on page 35:

> in most countries where rapid economic progress is occurring, net capital formation at home is at least 10 per cent of the national income, and in some it is substantially higher. By contrast, in most under-developed countries net capital formation at home is not as high as 5 per cent of the national income.[34]

may be the first time that Lewis or anyone else put numbers on the concept. In addition, there are lengthy discussions of agricultural as well as industrial productivity, and the institutional requirements for improving these,[35] and the familiar Lewis theme of mass education also puts in an appearance.[36] Notably, the report shows sensitivity to political as well as economic imperatives, and in particular its section on public finance notes that if taxation on middle- and low-income groups is raised too much this might provoke revolts that make tax reform politically infeasible;[37] this degree of political finesse, especially at that time and in what by its terms of reference was designed to be a narrowly economistic report, was rare. In its concluding policy recommendations, the report suggests an emphasis on aid in the form of technical assistance and knowledge transfer, which 60 years on, and after many changes of aid policy and fashion, donors have now returned to doing.[38] At the time, what caused the most controversy were chapters VIII and IX: 'Development Planning: Priorities' and 'Development Planning: Techniques'. However, the actual planning modalities recommended by the report are indicative and not directive, after the manner that was at the time being trialled in France, Italy, India, Pakistan and Sri Lanka, and in particular are careful to avoid any suggestion of the forced prioritization of industry over agriculture that had been catastrophic in Russia between the wars and was to cause an even greater disaster in China in 1958–62. The relevant paragraph reads:

> It is thus clear that there is no need to choose between developing agriculture and developing industry: both must be pursued. In countries that are short of labour the way to industrialisation lies through the improvement of agriculture: while, in countries that have a surplus rural population, the way to the improvement of agriculture lies partly through the development of manufacturing industry. In either case, both must figure largely in any development programme.[39]

In spite of the report's moderate tone, it excited a good deal of controversy and opposition from enthusiasts of the free market, one of whom, S. H. Frankel, the Professor of the Economics of Underdeveloped Countries at Oxford, wrote a lengthy denunciation of the Report's allegedly *dirigiste* tendencies in the August 1952 issue of the *Quarterly Journal of Economics*.[40] Frankel contested the premise of the UN report that, because of imperfections in the factor markets of developing countries, government action was needed to achieve economic progress by those countries.[41] He further accused the report of encouraging policies that would inhibit the flow of capital into low-income countries.[42] He warned that the aid flows which the UN group had sought to encourage should not be provided on demand, but rather should be conditional on governments 'refrain[ing] from pursuing autarchic and discriminating policies which undermine the movement of factors of production';[43] in so doing, as John Toye has shown, he anticipated the conditionality which the World Bank and other donors were to apply 30 years later.

Early the following year (1953), Lewis sent in his riposte, writing in a personal capacity rather than on behalf of the UN panel. In a letter sent to his old friend (and Director of the Institute of Economic and Social Research in Jamaica) Dudley Huggins, the main part of which cautions him not to pick a quarrel with Sir Arnold Plant (then advising the Colonial Office on development policy in Jamaica).[44] Lewis notes:

> As for Frankel, I have dealt with him in a forthcoming issue of the Quarterly Journal. C[olonial] D[evelopment] and W[elfare] never thought much of the line I was taking on development, and neither did the Colonial Governments, so it is quite normal for them to have criticised my industrialisation study. I am quite content to leave it to them to produce a better policy. Please let me know if I can help concretely.[45]

Lewis's way of dealing with Frankel is indeed dismissive: he accuses Frankel of disliking the very idea of speeding up development,[46] and of setting up a straw man in which stagnant developing countries would immediately transit to the growth rates which were beginning to be achieved in the Far East, rather than, as the UN report had advocated, seeking to move from per capita growth of zero to the 2 per cent growth being achieved by the USA and most other industrial countries.[47] He then accuses Frankel of setting up a second (political) straw man, 'that developed nations should transfer enough to underdeveloped nations to make possible equal rates of growth',[48] rather than simply seeking to measure the costs of closing the gap somewhat. Finally, we come to what Lewis describes as 'the heart of the matter', which, readers will not be surprised to discover, is mass education, as his main illustration of a policy variable which can be made better through purposive action by government:

> [Frankel maintains that] 'a whole people can no more be given rapid economic development by investment in mass education, than it can be given "democracy" by "investment" in mass political training'. Here we are really at the heart of the matter. I believe Professor Frankel to be in error. I believe, with the agricultural experts, that the yield per acre of Indian agriculture can be raised by 30 per cent during the next ten years by getting the farmers to use better seeds and by making available to them more fertilisers, pesticides and water. This requires the establishment of an agricultural extension service reaching into all the villages: mass education ... Professor Frankel believes that it will take a long time to bring about the necessary changes in the 'ways of doing, living and thinking' of the Indian farmers. Of course it will, if one means by this all their ways of doing, living and thinking. But if one means, as the report meant, only those ways immediately relevant to increasing the yield per acre of land, then he is being proved wrong every day in every underdeveloped country where these new techniques of mass education are being tried out in the countryside.[49]

All of this was, of course, a leap of faith, made before any developing country except Taiwan had experienced its 'green revolution'. But the experience of the whole of Asia since the 1960s shows that it was Lewis who was right.

Lewis's membership of the 1951 United Nations mission gave him more than the self-confidence that came from his intellectual leadership of the UN report. It also yielded him a dataset which filled what, he had had to confess, had been a yawning gap in his previous essay on global economic trends in the inter-war period – the *Economic Survey, 1919–1939* (Lewis, 1949a). This gap he filled by means of a time-series on world production and trade flows going back to the 1880s, compiled mainly on the basis of League of Nations data by Folke Hilgerdt, Assistant Director of Economic Stability and Development at the United Nations Secretariat. The data were provisional and unpublished, and Hilgerdt was to rebuke Lewis for publishing, in his paper 'World Production, Prices and Trade' (Lewis, 1952) analysis based on those figures without the necessary warnings of their provisional nature.[50] The paper measures the linkage between the quantity of primary products entering world trade, and world production of manufactures. By this means Lewis was able to specify the relationship between the terms of trade and world production of manufactures, on the one hand, and of primary products on the other. These two fundamental relationships – the terms of trade and the production of raw materials and manufactures – are, in Lewis's first venture into econometrics, estimated against global data for 1881 to 1960.[51] These estimations provided him with a basis not only for understanding the factors underlying the secular decline in the income terms of trade of primary producers, whose significance he was to emphasize in his writings on growth two years later,[52] but also for developing his inquiry into the reasons why production in different parts of the world responded in different ways to movements in the terms of trade, which was to be a preoccupation for the rest of his working life.

By that time, Lewis had far outgrown his former dependence on the British colonies as illustrative material for his development economics – as his weary remark to Dudley Huggins, quoted above, illustrates. However, he realized that he still needed to gather new material if he was to generalize across developing countries as he wished – especially in Asia, and that he could not depend on this material dropping into his lap as the result of consultancies materializing at the right time. He needed to make his own luck. In January 1952, therefore, he wrote to David Weintraub – another contact at the UN who had helped him gain the contract for *Measures for the Economic Development ...* :

> I have to go to Malaya this summer, to examine for the University through June. I plan to spend the summer wandering about Java, Bangkok and India, through July, August, September. (Indeed, I am on the lookout for assignments in that region, to help pay my expenses during those months, and look like having to accept an offer to write for a Sunday paper) ...
>
> PS Would ECAFE [the UN Economic Commission for Asia and the Far East] be interested in having me do a small job for them this summer? My air passage to and from Singapore is already provided for.[53]

According to Lewis's authorized version, his 'Eureka moment', in which he discovered the principle of unlimited supplies of labour, came to him 'while walking down a street in Bangkok' in the autumn of 1952, during the course of this fact-finding mission.[54] However, the genesis of his extraordinary discoveries of 1954 was a little more long-drawn-out, and had slightly more complex roots, than this, as we shall see below.

4.4 *Annus mirabilis*, 1954

When Lewis arrived in Manchester in 1948, development economics did not exist. Growth economics had only just begun, through the work of two men – the American Evsey Domar and the Englishman Roy Harrod – who, at the end of the war, wrestled with the Keynesian problem of unemployment and specified the conditions necessary for the absorption of new arrivals into the labour force, while sustaining full employment in the long term as the economy grew. Just as excitingly, Paul Rosenstein-Rodan, in his exploration of *Problems of Industrialisation of Eastern and South-Eastern Europe* (1943), had argued that industrialization in poor and war-damaged countries – such as Poland, Greece and Ukraine – would be unlikely to happen if left to market forces, because of a combination of lack of demand and entrepreneurs' uncertainty about each other's willingness to invest, as discussed in Chapter 3 above. On that basis, he had argued that the state needed to subsidize, and co-ordinate, industrial investments in the form of a 'Big Push' if poor countries were to transform their economies. Lewis himself, in his work for the Colonial Economic Advisory Council, had, of course, identified market imperfections and uncertainty as reasons why the market on its own could not deliver development to poor colonial economies, and drawn attention to the importance of selective industrialization and mass education (human capital) as the way forward. But this was in the form of isolated, and unpublished, flashes of insight. All of Lewis' published work, at this stage and for several years to come, was on industrial economics. The following year (1949), he published three books: *Overhead Costs, Economic Survey* 1919–1939 and *The Principles of Economic Planning*, none of them on development.[55]

However, possibly under the stimulus of the many students from developing countries whom he found himself teaching in Manchester, he now started to write up his ideas on development as a coherent story. His first effort in this field is an astonishing pamphlet, *Colonial Development*, which may have been first drafted in 1948 as a seminar paper at Oxford[56] before being presented early the following year, in amended form, to a meeting of the Manchester Statistical Society. The frame of reference is, as may be imagined from the title, Britain's tropical colonies and how they can be set on a path towards development. *Colonial Development* begins with a classification of the determinants of growth into their main components – knowledge, capital investment, 'ability to scale up', and enterprise[57] – which he describes as a 'rough map of the whole area as a guide to further exploration'.[58] It then goes on to argue that if these factors of production are to work together effectively, and if development is to happen, especially in the rural sector, not only purposive intervention in non-functioning markets, but a whole new economics, and indeed a whole new public administration, is required:

> I am concerned in this paper and in a large part of my life not with the text-book cases but with primitive societies, short of capital and entrepreneurship, lacking in roads and public facilities of all kinds, and looking constantly for leadership and guidance to the public officers sent to administer them with unrestricted powers. The economics that is relevant to their problems is not the economics of marginal utility, but the economics of laws, institutions, tenures, nationality, race, religion, ideology and kindred determinants of economic equity and of the rate of economic progress which were banished from the economic textbooks and seminars as disreputable topics over seventy years ago. In such societies leadership is not a political suspect [*sic*] but the most valuable quality that colonial governments can offer. In a fat rich country like the UK, where further progress is deemed unnecessary, and productivity is a shameful word, we need not think about such matters, and governments that seek to influence them are wicked. But in primitive societies the duties of government are large and positive and those who neglect these duties, or seek to belittle them, are guilty of a breach of trust.

> New jobs must be created outside agriculture. This is an urgent problem. Some people say glibly, looking at the poor state of agriculture in such places, that the first problem is to improve agriculture; but what they do not see is that this cannot be done without industrialisation. In the Colonies, as in every other country in the past, improvement in agriculture and industrialisation go together.

> If wages were equal to marginal productivity, as some economists actually believe to be the case, there would be no problem because labour in these places would be so cheap – [indeed] in many [places] wages would actually be negative – that entrepreneurs would be falling over each other offering employment in industry. But, outside the study and the classroom, wages bear no relation to marginal productivity. Although labour is superabundant it is also very dear.

Prices are therefore a false guide to the real economic situation, and policy must be in defiance of prices if the true economic situation is to be met. Industries ought to be established even though their costs of production may greatly exceed the money cost of imports.[59]

This brilliant polemic, and in particular this passage, contains the essence of the ideas for which Lewis was to be awarded the Nobel Prize thirty years later. Indeed, in a sense it contains more than that, since the demand to do away with 'the economics of marginal utility' had been replaced, by the time the ideas were formally written up in 1953–4, with the more modest claim that those rules do not apply (that is, wages are not equal to marginal product) in the subsistence-sector labour market only. The policy suggestions deriving from the analysis also go further than those encountered in later works, in particular in the capital market, where the observation that smallholders cannot get access to capital is countered by noting that village banks need to be created, using as a model Jamaica or Indonesia[60] (an idea which, as we have seen, Lewis had embraced from the Colonial Office's enquiry into mass education in 1941–3); the concept of large-scale, capital-intensive farming is mocked,[61] in a manner that in 1947 was enormously innovative; Rosenstein-Rodan's idea of balanced growth makes an appearance ('if an industrial centre can only grow by one factory coming to it at a time, it may never start at all. The economics of one step at a time is a very bad guide to policy');[62] and with a respectful bow to 'the Manchester School', to whom Lewis was delivering his paper, protection for colonial manufactures is defended.[63] Finally, the idea of 'mass education', which Lewis had adopted as a result of his CEAC work, and had persuaded the Colonial Secretary Arthur Creech Jones to introduce into his policy portfolio, also makes an appearance.[64] Moreover, the anger and savage irony mixed in to the objective analysis in phrases such as 'this fat rich country' and 'breach of trust' are unique to this period of Lewis's life and do not resurface in his famous publications of six years later, or at any other time.[65] And all this in 30 pages. The period from 1945 to 1951, when Lewis was able to make effective contributions, especially on education, to the aid policies of a Labour Colonial Secretary, was, as will be remembered from Chapter 3, the only time when he saw political argument as a way of making a difference to the well-being of developing countries. From 1951 to 1963, under the stress of several painful reverses, this hope gradually faded away, and with it Lewis's mocking rhetoric.

In 1950, as described above, Lewis was given the opportunity by the United Nations to develop these ideas, first at a comparative workshop and then as a member of the team that compiled the 1951 UN report, *Measures for the Economic Development for Underdeveloped Countries*. Both through contact with the Asians, Latin Americans and Africans whom he encountered there, and perhaps even more through 'wandering around Java, Bangkok and India' in the summer and autumn of 1952, he would gradually have discovered which elements of the economic experience he had encountered at the Colonial Office, and incorporated experimentally into *Colonial Development*, were capable of being generalized to other developing countries.

But by the following year, 1953, everything was ready for the sustained writing effort that was to bear fruit the following year in the form of the two works which are the twin peaks of Lewis's work as a development economist: 'Economic Development with Unlimited Supplies of Labour' (which we shall refer to hereafter simply as 'Unlimited Supplies of Labour') completed, and immediately published in *The Manchester School*, in the summer of 1954, and *The Theory of Economic Growth* (or *Economic Growth* for short), completed late in 1954 and published in mid-1955. The relationship of the two works is that of a house to its bay window: *Economic Growth* is an inquiry into the mainsprings of growth, of which capital accumulation is one, and 'Unlimited Supplies of Labour' illuminates the process by which capital is accumulated. Everything points to the larger work, *Economic Growth*, having been begun earlier, in late 1952 or early 1953,[66] and then laid aside, probably in the winter of 1953–4, at the point when Lewis decided to let his long-maturing ideas on capital accumulation have their head.

Like many insights of genius, the basic idea underlying 'Unlimited Supplies of Labour' is very simple. At its heart is a supply-and-demand diagram, of the kind that is found at the beginning of every first-year economics textbook:[67] in this case, a diagram of the supply and demand for labour supplied to the 'modern', or non-subsistence, economy. The demand curve is completely orthodox and downward-sloping; but the supply curve, instead of being upward-sloping, is flat, driven downwards by the many pressures that Lewis had observed generating a labour surplus in developing countries. The most famous and controversial of these pressures is 'disguised unemployment', in which the inhabitants of the subsistence sector of the economy share the product equally rather than paying workers according to their productivity as conventional profit maximization would demand – as a consequence of which,

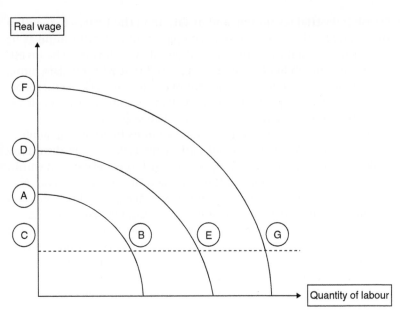

Figure 4.2 The Lewis model (as it originally appeared in *Unlimited Supplies of Labour*)

Note: C is the subsistence-sector wage. The lines AB, DE and FG correspond to successively higher levels of investment and productivity in the modern sector.

'surplus labour' remains in the village rather than being pushed out of it into the high-productivity modern economy. But, as Lewis often stressed, other pressures to keep the supply curve flat exist in many developing and industrialized economies, including casual part-term workers, household labour (notably women, but in poor countries also children) and population growth.

In Lewis's account of capital accumulation (reproduced in its original 1954 formulation as Figure 4.2) everything depends on the speed with which the demand, or marginal revenue product, curve moves outwards. The space between the supply and the demand curves (the 'surplus' between what capitalists earn and what they have to spend on labour costs, or the area ABC, on Lewis's diagram) is, in his interpretation, the source of all economic dynamism. If that surplus is spent well, in the sense of being invested in activities that will raise productivity, attract capital and increase competitiveness, as in the

British industrial revolution, and in Taiwan in the 1950s – to mention two examples that would have been uppermost in Lewis's mind as he was writing – then the economy will be led on to fortune: the investment rate will gradually rise over time, and that will translate into a rising growth rate. But if – for reasons of corruption, lack of enterprise, or flight of the 'surplus' into overseas bank accounts – the surplus is not invested productively, the economy will stagnate, or worse.

Once we look carefully at Lewis's model in its international application, as Lewis did in the second part of his article, some disturbing policy implications become clear, two of which Lewis elaborated within the body of his article. One of these is that different social classes may have opposite interests, and that this may widen social disparities and potentially cause political instability – the example Lewis gave was of capitalist landowners, who he had observed were often not motivated to invest in agricultural extension or better living conditions, since it increased the labour costs they had to pay.[68] A second is that, once surplus labour is taken into account, the conventional case for free trade collapses, and protection becomes the optimal trade policy for surplus-labour countries.[69]

Simple though this narrative might be, it managed to push outwards our understanding of development in four different ways at the same time. Before Lewis wrote this text, the economics of growth was based on single-sector, closed-economy models in which all markets cleared and the role of government was not specified. After the publication of 'Unlimited Supplies of Labour', all that had to change. A development economics that did not acknowledge the existence of market imperfection, disparity of productivity, political motivation and an open economy in explaining economic performance, as Lewis had done, was no longer a plausible way of explaining the gap between rich and poor.

However, if we glance back to Lewis's 1948 pamphlet 'Colonial Development', we find that Lewis had by 1954 scaled back his ambitions – no longer seeking to overthrow the whole of conventional economics in order to understand the development process, but simply amending the working assumption to be applied to two markets, those for subsistence-sector labour and subsistence-sector capital. All markets other than these – and indeed the labour market itself, in regions where the labour surplus has been exhausted or never existed – now conform to the conventional neo-classical assumption that prices are equal to marginal products. Lewis's revolutionary moment has passed, and he has gone back, for ever, to his reformist roots and instincts.

Indeed, both in 'Unlimited Supplies of Labour' and later in *Economic Growth* Lewis presents himself not as a revolutionary but as one harking back to a much older tradition of economic analysis. In classical economics, which Lewis had been taught by Robbins at the LSE, the focus is on the determinants of growth over the long term and on the distribution of income between its main components – rent, labour income and profit. Classical economics had always been preoccupied by the fear that, because rates of profit had a tendency to decline over time with increases in investment – as represented by Lewis in the curve AB in Figure 4.2 – enterprise and economic dynamism would expire, strangled by lack of profit opportunities, into a 'stationary state'. Lewis's answer for the developing world, of course, was that the flat supply curve of 'unlimited labour' was a big help for developing countries, and for the world, in avoiding the stationary state, and as long as technical change was sustained, the capitalist surplus would grow (as in curves DE, FG, and so on in Figure 4.2), and the stationary state could be put off. As Lewis established this proposition, he invited several of the classical economists on to the stage to help him make his point. 'Unlimited Supplies of Labour' includes an imaginary dialogue between David Ricardo, Thomas Malthus and Karl Marx concerning how the dynamic of capital accumulation could be maintained. But more influential on Lewis than any of these is John Stuart Mill, the one economist whom Lewis possibly revered above all others.[70] Mill's *Principles of Political Economy*, published in 1848, had been concerned with issues not only of growth but also of equity, between the sexes as well as between income groups, and indeed also of poverty. In his *Principles*, Mill had written:

> [Together with properly-regulated property rights] we must also suppose two conditions realized, without which [no] laws and conditions could make the condition of the mass of mankind other than degraded and miserable. One of these conditions is universal education; the other, a due limitation of the numbers of the community. With these there could be no poverty, even under the present social institutions.[71]

The line of descent from here to Lewis's impassioned advocacy of 'mass education', and indeed to the *Theory of Economic Growth* as a whole, is very clear. In his preface to *Economic Growth* Lewis insisted that 'the last great book covering such a wide range was John Stuart Mill's *Principles of Political Economy* ... After this economists grew wiser; they were too sensible to try to cover such an enormous field in a single volume'.[72]

Lewis goes on to insist that his book is not a unitary theory of economic growth and development, but rather a map 'on a scale more like an inch to a hundred miles'[73] than the one-inch scale of Ordnance Survey maps: the same metaphor as he had used to introduce his 'Colonial Development' pamphlet six years previously. This map, however, he continues, is by no means confined to economic theories of development, and Lewis particularly laments that the study of institutions 'ceased to be fashionable in the second quarter of the twentieth century, and [was] even authoritatively stated not to be the proper business of economists. All the rest of the field belongs to sociologists, to historians, to students of beliefs, to lawyers, to biologists, or to geographers, but they have done little more than to look at it, and to put in a spade here and there'.[74] Lewis has now moved a long way from the micro-economic preoccupations of his LSE years, and this is less a work of economics – indeed, it contains no econometrics, no diagrams and no tables – than of social science in relation to the historical experience of growth, and it is not surprising that Gluckman, as well as Mars and Martin, is acknowledged in the preface.[75]

In essence, *Economic Growth* is about capital accumulation – the theme of 'Unlimited Supplies of Labour' – the institutions that make it possible, and the policies which help to determine how productive it is. The starting point of the analysis is a magic number we have already encountered in Lewis's report for the United Nations of 1951:

> Communities in which the national income per head is not increasing invest 4 or 5 per cent of their national incomes per annum or less, whilst progressive economies invest 12 per cent per annum or more. The central problem in the theory of economic growth is to understand the process by which a community is converted from being a 5 per cent saver to a 12 per cent saver – with all the changes in attitudes, in institutions and in techniques which accompany this conversion.[76]

We have already heard a great deal in 'Unlimited Supplies of Labour' about one element in this process: 'If profit is the major source of saving, the conversion of an economy from a 5 per cent saver must be explained by an increase in the share of profits in the national income.'[77] However, if there is surplus labour and investment in the modern sector is embodied in state-of-the-art technology, then this increase in the share of profits will happen automatically, as illustrated in Figure 4.2, derived from *Unlimited Supplies of Labour*. What is much more of a worry in *Economic Growth* is what is done with the surplus: as Lewis puts it, 'where societies differ fundamentally is in what the wealthy do with their wealth'.[78] The whole of Lewis's third and fourth chapters, on institutions and knowledge, are concerned with this issue. The main building blocks of *Economic Growth* are, with minor amendments,[79] those presented in embryo in *Colonial Development* six years previously, as is the author's rejection of a mono-economistic frame of reference for his work.

Institutions and their functioning, which are merely offstage influences in 'Unlimited Supplies of Labour', are centre stage in *Economic Growth*; and the focus is squarely on rural institutions, and more specifically on the performance of smallholder agriculture, which he clearly sees as the centre of gravity of the economy. Here, an ambiguity arises, because when Lewis talks about small farmers, he is talking about a group that is nowhere formally defined or identified, but clearly overlaps the two parts of his 'dual economy' – neither multinational capitalists practising estate agriculture nor subsistence farmers with no marketed production, but entrepreneurial rural capitalists of modest means, often thwarted by innumerable obstacles in their attempts to grow. Systematically, in these chapters, Lewis enumerates the institutional obstacles that prevent the smallholder rural economy from realizing its potential – land tenure, religion (seen by Lewis as 'almost always restrictive' in this context),[80] the functioning of the courts, the maintenance of civil order (here we recall Gluckman's 'conflicts in one set of relationships [which]over a wider range of society or a longer period of time lead to the re-establishment of social cohesion'),[81] the functioning of labour markets (within which a notable role is given to women's limited participation in the cash economy[82]), and even insurance. Thirty years before microfinance, and 40 years before the suppliers of microfinance discovered that the poorest clients were made more rather than less vulnerable by having loans thrust at them, Lewis recommended an alternative form of finance as being much more protective of the weakest:

> Actually, the farmer probably needs insurance, even more than loans. Much debt is due to misfortunes of a statistically foreseeable nature – to sickness, or the cost of a wedding or a funeral, or fire, drought or hurricane, or accident to livestock. Such events happen regularly, and are not really suitable for loans, since if a poor farmer has to pay off the cost of an illness, or to replace crops lost in a

hurricane, it is most unlikely that he will be able to save enough out of future harvests to be able to pay off the debt. All such statistically foreseeable events should be covered by insurance.[83]

Lewis's affection for mass education as an instrument of institutional development, of which we have already observed several examples, continues *a fortiori* into these two chapters of his book. It is significant that, in his discussion of knowledge creation, Lewis spends little time talking about the education of the elite, and gives relatively little space to formal education of any sort, plunging directly into the world of night schools, applied training, apprenticeships, and, of course, agricultural extension. As in his controversy with Frankel two years previously, Lewis leaps into this field as a prime illustration of a case where market imperfection – here, the 'lumpiness' of agricultural inputs, and the failure of loan markets to lend to small farmers, especially for food production,[84] to buy those inputs – precludes the possibility that broad-based development can be achieved through the free market, and thus the state has to step in. At the time, the Asian green revolution was in its infancy or, in the case of India and China, not even that, and to make his point Lewis had to draw his exemplars from Japan.[85]

However, Lewis also gave plenty of space to the urban workforce and its own institutional support mechanisms – its health, in particular,[86] but also its technical training needs. It is of significance that, at the same time as he was drafting these centrepiece chapters of the *Theory of Economic Growth*, Lewis was engaged in his own attempt at hands-on institution building in south Manchester, less than a mile from his office. We discuss that experiment in Chapter 5.

Into the middle of a complex and nuanced argument, Lewis was always capable of injecting brutally blunt, often overstated, remarks for effect – as if to retain the reader's attention. 'Most governments,' he suddenly tells us towards the beginning of his section on institutions, 'are, and always have been, corrupt and inefficient ... In countries where government is corrupt and inefficient, *laissez-faire, laissez passer* is the best recipe for economic growth.'[87] This remark is interesting for more than its bluntness; it also communicates a scepticism about the merits of state intervention in development that is a long way from the position taken on this issue in 'Unlimited Supplies of Labour', and in particular from the remarkably powerful defence of 'strategic' protectionism he developed in that article.

Eventually, in chapter 7 of *Economic Growth,* Lewis does arrive at a more balanced picture of the role of government in development, and when he does so it is ground-breaking. He lists nine ways in which the state can harm the process of economic development:

1. failing to maintain order;
2. plundering the citizens;
3. promoting the exploitation of one class by the other;
4. placing obstacles in the way of foreign trade;
5. neglecting public services;
6. excessive *laissez-faire*;
7. excessive control;
8. excessive spending;
9. embarking on costly external wars.[88]

There is very little of the 1980s liberal critique of the state's role in developing countries, and of its incorporation into the modern theory of economic growth, that is not prefigured in this list, and indeed prefigured in a suitably balanced way: it will be noted that, in this list, 'excessive control' and 'plundering the citizens' are now joined by excessive *laissez-faire*. The role of the formal political process in development is not mentioned among the nine elephant-traps, but throughout *Economic Growth* and elsewhere, Lewis makes clear that he is not to be tempted into supporting undemocratic routes to boosting the rate of growth, 'not [because] it prevents tension, but because open discussion creates a healthier society than is achieved by suppression'.[89]

Beyond this, Lewis, for all his impatience with politics, had his ear closer to the ground than many academics or IMF staff, and was willing enough to see and warn governments of the political limits beyond which their intervention should not be pushed. He acknowledged that:

most governments find it easiest to tax those who oppose them and to exempt those on whose support they rely, and this fact plays as large a part in determining the distribution of the tax burden as considerations of equity, of incentives, or of savings. Yet the fact remains that in most of these economies it is impossible for the government to play the roles it needs to play in economic development unless it taxes all classes more heavily than at present. The major political problem in most of these countries is to persuade the people that this is so, and to gain their consent to the necessary measures. [In particular] the main problem is whether it is politically feasible to levy adequate taxation upon the peasants.[90]

By 'the peasants', as discussed above, Lewis meant neither the 'modern sector' nor the 'subsistence sector' of his dual economy, but a group at the interstices between the two, namely small-scale rural capitalists producing for the market. But at that time, before the coming of the green revolution, hampered by innumerable problems of poor infrastructure, market access, and sometimes state discrimination as well[91] this group had the ability to abort a process of take-off sustained growth, by capital flight or otherwise. Lewis saw this clearly, and in his judgement the 'social wage' was one of the most important pre-emptive assets available for managing that risk.[92] 'The greatest political question which a country such as India now has to face,' he wrote in 1955, 'is whether it can force a doubling or trebling of domestic saving without involving its people in hatred and violence on a large scale.'[93] These political limits to development have notably been observed in the 'East Asian' crisis, the most recent global crisis to impinge on developing countries. In Bolivia in February 2003, the flashpoint for political disturbance, involving more than 30 deaths, was a proposed extension of the income tax net, as in Lewis's example;[94] in Argentina the previous year, a freezing of domestic savings deposits; and in Indonesia in 1998, a rapid devaluation accompanied by a loosening of capital controls and other measures such as user charges designed to satisfy the IMF's targets for the financial deficit.

It is fascinating that, while the components of Lewis's models – in particular the flat supply curve of labour and the correlation between physical investment, human capital investment and growth – have been backed up by a large amount of subsequent research,[95] both comparative and by case study, Lewis at the time he was writing had little to hand apart from intuition, having no hard data available. (As we have mentioned above, neither of the 1954 masterpieces contains any statistical tables.) On Britain, his reading of the three-volume study by John and Barbara Hammond had told him that real wages during the Industrial Revolution period were more or less static – but this was impressionistic observation and not statistical measurement.[96] Lewis subsequently told Phyllis Deane of his relief on discovering that her study of UK real wages found no clear trend between the years 1760 and 1840,[97] but this was not published until 1962. For developing countries, Lewis would have picked up ideas from his trawl round Asia in the summer of 1952, and he had personal impressions about wage trends in Africa and, in particular, the Caribbean; but nothing that amounted to a time series. The one relevant body of material created during Lewis's writing of 'Unlimited Supplies of Labour' was Gisela Eisner's study of

Jamaica, researched under Lewis's supervision between 1952 and 1955, and eventually published in 1961 – an exceptionally innovative work and the first quantitative economic history of any developing country. However, while Lewis paid generous tribute to Eisner's work in *Economic Growth*,[98] only the bare bones of her research had been completed at the time Lewis published 'Unlimited Supplies of Labour', and he did not use it to support his argument. When finally it was published, it revealed the first concrete evidence in support of a flat labour-supply curve in any developing country.[99]

In a quite different context (Keynesian economics, not development economics) Lewis had earlier written: 'I am all for making brilliant guesses of the Keynesian type. I know of no way of arriving at the truth other than to make such brilliant guesses and then to test them out against the facts.'[100] It was a brilliant guess, rather than an empirically-supported hypothesis, that Lewis had published as *Unlimited Supplies of Labour*.

Lewis's proposition that a part of the labour surplus was caused by 'disguised unemployment' caused much greater controversy than the other parts of his argument, even though Lewis had always emphasized that the surplus had many other causes beyond market imperfections in the subsistence sector. Theodore Schultz – Lewis's ally on the UN mission of 1951 – now took exception, in his book *Transforming Traditional Agriculture*, to the idea that market imperfections in smallholder agriculture existed, and produced evidence from India and Pakistan from the 1918–19 influenza epidemic which he insisted demonstrated the reverse.[101] A. K. Sen weighed in on the opposite side of the argument,[102] and the controversy was never properly resolved. After Gustav Ranis and John Fei had produced a model[103] which extended and formalized the story presented in 'Unlimited Supplies of Labour', various economists, including Dale Jorgensen (1967) produced dual-economy models that did not depend on the existence of surplus behaviour or non-maximizing behaviour in the traditional sector; but, in demonstrating that they did not like non-maximizing assumptions, they did not suggest anything other than that, in a good number of low-income economies, the real wage of unskilled labour had been flat across a long period of time. Harry Johnson attempted, in private correspondence with Lewis, to pick holes in his trade theory as presented in the second part of 'Unlimited Supplies of Labour',[104] which he later retracted, and Peter Bauer of the LSE, taking over Frankel's neo-classical fundamentalist mantle, accused Lewis, somewhat in the same vein as Schultz but without statistical evidence, of maligning small farmers by representing them as irrational and undynamic.[105] In fact, this claim could not have been wider of the mark: if there is one thread that runs consistently through all Lewis's writings on development policy, it is the insistence that the salvation of the poorest economies lies in providing proper support to agricultural smallholders. In the main, however, both 'Unlimited Supplies of Labour' and *Economic Growth* got a good press: remarkably so, in view of the radicalism of what they were saying.

5
The Manchester Years: Lewis as Social and Political Activist

5.1 The South Hulme and Community House Social Centres, Moss Side

In Manchester, unlike London, the conditions in which the most distressed people live are not well screened off from the wealthy central area and university precinct. This is still true now, but was even more the case in 1951, when the welfare state was in its infancy, when thousands of vulnerable, sick and old people were killed off each winter by the smogs;[1] when the housing stock of the inner-cities (and in particular Manchester)[2] was dilapidated; and when anyone looking west or south-west from an upstairs window anywhere on the Manchester University central campus would find themselves looking not at comfortable, middle-class housing but at Moss Side, the poorest suburb of Manchester, where

> many newly-wed couples still lived with their parents for lack of any other home; where tenement slums still existed, terraced houses could still shelter several families sharing a gas ring and a single lavatory and where families would still find they would have to wait up to 10 years for a council house.[3]

If this was the situation of most inhabitants of Moss Side, it was even more so for the ethnic minority people who lived there. In Manchester, Birmingham and other cities that were beginning to experience something of a post-war manufacturing boom, gaps in the labour market were often filled by immigrants from developing countries, especially at that time, from the Caribbean.[4] These people, arriving full of hope of at least escaping from even worse conditions in their home countries, typically had few skills to offer; were open to exploitation and sometimes, as we shall see, outright discrimination by slum landlords; enjoyed little or no protection from membership of trade unions;[5] and often were unaware of the welfare benefits to which they were now entitled. And it was very cold in winter. This was before the time of controls on Commonwealth immigration at the national level, and the main problem facing West Indian and other immigrants was not national policies, but the discrimination practised informally and illegally by many employers with the encouragement of the unions.[6] For all these reasons, many immigrant workers experienced a standard of living well below that enjoyed by the white working class, and could be seen in Manchester, as well as the Third World, to be part of the underclass or reserve army which Lewis was analysing at exactly this time in what became 'Unlimited Supplies of Labour' (Lewis, 1954).

Lewis, academically over-extended as he might be, was determined to do something practical about this situation, which he felt to be the predicament of his own people. Of the 3,000 or so black people in Manchester, most were from the West Indies and a good few from his own island of St Lucia,[7] seeking to escape the kinds of conditions he had himself experienced and described in *Labour in the West Indies* (Lewis, 1939). The late 1940s and early 1950s were the years when Lewis was most outspokenly angry about the disparity between rich and poor, and its strong overlap with the disparity between black and white. He had been contacted early in 1950 by the Rector of Moss Side, who had tried and failed to attract the interest of the Colonial Office to the problems there.[8] In his work for the Colonial Office, Lewis had, as we saw in Chapter 3, become so riveted on the idea of mass education – the phrase then fashionable in the Labour Party – as the key to development that he devoted an entire report on national economic planning to this theme[9] and so it was natural that further education would become the focus of his efforts for Afro-Caribbeans in Manchester. By early 1951, Lewis had been in touch with both the Bishop of Manchester and Manchester City Council's education department and had discovered that a proposal already existed on the file, never acted on, to establish a community centre in Moss Side.[10]

In spite of somewhat discouraging initial reactions from the City Council,[11] Lewis decided to revive the idea, and in particular to get the community centre established as a meeting-point and training centre for the Afro-Caribbean group who were the main minority then living in Moss Side. Politically, his strategy was to enlist support from the business, academic and voluntary sectors – especially the churches[12] – and then use that support as a lever to convince a sceptical City Council that demand, and potential co-finance, for an Afro-Caribbean centre existed.

Within the business sector, his main approach was to Sir Thomas Barlow, the chairman of the District Bank, whom he succeeded as involving not only as co-sponsor, with the Bishop of Manchester, of an appeal to raise £3,000 for a new building, but also as a small-business adviser, knowing that financial intermediation would be needed if the centre was to be able to create self-employment among Afro-Caribbeans, in augmentation of what was already being raised by the West Indian rotating savings and credit associations (known as the 'pardner system') and their West African equivalent, the *susus*.[13] Within the voluntary sector, Lewis was given support by all church denominations, and also convened meetings, in his office, of the leaders of black secular associations across the city, including the Negro Association, the Coloured Seamen and Industrial League, the Ibo Union, the Gold Coast Brotherhood, the Kroo Friendly Society, the West Indian Friendly Society and the African Students' Union.[14] Within the university, Gluckman and his wife Mary were to be Lewis's main allies. When Lewis asked Gluckman for help in finding a researcher who could help him understand the social relations of Moss Side, with a view to designing a community centre that would be effective in fighting discrimination, Gluckman found for him a Sierra Leonean anthropologist from Edinburgh University, Eyo Bassey Ndem, who was carrying out research in the area. Mary Gluckman agreed to be on the organizing committee of seven members, balanced between private, government and voluntary sectors, with Ndem as the only academic representative apart from Lewis. Given Lewis's lack of experience in field research and in the voluntary sector, it is remarkable to observe the trouble he took to make sure that all parties 'owned' the proposal and to pre-empt the inevitable charges of airy-fairy social experimentation. The council gave approval in principle for the new centre in December 1952.[15]

In late 1952, before settling on a curriculum for the new centre, Lewis circulated alternative models for community centres set up in other cities with a high proportion of ethnic minorities, including Birmingham and Liverpool.[16] However, the eventual design he hit on was not simply a social centre and youth club with training added – the model piloted in Birmingham and Liverpool and subsequently applied in many other places – but something much more ambitious.

As we have seen, Lewis believed passionately in 'mass education', and he naturally saw the educational exclusion of many Manchester immigrants as a test case of the factors that caused underachievement everywhere. However, he knew that if the centre was to be able to make a difference within the labour market, it needed not only to provide formal education and training, but also to tackle the problem that those black people who did have qualifications and experience were, because of discrimination, not being recompensed for them. This led him to ask how people in Moss Side who were managing to fight discrimination effectively and obtain proper recompense for their skills were achieving this, and this in turn led him to see that adequate information (especially about rates of pay and availability of employment) and proper access to social support were crucial. In particular, if social support could be used not just to provide solidarity and sympathy but also to exercise leverage – as it was by bodies such as the Citizens' Advice Bureau, the churches and sympathetic lawyers, and by members of the Afro-Caribbean community – and, if they could make available the benefit of their experience, that, he realized, might transform the bargaining power of Afro-Caribbeans. In a more detailed study of Moss Side than is possible here (Mosley and Ingham, 2012) we refer to this kind of support, which provides social leverage out of poverty, as *vertical social capital*. Lewis's key innovation was to make vertical social capital available alongside education by providing access to it in-house.

Ndem's inquiry into the labour market in Moss Side, entitled simply 'Memorandum', commissioned by Lewis in 1952 and circulated to members of the organizing committee, gave a graphic picture of discrimination in the neighbourhood. He reported that:

- black people universally experienced difficulties in being promoted to positions of responsibility;[17]
- the Manchester Corporation transport department 'has decided on a fixed quota of Coloured drivers and conductors to be employed even though there are shortages of men in these categories';[18]
- many of the gains made during wartime in integrating Afro-Caribbeans into the forces were being undone. In the particular case of the Merchant and Royal Navy, 'Whites have ousted Coloured with the connivance of and, at times, open encouragement by the National Union of Seamen [of] which practically all Coloured Seamen are members';[19]
- five named public houses (all of them on the south side of the city and two of them in Moss Side) refused to accept black people. Restaurants would normally accept black customers but not always, and typically 'not without discourtesy';[20]
- there were a number of complaints of brutality by white police against black suspects. Investigation of these cases yielded some bizarre excuses such as 'you black men are very strong so [the police] have to use force'. As Ndem commented, 'the result is that

coloured people have also developed stereotypes about the administration of justice in this country. And in consequence they have
grown to distrust the Police. Viewed from a wider social context
it means that justice is determined by skin colour. This tends to
exacerbate Coloured feeling of frustration and exile.'[21]
- often a gender barrier was superimposed on a racial one, with some
dance halls (including the Astoria in Plymouth Grove, near the
Department of Economics in Dover Street) being closed to black men
but not to black women. As Ndem commented, 'there is an intense
sex jealousy. Most white people resent the idea of Coloured male
workers fraternising with White girls. This is a very common excuse
among employers who refuse employment to coloured [people].'[22]

In the conclusion of his report, Ndem, like his contract employer Max
Gluckman, tried to argue Lewis over to a more radical view of what
needed to be done to achieve social justice in Moss Side. He wrote:

I do appreciate the views of Professor Lewis, that the less publicity given
to anti-Negro practices in our society the more will be the possibilities
of harmonious relationships between white and coloured. But contemporary events have shown that we cannot altogether depend on the
'good nature' of those with whom Coloured have to argue for a more
civilized treatment. Publicity, in the main, is to reveal the obscured
fact – the illusion under which most White live – that all is well with
Coloured British citizens. Secondly, it is to invite the attention of those
liberal-minded British who are in a position to bring pressure to bear,
directly or indirectly, on the present unhealthy relationship of White
and Coloured. Thirdly, it is to help educate the public (for there are
many Whites who are no less ignorant of the constitutional position of
Coloured in Britain than their opposite number in the remotest parts
of West or East Africa) about their moral responsibilities.[23]

His argument won Lewis over. His analysis encouraged Lewis to identify
the fundamental problem of Afro-Caribbeans in Moss Side as being not
just a lack of skill (human capital) and a lack of social facilities specific to
the community ('bonding social capital') such as was provided by other
inner-city social centres like Stanley House and the Clifton Institute – and
indeed by the pardner groups. Rather, with the help of Ndem's research,
he saw the core problems as Afro-Caribbeans' inability, because of discrimination, to link to the social networks that would enable them to
climb the ladder to higher grades in the labour market, compounded

by lack of the required specialized legal and technical advice that could enable them to gain redress from the government and the courts. Lewis therefore resolved that the new centre needed to provide these linking services – 'vertical social capital' as we have called it – and where necessary to conduct its own research, as Ndem had done, to increase public awareness of the problems the community was confronting. In his letter to Sir Thomas Barlow, Lewis specified that, in addition to being a meeting-place and a college, the proposed centre would need to be

> a place where social service agencies could be brought into contact with the African population. The Citizens' Advice Bureau would like to send someone there regularly. WEA [Workers' Educational Association] and extra-mural classes could be arranged. The various organisations working among children would welcome an opportunity to meet the population in their own place. The churches have expressed interest in holding religious services there from time to time.[24]

In early February, under the impetus of this barrage of advocacy and fund-raising effort, permission to open the institute was finally granted by Manchester City Council, as a centre open to all, which would cater principally for the needs of ethnic minorities.[25] The City Council agreed to allocate a wing of Bangor Street Boys' School for use as a community centre, to be known as the South Hulme Evening Centre, insisting that these were the best premises it could make available. They had one important disadvantage. They were not in Moss Side, but in Hulme, a mile and a half to the north-west (Figure 5.1) – at that time an almost entirely white working-class area.

Once permission to open the centre had been granted by the City Council, Lewis lobbied hard to establish the institute as a full-time operation, insisting that was the only way in which the various companies and voluntary organizations with an interest in the centre could be persuaded to establish a presence.[26] Initially, he was forced to settle for running it as a night school, open two evenings a week and offering school-certificate-level training (of a standard that met the requirements for admission to a further education college) in English language, arithmetic, music, art, handicrafts, needlecraft, physical training, folk dancing and ballroom dancing.[27] Apologising for this restriction, Norman Fisher, the Director of Education, by now converted to the idea, wrote:

> I am guided in putting the proposal in this form by the failure of our previous attempts at a more ambitious scheme. My idea is that the

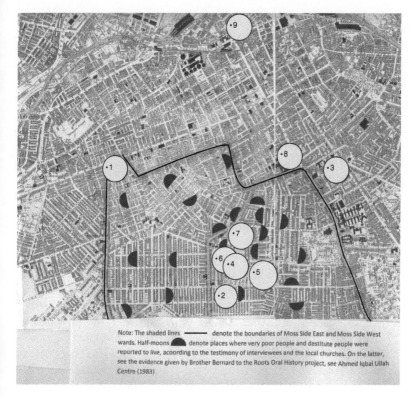

Figure 5.1 Key locations in Hulme and Moss Side

Source: Reproduced by kind permission of Manchester City Libraries.

Key to locations:

South Hulme Evening Centre, Bangor St (formerly the Evening Centre for Coloured People) (see also Figure 5.3 below)
Moss Side: main residential concentration of Afro-Caribbeans in Manchester
Lewis' office in the Department of Economics, Dover St
Community House Social Centre, Moss Lane East (see also Figure 5.2 below)
Christ Church Moss Side, Monton St./Moss Lane East
West Indian Sports and Social Club (formerly Cricket and Sports Club), Darcy St, then Westwood St (merged with Community House in 1961)
St Gerard's Overseas Club, Denmark Rd
University of Manchester
Manchester City Centre

biggest and hardest step is the first one. Once we can get the Evening Institute established then it will not, I think, be particularly difficult to let it grow. Two nights a week is intended only as a start. I am hoping that once we have established a demand and made a start with the work of the Institute, then we can greatly expand its scope.[28]

A local headmaster, Eric Blackburn, principal of Lily Lane Boys' School in Harpurhey, was recruited in July to be the part-time principal of the new centre.[29] By that time, permission had been given to open the centre on three evenings a week.

Meanwhile, other proposals for Afro-Caribbean social and educational centres were emerging. In that same summer of 1953, 'under a tree in Platt Fields' (immediately south of Whitworth Park in Figure 5.1), Aston Gore, a Jamaican railway shunter who had been in the air force in Manchester during the war, conceived the idea of bringing together the affinity groups of the different West Indian islands:

> –I felt all associations in the area should come together. I remember calling the Jamaica Society for a meeting and the Barbados Society ... we are all predominantly Jamaican [but] we had two Barbados people and two Trinidadians ... but we have our nationality here and they must be protected. At the time there was a federation movement going on in the West Indies, Trinidadians, Jamaicans, so one said let us find our own thing and we put in a little house.
> [*Interviewer*] Where was that?
> Darcy Street, and that is how Jamaica Society come. Then we change for the times now, from Colonial to Social Club.[30]

At this stage, the membership of the West Indies Cricket and Sports Club, as it was initially known, was mainly male, and with its activities heavily focused on sport, specifically on cricket, in which the West Indies side, and the West Indian members of the Lancashire League, were at that time experiencing remarkable success.[31] It was not yet running evening classes of the kind planned by Lewis, but, as we have seen, it was already operating a pardner association. Also, it was positioned, as Aston Gore mentions, not in Hulme, but in Darcy Street (position 6 in Figure 5.1), right in the heart of Moss Side.

In addition, Brother Bernard, a Catholic missionary recently returned from Africa, agreed during the summer of 1953 to establish a non-denominational social centre, to be known as Community House, almost opposite the premises of the Anglican Christ Church, in Moss Lane East, also right in the heart of Moss Side (position 4 in Figure 5.1). From the first, this centre announced its intention to run vocational evening classes and to establish an advice service, using the model pioneered by Lewis; indeed, Lewis agreed to join the board as vice-president. Not only this, but the appeal for a new building that Lewis had made in 1952 to Sir Thomas Barlow and others on behalf of a

COMMUNITY HOUSE
SOCIAL CENTRE

President: THE LORD BISHOP OF MANCHESTER
Vice-President: PROFESSOR ARTHUR LEWIS

Tel. MOS 3912

COMMUNITY HOUSE,
55, DARCY STREET,
MOSS SIDE,
MANCHESTER, 14.

SPONSORING COMMITTEE

Chairman: Revd. Canon T. F. Ethell (Rural Dean)

The Ven. the Archdeacon of Manchester.
Revd. Michael Meredith.
Revd. Bernard Markham.
Brother Bernard, B.H.C.

Ald. Miss M. Kingsmill Jones, J.P.
Frank Chaplin, Esq.
D. Walton, Esq.

CENTRE COMMITTEE

Brother Bernard, B.H.C. (Warden)

George Bennett, Esq. (Hon. Treasurer).
Jean Trevor Jacques, Esq. (Hon. Sec.).
Laud O. U. Dieah, Esq.
Aubrey Williams, Esq.

Mrs. M. Bennett.
Mrs. K. Stanton.
Mrs. K. Samuels.
Victor Lawrence, Esq.

Proposed New Hall

Figure 5.2 Community House Social Centre prospectus, 1954

Source: Reproduced by kind permission of Lewis Archive, Mudd Library, Princeton University, NJ.

putative South Hulme Centre had by then been transferred to the new Community House, which published the designs for the new centre as a proud and shining contrast to the gloomy and indeed rather correctional atmosphere which (as Figure 5.2 shows) prevailed at that time in Moss Lane East.

The atmosphere was by that time bubbling with excitement: there were, in August 1953, three Afro-Caribbean welfare societies operating or about to operate in Manchester, by contrast with only two (in Birmingham and Liverpool) in the entire remainder of the United Kingdom outside London. Lewis's name was on the masthead of two of the Manchester societies, South Hulme and Community House, but in August and September he put most of his energies into South Hulme. Sometimes on his own, sometimes with the help of Mary Gluckman and her advisory committee, he publicized the centre, not just through leafleting and the newspapers, but also by walking around Moss Side together with members of the organizing committee to explain to sometimes puzzled and sceptical residents what the centre was about. A memorandum submitted by Lewis to a meeting of the Manchester Council on African Affairs on 20 August 1953 explains his modus operandi. It began by noting that the 'student [black] population need claim less of the Council's attention than the working class population' (as it was catered for by the university, the British Council and the International Club). It continued:

The problems of the working class population can be subdivided under recreation, employment and housing.

Recreation. Two new ventures are being started, a social club by Christ Church ... on a non-religious basis, and an Evening Institute and Social Centre by the Corporation of Manchester in Bangor Street. I think the best thing we can do at present is to support these two ventures in every way that we can. Brother Bernard will be able to tell us what further support he would like from the Council for the social club. As for the Evening Centre it requires practical support in two ways. (a) Some time in the week beginning September 14th the Corporation will wish to distribute about 1,500 leaflets in the Moss Side and Cheetham Hill areas, giving details of the Centre. The best way to do this is for a number of people each to take two or three streets, and to walk down the street at about 7.30 pm, giving a copy to each coloured person seen in the road. I have undertaken to organise this distribution for the Corporation, and need about a dozen volunteers. (b) If the centre is not to be for coloured people only, sympathetic white people must be urged to join, and especially to take part in the social activities (table tennis and other games), discussion groups, and group visits. For this purpose the existence of the Centre should be made known to people who are likely to be sympathetic and interested in these activities. Suggestions for doing this will be welcome. One or two Manchester restaurants and I think public houses and dance halls do not accept coloured customers. A volunteer is needed to collect information (Mr Ndem probably already has it).

Employment. I understand that there was virtually no unemployment two years ago, but that the ratio is now quite high. The best way to proceed is to establish friendly relations with employers, to the extent of having a panel of employers known to be sympathetic, to whom unemployed people can be sent. The nucleus of this panel would be those who already offer such employment, and it would be helpful if some volunteer could be found to prepare such a list. This will tell us the sort[*sic*] of firms and jobs involved, and facilitate approaching others in similar trades. The approach will have to be done individually and tactfully, and much of it will fall upon Brother Bernard and the Warden of the Evening Centre, who are the two persons who will receive the greatest number of requests for help in finding jobs. It should probably be left to them to organize these contacts, but suggestions for getting in touch with possible employers will be welcome.

At some point the Corporation should be approached to widen the scope of the employment it offers. But first we first must know what it already offers and refuses, and thus should come out of the survey suggested in [the paragraph above]...

Housing. The best way to help here also is to make a list of persons outside the Moss Side area who would be prepared to take coloured lodgers, and to give this list to Brother Bernard and the Warden of the Centre ... A volunteer to organize this would also be necessary.[32]

Thus Lewis was proposing, and playing a large part in the implementation of, an integrated programme of action in the fields of social cohesion (styled as 'recreation'), employment and housing, with the aim of using the information intended to be provided under employment and housing to support the work of the two social centres. All this was done in the intervals of writing the first drafts of 'Unlimited Supplies of Labour' and *Theory of Economic Growth*, administering the Manchester University economics department, teaching students at all levels including, for the first time, Ph.D. students,[33] advisory work for the Labour Party, the Commonwealth Development Corporation and the United Nations, an already voluminous correspondence with all parts of the world on a large range of subjects including not only economics but also education, the politics of the West Indies and the UK, and the BBC's music policies,[34] and raising (with unusual devotion to duty, according to one contemporary account) two very small children.[35] During his work locally, his attention was drawn to the existence of West Indians who had fallen on hard times, or even ended up 'in Prestwich' (the County Asylum) or similar institutions, and he became, unintentionally, a kind of 'agony uncle' for the Manchester Afro-Caribbean community. In October 1953, a couple of weeks after the launch of the Evening Centre, he received a letter from the matron of a nursing home in Chorlton, asking him to find a home for the child of 'a single girl, well educated, age 21, English and RC religion, she has a baby girl aged one week of whom the father is a native of the Gold Coast who went off, his friends say to his home, when she was three months pregnant' who had been unable to find anyone to adopt the child.[36] Lewis's answer (he was invited to reply by telephone) is not recorded.

The South Hulme Evening Centre opened for business, in an atmosphere of great elation, on 28 September 1953. Lewis naturally insisted on taking personal charge of the musical arrangements for the launch, and a singer and pianist of his acquaintance were, on his insistence, hired from London at substantial expense,[37] and performed at the launch event that evening. He was also successful in getting white people from Moss Side to join the celebrations in numbers, and indeed to take on the black members at table tennis, as he had suggested (see Figure 5.3).

Figure 5.3   Table tennis at the South Hulme Evening Centre, shortly after opening, autumn 1954

Source: Reproduced by kind permission of Greater Manchester Archives.

Initially, the centre did well. Thirty-seven people enrolled on the opening night, and by 15 October this figure had risen to 60, 38 of whom were of West African descent, 19 were Afro-Caribbeans, and the remaining three were white British. Some students from outside the neighbourhood had decided to attend the centre, and were commuting from places as far afield as Wythenshawe (six miles to the south) and Cheetham Hill (four miles to the north), 'and there appears to be a steady increase weekly'.[38] Eric Blackburn, the principal, proudly noted that 'there are no disciplinary problems whatsoever in the Centre and the tone is one of deep respect and intense interest in all that goes on'.[39] Political opposition to the centre emerged, however, including a faction on the city council hostile to the prioritization of the Moss Side centre, and Lewis and the other members of the organizing committee were forced to issue a statement denying that the centre was responsible for the encouragement of prostitution in Moss Side[40] – at that time, as we describe elsewhere (Mosley and Ingham, 2012), an issue that was obsessing the council. They were also forced to deny any sinister connotations arising from the fact that the only other organization sharing the South Hulme Boys' School was the Hulme Communist Party.[41] Blackburn noted other practical difficulties, including the tendency of students who were working evening shifts to arrive late and/or leave early, and decided to try to deal with this problem by changing the opening times of centre, to run from 7.30 p.m. to 9.30 p.m. He also believed that the centre's catchment was limited by lack of publicity, and the organizing committee, on which Lewis continued to sit, agreed to help him by publicizing the centre through local employment exchanges. Blackburn concluded his first quarterly report proudly: 'The interest shown is proof positive of the necessity for such an establishment and its future seems assured.'[42] By the end of the year Blackburn's optimism seemed justified, and there were 97 paid-up students, fourteen of them female.[43]

In various ways, however, the way the centre was evolving diverged from the blueprint designed by Lewis, Ndem and their colleagues. In the first place, there was a great deal of drop-out from the nominal roll – only 29 of the 60 students who had enrolled by mid-October 1953 were actually present at the start of the class –a drop-out rate of 53 per cent, and by the end of April 1954 the drop-out rate was approaching two-thirds.[44] Second, enrolment during this period was mainly in craft subjects (such as woodwork and dressmaking), music and English, whereas only nine students attended classes in the technical subjects such as engineering, metalworking and car repairs, which had been expected to provide the spearhead of the centre's drive to place Afro-Caribbean people in skilled jobs, and thereby combat racial discrimination.[45] Third, and perhaps crucially, the hoped-for multiplier deriving from the invitation to social organizations to set up on the premises of the evening centre on teaching nights did not materialize as planned. Representatives from the City Council's social services department and the Citizens' Advice Bureau sent representatives, but the Poor Man's Lawyer Association attended for a few weeks and then gave up, as did the African welfare organizations that had helped to set up the centre, and the Workers' Educational Association (WEA), after promising to participate, never did.

Having drawn attention to all these problems, Blackburn urgently sought help, 'especially in relation to Housing and Employment ... I find it difficult to obtain casual labour for my students while their financial standing does not allow the Housing problem to be easily overcome'.[46] Thus there was a problem of financial exclusion – not an issue with which the centre was ever able to come to terms. Blackburn also worried constantly about the fact that the centre was located away from Moss Side, and mused how nice it would be 'if only we could move the Evening Centre a mile south' to Moss Side, where the main concentration of Afro-Caribbeans was' (see Figure 5.1, position 2). But he acknowledged that 'the facilities available at the centre more than offset this handicap'.[47] There is evidence during this period of constant adaptation and creativity by Blackburn and his staff, in the form of field visits by Evening Centre groups to the theatre (including *Macbeth* at the Library Theatre[48]) and the Hallé Orchestra, invitations to visiting lecturers, and the creation of a new scheme for social membership in which groups as well as individuals could enrol as members of the centre. It was proposed that 'heads or representatives of societies and associations most interested in the welfare of Manchester's coloured people should meet the Principal [of the South Hulme Boys' School] regularly for discussion; Professor Lewis undertook to supply the names of appropriate people'.[49] The principal, indeed, was a big supporter of the centre, and Blackburn recorded that 'the hour given by the Principal and various staff members from 6.30 to 7.30 for games, friendly discussion, chats in the canteen and piano-playing instruction is still very popular, and the tone of the centre was developed into one of which I am extremely proud'.[50]

None of these initiatives, however, was able to stem a collapse of involvement, and momentum, over the summer and early autumn of 1954. By the end of the year, enrolments had dropped to 77, and actual attendance was only a quarter of this, at around 20.[51] The Further Education Committee now began for the first time to have serious doubts about the viability of the centre, and minuted that 'arrangements at the centre be kept under review'.[52] To Blackburn, it was clear that one of the causes of what was wrong was competition, from the fourth Afro-Caribbean social centre to open in Manchester, namely:'The opening of St Gerard's Overseas Club in Denmark Road [which] has in my opinion been one of the causes of our small roll. This club *is purely social in character* and as it is right in the centre of the area where the majority of the coloured people live it certainly has first call on their affections.'[53]

Worse than this, of course, and not mentioned by Blackburn, there was also competition from the West Indian Sports Club, and from Community House, which, unlike St Gerard's, was not 'purely social in character': indeed, with Lewis's encouragement it had modelled itself very closely on the South Hulme Community Centre. Like the South Hulme Centre, it offered classes in 'English, arithmetic, housecraft, music, and so on'; posted on its notice-board a list of employers willing to hire Afro-Caribbeans, and landlords willing to take them in; and found 'several solicitors (willing) to give legal advice at the centre'.[54] And, crucially, it was located a mile south-east of the South Hulme Centre (at point 4 in Figure 5.1), much closer to where the critical mass of Manchester Afro-Caribbeans lived and worked. Lewis was now dividing his time between South Hulme and Community House, and frequently attended, with his wife, social events at Community House (see Figure 5.4), where he was frequently seen on the dance floor.[55]

The combined impact of these centres, all better-located than South Hulme, appears to have had a disastrous effect on the viability of the pioneering operation, and a decision to close the South Hulme centre in its original form as an educational centre was made at the end of March 1955. On 7 April 1955, the new Chief Education Officer wrote to Lewis, in a sympathetic tone, confirming this:

I expect you will already have heard that the Education Committee have felt obliged to discontinue the new Evening Centre at South Hulme on account of the very low attendances during the past few months ... As you know, the Committee went on with the Centre for a second year in the hope that numbers would increase, but I am afraid they have declined still further and the Committee, even with the best will in the world, did not feel that the Centre could continue after Easter.[56]

Figure 5.4   Social gathering at Community House, 1954

Photograph: Brother Bernard is third from left in the front row and the Bishop of Manchester fourth from left in the back row. Gladys Lewis is standing at the right-hand end, with Arthur Lewis, half out of shot, behind her. Victor Lawrence is second from right in the back row, next to Lewis.

Source: Reproduced by kind permission of Victor Lawrence and the Ahmed Iqbal Ullah Resource Centre, University of Manchester.

Lewis replied: 'I am sorry that the Committee had to close the Evening Centre at South Hulme, but this was inevitable in view of the attendances ... We are all grateful to the Committee for agreeing to make the experiment.'[57]

However, the Corporation did encourage Afro-Caribbean students who wished to continue their studies to move to other social centres (including St Gerard's and Community House) or further education colleges elsewhere in South Manchester, and offered to provide specialist teachers for them.[58] It also allowed the South Hulme Evening Centre to continue as a recreation centre open on one evening a week, which it was continuing to do at the end of 1957, when Lewis left Manchester[59] – indeed, in this capacity, it had much the highest attendance (237) of any of the seven recreation centres supported by the education committee across the entire Manchester conurbation. The mantle of providing evening classes and advice now passed, in the first instance, to Community House, of which Lewis was still the vice-president. After 1957, the West Indian Sports and Social Centre

(WISSC), as the Cricket and Sports Club had now been renamed, began to emulate Community House in providing training specifically in technical innovation. It also became involved in political action of a kind that, one suspects, might have horrified Lewis. As the warden, Aston Gore, later related:

Interviewer: Did you have Saturday schools?
–Lecture? We didn't have a school to teach the young ones, no, because at the time we didn't have young people, young kids, mostly adults. But there were women coming into the machine industry, because that's all they can get. We had actually started classes in that by buying a power machine and get you to learn on it, because they used a pedal machine at home; they don't use the electric one; and this is how they can't get a job. They can use a machine but they can't use a power one. So we get a power machine to teach them. We were the first to teach, I remember we used to get qualified people and ... we get an English person because we were not afraid to use anybody. We get an English person and a Black person to go for the job to prove a point. I remember one particular case. We had a television, a radio mechanic who teach a Scotch fella the job and we send the two of them and the Scotch fella got the job. We even boycott the bank. Barclays Bank out here, it was our bank in those days and we say we won't put we money here unless you employ, put a Black face. I remember once we had a cinema [and secured an agreement] with employers that they must employ Black faces in stores and things like that. Some weeks after they are writing back and saying we have employed a Black. The point is taken.[60]

Eventually, tensions emerged between the politically activist approach being pursued by Gore (and later by Beresford Edwards in the Carmoor Road branch of the Sports and Social Centre) and the quietist, politically neutral approach being pursued by Brother Bernard as warden of Community House. Matters were aggravated by the fact that both Gore and Edwards shared Marx's view that religion was the opium of the people, and when, in 1961, Brother Bernard was moved to another diocese, Gore took the opportunity to propose a merger of the two institutions (interviews, Victor Lawrence and Yvonne McCalla, 10/10/12).[61] The merged centre, on the expiry of the lease at Moss Lane East, then split into two branches: a western one at Westwood Street in new premises, which it still occupies, immediately opposite the original Moss Lane East premises of Community House, and an eastern one at

(a) What became of Community House's 'new hall' (compare Figure 5.2 above);

(b) WISSC's current premises, opened 1983

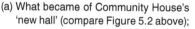

Figure 5.5   The West Indian Sports and Social Centre, 2012
Source: Author photograph.

Carmoor Lane, Longsight, run from 1963 to 1990 by Beresford Edwards (see Figure 5.5). Both centres continue, fifty years on, to pursue the functions of social support, training and liaison with the City Council and other authorities which Lewis encouraged them to combine. We have calculated (Mosley and Ingham 2012, tables 1–3) that membership of the centres significantly reduced the likelihood of their falling into the poverty trap. Thus, by contrast with Lewis' frequent experience (for example with the CDC, and also the Ghana and West Indies cases to be recounted below) this was a case where Lewis' attempts to make a difference in practical terms really worked.

Thus an upward shift in the supply curve, and an increase in the real earnings of Afro-Caribbean skilled labour through applied education mixed with vertical social capital – the strategy that Lewis wanted, which had enabled Lewis himself to break through the colour bar – was eventually achieved in Manchester by the voluntary rather than the state sector, as has also occurred in many of the poorest parts of the developing world. Analytically, Lewis's innovation built on his realization that Moss Side, like many another inner-city ghettoes, was itself part of a dual economy, separated by many invisible barriers from Manchester's 'modern sector'. It also developed a model of how to build social cohesion through 'adult education plus' beyond the point it has reached in many, if not all, UK inner cities even today, 60 years after Lewis's time.[62] But even more fascinating, it also shows Lewis not just as a scholar and a writer, but also as a man of action, – which he often denied even attempting to be – trying to shift with his own hands the institutional barriers that prevented the city's Afro-Caribbean citizens from getting a fair deal. As a man of action, however, he was to encounter many more reverses than as a scholar. After the high point of the end of 1953, we can observe Lewis putting progressively more emphasis on the scholarly rather than the practitioner role: accepting fewer consultancies, writing less to the newspapers, and certainly never again canvassing on doorsteps as he did in Moss Side. By the early 1960s, indeed, Lewis had given up trying to 'make a difference' at the level of practical action, and had reverted to being a full-time intellectual.

5.2   Political action and the Labour Party

Lewis had a long association with the Labour Party that dated from his undergraduate days at the London School of Economics in the 1930s. During the 1950s, as Professor of Political Economy at the University of Manchester, his relationship with the party developed significantly. Not surprisingly, perhaps, he was called upon frequently by the party for comments on matters relating to developing countries. Lewis was the recognized expert on development issues. In 1952, for example, he submitted to the Commonwealth Sub-Committee of the Labour Party National Executive a substantial Report on Aid to Under-Developed Countries, in which he recommended that the UK support proposals then before the UN, to establish an International Development Authority to make grants-in-aid to developing countries.[63] Lewis's Report to the Labour Party National Executive drew heavily on the work of the UN Panel of Experts (of whom Lewis was one), who had delivered the document *Measures for the Economic Development of Under-Developed Countries.* The UN Panel had proposed that, in addition to national agencies, aid should be delivered through the UN. When this proposal came before the General Assembly it did not receive support from the Labour government in the UK, which was profoundly disappointing to Lewis, as he made clear in his 1952 report to the National Executive.

In 1953, Lewis again made clear his position on aid in a draft chapter on *Aid to Underdeveloped Countries,*[64] submitted to Hugh Gaitskell, by then Labour Party Shadow Chancellor, for the New Fabian Essays on Overseas Development.[65] At the request of the National Executive Committee of the Labour Party, Lewis prepared a report in May 1952.

The transformation of colonial development and welfare into what is now called overseas aid was at an early stage, and Lewis was one of the first people to think systematically about how aid should be allocated. Already, he could see how inequitable the allocation of aid had become, but he was optimistic that the inequities could be removed:

> The total movement of capital from the developed to the underdeveloped world is now thought to be about the equivalent of £500 million a year– about enough to raise the standard of living by rather less than one per cent per annum, if it were evenly spread. It is not, however, evenly spread. The lion's share goes to Latin America, and to oil investments in the Middle East. Asia and Africa get only a trickle, in relation to their needs and populations.[66]

It should be allocated on the principle of most to the poorest, Lewis argued,[67] anticipating the 'pro-poor' policies of Robert McNamara (president of the World Bank) in the 1970s and later generations. Lewis then brings into the aid debate two principles that will be familiar from his 1943 paper on colonial development: 'The task of the second half of the twentieth century is to reach millions of small farmers, with better seeds, fertilisers, pesticides and water. It is a formidable mass education campaign, but it could double food production.'[68] Production and welfare (in the shape of health and education) Lewis saw as being 'irretrievably mixed, both as ends and as means. All the same, most under-developed countries now approach the problem through production rather than through welfare'.[69] So, even though aid donors need to encourage development both through 'production' (smallholder agriculture) and 'welfare' (mass education and health), the former is typically to be seen as the prime mover. 'Production', of course, needs to be encouraged through industrialization as well as through smallholder agriculture. Lewis tackled head-on the 'misplaced'[70] protectionist fear that industrialization in the Far East and elsewhere would drive Britain out of its traditional markets, thereby issuing a warning against using the aid programme as a subsidy for British exports, which was to be ignored, at great cost to the integrity and effectiveness of the aid programme, throughout the 1960s, 1970s and 1980s.[71] He also warned against setting targets for aid volume (such as the 0.7 per cent target ratio of aid to GDP adopted by the United Nations shortly after Lewis was writing, and still in force), on the grounds that 'the present capacity of under-developed countries usefully to absorb capital is nowhere near this sum ... [because] skilled people do not exist in anything like the numbers required for economic development on a large scale'. *The starting point of economic development is education, at all levels*: administrators, scientists, teachers, doctors, typists – every category of skill has to be taught.[72] The balance between vision and realism is admirable, and after 60 years still offers insights for aid donors.

In this draft chapter on overseas development, Lewis argued that Britain must make aid available through the UN, in addition to any funds it channelled through Commonwealth agencies. According to him, 'the main argument for a substantial British UN contribution is "pour encourager les autres" … In other words, the more aid the UK channels through the UN, the more it may succeed in persuading other countries to contribute to overseas development'. Pragmatically, Lewis went on to point out that Britain had an interest in persuading other countries to make contributions to aid through the UN, 'both because of its general interest in development, and also because the Commonwealth covers such a large part of the underdeveloped world that it is likely to receive more from any UN agency than it puts in'.[73]

That the Labour Party called on Lewis for advice on development issues during his Manchester years is hardly surprising. After all, he was widely acknowledged as the expert on the subject, and was increasingly in demand as a consultant by the major international bodies. What is perhaps less well-known is that during the 1950s Lewis came very close to the heart of domestic economic policy in Britain, advising the Labour Party, and Hugh Gaitskell in particular, on important aspects of socialist economic policy. Had Gaitskell become prime minister in the 1950s it is not inconceivable that Lewis's career might have taken a different path.

In a 1970 speech on socialism and economic growth (Lewis, 1971; further examined in Chapter 6), Lewis was to demonstrate his commitment to a distinctive strand of socialist thinking, one that encompassed the redistribution of wealth in Britain. Lewis identified this strand of socialist thinking with the late Labour leader, Hugh Gaitskell. Lewis was exceptionally generous in his acknowledgement of the contribution of Gaitskell, a generosity he rarely extended in other circumstances to his academic colleagues, at least not in print. Gaitskell, born in 1906, was a decade younger than Lewis.[74] He belonged to what one of his biographers, John Saville, described as the 'middle stratum' of Labour Party leaders, mostly university or professionally educated men, which emerged in Britain after 1945. Educated at Winchester and Oxford, Gaitskell took a First in Philosophy, Politics and Economics (PPE). He was tutored in economics by Lionel Robbins, and in history by G. D. H. Cole. The latter tutored him in his special paper on the British Labour Movement. Following a brief spell as WEA lecturer in Nottingham (where Gaitskell later recalled that he had lectured miners on thrift, saving and economic growth) he was appointed as economics lecturer at University College, London. He held this post from 1927 to 1938, and it is likely that it was during this period that he first met Lewis, possibly through the Fabian Research Bureau, in which Gaitskell took an active interest, or possibly through Lionel Robbins' lectures at the LSE, which Gaitskell attended to improve his understanding of economic theory. Gaitskell was never regarded as anything more than an economist of average ability, unlike his closest friend and colleague, the socialist Evan Durbin, who was widely regarded as a brilliant theoretician.

Looking through the documents and letters that survive between Lewis and Gaitskell, it is clear that during the Manchester years the relationship between the two men, both of them economists by training and on the right wing of the Labour movement, was a remarkably close one. It was a connection that must have been very valuable to Lewis. In 1950, when Lewis was at the start of his career at Manchester, and also closely involved in colonial matters through the CEDC, Gaitskell was appointed Chancellor of the Exchequer as successor to Sir Stafford Cripps in the Attlee administration. Gaitskell's period in office as Chancellor of the Exchequer was brief, as Labour was forced into Opposition for 13 years following the 1951 election. However, Lewis moved very close to the centre of power in the Labour Party when Gaitskell was elected as leader of the party in 1955, in succession to Attlee. Lewis wrote to Gaitskell in December 1955:

My dear Hugh,
I rejoiced to hear of your election as Leader. We look forward to having you as Prime Minister for most of the next 25 years.[75]

Had the Labour Party succeeded in taking power during the 1950s (it was defeated both in 1955 under Attlee and in 1959 under Gaitskell), it is possible that Lewis's subsequent career might have followed a very different course, since it is likely that he would have been encouraged to take on an increasingly influential role in domestic policy-making in Britain. However, Lewis's prediction of a future prime-ministerial role for Hugh Gaitskell came to nought. Gaitskell died suddenly in 1963, at the early age of fifty-six. He was succeeded by Harold Wilson, his long-standing political opponent on the left of the Party, who had challenged Gaitskell, unsuccessfully, for the leadership of the Labour

Party in 1960.[76] Harold Wilson, like Gaitskell, was an economist by training, and indeed had a much stronger interest in Third-World issues than had Gaitskell, but there is no record of any significant policy links between Harold Wilson and Arthur Lewis.

The policy issue on which Gaitskell sought the contribution of Lewis, to which Lewis referred in his LSE speech, was the distribution of wealth in Britain. When Gaitskell succeeded Cripps as Chancellor of the Exchequer in 1950 he told his Parliamentary Private Secretary (PPS) William Armstrong that the principal task of the Labour Chancellor would now be a redistribution of wealth, and not a greater equalization of income. Gaitskell belonged to the right wing of the Party, a position also occupied by Douglas Jay, George Catlin and Evan Durbin (until the latter's untimely death in 1948). This right-of-centre cohort was headed by Hugh Dalton. Equalization of income was important to this group, but they believed that it was already being taken care of through social-ist policies of increased educational opportunities, welfare spending and full employment. Moreover, too much emphasis on redistribution of income could damage incentives and growth. The socialist agenda in this view should not be the extension of nationalization, and should instead be the elimination of an unequal distribution of private property. In his 1970 speech, Lewis set out the principles that would govern this agenda:

1. The socialist creed of 'from each according to his ability and from each according to his need' is no longer appropriate as it is incom-patible with incentives and economic growth.
2. The right of the worker to the whole product of his labour (Ricardo; Marx) results in inadequate savings. The modern socialist agenda is to increase the surplus over wages so as to have the resources for capital formation.
3. The volume of saving is a matter for collective decision and is not a matter for individual determination.
4. To increase public saving nationalized industries need to make profits, and there needs to be a budget surplus with strict curbs on public expenditure.
5. Taxing business corporations very heavily is unwise, as it weakens their power and incentives to invest.
6. Collective bargaining to determine the level of real wages is incompatible with a socialist economy in which the rate of saving is collectively determined.
7. It is the unequal *inheritance* of private property that is at the base of the class system.

The correspondence between Gaitskell and Lewis in the 1950s indicates what the left of the party suspected, that following successive defeats at the ballot box, the leadership on the right was looking for a new programme that would get Labour back into power. 'Equality of ownership' was the concept being explored by Gaitskell with the assistance of Lewis. Nicholas Kaldor, later to be a prominent adviser to Chancellor James Callaghan in the Wilson administration in 1964, had already written to Gaitskell to the effect that a draft of a book on the future economic policy of a Labour administration required 'fresh thought and an elasticity of mind that is capable of adapting itself to new situations ... we should have something new and constructive to say' According to Kaldor, the draft document on socialist economic policy was in danger of revealing 'intellectual bankruptcy'.[77] Gaitskell took what we may imagine was the rather unusual step of forwarding Nicholas Kaldor's letter to Lewis at the University of Manchester, for his reactions. Lewis replied that he was 'embarrassed' by the request for comments on Kaldor's letter. He explained, 'The reason for the embarrassment is that my comments are like his destructive, and it is embarrassing to comment destructively when one is not up to date and cannot quote chapter and verse'.[78] Lewis continued in this letter to set out what he believed to be the three crucial internal problems of the British economy:

- the need for capital formation and innovation in the private sector;
- the need for restraint in private and public consumption; and
- the question of what to do when there was a slump in the export trades.

Lewis went on:

On the private sector ... the important thing is to get it to invest heavily and put forward any innovations. This is much more important than where to draw the line in nationalization ... Restraint in private and public consumption is necessary if we are to have adequate capital formation and adequate exports. Is there any means of preventing the Labour Government from continuing to use up more and more of the country's resources for social services etc.? Is there any means of preventing the Trade Unions on the one side and capitalists on the other from insisting on an annual rate of increase of money incomes and of real incomes larger than the economy can carry? If we cannot offer answers to these two questions not much else that we can say is helpful.[79]

Lewis's diagnosis of the problems of the British economy, though close to the mark, would have presented Gaitskell with political problems, were his solutions to be implemented. From the date of Gaitskell's appointment as leader, to his death in 1963, he was under pressure from the left of his party, and from the trade unions whose contributions underpinned Labour Party finance, to maintain the commitment to public ownership and not to pick a fight with the unions over wage restraint. Nevertheless, the correspondence between Lewis and Gaitskell was warm in tone: Lewis was 'My dear Arthur'; Gaitskell was 'My dear Hugh'. There were requests from Gaitskell for Lewis to contribute to National Executive studies on Equality, on the Co-operative Movement and invitations to meetings in London.

In December 1955, Gaitskell wrote to Lewis to congratulate him on a recent article he had published in *Socialist Commentary*, entitled 'The Distribution of Property'. Gaitskell wrote that he agreed with a great deal of it, and substantiated Lewis's statement that two-thirds of property in Britain was owned by less than 4 per cent of the population. Tellingly, however, Gaitskell went on to say that the real objection to the capital levy that Lewis proposed was 'the difficulty of getting sufficient political support for it under normal conditions'.

I am afraid that the British people are not normally specially interested in redistribution for its own sake. They might back you if a capital levy were necessary as part of a programme associated with increasing the standard of living, or giving some obvious benefits. But – and this is to their credit in a way – they are not simply interested in taking money from the rich.[80]

As to Lewis's proposals for increasing public saving via a budget surplus, Gaitskell reminded Lewis that

it is no use pretending that it is politically at all easy. Similarly, while I think you are perfectly right in saying that the nationalised industries ought to do more of their own saving, the political difficulties of this are unfortunately very great. The ordinary public tend to judge a nationalised industry by its prices, and to ask the industry deliberately to put them up in order to finance saving is to ask it to incur, and the Labour Party to incur, great unpopularity.[81]

Lewis replied to Gaitskell in characteristically robust fashion:

> I do not think that the Party should have only policies which command an immediate majority. If we take that line, our role as a movement will be ended; we shall have nothing to look forward to; and we shall be indistinguishable from the Tories, since they adopt whatever policies prove to be popular. Our forefathers took pride in being in a minority in advocating policies (now generally accepted) which they thought to be right, and in doing so they gave moral fervour to our movement ... Of course your position is quite different from mine. You have to weigh every word and count every vote. Chaps like me have a long run educational job to do, which we do not expect to bear fruit immediately, and to which we do not expect the Party's leaders to commit themselves until the spade work has been done.[82]

Soon after this letter to Gaitskell at the end of 1955, Lewis left Manchester for a one-year Fellowship at the University of California at Berkeley. In effect he never returned to Manchester in a full-time capacity, as a secondment to Ghana in 1957–8 and a spell with the UN in New York in 1959 were succeeded by three years at the University of the West Indies, and his final appointment at Princeton in 1963.[83] Gaitskell lost the 1959 election, and thus the tantalising possibility of Lewis exercising significant influence over the making of UK economic policy melted away.

6
Why Visiting Economists Fail: The Turning Point in Ghana 1957–8

6.1 Introduction

'Many have sought to interpret the world; the point is, to change it.' In the field of development policy, Lewis was one of the first people to pick up on Marx's dictum by providing advice to policy-makers wishing to intervene in or speed up the development process. We have already observed some examples of this policy advice and its results in previous chapters, in particular Lewis's (1942b) report 'Some Aspects of the Flow of Capital into the British Colonies', which was his starting-point as a practitioner; his intellectual leadership of the 1951 UN mission that resulted in *Measures for the Economic Development of Underdeveloped Countries* (United Nations, 1951), which for the first time gave him a global reputation as a development economist; and his institution-building in Moss Side, Manchester in 1953, which sought to overcome racial discrimination against the Afro-Caribbean population of Manchester. These were all short-term assignments lasting six months or less; and yet, as we have seen, they are a key part of Lewis's creative contribution to development.

In addition, Lewis undertook some longer-term assignments lasting a year or more during his LSE, Manchester and Caribbean years, involving secondments from his academic work; these relate to the process of transition to independence for African and Caribbean countries, and the economic consequences of this. In 1943 and 1944, as discussed in Chapter 3, he acted as Secretary for the newly established Colonial Economic Advisory Committee; between 1951 and 1953 he served on the board of the Commonwealth Development Corporation (CDC); and, as we now relate, between 1952 and 1958 he was on several

occasions a senior adviser to the government of Ghana. All these experiences ended in frustration, which Lewis perceived as failure: he was
removed, as we saw in Chapter 3, against his wishes from the board
of the CDC and resigned before his contract was up from the other
assignments. And the cumulative effect of all these frustrations, as we
shall see, was to bring about a radical change in the pattern of Lewis's
working life from the mid-1960s onwards. Why, when his ideas were
so good, did they work out so badly in practice? And what implications
does the answer have for development policy-making generally? These
are the main questions with which we shall be concerned in what follows. In this chapter, we examine Lewis's experiences as adviser to the
government of Ghana.

6.2   Lewis in Ghana, 1952–8

Of the many developing countries preparing for independence in the
late 1940s, the Gold Coast (now Ghana) struck many expert observers
as being the most promising. Its export earnings were buoyant, its living standards (in particular its health and education indicators) which
were a disaster in very many colonial countries, were on a distinct
upward curve; and its indigenous public administration was far bet-
ter-trained than that of most African countries.[1] Within the Colonial
Office, the conviction was that the Gold Coast would be one of the first
countries to become independent, a conviction that became stronger
during the riots of 1948, when 29 people were killed. The riots were
a protest against the government policy of destroying cocoa plants
damaged by swollen shoot disease, but they were also a demand for
a quicker transition towards self-government. They brought to prominence a young politician, Kwame Nkrumah, whom Lewis had met in
London during the war years and for whom Rita Hinden had organized
a Fabian Colonial Bureau meeting in 1946, with Lewis helping to organize the guest list, as discussed in Chapter 2 above (Tignor, 2005, p. 110).
Nkrumah, as Secretary of the United Gold Coast Convention, argued
eloquently during the riots for self-government, and founded his own
party a year later – the Convention People's Party (CPP).

One of the underlying political issues that had caused persistent
tension since the inter-war period was the export levy. Cocoa farmers
in the Gold Coast, as in other primary-product-exporting countries,
did not receive the full export price for their crop, but only a fraction
of this price, which was generally less than half – and in boom years,
such as those leading up to the 1948 riots, could be less than a quarter.

The balance – in effect an export tax – was skimmed off by the government, on the understanding that it would be used 'for the development of the colony'. But this phrase clearly has many meanings varying with the interest group with which one identifies, and an issue of urgent political debate in the Gold Coast in the post-war years was how these cocoa export surpluses should be used. One option strongly advocated by Lewis, as we have seen, was that colonial countries needed to design proactive industrialization programmes, which could not be expected to come about through laissez-faire. In 1952, Lewis received an invitation to design such a programme for the Gold Coast.

Lewis was not the first 'visiting economist' in the Gold Coast in the 1950s, in the run-up to Independence in 1957. Dudley Seers and C. R. Ross of Oxford had been appointed by the Colonial Office to visit the Gold Coast in 1951. Since Dudley Seers features later in this chapter on 'why visiting economists fail' it is useful to begin our account of Lewis's experiences in the Gold Coast with their report. Initially, Seers and Ross had been appointed by the Colonial Office to examine building costs in the Colony. However, their terms of reference were widened repeatedly into a comprehensive development agenda: the mechanics of inflation in a poor agricultural economy; the role of capital accumulation; foreign investment; development finance and, most important, the selection of priorities for development policy. Of these, it was the treatment of inflation that received the most attention in their report. The treatment of inflation, with its detailed account of the various sources of inflationary pressure, indicated a heavy Keynesian influence. Also novel was the use the report made of the Keynesian three-way accounting procedure that had been developed in Britain during the Second World War. National accounts were prepared for the Gold Coast for each of the years between 1948 and 1951. Despite the fact that it was almost impossible to calculate the output of domestic trade and agriculture in the short time available to the visiting economists, the statistical element of the report was lauded as a breakthrough. It ensured that the report was well received in academic circles in the UK.

In the Seers and Ross report,[2] development was equated with capital accumulation: specifically, spending on building and construction, water supply, transport and industry. Because of the presumed shortage of domestic savings, development expenditure was perceived to be essentially a public function. Indeed, in some areas, of which private construction was one, there was a presumption against private investment altogether, arguing that it would compete for scarce labour and materials. In those parts of the economy where private investment was to be more welcome, it should none the less be recorded centrally to make it more amenable to public regulation and control. Seers and Ross stayed in the Gold Coast for only two months – very much the visiting experts, and it is hard to escape the conclusion that they did not understand West African society, or the way its economy functioned. Even more seriously, they did not know what they did not know. Take the following passage from their report: 'the task of economic analysis, as such, is not hard: the Gold Coast economy, considered purely as an economy, is one of the least complicated in the world, and its main problems should soon be obvious to anyone with a professional training'.[3]

Academics like Seers and Ross, trained in the complex economic structures of mature societies, may well have assumed that they were dealing in the Gold Coast with a stable and uncomplicated form of economic organization. Lewis would have made no such assumption; indeed, he may well have had this report in mind when he said in a lecture in Ghana in 1968: 'An intellectual in Europe can say anything he likes because it will not matter. But the intellectual in Africa ought not to open his mouth on public questions unless he has studied all the facts and is quite sure of what he is going to say.'[4] Lewis's own *Report on the Industrialisation of the Gold Coast* (Gold Coast Government, 1953a), gave him a wonderful opportunity to put into practice, in the most favourable of settings, the policy framework he had sketched out while working for the Colonial Economic Advisory Council (CEAC) in 1943. In particular, it embodies all of his 'four principles', though the first principle, the idea that the market alone will not bring about development, appears only in veiled form.

On the theme of *selective industrialization*, Lewis recycles a good deal of material, and in particular his methodology for being 'selective', from the CEAC and in particular from the paper on *The Analysis of Secondary Industries* (Lewis and Meyer, 1946), which he and F. V. Meyer drafted in the hope of waking up the 'dormant' Industry Sub-Committee.[5] The approach taken was to make an estimate, from import statistics, of the size of the local market for consumer goods, and then to go down the standard list of industrial products one by one, to decide whether it would be economic to supply the local market for each of those goods (that is, whether the estimated costs of local manufacture, at the current market size, are more or less than the current market price). Because few data on local (or any other) costs of production are available, we are in the realm of 'planning without facts', and therefore of inspired guesses. The first big contribution, however, that

Lewis makes is to take the discussion away from an ambitious drive into capital-intensive industrialization (on the Russian and Brazilian model, in the process of being emulated at the time Lewis wrote by India and China), or even the Hong Kong/Puerto Rico model of exporting manufactures, on the grounds that labour costs are too high,[6] and to settle for a more modest model of primary export-processing and consumer goods-led industrialization, preferably making extensive use of small-scale, labour-intensive methods. On this basis, the most promising options for export processing emerge as bauxite (which was outside Lewis's terms of reference), cocoa and timber, and the most promising options for home-market-based manufacturing emerge as salt, sugar, glass, textiles, beer, cement and glass (Gold Coast Government, 1953a: paras 62–65). Indeed, for the first time, Asian (not only Japanese and Far Eastern, but also Indian and Burmese) motifs are everywhere in this report. When it was drafted, Lewis was just back from his highly productive Far East tour of late 1952, and had picked up there the central idea that there was 'another way' in industrial technology, intensive in both labour and human capital, which could at the same time make industry more competitive and, by absorbing a lot of labour, reduce rural and urban poverty.

Second, Lewis goes back to basics: 'a high standard of living cannot be built upon an economy in which half the people are scratching the ground with a hoe' (Gold Coast Government, 1953a; para. 25). This, he argues, is an area where the Gold Coast is not only backward, but also unprogressive: 'In the Gold Coast there is very little sign of an increase in agricultural productivity, except in so far as the improvement in the world price of cocoa since the war is an improvement in agricultural productivity' (Gold Coast Government, 1953a, para. 21). From there, he returns to his (third) CEAC theme of smallholder agricultural productivity before everything, and then builds links from this to industrialization and his fourth theme, of mass education:

> The most certain way to promote industrialisation in the Gold Coast is to lay the foundation it requires by taking vigorous measures to raise food production per person engaged in agriculture ... The surest way to industrialise the Gold Coast [*here Lewis repeats himself – it is not clear whether for deliberate emphasis or by accident*] would be to multiply by four or five the resources available to the Department [of Agriculture] for fundamental research into food production. And then, as the results become available, to multiply five-fold the funds available for extension work in the villages.[7]

He enthuses about mass education for some time, drawing attention to the innovative People's Educational Association model of the Gold Coast which Creech Jones had uncovered (and identified as 'in constitution and organisation almost identical to the W[orkers']E[ducational] A[ssociation])'[8] during the mass education campaigns four years previously. It is not only the mass education of the rural workforce that is important in this context, but also of the urban workforce, and the Industrial Development Corporation of the Gold Coast is castigated for throwing away money on subsidized loans: 'Had the emphasis of the Industrial Development Corporation been more on managerial assistance and less on lending money the results would have been different' (Gold Coast Government, 1953a, para. 151).

Third, looking ahead, industrialization, Lewis argues, cannot be financed only by the Colonial Office (independence was only five years away), nor by the government of the colony: it must come from local and international private enterprise, which requires policies to encourage both of these. At this point, the analysis starts to prefigure not only the emphasis on local reinvestment, but also the political economy, of 'Economic Development with Unlimited Supplies of Labour'. Local industries need not only to generate a surplus, but also to reinvest it locally ('what matters with profits is not how large they are, but how much goes out of the country', Gold Coast Government, 1953a, para. 103), potential overseas investors need to be encouraged rather than nationalized or intimidated (ibid., para. 255, recommendation 3), and the government needs to think about how to create the necessary fiscal base, and the economic and political implications of creating one. At this point, Lewis returns to the agricultural productivity leitmotiv, once again taking his inspiration from the Far East:

> To the extent to which industrialization is financed from domestic savings, it is, in the ultimate analysis, the farmers who provide the wherewithal. In Japan, this was accomplished by levying high taxes and rents upon them; [however, this was only possible because] in Japan, in the period 1880 to 1920, the yield of an acre of land increased on the average by 1.3 per cent per annum and the output per person engaged in agriculture increased even faster than this, namely by 2.4 per cent per annum. (Ibid., para. 98)

It is possible to argue that this is much more than a report on the industrialization of the Gold Coast: it is also a manifesto seeking to create for the new Ghana what would now be called a developmental state.[9]

A developmental state (the term was coined in 1962 by the American political scientist Chalmers Johnson, with Far Eastern examples principally in mind) is one in which the balance of political forces is such as to motivate, through transformation of the industrial structure, a rapid rate of economic growth, maximizing the possibilities for inclusion of vulnerable groups.[10] It is a merit of Lewis's analysis that he goes beyond simply specifying an industrialization strategy to spelling out the governance requirements for equitable growth, and this was, for the time, an extraordinary step forward.

The report was generally welcoming of foreign investment in the Gold Coast, and clearly regarded it as providing a supplement to domestic savings. The report also argued that foreign investment would provide some of the commercial experience sadly lacking in the Gold Coast. Hence Lewis's recommendation that overseas firms should be allowed into the Gold Coast only if they were willing to take on a proportion of Africans in senior posts.

How was the Lewis Report received? From the point of view of the Colonial Office and of the Gold Coast government, the paragraphs dealing with foreign investment proved to be the only difficult areas in the report, which was otherwise welcomed quite genuinely. By 1953, the Colonial Office seemed not to be unhappy with foreign investment in the Gold Coast, providing it did not impinge on the institutions of the rural economy. Thus those paragraphs in the report, in which Lewis argued for favourable attitudes to foreign investment in the Gold Coast were described as 'refreshing' and 'sensible' in the Colonial Office. However, there was an important qualification. Lewis's recommendations for the compulsory employment of local labour were treated with caution. In 1949, proposals for the compulsory training and employment of local labour had been considered by a sub-committee of the Colonial Labour Advisory Committee, and the idea had been rejected in favour of voluntary procedures. Similar reservations about statutory requirements for labour employment were expressed in the Colonial Office response to the Lewis Report.[11] Paragraph 150 of the Lewis report contains a very sad reflection on British attitudes to colour in the early 1950s. It states that, to expand administrative skills through business experience 'The Gold Coast should ... place young people in firms in Britain, or if colour prejudice stands in the way of this, by sending them to India, or to Japan, or to the United States, or any other country which will agree to have them.'

In nationalist circles in the Gold Coast, the overall response to the Lewis report was lukewarm. It was thought to be too cautious, not radical enough, to take the Gold Coast to independence. In government circles in the Gold Coast, however, there was rather more enthusiasm. The report was warmly received by the minister for commerce and industry, Komla Gbedemah (later to fall victim to Nkrumah's anger), as 'a lucid and comprehensive document, of the greatest value to the Gold Coast in formulating an economic policy for future industrial development'.[12] Interestingly, in the light of his later trajectory, Nkrumah at the time accepted the idea of private-sector-driven industrialization.[13] However, the response to the Seers and Ross report in Gold Coast government circles was unequivocally hostile. Nkrumah and the party regarded it as anti-development, offering few opportunities to speed up the pace of change, and not to be taken seriously.[14] Nevertheless, the Seers and Ross report may have sown in the mind of Nkrumah positive thoughts on a future policy of taxing cocoa incomes. Seers and Ross had referred to Marketing Board surpluses as a possible source of domestic saving. Nkrumah was to report later, in his autobiography, that 'about this time it became clear to me that further steps were necessary to control the price paid locally to the cocoa farmer, otherwise we would shortly be faced with inflation'.[15] For the Colonial Office, it is fair to say that officials were broadly supportive of the Lewis report. It was written in the style of economics with which they were familiar: non-technical, easy to understand, full of what Harberger was later to describe as the 'nuggets of wisdom' associated with Lewis. The Seers and Ross report, on the other hand, was difficult to understand without formal economics training. It was technical and abstract in parts, marking, for better or worse, the growing professionalization of economics, and particularly development economics, as a discipline. For the Colonial Office it is fair to say that their development policy for West Africa in the 1950s often came very close to Lewis. It was political considerations and Treasury economics that were the countervailing forces.

The state created in Ghana during the 1950s, prior to and increasingly after independence, was very different even from an attempt at a developmental state. In place of Lewis's selective, labour-intensive industrialization, what were created during the decade were plans for a gigantic, and highly capital-intensive, aluminium and power project (the Volta River Project, a combined hydroelectric power and aluminium-smelting project similar in scope to Owen Falls in Uganda) and little else, the premise being that infrastructure should come first.[16] In place of Lewis's smallholder-agriculture-led industrialization, what the Ghanaian state attempted to create under Nkrumah was large-scale mechanized agriculture, which failed to raise agricultural productivity and never had any hope of promoting equality. This gigantism, in turn, was fatal for the agricultural extension services that were at the heart of 'mass education'. In Tony Killick's description:

> [Nkrumah] called for 'a total break with primitive methods' and for 'gigantic agricultural schemes' ... He had little faith in the modernizing capabilities of Ghana's millions of small-scale peasant farmers. 'Small-scale private farming,' he was to write later, 'is an obstacle to the spread of socialist ideas. It makes for conservatism and acquisitiveness and the development of a bourgeois mentality.' This, no doubt, explains why he dismantled agricultural extension services designed to help the peasant farmers.[17]

Despite these contradictions, Lewis was happy to continue in an advisory role to the Gold Coast government as it prepared for independence. In 1956, he returned a couple of times to Ghana, to advise on planning for the Volta River Project, which was strongly supported by Nkrumah's chief economic adviser as a way of using the government's cocoa surpluses. Indeed, by March 1957, Lewis was urging that the Volta project should be speeded up:

> *Reopening negotiations.* The [Volta River] scheme has now been in cold storage for nearly a year, and it is time to take it out. The recent fall in the price of cocoa serves only to strengthen the case for getting the project started as quickly as possible.[18]

Lewis allowed himself to become quite rhapsodic about the possibilities for the proposed hydroelectric–metal manufacturing–railway complex, and enthusiastically pressed on Nkrumah the importance of levering in UK government capital, as well as the World Bank capital which was being offered at the time.[19] For his part, Nkrumah, anxious to cement the relationship with Lewis, offered him the post of first professor of applied economics at the new University of Ghana,[20] and then, when this was refused, floated the idea that Lewis might like to come and assist him as his chief economic adviser. It was arranged that the UN Special Fund for Technical Assistance would pay Lewis's salary, and he arrived in Ghana in October 1957. In spite of clear differences between Lewis and Nkrumah in preferred economic strategy, there is no evidence that Lewis had any misgivings about committing himself. In contrast to Lewis's two previous experiences of long-term consultancy, the invitation was a personal one, to advise the prime minister directly: this time, he hoped, the layers of intervening bureaucracy could be eliminated. There was much excitement associated with launching the first and most promising African colony into independence and development. There were romantic loyalties associated with the group of African exiles now in the process of becoming national leaders, not only Nkrumah but also Eric Williams of Trinidad and Tobago, and Jomo Kenyatta of Kenya, with whom Lewis had socialized in or around the LSE during the war and post-war years. And there were, if needed, intermediaries within Ghana, notably Gbedemah, whom Lewis liked and trusted. In many ways, it was the biggest advisory opportunity Lewis ever got.

Lewis's terms of reference were not lacking in breadth. Nkrumah wrote to him:

It seems to me that probably the most important task ahead is to carry out a general stock-taking of our entire economic and financial policy. This major survey would clearly involve (amongst other things) consideration of:

(a) Current economic and financial policy;
(b) The Budget;
(c) Development Policy with particular reference to:

    (i) the preparation of a plan covering a period (say five years) from 30th June 1959 ...
    (ii) The Volta River Project.
    (iii) The development of Industries, particularly smaller industries.
    (iv) The construction of the new port at Tema and particularly the new Township ...

I know that you intend to train two or three young economists whilst you are with us, so that the work which you initiate with us may be carried forward into the future ...

I intend to recommend to Cabinet that you should attend meetings of the Standing Development Committee.[21]

The (main) members of the Standing Development Committee were Gbedemah, now promoted to minister of finance, Nkrumah, Kojo Botsio (general secretary of the CPP) and Krobo Edusei. But on both on budgetary and planning issues, it was Gbedemah whom Lewis regarded as the most knowledgeable and trustworthy colleague, and with whom he formed the closest relationship. After scoring an initial hit on a mission with Gbedemah to London for the purpose of repatriating Ghana's currency reserves into the Bank of Ghana, the two men returned to the familiar territory of industrial policy. The industrial and agricultural development corporations, which Lewis had criticized in 1952 for not paying sufficient attention to staff and management training, were reorganized under the direction of a trusted Ghanaian business leader, Ayeh Kumi, and expatriate directors were brought on to the boards of both corporations. In his budget speech, on 7 July 1958, Gbedemah emphasized the importance of company tax remissions for emergent ('pioneer') industries as a means of signalling the importance of involving private capital in development.[22]

The first hint that something was amiss came in a letter by Lewis to David Owen of the United Nations in February 1958:

> One cause of trouble is that the administrative machine is not at present working smoothly. This is because relations between Ministers and Civil Servants have deteriorated sadly ... Civil servants *dislike some of the political events of the last few months,* and leading Africans, in particular, are at loggerheads with the government for this reason. Finally, the decision to postpone starting a new development programme for two years was a political mistake of the first order. It has meant there are no plans for development, just at the moment when Ministers, having achieved independence, are straining at the leash to announce and execute new plans. Naturally, they blame their civil servants for this.
>
> Development expenditure was £18 million two years ago; and is now only £13 million. I cannot discover why. Partly the Ministry of Finance took fright when the price of cocoa dropped below £250 a ton. More important, I suspect, because Jackson persuaded Ministers to hoard all their reserves (then standing at £120 million) for the Volta River Project. Economically, the building contractors laid off workers, and have been contemplating leaving the country. Important projects like rural water supplies and scholarships for university training were cut. It is not the economic but the political result which has been disastrous, namely the sharp deterioration of confidence between ministers and their advisers.
>
> My first task was to explain to Jackson that I considered the development of the country to be more important than the Volta River Project, *which I consider to be of only marginal significance.* (If others will put money into it, o.k; but Ghana doesn't get enough out of it to justify putting much Ghana money in.) To my complete surprise,

he agreed. So Ministers were advised to launch a new £100 million development plan, which we are now in the middle of preparing.[23]

At that point, this was only a gripe, rather than an alarm signal; but the passages in italics draw attention to two important factors that determined the ambience of Lewis's policy advice. The remark about 'the political events of the last few months' relates to the increasing illiberality of Ghanaian politics. Also, Lewis is now throwing cold water on the Volta River Project, which, as we saw, he so enthusiastically backed only a year before.

While the political situation of Nkrumah's CPP at this time was quite secure, Nkrumah himself saw it as being threatened, and 'the political events of the last few months' were attempts to crack down on dissident elements within the opposition. The opposition was of two main kinds: an alliance between Ashanti cocoa producers, and professionals led by Kofi Busia and the lawyer and veteran figure of Ghanaian nationalism, J. B. Danquah. At the end of 1957, just after Lewis's arrival, the government passed the Emergency Powers Bill, allowing it to proclaim emergency powers in designated regions. And in July 1958 the government extended the Bill so as to give it powers to imprison individuals deemed to be a threat to security. As a consequence, a climate of fear and 'whispering' began to infect the Ghanaian political scene. In particular, it infected the 'new £100 million development plan', and this was to bring about the final breakdown in relations between Lewis and Nkrumah.

The issue that caused the rupture, as in the cases of Lewis's involvement with the CEAC and CDC, was the functional allocation of government expenditure. As the first drafts of the plan began to materialize in late July and August 1958, it became clear that (1) they demanded expenditure that was unaffordable (£340 million over the five years 1959–64 instead of a planned £160 million, including the Volta River Project); (2) they contained too little for developmental essentials such as agriculture, mass education and industrialization (only 8 per cent for agriculture and just 12 per cent for manufacturing); (3) these developmentally essential expenditures had been crowded out by the enormous and capital-intensive Volta Project, which Lewis no longer saw as a priority;[24] and (4) – the clincher – another thing that was crowding them out was low-priority luxury expenditure prioritized, in some cases for reasons of personal patronage, by the prime minister himself. In happier times, Lewis would have used Gdebemah, his trusted link-person, to convey this to the prime minister, and he continued to attempt to do so now. However, it seems clear that he gradually became less successful in this; that Nkrumah used Kojo Botsio, his enforcer, to intimidate Gbedemah and discourage him from pressing his case,[25] and that Lewis's only hope was to go to the prime minister directly.

This he finally did, on 1 August 1958, beginning with the strategy he had used with the Colonial Economic Advisory Committee in 1943 and then, as a last throw, appealing in solidarity to Nkrumah's loyalty and moral sense. He sent a five-page handwritten letter to the prime minister, describing the Plan as 'awful' and emphasizing that the blame for this rested with £18 million worth of 'toys', including a royal palace for visiting dignitaries and a yacht for VIPs, inserted into the 'special list' within the development budget at the prime minister's behest. Lewis appealed to Nkrumah – as a socialist, as a prime minister eager to promote development, and as the figure who 'according to the Bible should set an example of self-interest' – to scale down his personal demands on the budget from £18 million to £5 million.[26]

Once Lewis was finally able to confront Nkrumah, in October 1958, Lewis repeated his accusations at a meeting of the Standing Development Committee (SDC) and received a flippant response:

> When I remarked two months ago at a meeting of the SDC 'Nearly half the Development Fund is to be spent on beautifying Accra which has only 4 per cent of the population, he replied 'So what? When you think of England you think of London, and when you think of Russia you think of Moscow; so, when you think of Ghana you must think of Accra.' I forgot to tell him that when I think of England, I think of Manchester.[27]

Later that month, replying to a memorandum on the Volta project, Nkrumah became more imperious. When Lewis pleaded with him not to commit large domestic resources to the Volta project because it was marginal, and because 'as far as general industrialisation is concerned, we will make enormous progress *whether a dam is built or not,* because the industries that will come here do not care whether power costs 0.5d. or 1.5d.', Nkrumah scribbled on Lewis's note, in longhand: 'E.A. I did not ask Taylor to persuade you about any cheap power. My mind is finally made up and irrespective of anybody's advice to the contrary, I am determined to see that at all costs the Dams at Bui and Ajena are built in the shortest possible time. K.N.'[28]

The final break between them came in December. Lewis learned that the vital budget for spraying cocoa plants with protective insecticide had been transferred from the Ministry of Agriculture to the Cocoa Marketing Board. This he interpreted as only being likely to create 'immense corruption'; he appealed to Nkrumah to change his decision; but rather than doing this, he fudged it by referring the matter to a Committee of Ministers. In the letter in which Lewis reported all this to Hugh Keenlyside, the UN's head of technical assistance, he illustrated how far political intimidation had gone:

> I considered it wise to give advance notice [of my intention to resign] to the Ministers on the other side, especially Mr Krobo Edusei, of worldwide fame for the ease with which he imprisons or deports, and Mr Ofori-Atta, whose main task has been the terrorising and destooling of non-CPP chiefs ... The fascist state is in full process of creation, and I find it hard to live in a country where I cannot protest against imprisonment without trial, or the new legislation prohibiting strikes and destroying trade union independence.[29]

He begged Keenlyside to find him a job, any job, within the UN system for the remaining six months of his contract that would enable him to serve out his time and make it seem that he had been seconded, rather than resigning from his Ghana assignment.

This was not quite the end. In telling Nkrumah about the job Keenlyside had found for him within the UN system (as an adviser on the Special United Nations Fund for Development), Lewis decided to offer Nkrumah one last olive branch; but it was a conditional one. He presented a final report on his efforts:

> You and I would not be justified in turning down this new opportunity for me to do important work, unless it were clear that I could achieve something nearly as important by remaining in Ghana. I presented you with the first draft of the Development Plan in June. Since then, and for the past six months, I have achieved practically nothing here, since all my advice has been ignored. Neither you nor I could justify my staying here, if the next six months are to be like the last six months.
>
> There is no point in my staying unless you and I are in agreement on the fundamentals of economic and financial policy, which seems not to be the case; and unless my advice will be given serious consideration, and not callously brushed aside as it is at present. I will stay only if there is enough agreement between us to ensure that I will be able to do useful work.

Whether such agreement exists can be tested by asking whether you will agree to the following three propositions:

(1) Whenever the Government is discussing an economic paper, I shall be sent for and be present for that item.
(2) The Ghana government should not invest in the Volta dam more than £25 million of its own money.
(3) Phase I of the Second Development Plan, as published, should not exceed £120 million.

If we cannot agree on these propositions, there is no point in my remaining. Let me elaborate.

Attendance at Cabinet Meetings. I know of no other country in the world where the Cabinet makes technical decisions without consulting its technical advisers ...

The Volta Dam. It was never proposed that Ghana should find all the money (£70 million) required for building the dam. In the White Paper scheme we were asked only for £8 million. It would be madness for us to use up all our resources in building this dam, and have to abandon all other development schemes. The benefits which this dam will bring are not great enough to justify such a sacrifice. We would be ruined financially, and would become a laughing stock in the world's money markets, and such an example of financial mismanagement, that we would be unable to borrow for other purposes. We should build the dam as soon as we can, but only on condition that others who put up most of the money, on long terms (25 years or more), and at interest rates which enable us to sell power cheaply and without loss. The limit of our investment in the dam should be £25 million.

The Development Plan ...We have only £60 million. If we are to succeed in borrowing the remaining millions, potential lenders must be convinced that we are a good investment – that we are realistic, and will be spending most of the money wisely on productive projects. I know that you have fastened your eyes on the political kudos to be gained in Ghana using illiterate people by naming the largest figures we can think of. Unfortunately, these are not the people who have to lend us the millions. However, the chief effect of overloading the programme is to make planning impossible. What will happen – it is already happening – will be that the prestige projects will all get done first, and there will be no money left for the really important ones. I cannot lend my name to a programme which is grossly inflated, obviously unrealistic, and over-balanced with projects which neither develop the country nor add anything to the welfare and comfort of the people of Ghana: and indeed, only more and more taxes to meet the rapidly growing recurrent expenditure. If you wish to insist on the programme as it now stands, you must publish it without me. As I see it, Phase I of the Development Plan, which now stands at £141 million (excluding defence), should not in the published plan exceed $120 million ... This should be achieved by pruning the following list of projects, now totalling £31 million, to £10 million:

[there follows a list of eighteen projects, most of them in Accra, and including several of the 'toys' that Lewis had vainly tried to eliminate in August, including a casino, an esplanade and a palace for heads of state]

Personally I would have no difficulty in pruning this list to £7 million. In the first place I find it immoral to tax poor people all over the country, and use the proceeds to beautify Accra, when 80 per cent of our people still live in towns and villages with no water, or other elementary amenities. And secondly, wasteful expenditure on prestige objects seems to me the worst form of inferiority complex. The only prestige I care for is the country's reputation for putting first and foremost the economic and social welfare of its people. If our sense of values differs so greatly in this respect, there is very little I can do for you in the next six months.

If you would promise me to accept these three propositions enumerated above, I should be only too delighted to stay, and to continue to serve you in every way that I can. But if we disagree on these fundamentals, it seems better that I should take on this new job, and try to help the poor countries of the world to build up their productive capacity.[30]

Nkrumah's reply arrived the following day. It was much shorter, and perfectly summarized the fundamental problem Lewis had confronted, and vainly tried to finesse, throughout his stay in Ghana:

The advice you have given me, sound though it may be, is essentially from the economic point of view, and I have told you on many occasions that I cannot always follow this advice as I am a politician and must gamble on the future.[31]

Lewis left Ghana on 28 December 1958, having served 14 months of his UN contract. Gbedemah, already marginalized before Lewis left, was demoted to minister for health in 1961, and six months later was subjected to a sneering attack in the press denouncing him as 'one who has relied the utmost and has stuck persistently to expatriate advisers'.[32] Shortly after this he was forced into exile, one of many seeking to avoid rougher treatment within Nkrumah's new political kingdom. From that point, Nkrumah embarked on an orgy of unselective state-financed industrialization and mechanization of agriculture, the results of which have been entertainingly described by Tony Killick in *Development Economics in Action* (Killick, 1978).

While in the thick of this controversy, Lewis had received a letter from his old Fabian Colonial Bureau ally, Rita Hinden, enquiring after him and asking whether he wanted to remain on the editorial board of *Socialist Commentary*, of which she was editor. The beginning of the letter read:

My dear Arthur
I was delighted to hear that you would eventually be taking up a post at the University of the West Indies. I can remember years and years ago, when you visited my flat in Hampstead, telling me that that was your ultimate ambition. And now it has come true. I am sure that you will have a most interesting, as well as influential and happy time out there. It is always exciting to work in young institutions, and particularly in young countries as well. I don't have to explain what I mean when I call the West Indies 'young'.

I never followed up your suggestion that we invite Krobo Edusei to speak at the conference on socialism and democracy ...

I have been longing to hear something of your impressions and experiences of Ghana. I wonder if there will ever be a chance?[33]

Lewis never gave her the opportunity. He replied rather brusquely a few days later, on 29 May, asking for his membership of *Socialist Commentary* to be cancelled. His last words to her were 'There is still too much work for me to do. We are in [a] hurry to get everything finished by tomorrow.'[34] Though a measure of mutual respect remained between them, he responded to her affectionate approach with a brevity bordering on waspishness.

6.3 Was Lewis an exemplar of 'why visiting economists fail'?

As the above account will have indicated, Lewis's impact factor as a policy adviser in Ghana was not large, even though his ideas were brilliant, well-articulated and practical. Taking Lewis's experiences in Ghana in the context of his policy advice elsewhere, what can we learn from these experiences? Shortly after his Ghana experience, two eminent economists with experience of the advice business made independent attempts at systematizing the reasons 'why visiting economists fail', and it is worth examining whether these analyses and others deriving from them shed any light on Lewis's own setbacks. To repeat, we are concerned here only with Lewis's *long-term* advisory missions; much of his short-term advisory work in the 1950s and 1960s, as we have seen, had much less pain and discord.

The first of these inquiries was by Dudley Seers, at the time working at Yale University and soon to become director of the new Institute of Development Studies at the University of Sussex. Like Lewis, he had been involved in a number of consultancy assignments that had ended less than happily – in his case mainly in Latin America– and his paper represents his assessment of what went wrong. Seers identifies three major 'consultancy-related pathologies': personal failings in the consultant; errors in professional technique; and getting the politics wrong.[35] *Personal failings in the consultant* include a failure to identify who is the correct decision-maker, remaining fundamentally loyal to one's own organization or country rather than the country one is advising,[36] lack of relevant qualifications, or simply a failure to learn the local language. *Technical errors* include the imposition of a model of 'what works' on the basis that it works in the adviser's country, which turns out not to work in the advisee's; for economists, whose modus operandi is to get the best they can out of scarce resources or 'to maximise an objective function subject to a constraint', this kind of error divides into disagreement about principles and about how the local economy works and in particular responds to specified policy instruments.[37] (As discussed above, in poor countries the data are very defective, and were even more so in the time of Lewis and Seers, and this opens up a great deal of scope for disagreement about how the local economy works.) And *political mistakes* embrace the two polar cases of never getting close enough to the local political scene to be able to suggest an intervention with any hope of being persuasive, and getting so close that one loses objectivity and becomes captured by a special interest rather than being able to arbitrate credibly and justly between all of them.

Albert Hirschman, in *Journeys Towards Progress* (1963), also reflected on the tribulations of visiting advisers on the basis of his experiences in Latin America, in his case working for the Ford Foundation in Brazil, Colombia and Chile in the late 1950s and early 1960s. Hirschman 'highlights the names of the economists Jean Gustave Courcelle-Seneuil,

Edwin Walter Kemmerer and Lauchlin Currie as economic advisors and/ or heads of foreign missions' to Latin America,[38] and finds that all of them – even Currie, who took Colombian nationality – spent too much time hectoring the Latin-American host government, and inflicting their favourite reformist wheezes on it, and much too little time listening to the different interest groups within it – let alone civil society – and as a consequence failing to perceive political changes that are already on the way.[39] Much later, in 1984, Hirschman was to coin the phrase 'visiting-economist syndrome'[40] to criticize the tendency that specialized missions had of issuing policy recommendations based on supposed universally valid economic principles without taking into account the special cultural conditions prevailing in each region,[41] and this critique comes close to Seers' first category, of consultancy spoilt by personal failings in the consultant, otherwise put the imposition of an Ugly American (or British-imperialist, or imposed by other donor) model of technical assistance. Both Seers and Hirschman use Freudian metaphors to describe the psychological bind in which visiting advisers can become involved, as well as possibilities for an alternative model of the adviser – advisee relationship: Hirschman describes Latin American countries as 'like children involved in disputes, looking for a fatherly adviser', yet maintains that 'the exercise of this kind of parental authority is humiliating for the children';[42] and Seers had known cases 'where the main achievement of an economist, but not a negligible one, has been simply to let a minister think aloud about his problems and bring to the surface his real motives and his judgments on economic and social policy: the economist can carry out the function of a psychotherapist'.[43]

Most development writers since Seers and Hirschman have not attempted to cover the same wide canvas. But a number of lively debates have continued to proliferate in relation to elements of the visiting-economist problem. George Abbott, a Trinidadian who on several occasions tried without success to persuade Lewis into writing academic references for him, insisted that trying to occupy the middle ground between being a statesman-adviser, or 'detaching oneself from local politics' and being a party adviser, or 'getting too close to local politics', which Seers had advised visiting advisers to do, was in fact a recipe for failure, because the 'ability to manipulate the political machine neither ensures nor safeguards success ... It does precisely the opposite'.[44] Gerald Meier, who later collaborated with Seers in writing profiles of the founding fathers of development economics, including Lewis, has asked whether the 'New Political Economy', by which he means objective analysis of why governance failures occur, might be capable of addressing the problems embodied in Seers' third problem of 'getting the politics wrong',[45] and this same problem area has been decomposed by Ravi Kanbur, in the context of the implementation of the 'new poverty strategies' of the 1990s and 2000s into the two separate cases of policy disagreements between adviser and advisee about *objectives,* as when the advisee is more preoccupied with growth and the adviser with income distribution, and disagreements concerning the balance of *interests* within the advisee group towards whom the advisee leans, as in the case of the two tendencies that Kanbur calls 'Finance Ministry', more concerned with macro-economic stability, and 'Civil Society', more concerned to promote special interests including those of the under-privileged (Kanbur, 2001).[46]

In relation to the kind of scenario of failure which Seers and Hirschman had in mind, namely the 'ugly American' who imposes a reform agenda on a foreign country that he does not know well enough, Lewis had two enormous advantages. First, he was not only technically competent, but he also had a coherent and inclusive vision of how development should happen, and this vision, in the shape of his 'four principles': agricultural productivity first; selective industrialization; not relying on the market alone; and mass education – shines through all of the four examples above, albeit with learning from case to case. Second, as a black West Indian Lewis was, prima facie, not open to the charge of imposing neo-colonialist solutions on African or West Indian governments – indeed, except in the Ghana case, he was not formally a 'visiting economist' and had stronger ties to the advisee than the label of visiting economist implies, which ought to have increased his effectiveness. And yet in these four missions (we here jump ahead of the argument to bring into the story his forthcoming experiences in the West Indies) he was not successful: the question is, why not?

Before we start, let us stress that in some cases the reason why Lewis got into difficulties lies, especially in the last two cases with the external environment, which in the years of decolonization was associated with rapidly-changing demands imposed on inexperienced political leaders as they made rapidly-changing calculations – or 'gambles' as Nkrumah called them – on what policies were needed in order to survive. These not only inflicted frequent changes on Lewis in what he was asked to do, but also impossible wish lists, such as that inflicted by Nkrumah on Lewis and cited on page 156 above. A perfectionist might retort that Lewis accepted these impossible terms of reference, which he did; but the fact remains that the reason why visiting economists fail often rests with the advisee rather than the adviser, as Seers acknowledged;[47] and especially so under the testing circumstances of a change in regime to a totally new constitution.

Bearing this in mind, Table 6.1 makes a preliminary attempt to classify Lewis's four long-term advisory missions, in the light of the above discussion, to see which of them corresponds to the pathologies discussed by Seers and Hirschman, listed above.

There are some cases where Lewis does fall fairly clearly into one of Seers' elephant traps. He changed his mind without warning or explanation over the Ghana Volta River Scheme in 1957: this falls into Seers' second category, technical error, and the Ghana government would be been right to complain that his savage 1958 critique of the Volta scheme came out of nowhere. In the case of the CDC, he failed to realize how politically exposed he was to a backlash from the Colonial Office 'insiders' on the CDC board, and did not foresee, in an environment where he had not made any attempt to cover his back by canvassing support on the board, the political risks associated with speaking his mind about the excessive employment of expatriates. However, most of the cases in Table 6.1 do not, we find, fit the Seers–Hirschman template.

Rather, we find that the problem often lay elsewhere; and, most important, we would argue, on the evidence presented in the table, the key was whether a third party existed, with the credibility to mediate between the adviser, Lewis, and the ultimate advisee. In all the cases examined in the table this is a critical issue, and it is not one that emerges from models of the adviser–advisee relationship portraying it as a two-person game. In the CEAC, Durbin's credibility and willingness to act as intermediary between Lewis and the Colonial Office committee members was vital to getting the Durbin–Lewis strategy document placed before the Secretary of State. In Ghana, so long as a line of communication existed between Lewis, Gbedemah the finance minister and Prime Minister Nkrumah, there was some hope of Lewis's ideas being implemented, as they were partly in early 1958, and it was only when, in the summer of that year, the leverage of the intermediary, Gbedemah, began to wane that Lewis' influence also began to crumble. In the Caribbean in 1961–2, the political support of prime ministers Errol Barrow and Vere Bird provided the essential intermediation between Lewis's economic vision and the Colonial Office's money. Finally, in the CDC, the fact that Lewis did not have an intermediary able to build social capital, in the shape of lines of communication accompanied by goodwill, between himself and the rest of the board was directly responsible for his ineffectiveness and eventual removal. So

Table 6.1 Lewis as 'visiting economist': incidence of type 1, 2 and 3 errors and their causes, 1943–62

Case and date	Client	Task (as designated in terms of reference)	Contextual factors	Incidence of type 1 errors (personal failings of the consultant); type 2 errors (technical flaws); and type 3 errors (political mistakes)	Problem-solving intermediaries and their roles
Colonial Economic Advisory Committee (CEAC) 1943–4	UK Colonial Office	Secretary, CEAC	(1) Lewis (and the other members of the Committee) were not 'visiting economists': they were debating the conduct of economic policy from a UK base. (2) Lewis was Secretary to the Committee, and trying to make the most of rather imprecise terms of reference from a junior position.	Type 1: Lewis walked out on the CEAC before it was known whether his recommendations would have influence (he may have feared being outmanoeuvred, and decided to jump before he was pushed).	Evan Durbin and Sir Bernard Bourdillon (Committee members sympathetic to Lewis's position): managed to articulate a 'development plan' embodying Lewis's preferred strategy. They were not able to persuade him to stay and see the proposals through.
Colonial (later Commonwealth) Development Corporation (CDC) 1951–3	Colonial Development Corporation (a quasi-autonomous public body, reporting to the Colonial Office, which establishes and manages commercial	Board member	Lewis was a 'visiting economist' only on a short trip to Malaya in September 1952, during which he was considered to be giving too much support to the Malayans in opposition to the Colonial Office.	Type 3: Lewis did not realize how politically isolated he was. Believing that he was free to speak his mind both on matters internal to the Corporation (the excessive high cost of European labour employed by the CDC) and on global politics, he found that he was seen on both counts as a troublemaker, and	Conspicuously absent. There was no empathetic Board member who could mediate between Lewis and those hostile to him.

| Ghana 1952–8 | Ghana Government | (1) Visiting adviser on industrialization policy (1952) (2) Chief economic adviser to prime minister (1957–8) | Before his long-term secondment to the Ghana government in 1957, Lewis had made three previous visits to the country, one of which was to report on the industrialization of the Gold Coast. Even before this (late 1940s) he had met Nkrumah in London. However, by 1957 he would have been aware that Nkrumah's insistence on the priority of political over economic criteria would lead to trouble. | Type 2: Lewis switched from being enthusiastic about the Volta River project to becoming a sceptic in the course of 1957 (this might be justified by the falling price of cocoa, but the case for changing his mind is not presented in this way). Also, in association with other decision-makers, Lewis put too much trust in 'enforcers' (for example, Ayeh Kumi) who eventually turned out to be corrupt.

Type 3: Lewis knew he was at odds with Nkrumah, but gambled that the gap could be bridged, either through intermediation by Gbedemah, or through personal appeals to the prime minister on moral grounds. Both these surmises turned out to be wrong (see right) | Critical. Komla Gbedemah, the minister of finance, was trusted by Lewis and had done joint missions to London with him. But during the summer of 1958 Gbedemah found himself marginalized by Botsio (the party secretary) and other members of the Cabinet, partly on the grounds that he was 'too sympathetic to expatriates'. From this point onwards he found himself unable to influence Nkrumah. |

(Continued)

Table 6.1 Continued

Case and date	Client	Task (as designated in terms of reference)	Contextual factors	Incidence of type 1 errors (personal failings of the consultant); type 2 errors (technical flaws); and type 3 errors (political mistakes)	Problem-solving intermediaries and their roles
West Indies 1961–2	Commonwealth West Indies governments, excluding Jamaica after September 1961, and excluding Trinidad after January 1962.	Volunteered to help salvage a West Indian closer union after the defection of Trinidad from the existing federation, in January 1962, had put all plans for economic and political collaboration at risk.	As vice-chancellor of the University of the West Indies, Lewis had a vested interest in making economic collaboration between the West Indies countries work (but possibly also in limiting entry into the market).	Type 3: Lewis was not completely impartial, as he had a vested interest in federation and was therefore considered 'too close'. Also, not really Lewis's fault, the moment was not seized. All the conditions for federation were there in summer 1962, apart from money. Because the Treasury did not immediately underwrite the budgets agreed at the Lancaster House meeting of May 1962, momentum towards federation was stalled for a year and a half. Possibly a 'step-by-step' approach, implementing measures such as customs union which were already agreed and leaving the rest till later, might have salvaged the agreement.	After the defection of Trinidad from the federation, Lewis relied heavily on Errol Barrow (prime minister of Barbados) and Vere Bird (prime minister of Antigua). Though both remained loyal to him throughout the period October 1961 to May 1962, there is indirect evidence that Lewis felt slighted by Bird later (see text).

often, in the recent history of policy reform, what began as a stalemate between an adviser (often the IMF or the World Bank) and an advisee, typically a head of state, has hinged on there being, or not being, an intermediary who is able to translate what the adviser needs into a language that the advisee 'understands'.[48] This is not the same thing as Seers getting the politics wrong, because it introduces a third party, on whose presence, survival and continued influence everything depends. In all of the Lewis cases, whether such a third party was allowed into the game and what role they were allowed to play was responsible to a large degree for the success or failure of the enterprise.

A second issue relates to compromise and flexibility; put another way, whether the game between donor and recipient is played as a 'winner takes all' ultimatum game, or whether either player is willing to make intermediate offers that provide a lower payoff but also have a lower risk of the game collapsing. As Lewis tells the story (see pp. 199–203 below), the union of the 'little Eight' fell apart because the Colonial Office did not provide the agreed amount of money, and therefore momentum was lost. (The 'Eight' are the British East Caribbean Territories, which made an attempt to federate in 1962–63. The 'Little Eight' are the same countries minus Trinidad. The negotiations surrounding the attempted federation are discussed in Chapter 7.) But could the deadlock not have been broken by proceeding in stages or 'tranches', thus securing a part of the agreed budget in return for the progress already made (for example, the customs union) and postponing the remainder of the agreement until the rest of the package had been delivered, rather than persisting with all-or-nothing negotiations? It may be significant that it was not Lewis's style to offer his advisees a range of options, or to compromise; he made definite and precise recommendations, which the advisee could either take or leave. The idea of Lewis listening patiently to his advisees like a psychotherapist à la Seers–Hirschman, encouraging them to express their repressed anxieties and inner conflicts, does not fit his observed behaviour, and would almost certainly have appalled him. The Harvard Institute of International Development advisory team approach of 'you tell us what you want, we'll show you how to do it',[49] in which the choice of objectives is left to the advisee and the adviser recommends (not dictates) the means, which has become increasingly salient as World Bank and other programmes have put increasing emphasis on 'recipient-country ownership' of reform programmes as a condition of their effectiveness, similarly found no favour with Lewis, who was concerned with objectives and tended to pursue a take-it-or-leave-it negotiating style.

Finally, and an expression of this take-it-or-leave-it style, it has to be acknowledged that if Lewis's recommendations did not happen, it was often because he took himself off the case, and did not persist to see it through. This is very clear in the CEAC case (see pages 62–5), where he resigned before even waiting for the Secretary of State's response to a paper he had spent months writing and scheming about to enable it to achieve some political influence. But, less obviously, it also applies to the 'Federation of the Eight'. The Lancaster House Conference, which agreed the union, ended on 16 May 1962; barely two months later, on 19 July, while budget negotiations were still ongoing, Lewis announced that he had accepted a job offer from Princeton University. This is not to blame Lewis; simply to argue that on each of these occasions, having done what he thought he could, he decided to exercise his exit option rather than to commit more resources to what he feared might be a losing cause.

Sometimes, the reason that visiting economists fail is not a flaw in the advisee or in the adviser's advice; but rather that the adviser, a human being who knows his resources are limited, eventually opts out of the game rather than follows it through to its end and, just as advisees often put political survival before long-term policy impact, the advisor puts self-preservation (personal survival) ahead of long-term policy impact. An uncharitable observer might put this behaviour into the first of Seers' categories and characterize it as a 'personal failing in the consultant'. We, who also have ample experience of failure as visiting economists, would not.

7
Disenchantment in the Caribbean, 1958–63

7.1 Introduction

In 1960 at the University College of the West Indies in Mona, Jamaica, Arthur Lewis, as Principal, addressed students on their Matriculation. In his Address, Lewis described himself, like most of his audience, as a 'new' student, but in his case one who had been away from the West Indies for 27 years. The theme of his Address was the question of West Indian 'identity':

> 'What is a West Indian?' he asked the students in his Address. 'What are we trying to be? These are the speculations of a West Indian who has been away from these islands since before you were born, and who has only just returned. It is not I who will make the image of the new West Indian, but you.'[1]

The nature of West Indian identity was an important question for Lewis. It is a question that recurs throughout this chapter in relation to Lewis himself. To what extent should we regard Lewis as a West Indian economist? Indeed, to repeat his own question to the students: what is a West Indian?

Lewis's claim in the 1960 Address to be a 'new student' in the West Indies could have been misunderstood by his audience, given his long personal involvement with Caribbean affairs that dated back to his undergraduate student days in London in the 1930s. Though Lewis had lived outside the West Indies for almost 30 years, he had made frequent visits back during that period, some of short duration, others lasting several months. There had been visits connected with personal and family matters – for example, leading up to his marriage in Grenada in May 1947. Others were of a professional nature, beginning with the travelling scholarships he was awarded as a student. Then, from the mid-1950s, Lewis began a new chapter in his engagement with the Caribbean. In 1956, the passing of the Caribbean Federation Act set in motion the intention of Britain to create a fully independent state – the West Indian Federation – comprising the British West Indian dependent colonies of Barbados, Jamaica, Trinidad and Tobago, the British Leeward Islands and the British Windward Islands. Lewis, for reasons discussed later in this chapter, was a strong supporter of the Federation. For once he was closely aligned with colonial policy, and recognized as a useful ally by the Colonial Office. The failure of the Federation – it lasted for just over four turbulent years, from January 1958 to May 1962 – was one factor, but not the only one, contributing to Lewis's growing disenchantment with the Caribbean.

This chapter suggests that Lewis's return to the Caribbean in 1960 as Principal of the University College of the West Indies should perhaps be regarded as a watershed, following his long engagement with West Indian economics and politics. What turned out to be a very short spell at the highest level in the West Indies marked the beginning of the end of Lewis's active professional involvement with the Caribbean. Though he subsequently enjoyed a distinguished three-year appointment as president of the Caribbean Development Bank between 1970 and 1973, in a role that could be regarded as his lasting legacy to the Caribbean, and eventually retired in 1983 to his holiday home in Barbados, which he loved, the era of Lewis's close personal engagement with the problems of the Caribbean did not survive beyond the early 1970s.

7.2   Engagement with the West Indies, 1933–48

Between leaving St Lucia for the London School of Economics at the age of 18 in 1933 and taking up his post at the University of Manchester in 1948, Lewis was diligent in maintaining and building on his West Indian connections, both in London and in the West Indies, where he returned on several occasions. His return visits to the West Indies took place even during his undergraduate and postgraduate years, which was remarkable considering the cost and the difficulties of a sea voyage to the Caribbean at that time. Passenger lists record that the young Lewis sailed to Trinidad in 1934, which would have been towards the end of his second year of undergraduate studies. It is likely that he journeyed onwards by sea from Trinidad to Barbados and from there homeward to St Lucia. It was not possible in the 1930s to sail directly from England to ports in Barbados and St Lucia in the Eastern Caribbean. Though it is likely that the 1934 visit was primarily a visit to his family in St Lucia, Lewis took the opportunity to update himself on Caribbean problems and the stirrings of labour unrest. On returning to the LSE he prepared a paper, *The British West Indies* (1935) – subsequently published as *Labour in the West Indies* (1939) – which he sent to the Fabian Colonial Bureau.

On graduation in 1937, Lewis was awarded a Leverhulme Studentship, worth £350 for two years, for research leading to a PhD. It is probable that Lewis would have considered the British West Indies as a doctoral research topic. Certainly, his personal interests would have led him along that path. Career considerations would have deterred him, however, and encouraged him to stay within what was regarded as the mainstream of economics. In the event, Lewis's doctorate, under the supervision of Arnold Plant, was awarded in 1940 on the subject of Overhead Costs. Indeed, it is likely that Lewis was aware of the subsequent chequered career of an earlier student of Plant at the LSE – Ida Greaves from Barbados – who had produced a brilliant doctoral thesis on labour and tropical trade in developing countries, but who (as reported in Chapter 3) ended up very much on the margins of academic life at the LSE.[2]

In 1938, Lewis again sailed to Trinidad. On this occasion, one of his objectives was a job interview with the City Council in Port of Spain. Though highly qualified for the post, his application was unsuccessful. This rejection, quite clearly on racial grounds, was a snub that Lewis never forgot. It is likely that Lewis also took the opportunity during that visit to see his family in St Lucia and make other connections in the Eastern Caribbean.

Lewis's birthplace of St Lucia was, in the 1930s, still (as related in Chapter 1) an important coaling station for steam ships, even though coal was being replaced progressively by oil, and the demand for dock labour was shrinking over time as a consequence. Sailing eastwards from Kingston, Jamaica (in the Western Caribbean) Castries, the capital of St Lucia, was the only port where steam ships could enter the harbour and refuel alongside. The significance of St Lucia in the 1930s is often overlooked by Lewis's biographers, who stress the small size of the Colony and its relative isolation in the Caribbean. Though a small island in terms of area, St Lucia in the 1930s not only had the key dockyards of the Eastern Caribbean but also possessed significant sugar plantations. Even today, in spite of its small size and relative isolation, St Lucia often takes on a significant leadership role in regional affairs in the Caribbean. Important for an understanding of Lewis's later attachment to Fabian socialism, St Lucia in the 1930s was at the heart of labour unrest and social upheaval in the region. Strikes and demonstrations, often violent in character, were features of economic life throughout the British West Indies in the 1930s, and, as related in our opening chapters, led to the establishment of the Royal Commission (Moyne Commission) in July 1938 to investigate the social and economic conditions in the area.[3]

From what we know of Lewis's subsequent career, and from the later report of his visit in the periodical *Jamaica Arise*, it is likely that Lewis had made it his business to look closely at the labour situation in the West Indies when he returned to the Caribbean in 1938 after graduating. It is puzzling, therefore, that in his Nobel Laureate autobiographical account (Lewis, 1979) he was at pains to stress that the Fabian Society pamphlet he had subsequently drafted, *Labour in the West Indies* (1939), 'was based on newspaper research and on conversations with some of the union leaders'.[4] He did not specify where, or with whom, these conversations took place, and made no reference to any personal observations he might have made in the West Indies. As is evident elsewhere in this chapter, Lewis had a tendency to understate his involvement in Caribbean politics. Mark Figueroa confirms that, in the Caribbean, Lewis 'was more in touch with politics and political leaders than apparently he wished to reveal'.

As a young student, Lewis had nailed his colours firmly to the mast as a committed anti-colonialist. As early as 1935 he had written from the LSE students' union to John Parker, General Secretary of the new Fabian Research Bureau, 'If you need assistance on the West Indies I beg to offer my services. I am myself a West Indian student, and have recently been doing a not inconsiderable amount of research into the history, government and prospects of the West Indies.'[5] There was a positive outcome from this letter, leading Lewis into decades of involvement in various senior capacities in the Fabian Colonial Bureau. Here he was to meet influential people of the left such as Stafford Cripps and Arthur Creech Jones. Of more immediate significance for Lewis was the Fabian Society undertaking to publish in 1939 his paper *Labour in the West Indies : The Birth of a Workers' Movement* as a Fabian Society pamphlet. This was Lewis's first published paper on the Caribbean and it merits consideration because it set out Lewis's socialist and anti-colonial sentiments within that gradualist and reformist Fabian framework that characterized many of his later policy pronouncements.

When discussing Lewis as a specifically Caribbean development economist, it is important to recognize from the outset that there was great hostility among radical Caribbean social scientists in the 1970s to Lewis's reformist Fabian-style anti-colonial policies. The best-known criticism was that from the Tobago-born sociologist, Susan Craig, in her 1977 'Afterword' to a 1970s reprint of Lewis's Fabian pamphlet. Susan Craig indicted Lewis and Fabian socialism in general as a malign influence on the immediate post-colonial period in the Caribbean. By supporting the 'responsible' trade unionism of Walter Citrine and his socialist colleagues in the British Labour Party and Trades Union Congress, she believed that Lewis and other Caribbean intellectuals such as Grantley Adams and Hugh Springer had sold out the Caribbean, undermining the efforts of radical nationalist politicians. Lewis and his colleagues had perpetuated neo-colonial relationships in the newly independent states of the Caribbean.[6]

We have no doubt that in part this hostility to Lewis stemmed not so much from his Fabian outlook as from his elitist attitudes to Caribbean society and culture, which made him many enemies and can make uncomfortable reading even in the present day. *Labour in the West Indies*, discussed in Chapter 3 above, provides an example of the type of social analysis he employed. The pamphlet introduced readers to what Lewis referred to as the West Indian 'bourgeoisie': an element of Caribbean society that 'includes those educationally most fitted to lead the West Indies'. He sees the bourgeoisie as largely comprising 'coloured professional men – lawyers, doctors, secondary school teachers, engineers and other university graduates, [plus] a small number of people who have managed to become large landowners, [and] a sprinkling of men who have made big money in business' (Lewis, 1939, p. 7). This was the class judged 'fit to rule' by Lewis and his colleagues in the Fabian Society.

According to Susan Craig, 'many of the major political figures of the 1930s and 1940s embodied the same coincidence between intellectual and political pursuits, since they were the educated minority in a colonial situation ... Within the Caribbean, Munoz Marin, Aime Cesaire, Grantley Adams and Hugh Springer, Norman Manley and Eric Williams all come to mind as the leading figures of that class. Arthur Lewis is of their generation, is close to them in temperament, background and activity' (Susan Craig, 1977. p. 61).

The strongly elitist approach that first appeared in Lewis's writings in the 1930s often surfaced in his life, in his personal dealings and in his correspondence. Caribbean academics have commented unfavourably on what they believe is a middle-class bias in Lewis himself and in his work. Some quotes can give a flavour of their criticisms:

'the world view of Sir Arthur Lewis represented that of the middle class'

'unambiguous support for any system of government dominated by those with middle class skills'

'middle class domination justified by Lewis in terms of the rationality of its system of beliefs, value and practices'

'the educated middle class alone [is perceived] to have the necessary skill prerequisites [for government]'[7]

Even as a young student, Lewis had little sympathy with different tribal, cultural or religious identities in the Caribbean if they failed to deliver the liberal middle-class values he believed were essential if the West Indies was to be brought out of poverty. This did not compromise in any way his anti-colonial sentiments, but it goes a long way towards explaining why there is still a degree of ambivalence regarding Lewis even today on the part of some Caribbean intellectuals.[8]

It is important to recognize, however, that this bias towards middle-class values in Lewis's work was widely shared by his colleagues (and friends) at the time, even among those at the further end of the political spectrum. C. L. R. James was a radical Marxist colleague of Lewis who had come to Britain from Trinidad. Aged 31 in 1932, James was of a different generation from Lewis. He had come to Britain with encouragement from the Trinidad cricketer Learie Constantine, just a year before Lewis arrived as an undergraduate at the LSE.[9] James hoped to pursue a new career in London as a writer and political activist. In his autobiography, he referred to the social milieu in which he was brought up and educated in colonial Trinidad, where, like Lewis, he had been a recipient of the prestigious Island Scholarship, the 'narrow gate' through which the most academically gifted could pass. Like Lewis, James was the son of a teacher, a profession he himself followed initially in Trinidad.

James records that in Trinidad as a young man he was a teacher

known as a man cultivated in literature. I was giving lectures to literary societies on Wordsworth and Longfellow. Already I was writing. I moved easily in any society in which I found myself. So it was that I became one of those dark men whose surest sign of having arrived is the fact that he keeps company with people lighter in complexion than himself. Faced with the fundamental divisions in the island,

I had gone to the right and, by cutting myself off from my popular
side, delayed my political development for years.[10]

James had a great respect for Lewis's intellectual powers, describing
him in 1960, when Lewis was Principal of University College of the
West Indies, as one of those rare people with a capacity in conversation to concentrate all the forces available and needed on the matter
in hand.[11]

Another colleague and friend of Lewis, of a younger generation than
James, was the novelist V. S. Naipaul, born in Trinidad in 1932. In 1960,
Naipaul returned to Trinidad from London, where he had been living.
He had been granted a three-month scholarship by the government of
Trinidad and Tobago. The inspiration appears to have been the Trinidad
premier, Eric Williams, who had suggested that Naipaul write a non-
fiction book about the Caribbean. The result was the controversial book,
The Middle Passage (Naipaul, 1962). In the final chapter of that book, 'On
To Jamaica', Naipaul tells how Lewis, in his capacity as Principal of the
University College of the West Indies, had arranged with the wealthy
Grainger Weston for the ascetic Naipaul to experience three days free
of charge at the luxury resort of Frenchman's Cove in Jamaica, which
Grainger Weston owned. Naipaul describes the ultimate in luxury tourism; a resort where guests could order whatever they wanted to eat and
drink, at any time of the day or night. Caviar was on order for breakfast;
the best champagne at lunch. Aircraft, yachts and cars were placed at the
disposal of guests. Naipaul learnt, however, that his experience of poverty in the Caribbean ruled out for him the life of a luxury tourist. After
24 hours, he reports, even his interest in the food and drink available at
Frenchman's Cove had disappeared.

The Middle Passage is deeply anti-colonial: 'the pressures in Jamaica
were not simply the pressures of race or those of poverty. They were
the accumulated pressures of the slave society, the underdeveloped,
over-populated agricultural country'. Significantly, however, Naipaul,
like Lewis, has frequently been criticized for what has been interpreted
as unhelpful elitist attitudes, those middle-class values which Naipaul
believed gave society its purpose and direction. Naipaul concluded his
book with a warning:

Dr Arthur Lewis has drawn the distinction between 'protest' leaders and 'creative' leaders in colonial societies. It is a distinction of
which the West Indies are yet scarcely aware. In the West Indies with
its large middle class and abundance of talent, the protest leader is

an anachronism, and a dangerous anachronism. For the uneducated masses, quick to respond to racial stirrings and childishly pleased with destructive gestures, the protest leader will always be a hero. The West Indies will never have a shortage of such leaders, and the danger of mob rule and authoritarianism will never cease to be real. The paternalism of colonial rule will have been replaced by the jungle politics of rewards and revenge, the textbook conditions for chaos.[12]

Eric Williams, who had suggested that Naipaul write a non-fiction book about the Caribbean, was a close friend and ally of Lewis in the Caribbean. He belonged to the well-educated coloured elite indicted by Susan Craig. Williams, like Lewis, was an Island Scholar. On his mother's side he was from the influential French Creole minority. His father was a lower grade civil servant. Though he was four years older than Lewis, his time in Britain was roughly coincidental with that of Lewis at the LSE. He went up to Oxford (St Catherine's) in 1932, and graduated with a first class honours degree in history in 1935. His DPhil was awarded three years later. In spite of his distinguished academic career, Williams was unable to secure employment in Britain for racial reasons, and eventually he returned to Trinidad via a spell as an academic in the USA, during which (in 1944) he published his major work, *Capitalism and Slavery*, his controversial study that secured his radical credentials. In 1944 he was appointed to the Anglo-American Caribbean Commission, and it was through his good offices there that Lewis was appointed as Consultant to the Commission in 1948, an important stepping stone in Lewis's career. Williams became Chief Minister of Trinidad and Tobago in 1956, taking the country to Independence as leader of the radical political party he had founded. His withdrawal of Trinidad and Tobago from the West Indian Federation in January 1962 was a great disappointment to Lewis.

In May and June 1938, while Lewis was pursuing his research in London, events were reaching a climax in Jamaica. There were riots on sugar estates and business in Kingston came to a halt as a state of emergency was declared. In response, as related in Chapter 3, the Moyne Commission was set up in July 1938 to investigate conditions in the West Indies, and to make recommendations. The Moyne Commission was a comprehensive investigation covering not only the immediate labour issues, but also the deeper questions such as the role of agriculture, land settlement, housing and social welfare. The Commission received over 700 submissions, including one from Lewis, whose aim was, in his own words, 'to analyse some of the main issues relevant to social welfare in the British West Indies, and to suggest steps likely to increase the material and cultural well-being of the population'.[13] On reading the Lewis Memorandum, which is presented by Lewis as being highly critical of the Moyne Report, what is striking is the very large measure of common ground between Lewis's memorandum and the report of the commission.

John LaGuerre, in his study of the Moyne Commission, suggests that Lewis and the members of the Moyne Commission shared a common intellectual heritage:

> Lewis belonged to an intellectual class from the Caribbean that necessarily had to work within the assumptions and framework of colonial rule. By and large that class accepted the basic premises surrounding the concept of 'fitness to rule' which incorporated a gradual approach to self-government ... to sneer [at Lewis and others] for their middle class origins or to belittle their contribution to the intellectual development of the Caribbean is to misunderstand their time and place.[14]

Lewis was strongly anti-colonial. He never compromised on colonialism, imperialism or racism. But there was common ground between Lewis and the Moyne Commission on many aspects of development policy, including, among other things, an extension of the rights of workers to engage in collective bargaining, peaceful picketing and strikes. Moyne and Lewis were also strongly committed to increasing expenditure on welfare, and on improving the productivity of peasant agriculture. In the long run, however, Lewis saw the economic future of the West Indies very differently from Moyne. Lewis was an advocate of industrialization for the West Indies, claiming that 'the policy which seems to offer most hope of permanent success is for these islands to follow in the footsteps of other agricultural countries in industrialising'. The Commissioners did not concur in this. With a few exceptions, such as the Jamaican cement industry, the Commissioners saw little potential for industrialization in the British West Indies. Nor did they accept the need to direct West Indies exports of foodstuffs and raw materials increasingly towards US markets, as Lewis had suggested. His plea for higher prices for sugar, based on 'special treatment' in British markets, was similarly ignored.

Following from the Moyne Commission, the Colonial Development and Welfare Act (CDW Act) was passed in London in 1940. This invited positive proposals from colonial governments for policies to raise standards of living in the Colonies. As Lewis was to write a few years later, the act was seen as 'a symbol of great change in colonial policy, as a symbol of Britain's recognition that positive measures to raise the standard of living in the Colonies should have a high priority'.[15]

Writing in 1944, however, Lewis expressed his strong disappointment at the quality of the official reports that had been submitted to London by the colonial governments in response to the CDW Act. Lewis made a valid point. The proposals in the reports were almost entirely for increased welfare spending, on schools, hospitals and other social benefits. As he pointed out, the needs here were obvious but resources were limited:

> Health is poor, and public health facilities worse; schools vastly inadequate in number and quality; child welfare, old age, labour, 'social security', community centres – on all these matters £13,000,000 a year [the budget allocated in the Act] could be spent several times over. The unfortunate result is that nearly every plan concentrates on welfare services on which money is to be spent; economic development gets only a few paragraphs, and a small proportion of the funds.[16]

What Lewis was arguing was that economic development must be a priority. Only through a higher national income could the enormous social needs of the Colonies be met:

> The principal object of colonial policy should be to enable the Colonies to stand on their own two legs as soon as possible. This can be done only through their rapid economic development. Expenditure on social services, e.g. on health and on certain types of education, assists and is necessary to economic development. But social services are not the whole, or even the principal content of economic policy. As matters are tending at present, the Development Vote is going to be frittered away on a number of schemes, mostly unrelated. (Lewis, 1944)

In the context of development planning, Lewis was later to argue convincingly throughout the 1950s and 1960s that sound economic policies were more important to economic development than mere expenditure of money by the government. His argument was that, given how little money governments in developing countries had in relation to their needs, they must create an 'encouraging framework' for private investment.[17] His 1944 paper, 'An Economic Plan for Jamaica' was a critique of the patchy and uncoordinated response of the colonial government in Jamaica to the Colonial Development and Welfare Act. It also shows the young Lewis at his most acerbic, penning a bitter and cutting attack on the competence of the economist Frederic Benham, a senior colleague of Lewis at the LSE, who, as chairman of the relevant committee in Jamaica, authored the Jamaican response.

Frederic Benham held the Chair in the Commerce Department at the LSE. He took temporary leave in 1942 and travelled to Jamaica when he was appointed as economic adviser to the new Economic Policy Committee set up in Jamaica following the passing of the Colonial Development and Welfare Act. In 1944, he was appointed chairman of this Committee, and it was the report of this Committee that Lewis attacked so vehemently in his 1944 paper. At first reading it is tempting to conclude that what annoyed Lewis in relation to the Report from Jamaica was its failure to entertain seriously any proposals for industrialization in the West Indies. Indeed, Lewis was correct in saying that 'a strong prejudice against local industries runs throughout the Report'. However, it is perfectly possible to construct a respectable economic case against infant industry protection in a developing country, as Lewis was no doubt fully aware. Perhaps the authors should have done this. They did not, and Lewis was right to point this out. However, he went beyond this with a strong attack on Benham's competence as an economist. He described the report as 'a tragedy of errors and omissions', and more:

> What [the Report] has to say on industrialisation is not worth the paper on which it is written ...
>
> This Report is one of the worst examples of misapplied economics that has ever come from an official press ...
>
> Has the Committee ever heard of Keynes? Nay, has the Committee ever heard of Robbins, stern champion of the opportunity cost approach to economics?[18]

Nor was Lewis content to let the matter rest with a paper in an academic journal. He was keen to take up the issue in *The Manchester Guardian*, producing a long article, which the editor, probably wisely, politely declined to publish.

The attacks on Benham cannot have helped Lewis's career prospects at the LSE, and it is tempting to conclude that there must have been a degree of personal animosity between the two academics, if not before the report was published, most certainly afterwards. This is not to under-estimate Lewis's strong commitment to industrialization as a means of increasing employment in the West Indies, and his disappointment with the committee for failing to address the scale of the problem:

> Where does the Committee hope to find jobs? Frankly it has no hope. It reviews the agricultural prospects, and concludes that, thanks to banana diseases, agriculture may offer fewer jobs than it did before the war. Public works, housing, factories, bauxite, and tourists may absorb a few thousands, but nothing like what is necessary. This said, the Committee merely shrugs its shoulders and goes home. (Ibid.)

In his various capacities as adviser to the Colonial Office in the 1940s, Lewis was often asked to comment on Caribbean matters. Where development planning was involved, he was regarded as the expert, one moreover with a good understanding of agricultural conditions in the West Indies. In 1948, as a member of the Colonial Economic Development Council, he was asked for his comments on the British Guiana Ten Year Plan. He had visited the Caribbean quite recently, for his wedding, which took place in Grenada in 1947. It is clear from the report he submitted in 1948 to the Colonial Office that he had made use of the opportunity of his visit to the Caribbean the previous year to draw together some observations and opinions on the draft British Guiana Plan.

The report Lewis submitted to the Colonial Office was particularly strong in the comments it made on the recommendations in the Plan for agricultural development. The comments could have been written only by someone like Lewis, with a sound knowledge of the practicalities of peasant farming in the Caribbean. Lewis took the Plan to task for its anti-malaria proposals, pointing out correctly that the emphasis needed to shift from curative to preventive measures:

> Poor health is one of the scourges of British Guiana, militating both against human happiness and against a high level of production. At this stage of the Colony's development, curative work can make only a small impact on the people and I suggest that the emphasis of the Plan still needs considerably to be shifted in the direction of public health work and propaganda. (Lewis, 1948, para. 6)

The other significant part of Lewis's 1948 report is in the comments he made on land settlement schemes. To solve the problem of high population growth in British Guiana, made worse by the adoption of labour-saving investment techniques on the sugar estates, Lewis recommended orderly land settlement schemes. He hoped they would be more successful than elsewhere in the Caribbean, where the units of settlement had been too small, and settlers had been put on the land without any capital:

> Investigations in the West Indies and elsewhere lead to the conclusion that the minimum unit should be ten to twelve acres, and it is also desirable that settlers should be assisted to build houses and water tanks, to purchase livestock, and to have at least a minimum of agricultural implements. (Ibid., para. 14)

Lewis also advocated some larger units, worked by individually selected farmers or groups of farmers on a co-operative basis. Such farms could act as model demonstration units for settlers on smaller holdings.

It was not necessary to agree with Lewis's recommendations to appreciate that here was an economist deeply committed to practical policies that would raise living standards in the Caribbean. He also understood the Caribbean, and the opportunities and constraints under which peasant farmers laboured. This was why he was so valuable to the Colonial Office, and why he continued to be called upon as an adviser despite his well-known tendency to be critical and outspoken in his comments on official policy.[19] He was lucky too, in the sense that his time at the LSE coincided with the seven years of Labour government following the 1945 election, with politicians such as Creech Jones, a member of the Fabian Colonial Bureau, in charge of colonial policy.

7.3   Consultant on Caribbean development, 1948–58

In 1948, Lewis took up his professorial appointment at the University of Manchester, a move that marked the beginning of extensive consultancy work overseas. The Caribbean Commission, at its Eighth Meeting, held in Trinidad in June 1948, agreed to approach Lewis, who was described by the Secretariat as 'the distinguished British West Indian economist', to carry out research into the potential for Caribbean industries. Lewis accepted the appointment. In the course of his research he visited Trinidad, Puerto Rico, Jamaica and British Guiana, and published two reports in 1950, namely 'Industrial Development in Puerto Rico' (Lewis, 1950a) and 'The Industrialisation of the British West Indies' (Lewis, 1950b).

As related in Chapter 3, Lewis had seen Puerto Rico as a way forward for export-based industrialization since his first visit in 1940. Puerto Rico had established an Industrial Development Corporation in 1942, and a Government Development Bank in the same year. Initially, the government had operated factories, for cement, glass bottles, cardboard, clay products and shoes. In the second stage, the government constructed factories but leased them to private investors to operate. Finally, the government was attempting to encourage established US companies to set up manufacturing businesses in the country, with the Government Development Bank as the main source of loans for industry. With the small size of the domestic market, however, the industries needed to export or they would fail, therefore the priority was to attract companies with established market connections:

> For a firm to establish in Puerto Rico and then try to get a footing in the market, whether local or overseas, is an exceedingly risky and costly business ... vigorous persuasive efforts are mainly directed at those who can bring market connections with them as well as 'know how'. (Lewis, 1950a, para. 45)

Lewis was much less satisfied with the prospects for industrialization in the British West Indies. His second report on the British West Indies suggested that, in terms of overpopulation and unemployment, the need to industrialize was, if anything, greater in the British West Indies than in Puerto Rico. But there was very little in the way of practical support for such a policy in the British West Indies. Instead, Lewis said, there was 'violent prejudice against the development of industries in the islands ... common in powerful quarters' (Lewis, 1950b, para. 77).

Lewis elaborated on this theme in his report:

> It is not only the West Indian governments who fail to realise this [the need to industrialize]. On the contrary, the blindness of many of the West Indian nationalists in opposition is even greater. They speak frequently as if manufacturing in the West Indies offered a large profitable market which greedy foreign capitalists are anxious to rush in and exploit. They discuss industrialisation in terms of the close restrictions which they would like to impose on such capitalists ... The facts are exactly the opposite of what they suppose. The West Indies does not offer a large market. There are very few manufacturers who wish to go there ... these islands cannot be

industrialised without a considerable inflow of foreign capital and capitalists, and a period of wooing and fawning upon such people. (Ibid., paras 112 and 113)

Sentiments such as these undoubtedly underpinned and reinforced the criticism Lewis was to attract in later years, from radical academics, when he took up his appointment as Principal of the University College of the West Indies (UCWI).

These early reports that Lewis produced for the Caribbean Commission are also significant in that an element of frustration, even exasperation, was beginning to surface in Lewis's attitude to the British West Indies. He contrasts what he sees as the drive and enthusiasm of Puerto Rico with the lethargy of the British West Indies, a visit to which he describes as a

> depressing experience ... Everyone seems to be waiting for something to happen, but the traveller is never quite able to discover what it is they are waiting for ... the British West Indians can solve their problems if they set to them with a will. But first they must find the secret that will put hope, initiative, direction, and an unconquerable will into the management of their affairs. And this is the hardest task of all. (Ibid., p. 153)

From the 1950s onwards until he returned as Principal of the University College in 1960, Lewis's professional ties with the Caribbean necessarily had to give way to other demands. There were consultancies in different parts of the developing world – in West Africa, the Far East and Egypt – and in 1956/7 a one-year Fellowship at Berkeley, California. His ties with the Colonial Office were also becoming significantly weaker, as he made clear in a letter to Dudley Huggins, first Director of the Institute of Social and Economic Research (ISER) at Mona.

The ISER was founded at Mona in 1948 with a grant from the Colonial Development and Welfare Fund. Modelled on similar Institutes at Oxford, Cambridge and London, it aimed to promote academic research on social and economic issues in the British West Indies. In 1953, Dudley Huggins wrote to Lewis soliciting help in ISER's dealings with Arnold Plant, Lewis's mentor when he was an undergraduate at the LSE. Both Plant and Herbert Frankel appeared to be hostile to the work being carried out at the ISER, and Huggins was concerned that the Colonial Office grant would not be renewed. He believed the reason was that the ISER's pro-industrialization development philosophy, which was closely aligned to that of Lewis, was deeply unpopular in Colonial Office circles. He asked Lewis for support and advice, but Lewis' reply, as related in Chapter 3, was unsympathetic and warned Huggins of the dangers of getting on the wrong side of Plant. On the positive side, however, Lewis gave a great deal of practical support to the ISER at Mona. He was diligent in reading and commenting on the papers submitted by 'your young people' at Mona. One year after the discouraging letter to Dudley Huggins, he was writing to compliment Huggins on the quality of the submissions to the ISER journal, *Social and Economic Studies*:

> The articles contain much new, useful and interesting material, and it is a considerable achievement to be able to publish so much good stuff within three years or so of effective operation. I cannot think of any other Economic or Social Research Institute anywhere in the world which has given so much value for the money.[20]

7.4   University College of the West Indies, 1960–3

By the mid-1950s, Lewis was looking outside the United Kingdom for his next appointment. His relations with the Colonial Office were significantly less congenial after the election of 1951, when a Conservative government took the place of Labour. The culture and mood of the Colonial Office had changed, and Lewis's policies, especially on industrialization, were being questioned increasingly by officials.[21] Nor, as we have seen, was Lewis particularly happy by this stage in the Department of Economics at Manchester. It is likely that Lewis already had in mind a move to the USA, a move that in the event was postponed until 1963, when he took up his final appointment at Princeton. In 1956, he had leave of absence from Manchester for one year, with a Fellowship at Berkeley, California. The following year, in April 1957, the Department of Economics at Chicago met to discuss an appointment for Lewis. He was the front-runner. There was another candidate, however, Lewis's Manchester colleague Harry Johnson, who was also anxious to leave the UK.

Johnson's biographer, D. E. Moggridge, quotes Johnson as saying the reason he wanted to go to Chicago was that economics in Britain was dominated by Keynesianism and Labour Party socialism. Whether he had Lewis or others in mind when he made this complaint is difficult to say. Moggridge reports that when the names of the two candidates, Lewis and Johnson, were put to the vote in the Department at Chicago the vote was split: six of the thirteen alumni present favoured Johnson, while five favoured Lewis. The Department met again one month later, when 'a motion was passed unanimously authorizing the chairman to proceed to negotiate the appointment of Harry Johnson to a major tenure post in the Department'.[22]

Lewis's feelings when he learned that he had been passed over in favour of his junior colleague Harry Johnson are unknown, but we can speculate that it is more than likely to have strengthened his resolve to leave Manchester. The Chicago appointment failed to materialize in May 1957, and by March 1958 Lewis was writing to Ely Devons to say that he had accepted the Chair of Economics in Jamaica. The long-drawn-out move to Jamaica, however, does not suggest that Lewis was overly keen to take up the appointment. In his letter to Devons, Lewis said that the Chair was to be effective from October 1958, but that he would not arrive in Jamaica until a year later, in October 1959. The terms of the appointment were subsequently changed to 'Principal of the University College', and the starting date postponed to April 1960. The Lewis family finally arrived in Jamaica on 14 April 1960. The intervening period between leaving Manchester in 1958 and arriving in Jamaica in 1960 was spent by Lewis, first on secondment to the Ghana government, as described in the previous chapter, and then at the UN in New York.

While in New York, however, Lewis had once more demonstrated his commitment to the Caribbean by taking a leading role in establishing a second Institute of Social and Economic Research, this time in Barbados. Lewis was increasingly anxious to bring to the Eastern Caribbean some of the benefits hitherto enjoyed by Trinidad and Jamaica in the Western Caribbean. The ISER (Eastern Caribbean), set up in 1959 with money Lewis obtained from the Ford Foundation, is still remembered fondly in Barbados as the institution (pre-dating the Cave Hill Campus of the University of the West Indies) that opened up higher education in the Eastern Caribbean. True to his academic philosophy, Lewis saw independent research as the primary function of the ISER. In his own words, the purpose of the ISER (Eastern Caribbean) was to conduct its research, 'in accordance with the traditional policy of the University and its scholarly standards ... non-partisan and non-political'.[23]

Though Lewis was still engaged in the development problems of the Caribbean, it is not certain that he was keen to return to the region in a permanent capacity. In May 1958, his Fabian colleague, Rita Hinden, as we recall, had written to Lewis in Accra to congratulate him on his new appointment and had predicted 'an influential and happy time' for him at the University College of the West Indies. She was wrong, however.

She may also have failed to realize that the passage of time had damp-
ened Lewis's enthusiasm for a post in the Caribbean.

This supposition of diminished enthusiasm for a permanent appointment in the West Indies was confirmed in interview with Phyllis Deane,
who had worked with Lewis at the National Institute of Economic and
Social Research (NIESR) and the CEDC in London during the Second
World War. On the strength of her research on national income statistics, Deane was invited to Jamaica in the 1950s, to draw up national
income accounts to be used in development planning. Her adviser on
the research in Jamaica was Lewis. Interviewed in Cambridge in 2006,
she was adamant that even in the early 1950s Lewis had no enthusiasm
for a return to the West Indies on a permanent basis.

One of the most intractable problems of the UCWI was that it had a
very small population of privileged, high-income, high-cost students. The
student population, only 600 in 1957, could have fitted comfortably into
a large lecture hall anywhere in the world; and, as Lewis told the students, in the presence of such diseconomies of scale, it would have been
cheaper to close down the entire university and send all the students to
get their education overseas than to carry on with such tiny numbers.
Consequently, he needed to expand rapidly. He was able to get numbers
up to around 2,000 by the time he left six years later, but each attempt
either to reduce costs or to increase revenue was met, as we shall see, with
uncoordinated howls of protest, which confirmed in him quite early in
his tenure the feeling that he had chosen the wrong job and should get
out as soon as possible for the sake of both his health and his sanity.

Indeed, less than a year after arriving in Jamaica with his family in
April 1960, Lewis had submitted a formal letter of resignation to the
Chancellor, Princess Alice, from his post as Principal. The letter, sent on
23 January 1961 (his 46th birthday) sets out at some length the reasons
for the resignation, which were also given in writing to members of the
University College Council:

> I suppose the basic reason for going must be that I do not feel at home
> here ... The job here is especially hard for two reasons. First, the new-
> ness of the College and the expansion of its activities means that
> there is something new to settle every day ... Secondly there are not
> enough top people sharing the burden ... However, I am not leaving
> the job just because it is hard ... my vision of what the College should
> be like is shared neither by staff nor by students ... I long ago ceased
> to want to organise people or institutions. My work has been to study
> data and ideas, and to teach and write ... Perhaps I should never have

taken on the job; I did so reluctantly, and only under pressure from people outside the College.[24]

Lewis rescinded his resignation very quickly, however. The Chancellor reported to Council on 16 February 1961 that the Principal had asked permission to withdraw his resignation. Lewis wrote to Council:

> I still feel that my talents are more appropriate to teaching than to administration, but I cannot ignore the communications I have received from people in all walks of life, inside and outside the College, urging me to remain in the post at this critical time in the history of the College and of our country.[25]

Lewis received support from key individuals in Jamaica, who expressed confidence in him, with requests that he remain. The support of the premier, Norman Manley, was critical. Manley, it will be recalled, was one of the people cited by Susan Craig in the 1970s in her critique of the elite who had taken the Caribbean to independence. Manley was a highly educated Jamaican of mixed race, with English and Irish ancestry. He was a Rhodes Scholar at Oxford, trained as a barrister, and by the 1920s was a leading lawyer in Jamaica. He founded the left-wing People's National Party (PNP). Lewis was in touch with the PNP during the 1940s and corresponded with N. N. Nethersole, who was an important leader of the PNP.[26] When Lewis arrived at the UCWI in 1960 he could count on the valuable support of Manley, by then serving as Jamaica's first prime minister.

Manley wrote to Lewis on 26 January 1961:

> I do not think you will be surprised to know that I have heard something about your difficulties at the UCWI. Some time ago when you were talking over some matters with me you hinted of them to me and I found it easy to understand how difficult you found the change from a life of scholarship and teaching and advice to a life beset with problems of administration and management and public relations and money raising and all those disagreeable things ... I would welcome the opportunity of having a talk with you about it ... at this moment in West Indian history and for the next couple of years there is so much at stake that I feel that I would like to explain why I think that you in your present position at any rate for the critical years ahead are in a peculiar position where we just could not afford to do without you.

The meeting did take place. Manley wrote again to Lewis on 4 February 1961:

> I am glad we were able to talk the other night and I hope good will come out of it. I have no doubt about two things
>
> (1) You should stay where you are until at least one year after the West Indies achieve independence
> (2) You should demand that things be so arranged that you are free to do your own research work, and your own advisory work and not be burdened with administrative detail
>
> ... I can only hope that your inner convictions will in the end go with what the whole of the West Indies need at this time.[27]

In fact, Lewis did stay on in Jamaica until 1963. From February to October 1961, he threw himself into the expansion and reform of the UCWI, against the shadow of the larger political problems of the British West Indies which, as Manley had suggested, were at a critical juncture. The constitutional position of the West Indies had changed in 1958 with the setting up of the West Indies Federation. This comprised most of the islands of the British West Indies, large ones such as Jamaica and Trinidad, and smaller ones such as St Kitts and St Vincent. It was expected that the Federation would be a unit, and as a unit it would be granted independence from the Crown. It was a weak Federation from the start. Grantley Adams of Barbados was elected the first premier, because neither Norman Manley, premier of Jamaica nor Eric Williams, premier of Trinidad, stood for office. Trinidad was granted independence as a political unit on 31 August 1962. Jamaica had already been granted independence as a political unit on 6 August that year. The first premier of the newly independent Jamaica was not Manley, who was defeated in the election, but his cousin, Alexander Bustamante, who had stood on an anti-Federation ticket. Given his political difficulties, it is likely that Manley had indeed needed Lewis, much more than Lewis needed Manley, when they met to discuss Lewis's intention to resign in 1961.

Lewis's personal files in the Archives at the University of the West Indies (UWI) indicate that local and domestic concerns were at least as important to him as the larger political issues. First, much of his time between his arrival in April 1960 and his 'resignation' in January 1962 was taken up with travel, both within the Caribbean and beyond, leaving little time to deal with administrative matters at the University. His calendar of travel during that period included New York, Israel, Vienna, London, Washington, Barbados, Antigua, and Pittsburgh and Boston in the USA. Most of this travel, as far as we can tell, was for fund-raising rather than academic purposes. In spite of Manley's pleas, he attempted little research at this time, although, as we shall see, he still sought through his overseas links to give a developmental thrust to higher education in the West Indies.

Relations with academic and senior non-academic staff were also a problem for him. There were important differences on development policy between Lewis and the radical social scientists at Mona, but there were also divergences of a baser material kind. As indicated above, Lewis on arrival made it clear that he saw the University as a non-viable institution, partly as a consequence of the high cost of salaries for staff, which, as was customary in universities in the Colonies, were pitched at levels necessary to attract expatriates. In a Memorandum of the University of West Indies, he objected to the fact that 'This University pays the same basic scales as British Universities, and then adds benefits which for the average staff member with two children comes to £940 per year.'[28] At this time the basic salary for a mid-scale academic or academic-related post was of the order of £1,200 per annum.

Lewis's objections might have been more acceptable to his colleagues had his own remuneration, widely known in the University, been less generous. In January 1961, prior to his resignation, the remuneration Committee raised his basic salary from £3,500 to £4,000, backdated to the start of his appointment in August 1960. In addition to his salary he received family allowances, an entertainment allowance, and occupied the Principal's house rent-free with a car, driver and gardener provided.

Lewis wrote to the UWI Senate, which he accused of being 'irresponsible', on the subject of academic salaries not long after he withdrew his resignation letter. The tone of his letter can be judged from the following extract:

For my part I am disgusted that our West Indian staff should demand these premiums above British salaries. If this is the moral atmosphere of UWI, let us close the place down, and use the money to send twice as many students to older universities, where they will learn something about the responsibilities of citizenship. If this is the best we can do, there is no prospect of my appearing before the Triennial Advisory Committee [which advised on salaries] to ask that one more penny be put under the control of so irresponsible a Senate.[29]

There is a certain irony in Lewis's moral indignation over the allowances being paid to West Indian staff, since the files indicate that he himself had many disputes with senior staff in the Registry over the expenses he claimed. The Bursar queried personal expenses that had been charged to the College on a number of occasions. There were disagreements with the Registry over Lewis's claims for expenses in moving from New York, which included the transport of his wine cellar, and the losses incurred on the sale of the family car. The maintenance and decoration of the Principal's house was another source of disagreement. A letter has been retained in the files, mischievously perhaps, in which an interior decorator, one Susie Latreille, writes to the Registrar complaining that at Mrs Lewis's direction she had had to take back furniture she had supplied to the Lewis household and replace it with costly items such as an 'expensive mahogany empire couch' and damask curtains. There is no doubt that the Lewis family lived well in Jamaica, but equally it is likely that Lewis's enemies in the University were skilful in exploiting the situation.

Lewis did not confine his moral indignation to salaries. He wrote to the Deans in November 1961 complaining that 'this college has an unsavoury reputation because of rumour, gossip and speculation about the irregular sex lives of some of our staff members'.[30] The letter referred to a case in which an unmarried female staff member was sharing her room on campus with a married staff member. Nor did students escape censure. Students who were 'caught' in a similar situation on campus would be expelled. The serious side to Lewis's moralizing is the struggle he had with the image of the West Indian. This was demonstrated most clearly in his Address to Students on the Occasion of their Matriculation in 1960. He asked the students 'What is the image of the West Indian? What do we say about ourselves?'

His answer was:

> when I was a boy the image of the West Indian was that he was a happy go-lucky character. A good cricketer ... A good dancer ... Irresistible to women ... I think we took a certain pride in understanding that life was meant to be enjoyed, and not meant to be taken seriously ... This is one side of the penny. The other side consists of what foreigners say about us. A happy-go-lucky person is unreliable ... unpunctual ... never put a West Indian in any really responsible job.
>
> If this is the correct picture then we need a new one, and I can think of no better place for creating a new image than the University College of the West Indies.[31]

Unfortunately, there is no record of how the students of UWI in 1960 responded to their Principal's moralizing. The Caribbean poet, Derek Walcott, his biographer notes, found the University College at Mona, which he attended for four years as an undergraduate in the 1950s, to be narrow and stuffy, and the attitudes of many of its British staff offensive to West Indian culture and achievements. Walcott felt that the College was an imitation of England, at a time when young people like himself were discovering the Caribbean and its culture.[32] If Lewis's 1960s student audience shared Walcott's perception of the College, then Lewis's Address is unlikely to have been received with great enthusiasm. Lewis's lack of empathy with certain aspects of West Indian culture, especially on the musical front, is well known. This was a serious problem, since black music is central to the Caribbean identity. Lewis had a particular dislike of steel bands, on which his observation was that 'a false nationalism has persuaded us that the steel band is a significant contribution to the world's heritage of music'.[33] This led Lewis during his time as Principal into heroic efforts to establish a Jamaica School of Music in Mona, to promote violin and piano playing. He recruited William Primrose, the distinguished American violist, to be the founding Principal of the Jamaica School of Music, and thereafter as a special adviser to the school,[34] and searched around the world for talent that might help the school achieve international excellence. Having failed to recruit Pablo Casals,[35] he was able to call on the support of a wide range of distinguished musicians in Britain, including Arthur Bliss, Adrian Boult, Myra Hess and Yehudi Menuhin.[36] The Jamaica School of Music assignment was dear to him, and he continued with it for a number of years after his departure for Princeton in 1963.

One of the more attractive of Lewis's behaviours during this period of constantly rowing upstream against the current was his attempt, whenever possible, to implement within the West Indies the ideas of 'mass education' and giving priority to agricultural development that he had been propagating as an element in egalitarian development policy since the early 1940s. In the context of the UWI, of course, this had to be done mainly through teacher training in agriculture, animal husbandry, health and other applied technical skills, as Lewis had advocated in his *Principles of Economic Planning* document of 1948 (see Chapter 3 above). Twenty years of colonial economic planning work had given him a clear picture of where the crucial manpower gaps were in the West Indies' economies, and now, as Vice-Chancellor, Lewis could act to fill them. For example, in defiance of the stereotype of the West Indies as a lush tropical paradise where everything grows, there are some areas of the islands in which drought is a serious problem, and the only commercial crop that will grow there is citrus fruit (especially limes and grapefruit). In 1961, these drought-prone areas, which were also areas of severe localized poverty, were operating at very low productivity, and no local West Indian technicians were available to advise on how to increase it. Lewis immediately perceived an opportunity for practising what he had been preaching, and arranged for technicians to come to the University's Agriculture School from Israel on one-year contracts with a view to making the dryland areas of the West Indies bloom.[37] During this time, Lewis had no time to do academic research, but he did occasionally get the opportunity to give a talk at one of the UWI campuses in which some of his philosophy of development was allowed to emerge.[38] In these talks, Lewis makes clear that he sees the way forward for the university as being, not just expansion, but expansion of opportunities for those at the bottom of the pyramid as well for the privileged elite – in particular, through what the 1990 *World Development Report* (World Bank, 1990) was to call 'investing in the human capital of the poor'. This is the last and the climactic stage of Lewis's work as a development practitioner.

7.5   The Principal as an economist

So much happened to Lewis during his brief period as Principal of the University College that it is easy to overlook the fact that when he was appointed he was one of the world's leading development economists. It is a significant question as to how he related to his fellow economists at Mona during this period, because after he left the UWI, from the mid-1960s onwards, his economics, characterized as 'industrialization by invitation' came under persistent attack from Caribbean social scientists – what came to be known as the Plantation School.

In interview, Gisela Eisner, who was in the University College in Jamaica in 1953 and 1954 at the ISER, put forward the view that Lewis, who supervised her research at Mona in the early 1950s, was 'generally disappointed' with the expertise of many of the economists there. He made exception, however, for George Cumper, whom he may have taught as an undergraduate at Cambridge during the Second World War and who became a family friend. Cumper came to ISER in 1949. He had married a prominent Jamaican lawyer, also a Cambridge graduate. Cumper's economics was conservative but probably not very far removed from that of Lewis, in the sense that it was non-technical applied economics, with an emphasis on demography, national income accounting, household budget studies and rural development policies. As Figueroa reminds us, these topics were at the forefront of economics in the 1960s, though they may appear very mundane to us now.[39]

According to George Beckford, Cumper was part of the 'core of British researchers' who dominated economics at Mona until the mid-1960s.[40] In 1961, possibly with the support of Lewis, the core researchers were joined by yet another British economist, the young Keynesian, Charles Kennedy, who became the first head of the Economics Department in the new social science faculty. However, the mainstream economists were being challenged increasingly.[41] A group of young radical Marxist Caribbean social scientists wanted to teach what they believed to be a more relevant economics in the Caribbean. The leading names in this group were Beckford himself, Norman Girvan, Lloyd Best and Kari Polanyi Levitt, the daughter of Karl Polanyi, herself a former undergraduate student of Lewis at Cambridge. The radicals did not win over the faculty administration at Mona immediately, however, and the traditionalists prevailed for a few years. Kennedy departed in 1966, and by the 1970s radical approaches had taken over. The debates and disagreements rumbled on into the 1990s. Lewis's name was often mentioned in this context. He was alluded to as the father of development economics, who had, however, encouraged Caribbean economists to follow a tradition in economics in which the 'inherited toolbox of metropolitan economics' was misapplied to the Caribbean.

This was the hostile environment in which Susan Craig later penned her bitter attack on Lewis and the nationalist politicians of the 1950s and 1960s. How did Lewis himself view this scenario? Bearing in mind all the other issues that dominated Lewis's brief spell at Mona in the early 1960s, it is doubtful whether he would have had the time during his stay at Mona to tackle his young critics, even if he had had the inclination. But there were fundamental principles at stake here. Norman Girvan, who at an early stage in his career had been counted among the anti-Lewis rebels, later came to reassess his opinion on the 50th anniversary of the publication of *The Theory of Economic Growth*.[42] Girvan drew his audience's attention to two areas of West Indian development where he believed that experience has shown that the policies Lewis advocated for the Caribbean were correct, but years ahead of their time. First, there was Lewis's attitude to foreign capital. The Plantation School believed that multinationals were a problem in the Caribbean. Lewis had an eclectic attitude to foreign capital in the region. In some cases it worked, but in others it failed to generate development. Given the correct conditions and safeguards it could have a positive impact on development. The second area was regional integration, where Lewis was a strong advocate of collective regional sovereignty. Post-Lewis experience has shown that insular attitudes bring only a sham independence, especially to small economies, and are inappropriate in a globalized environment, which has a degree of interdependence barely contemplated in the 1960s.

In a paper in 1994, Mark Figueroa spoke for a generation of Mona-educated economists, taught by radical academics, who had been left in ignorance of Lewis's writings, in the belief that they had little relevance to the Caribbean:

> The impression that was conveyed to students at least at Mona was unfortunate as the representatives of the Plantation School themselves were at times quite aware of the breadth of Lewis's work and at least in the case of Beckford greatly influenced by aspects of his work. Indeed the discovery of the latter fact was one of the greatest surprises in my intellectual development. Long after graduating from Mona and absorbing the attitude to Lewis described above I was enquiring of George Beckford as to how he became turned on to economics. To my shock, he without hesitation referred to the work of Lewis in general and *The Theory of Economic Growth* (1955) in particular.[43]

7.6   The Agony of the Eight

The basic economic problem of the West Indies was, of course, that it consisted of a set of small, poor islands with diminutive populations. Because of the population sizes, their market was small; because their market was small their costs were high; and because their costs were high, industrialization was between difficult and impossible. Because of this predicament, the West Indian colonies remained poor and primary-commodity-dependent. The obvious way out of this quandary was some form of economic and political union. The obvious points of contention were how to design the economic union to best overcome the problem of small size, what forms of individual sovereignty should be sacrificed in the cause of political union, and how, if at all, it might be possible to persuade the stronger and richer countries within the union that it was in their interests to be inside the union rather than outside it. As we shall see, this third issue quickly came to dominate the politics of West Indian closer union in the early 1960s, to the detriment of a proper discussion of the other issues.

The position in early 1961 was that a federation project had been mooted, to coincide with preparations for independence in the territories most impatient for it: Jamaica and Trinidad. The project had received unexpected support from the Colonial Office, but was threatened by ever-increasing divisions between the individual islands, in particular Jamaica and Trinidad, which were separated by both ethnicity and economic philosophy. Jamaica was dominated by people of Afro-Caribbean origin, and Trinidad much more by people of Indian ethnicity. Politically, both Norman Manley and Eric Williams, the prime minister of Trinidad, were left-leaning, but whereas Manley depended strongly on his power-base in the trade union movement, Williams was more of a free-standing intellectual socialist – indeed, like Lewis, a former university academic. And where Manley wanted a federation in which all public expenditure was essentially delegated to the budgets of, and votes by, the legislatures of individual territories, Williams wanted a 'unitary state'; that is, a federal constitution (for which the USA, Mexico and Brazil provided models) in which a strong government at the centre determines defence, foreign and central economic policies, and only issues of purely local concern are delegated to the individual legislatures. In Williams' vision, Trinidad would be the leader of the federation and thus all the other East Caribbean states 'would be in the same position as Tobago'– that is, merely appendages of Trinidad.[44] After Manley's defeat by Alexander Bustamante in the pre-independence referendum of late 1961, the possibility of Jamaica being involved in any federation disappeared, and the question became whether to go with Williams' unitary state or to devise some alternative.

The issue was of concern to Lewis because, as discussed above, he was the principal of an institution – still based in the about-to-become-independent Jamaica – whose finances were at risk as the result of persistent threats by the governments of Jamaica, Trinidad and even British Guiana to reduce or withdraw their financial support. Rightly or wrongly, he believed that the preservation of a political federation was key to the protection of the finances of the UWI, in other words, to the University's survival. At this point (late summer 1961), after the departure of Jamaica, there were nine countries left in the potential West Indian federation – Trinidad, Barbados, St Lucia, Antigua, Grenada, St Kitts with Anguilla, Montserrat, St Lucia and St Vincent. Grantley Adams, the head of the West Indies federation, like Lewis, believed that Williams' centralized ('unitary state') federal model was unworkable and, in particular, extravagant, but Adams, already suffering from being constantly disparaged by Williams on intellectual and personal grounds, was losing faith in his own ability to hold the argument for federation together, and had done nothing to ingratiate himself with the University. Indeed, Lewis felt that the Federal government had 'let the [University] College down on every occasion that we have asked for support'[45] and shared Williams' contemptuous view of Adams.

Despite this, in October 1961, Lewis offered his services to Adams as technocrat-cum-mediator. His trump cards were, first, his long-standing friendship with Williams (who had edited books and journal articles to which Lewis had made contributions, describing him as 'our best box office attraction');[46] second, his command of the economics of closer union; and third, his renewed credibility with the Colonial Office, who appear to have been willing to listen to Lewis as long as he confined himself to West Indian matters and did not try to hector them on more general matters of economic policy.[47] So, it is natural that the Federation wanted Lewis to try to hold them together. But why did Lewis, so badly burnt in Ghana, want to involved himself in such a high-risk venture? One reason is that he saw severe downside risks of failure not just for his University, but also for the whole of the West Indies. As he wrote to his Vice-Principal on 22 September 1961: 'My own country [may] become another Congo. I have today taken up a new assignment as special adviser to the Prime Minister of the West Indies in an effort to hold the pieces together.'[48]

A second, and more bizarre, reason is that Lewis seems at the time to have entertained a high degree of optimism about West Indians having a special talent for peace-making, which sits strangely with the quotation above.[49] Thus he now committed himself to a formal attempt to re-stitch the West Indian federation (minus Jamaica) together, and took leave from the University for three months. The federation agreed to pay Lewis the sum of one dollar to hire him as a consultant for the period that he was free from university obligations.

Lewis had meetings with Williams and the leaders of the eight other islands on several occasions during the final quarter of 1961, and for a period of three and a half months sought to design a blueprint for a federal constitution that would provide the benefit of a wider market for the production of all of the nine territories and at the same time avoid the massive costs associated with Trinidad's unitary state model. At the same time, he sought to use his influence with Williams to accept this smaller-scale concept of federation, and crucially to avoid public briefings against that model while negotiations were ongoing. Lewis was able to do this until 15 January 1962. On that day, however, having won re-election as prime minister, Williams broke cover and announced publicly that Trinidad was intending to move straight to independence. If, however, he suggested, other East Caribbean territories wished to join Trinidad in a federation based on a unitary-state model, they would be welcome to so. The Colonial Office quickly confirmed that it would have no objection to Trinidad's independence, and thus another building block within the planned federation fell down. There were now only eight green bottles hanging on the wall.

Years later, Lewis was to write a post-mortem on these events, which reads as follows:

Williams' attitude was consistent from the day of the referendum onwards:

(1) He wanted the existing federation destroyed
(2) He wanted to associate with other territories
(3) He preferred a unitary state to federalism.

The record of our first meeting, September 22, says: 'It became clear at the beginning that he was so fed up with the whole of the existing federation and the kind of constitutional structure that had emerged from the discussions that he thought the best thing was to let the whole thing smash up, and then some time later the smaller islands would come crawling to Trinidad to create a new federation more like a unitary state. I sent him a preliminary draft of my report at the end of October[50] and saw him on November 3rd. By now he was completely obsessed with getting rid of the existing federation. I tried to persuade him to attend a conference. He said that he was willing to attend a conference but he would not agree to any date. I recorded: "I was left with the clear impression that he wishes to see the issue of the continuance of a federation come to a boil because he wants to get rid of the existing federal personalities, and that was the main concern." I pointed out that there is an infinite gradation between confederation at one extreme and unitary state at the other, and one could get what one wanted without calling it by names which aroused emotions.

Williams' stand-off attitude to Barrow [the premier of Barbados] was no doubt due to his knowing that Barrow would not be interested in a unitary state, so they were not likely to reach early agreement ... Barrow was therefore very angry when Williams did talk a few weeks later: he called him a double-crosser. This emotion did much to put Barrow into the English camp.

Maudling [Colonial Secretary] wrote to Williams the day after the election. Mordecai's [chief executive of the embryonic West Indies Federation] letter of December 13th mentions this and Williams' rebuff to Maudling. Mordecai's letter of December 27 reports that Maudling then informed Williams:

(1) That the federation would be dissolved, and
(2) That Trinidad could have independence if it wanted.

However Mordecai's letter indicates that even at this date Williams was saying that he was not yet prepared to talk about future arrangements.

Williams spoke to me on January 25 about the unitary state in terms which left no doubt that he was serious. Trinidad must leave[51] Grenada and St Vincent at least, to get Negro votes to counter the Indian vote which had now solidified behind the Opposition.

I had my small proof that he did not care, at the beginning of November. He was due to make a long broadcast at the end of the first week, giving his story on Federation. I said: forget how you feel about the Chief Ministers [of the islands], and think for the moment of the hundreds of small islanders who love you as a great national hero.[52] The referendum [which caused Jamaica to opt out of the federation] has been a great shock to them and they are worried and anxious. Please put in a sentence for them which says: I know how anxious you are, but don't worry, we will work things out. He promised to consider this. I listened to the speech most anxiously, but it was addressed exclusively to the people of Trinidad and Tobago, all references to others being hostile. At that point I wrote off the bastard.

[Williams' close advisers were all against any kind of association with the small islands]. I was convinced that it was important to prevent Williams from speaking, and that this was the only hope. My real achievement was that I succeeded in keeping Williams silent for four months. My failure which we all share was that his silence was broken in January. Why was it broken in January? If Williams had adhered to his stated plan of consulting various groups in Trinidad, and attending some sort of conference with the eight after the federation was dissolved, something might have been salvaged:

(a) As the election fever subsided the political temperature would have cooled and he would not have been so excited.
(b) The disappearance of Manley and Grantley [Adams] from the table would have left him a clear field with strong Colonial Office backing.

(c) The fact that a unitary state would cost the earth would have finally sunk in (in February 1963 he told me that he had not realized this until he got the Grenada figures from Demas).

(d) Given his need for Negro votes, his preference for a big puddle rather than a small one and his desire to have his name in history, he would probably have preferred federation to independence alone, if independence with a unitary state became obviously impracticable.

So THE GREAT QUESTION: what made Williams suddenly decide to break silence in mid January, 1962?[53]

On 19 January 1962, four days after Williams' formal announcement that he was proceeding with independence, the remaining eight East Caribbean territories (one of them his own St Lucia) announced their support for the idea of a political and economic association. It is clear from the short delay that Williams' announcement was something they had expected. In fact, we know from Lewis's diary that he and his allies, Vere Bird (the prime minister of Antigua) and Errol Barrow (the Prime minister of Barbados), had met on 13 January to organize a federation of the eight – that is, the nine Eastern Caribbean territories minus Trinidad. On 14 January this was explained to Grantley Adams, the incumbent chief executive of the Federation, whose reaction to being thus ambushed is described by Lewis as 'confused and inane ... [he just] sat there mumbling and deeply hurt'.[54]

Over the following four months, from January to May 1962, the eight countries of the Eastern Caribbean, with Lewis now working as a part-time rather than full-time adviser, having resumed his university post, worked in consultation with the Colonial Office to design a model for closer union. Lewis, according to his own account, drafted an outline constitution for the new federation in 24 hours, on 16 and 17 January 1962,[55] and appended further notes to it at the end of the month which are nothing less than a composite development plan for the eight Eastern Caribbean countries, projecting national income, government income and expenditure, aid flows, and major categories of agricultural and industrial production forward for the ten years from 1963 to 1973.[56] This document applied to the whole of the West Indies the blunt economic verdict which Lewis had caused so much offence by applying to his own University two years previously: 'the chief reason why the Windward and Leeward Islands are grant-aided is because that their governments cost too much'. The main element in excessive cost, Lewis goes on to argue, is excessive staff salaries, and as a result, 'the major effect of the British grants-in-aid has been not to improve the public services of the islands, but merely to enable civil servants to earn more than their next-door neighbours. The fiscal situation in the islands will not come right until this situation is corrected'.[57] Lewis advised the eight governments to plan for a fourfold reduction in aid flows, from US$9 million to US$2 million as a whole, over the following five years.[58]

Fascinatingly, the 'four principles' which Lewis and Durbin had used as a point of departure for their *Colonial Economic Development* document of 1944, much metamorphosed, are still visible in Lewis's testimony to the Marlborough House Conference. Protection was needed to set up industry on an Eastern Caribbean basis.[59] This industrialization would be selective, but the basis of selection would be the decisions of individual entrepreneurs, and not any plan imposed by a federal authority; indeed, Lewis insisted on this, saying 'If an attempt were made to impose centralised control over industrial development he feared this would lead to the break-up of the federation.'[60] Agricultural production could be expanded both by applying the techniques of agricultural engineering, and terracing, which he believed could 'expand the land at present under cultivation by about 20%'.[61] And, of course, agricultural education and enterprise were needed and 'could be encouraged by a unified agricultural service, by extension services, by provision for agricultural credit and by marketing arrangements adapted to the small-scale producer.[62]

The leaders of the eight territories, with Lewis in attendance as adviser, spent the week from 9 to 16 May in conference in Marlborough House, London, as guests of the Colonial Office, with Lewis attending for the first three days. Agreement was reached quite quickly on the principle (though not the fine print) of a customs union agreement, of free movement of people and goods within the Eastern Caribbean and of the centralized collection of customs and excise and (in the future) income tax duties.[63] When the conference disbanded it was agreed that many matters needed to be fine-tuned, in particular the unit constitutions of the eight states and, in particular, the fiscal arrangements;[64] but the mood was that these were things which could be resolved. The only rumble of thunder came from the prime minister of Grenada, who reminded delegates that 'a minor group' in his country had been campaigning for a unitary form of government with Trinidad; but even he expressed the hope that the nascent Eastern Caribbean Federation could be a nucleus to which even Jamaica and Trinidad might return 'for shelter'.[65]

It was not to be, however. The first problem was that the UK Treasury failed to consent to the financial formula agreed at Lancaster House, that the islands should receive the same amount of aid for the following five years as they were then receiving.[66] This caused momentum to be lost, which was never recovered, even though by February 1964 the Treasury had announced its intention to fund the Federation on the terms it had previously rejected. Grenada opted out of the federation after being offered, as it hoped, access to the riches of the Trinidad oil wells. The seven remaining partners continued to plan for a new round of negotiations in London, which kept being postponed. Lewis gradually realized, from a position of near-impotence because he was now back at the University full-time trying to hold that together, that the opportunity to catch a flood-tide had been irrevocably lost; how badly hurt he had been is visible in his pamphlet *The Agony of the Eight,* written some time in 1965. This relates in short, abrupt paragraphs, very unlike his normal fluent prose, the ill-fated history of the West Indies Federation from August 1960 to the point at which the story breaks off. It ends with a cry of pain:

> IF EACH LITTLE ISLAND GOES OFF ON ITS OWN, ITS PEOPLE MUST SUFFER…
> Any one of these leaders can break the present deadlock by initiating quiet talks with the others.
> HAVE WE NOT THIS MUCH STATESMANSHIP LEFT IN THESE LITTLE ISLANDS?[67]

However, Lewis had also moved quickly to reduce his vulnerability, and his personal involvement in the political affairs of the West Indies. A month after the Lancaster House talks, in June 1962, Lewis had been offered the Professorship of Economics and International Affairs at Princeton University, and on 20 August 1962 he formally resigned as Vice-Chancellor of the University of the West Indies, suffering from ulcers and high blood pressure. Both of these events occurred before there was any suggestion that the federation of the eight would not go ahead.

To a sympathetic Chancellor he said:

> I have had a terrible three years, unsupported by a weak Federal Government, struggling with other Governments to hold the place together, and trying to persuade the staff to adopt policies which would win outside support. The worst part has been not being able to rely on colleagues inside the college, except for a precious few. I suppose I have

tried to do too much in too short a time; on the other hand we would have sunk with the federation if we had not tried; and if I have erred, it was because my temperament does not suit this sort of thing.[68]

Ironically, the University of the West Indies was now financially secure, as the consequence of the decision to spread undergraduate teaching between multiple campuses; and it still survives. Lewis's conviction that the federal University could not survive without political federation was exposed as being inaccurate.

In August 1962 there were great celebrations in Kingston to mark independence for Jamaica. The British delegation was led by the Secretary of State for Air, Hugh Fraser, and the US delegation by Vice President Lyndon Johnson. Despite the fact that the University College had also been granted its independence as the University of the West Indies, Lewis as its first Vice-Chancellor was missing from the celebrations. In June 1962, he had written to the Governor-General, Lord Hailes, at in Port of Spain, Trinidad:

> It was good of you to write sending your congratulations on the university's independence ... The demise of the Federation is such a shock to me that, in our various territories, we are expected to turn around and dance to celebrate individual independencies. Fortunately, I have long-standing commitments to be out of the West Indies this summer, so I shall not have to turn up at various celebrations to grin and make hollow speeches.[69]

Lewis was bitterly disappointed with the failure of the Federation, and it would appear that in spite of his close political connections he had misread the popular mood in both Trinidad and Jamaica. Whether this disappointment played a major part in his decision to move to Princeton in 1963, however, is doubtful. In his letter to Lord Hailes he described the demise of the Federation as 'a shock'. It appears that it had not been part of his calculations in deciding to move to the USA, since negotiations were already under way for his move to Princeton when the Federation collapsed. Furthermore, a factor that is not generally recognized as prompting Lewis's move to the USA is the turbulent social situation in Jamaica in the early 1960s. Lewis was a family man. He feared for the safety of his family, and believed that he was being targeted by Rastafarians. There is no independent evidence that this was the case, but there had been serious violence in Kingston, prompting Lewis to request from the University 'a night watchman' to be placed by the Steward outside his house, 'since members of the Rastafarian movement have begun to take a special interest in me'.[70]

In *The Agony of the Eight*,[71] Lewis conceded in chapter 2 of the pamphlet, entitled 'The Mission That Failed', that he had been too easily persuaded that the other countries were keen to maintain the Federation. He went on to say, 'The reason for my mistake was ignorance ... As head of the University College I had kept scrupulously out of politics; had played no part in the federal wrangle; and did not know how deep the hatreds were' (Lewis, 1965a, p. 14).

Lewis certainly had misread the situation, but, as the above account makes clear, this was not because he had kept himself scrupulously out of politics, and his remarks may be seen as disingenuous. Norman Manley and Eric Williams were long-standing friends and colleagues. So close was Lewis to Williams, for example, that in December 1961, Hugh Fraser wrote to Lewis for advice on the likely future actions of Eric Williams. Lewis replied, signing off as Principal of the University College, with a remarkable three-page document outlining the likely future responses not only of Williams, but also of Vere Bird of Antigua and Errol Barrow of Barbados. It ends with the advice to Fraser that

> If he [the Secretary of State] considers Trinidad's terms to be unacceptable he should say so as soon as he has heard them; should say so to both Dr Williams, in the hope of getting him to be more reasonable, also to Barrow and to Bird, so that they can have some basis for putting up an alternative.[72]

7.7 Postscript: The legacy of the Caribbean Development Bank, 1971–4[73]

In 1963 Lewis took up his final appointment, at Princeton. In 1964, he published a series of seven articles in the Kingston paper *The Daily Gleaner* on Jamaica's economic problems.[74] Lewis was always keen to take on an educative role, and the articles covering topics such as land utilization, population pressure, unemployment, the growth of towns, and social breakdown, are models of lucidity, aimed at the general reader. It is interesting to note what he had to say about foreign investment, together with his preference for higher domestic savings rates, for 'the point of developing Jamaica is to give Jamaica more income, rather than foreigners. Foreign investment is better than none, since it raises Jamaican incomes too. But Jamaican investment is better, if the money can be saved at home.'

Between end 1970 and early 1974, Lewis returned to the West Indies, taking leave from Princeton on secondment as the first President of the Caribbean Development Bank (CDB). The Bank in effect gave Lewis a second chance to set in motion his ambitions for a regional solution to many of the Caribbean's economic problems. By this time, Lewis had published all the major works in development economics for which he was awarded the Nobel Prize in 1979.

One of Lewis's successors at the Bank was its third president, Neville Nicholls, who had served at the Bank in Lewis's day. In interview in 2005, Neville Nicholls claimed that it was Lewis's personality that established the character of the Bank. Lewis insisted that the president needed to approve all schemes. The Bank was not to come under the influence of politicians, and he was fearless in his criticism of politicians who tried to browbeat CDB officers. In the controversy over whether the CDB was a 'bank' or a 'development agency', Lewis always came down on the side of a bank, an attitude that went down well with lenders. Lewis also had the strength of a meticulous administrator. Unlike many economists, he put efficient administration on a par with economic analysis and policy. Before he arrived at the CDB in 1971 he visited its regional members. He spent time observing procedures in major lending institutions, including the World Bank and the Inter-American Development Bank (IDB), in his own words, 'wandering from department to department discussing administrative procedures and policies'. He recorded the roles of agriculturalists, engineers, loan officers, technicians, economists, financial analysts and lawyers. He noted the reports needed for each project: technical, financial, accounting and cash flow. He reported that cost–benefit analysis was the cornerstone of decision-making. No project was recommended unless it showed a social rate of return of at least 10 per cent per annum.

Accounts of the early years of the Bank indicate features that came to have an important bearing on its subsequent operation. In the 1950s and 1960s, the smaller colonial territories of the Eastern Caribbean did not have access to the major international lending institutions. This was a key factor influencing the establishment of the Bank, as it was empowered to negotiate soft loans on their behalf. This influenced the location of the Bank in Barbados, in the Eastern Caribbean, against the wishes of Jamaica. The early emphasis on lending to the smaller territories was in part because of the fear that, without economic and social development, political unrest could spread from one island to another. In this context, it is not surprising that the political situation in Grenada under the radical leadership of Prime Minster Maurice

Bishop and the People's Revolutionary Government became an issue for the CDB. Under Lewis, the Bank had received strong support from the United States Agency for International Development (USAID) and was regarded as a model development bank. In the 1970s, under the Carter Administration, the Bank received substantial US funding. This changed when, in 1981, the Reagan Administration demanded that the Bank exclude Grenada from the Bank's flagship student loan scheme. Even the most conservative Caribbean leaders were unwilling to accept this attack on the Bank's autonomy, and the US demand was rejected unanimously by the Bank's board.

When Lewis first arrived at the Bank's headquarters in Bridgetown, Barbados (see Figure 7.1) in February 1971 there was much to be done. His Princeton colleague and biographer, Robert Tignor, who was familiar with Lewis's workload at the time has described the challenges that Lewis faced. He needed to appoint new staff and train personnel in project management. He had little confidence in many of the existing staff members, including heads of divisions and other senior officers. These tasks, together with fund-raising and research activities, gave Lewis

Figure 7.1   The Caribbean Development Bank, Barbados
Source: Author photograph.

what he described as a fifteen-hours-a-day job. He made it clear that he expected the highest standards of work from all the staff. For example, letters had to be answered promptly, as punctuality was to be the norm. If staff failed to deliver as expected he 'ticked them off [like] children' (Interview, Neville Nicholls, Barbados, 2005).

At CDB headquarters, Lewis received many delegations from public and private organizations seeking finance for projects. Perhaps the letter that raised a wry smile from Lewis was the one from a representative of the Commonwealth Development Corporation. Two decades earlier, as the young Professor of Political Economy at the University of Manchester, Lewis had suffered the humiliation of 'non-reappointment' to the board of the then Colonial Development Corporation. He believed the snub was because of the stand he had taken on colonial policy in Africa. Now the tables were turned, and the Commonwealth Development Corporation representative was anxious to secure the support of the CDB president. 'There is much to learn', his letter runs, 'from [your] good, sound, commonsense approach to the problems of the Caribbean.' The Commonwealth Development Corporation 'noted with interest' the wishes of the CDB directors to invest in the equity of companies and 'hoped that this may lead to some joint partnerships'. If Lewis saw fit to respond to this letter, there is no record of his reply in the files.

The three statements that Lewis made in his capacity as CDB president provide insights into his views on how Caribbean development should proceed. Some of the policies he advocated have been overtaken by events, but many could appear without modification in current development agendas.

In 1971, the commitment of the president and his board was clear with respect to the agricultural sector: '[F]eeder roads, terracing of land, control of water flows, drainage, [and] irrigation (1971: 1473)' were the infrastructural projects that were accorded first place in lending to governments. More directly, farmers with fewer than 200 acres were to be assisted with capital schemes, though no money was to be loaned for land purchase. The Bank would also entertain applications from larger estates in the private sector, for livestock production and tree crops. Lewis's own commitment to the agricultural sector cannot be doubted by anyone who reads his first statement as president: '[O]ur agriculture needs massive new inputs of both biological science and capital; otherwise our fields will increasingly lie fallow while our people roam idly through our capital cities. Our Bank must do anything it can to support this agricultural revolution' (1971, p. 1474).

Manufacturing and services, however, were not to be neglected, and while Lewis nowhere used these words, it is clear that he favoured a form of balanced growth. There was to be provision for industrial estates, workshops, and vocational and technical training. As far as the tourist industry was concerned, the attitude of the CDB was more ambiguous. Many requests had been received for loans to build hotels and guesthouses, and while the Bank did not rule out loans for large hotels, there was a presumption in favour of small hotels run by West Indians. Similarly, the Bank was less than enthusiastic about the numerous requests it had received from individual Eastern Caribbean Islands for loans for deep-water ports, which threatened to overwhelm the 'soft' (concessional interest-rate) window. Some people may question the wisdom of his decisions with respect to priorities, but Lewis proceeded with his particular notions as to how the limited resources would best be allocated.

Lewis's second address to the Governors' Meeting was in St Lucia in April 1972. That year was significant for the global economy. It was the mid-point in the three years of instability associated with the collapse of the Bretton Woods fixed exchange rate system. Lewis's 1972 Presidential Statement was based on the assumption of a return to fixed exchange rates, and in this respect it appears somewhat dated to the modern reader. Nevertheless, it contains important macro-economic truths. In his Address, Lewis set out to give a lesson in economics. He decided to explain why the Caribbean was unable to provide full employment, a situation he described as 'an agonising human problem' which had a 'dangerous political potential' (Lewis, 1972, p. 1484). First he argued for the correction of overvalued exchange rates but went on to say that, by itself, this would not solve the unemployment problem. Without social discipline, which he linked to the development of incomes policies, devaluation would filter through into higher import prices and increased costs. Lewis had long been an advocate of incomes policies and often referred to the countries of Western Europe that made use of them. In the 1960s he had advocated such a policy for Jamaica. He was also of the view that low savings rates in the Caribbean constrained the accumulation of capital. Arguing in the classical tradition of economics, he always placed a stress on the role that domestic savings mobilization had played in the development of Western Europe, North America and Japan. His second Presidential Statement reinforced this view:

[W]e are a thriftless people. We are all trying to keep up with the Jones' and living to the limit of our borrowing capacity. In this we differ from say the average Japanese, who saves 20 per cent of ... disposable income; but we are not very different from other Third World people. Personal saving is low in the developing world, and will expand only as new standards of values and new institutions stimulate the habit of thrift. (Ibid., p. 1496)

Two months after the Bank's second Governors' Meeting in St. Lucia, Lewis was one of the signatories to a document in support of federation, 'Towards an Eastern Caribbean Federation (AGOWIMIT [A Group of West Indians Meeting in Tobago] 1972)' (Nicholls, 2005). It is difficult to say how much of this document originated with Lewis, but he was the senior academic and the pragmatism that characterized his approach to integration was well represented in the document. The Federation that was proposed included Antigua, Barbados, British Virgin Islands, Dominica, Grenada, Guyana, Montserrat, St Kitts, Nevis, Anguilla, St Lucia, St Vincent, and Trinidad and Tobago. The hallmarks of Lewis's perspective are there in the call for economic integration, the desire to safeguard civil liberties, proposals for federal control of defence, and a clear regard throughout on probity through the auditing of federal public accounts. The emphasis that Lewis placed on efficient and transparent administrative procedures, particularly in banking and the civil service, was also evident in the document.

In his third and final Presidential Statement at the CDB Annual Meeting in Jamaica in 1973, Lewis took on a topic that has engaged historians and developmentalists for generations. This related to the question of 'what it takes for a community to grow an adequate cadre of persons endowed with the qualities for successful business enterprise' (Lewis, 1973, p. 1503). Lewis must often have pondered this question, beginning with his early training in industrial economics under Arnold Plant at the London School of Economics. While 'enterprise culture' currently receives a great deal of attention, it was not a central topic within the discourse of mainstream economists when Lewis was writing in the early 1970s. He relies on the study by David McClelland, *The Achieving Society* (1961) to start his argument. The essence of his statement (which reads more like a lecture than a presidential address) is that 'differences in ... entrepreneurial capacity are a cultural and not a genetic phenomenon' (Lewis, 1973, p. 1504), and what we need to study is the type of cultural environment that fosters business achievement.

Lewis saw the mastery of business enterprise, whether exercised in the public or private sphere, as playing a key role in development. It requires the development of knowledge of business administration, market research, budgetary control and personnel management. It requires foreign enterprises to commit themselves to training and educating their local staff. This was a long-standing preoccupation of Lewis that clearly stretched back into his early years at the LSE and in the Colonial Office, and was to reappear in his book *The Theory of Economic Growth* (Lewis, 1955, pp. 196–200, 258). The availability of credit from institutions such as the CDB is important for enterprise, but the funds are unlikely to produce optimal results unless supported by technical assistance. Above all one needs the appropriate cultural environment to foster business enterprise, and it must be rewarded as an achievement in the same way as sport, music and academic success: 'We shall not be well endowed with business types until our society learns to appreciate the business like personality and absorbs this appreciation into the cultural framework of boyhood, girlhood and adolescence' (Lewis, 1973, p. 1516).

Lewis made limited reference to what we now call gender issues, but it is clear in this statement that the business personality was gender neutral. The cultural changes he envisaged would take time, but the Caribbean could 'catch up within two generations' if they were able to 'match ... deeds to ... words' with respect to placing an 'emphasis on performance' as against a history that has held up 'superior values of colour, class, masculinity and other non-achievement attributes' (Lewis, 1973, p. 1517).

8
Princeton and Retirement, 1963–91

8.1 'The pleasantest country club in America'

Traumatized and exhausted by the experiences described in previous chapters, Lewis was profoundly relieved to receive Princeton's offer of employment. It was to set his life on a different course. No longer would he try to 'make people do what they did not want to do'. He was done with consultancy – or certainly with the kinds of consultancy that involved these kinds of stress. He was done with trying to 'make a difference', in the sense of directly seeking to change the actions of policymakers in the interests of the world's poor. Rather, he was going to do the job he did best, being an economics professor, in an environment as far removed as possible from the world of telegrams and anger with which he had wrestled since his Colonial Office days.

No better place to do this than Princeton University could be imagined. The population of the town of Princeton, even now, is only about 30,000, less than Canterbury or Durham in the UK and, like them, originating in an ecclesiastical environment. The College of New Jersey, which became Princeton University in 1896, was founded in 1746 as a Presbyterian institution, and only in 1902 did a non-cleric, Woodrow Wilson, become president of the university. Something of an upper-class social environment and indeed something of the atmosphere of the great southern estates still pervades the place,[1] even though Princeton is a bare 40 miles south of New York. F. Scott Fitzgerald, who relished the atmosphere while a student there at the end of the First World War, described Princeton as 'the pleasantest country club in America',[2] pervaded by a system of social stratification of almost unparalleled complexity, in which one's caste is determined by the social groups, the dining clubs and the sports teams to which one belongs. However, there is another, more integrative, side to Princeton, which during the college's early colonial years could not have hoped to be viable on the basis of recruitment from thinly populated New Jersey alone. By taking students from the other twelve states it became, as the university's official historian puts it, 'a national institution before there was a nation'.[3] Integrative and elitist at the same time is, of course, what Lewis was too.

As in Britain's ancient universities, it took women time to penetrate this caste system, and they were only admitted to undergraduate programmes in 1969, some years after Lewis arrived. And while black students are now well represented in the university, with the undergraduate population rising from seven in 1962, when Lewis arrived, to about 200 in the 1980s (or about 7 per cent of the undergraduate student body[4]), they are scarcer in the town as a whole, representing barely 3 per cent of the population, or a quarter of the black ratio in the United States as a whole.[5] Since 1868, the colours of Princeton's scarves and football shirts have been black and orange – the orange allegedly derived from William of Orange[6] – and the Princeton Tigers, now carved into almost every coat of arms, gargoyle and waterspout around the campus, provide the university with one of the wittiest and most marketable corporate identities to be found in global academia. Even the writing paper in the library is black and orange.

Rationalist critic of caste systems though he might be,[7] Lewis was highly susceptible to this assault from old money in by far the most ancient university he had attended. As we shall see, he devoted considerable effort to attempting to persuade Princeton University's own caste system to work to his advantage, and in particular to getting his children into good universities.

Academically, Princeton has always been special. It is at the time of writing (2012) fifth in the global league table of universities (behind CalTech, Harvard, Stanford and Oxford)[8] and has been somewhere near that ranking ever since, in the 1930s, a series of charitable donations were used to recruit a number of world-famous scientists to the university – many of them refugees from Nazi Germany, including Albert Einstein.[9] The Department of Economics' contribution to this proud record includes five Nobel Prize winners, including Lewis himself in 1979, the controversial John Nash in 1994,[10] and Daniel Kahneman in 2002 ; all of these, interestingly, spent much of their time working in fields outside economics. When Lewis arrived in 1963, the department's main areas of excellence were in international finance, famous for the presence of Fritz Machlup and the *Princeton Papers in International Development*, which he had founded in the 1930s, and microeconomics, where Lewis's good friend, William Baumol, was, and where Oskar Morgenstern, who with John von Neumann had opened up the hugely influential field of game theory through his *Theory of Games and Economic Behaviour* (1951) (in which Nash had won his Nobel Prize) was still teaching. Development economics was frankly lagging, apart from the parts that overlapped with international finance: it had no competition to offer to Chenery at Harvard, Hirschman and Ranis at Yale, Schultz at Chicago, or even Dudley Seers at the recently-established Institute of Development Studies at Sussex.[11] Lewis was therefore brought in to give the burgeoning development area a lift, as much through recruitment of international postgraduates as through research.

Lewis contributed to the teaching and research of both the department of economics and the Woodrow Wilson School of International and Public Affairs, a school of Princeton University that, since 1930, has provided training in the area of government and international relations. In 1961, the university received an extraordinary donation of US$350 million from Charles Robertson, a Princeton alumnus, to expand and strengthen the Woodrow Wilson School's graduate programmes, and it was this that made possible the expansion of international development to which it was hoped Lewis could contribute. When the Lewises arrived, they moved into a university apartment on Harrison Street, near the wooded lake that divides Princeton's University precinct from the less privileged parts of the town, from where it was a pleasant 10-minute walk to work.

8.2   Picking up the threads, 1964–7

In 1964, at a time when he was easing himself into his Princeton schedule and did not as yet have any teaching obligations, Lewis received an invitation from McMaster University in Canada to give the Whidden Lectures early the following year. As his theme he chose the politics of West Africa. Academically, this was a new departure – very little of his *Theory of Economic Growth* had been about politics. But now there was an obvious incentive to write out of his system the puzzles he had failed to solve during his Ghanaian experience. However, the lectures are not just about Ghana, and as early as the summer of 1962, in the aftermath of Lewis's failed attempt to achieve an economic and political union in the Eastern Caribbean, he had arranged for himself a study tour of Senegal, Ivory Coast and Nigeria, all of them countries with which he was unfamiliar. As in the case of his tour of South-East Asia, he launched himself in a new academic direction by exploring new places.

The three lectures were published as a 90-page novella, with a sombre tone. Lewis's main encounter with West Africa had been the cause of severe personal anguish, as described in Chapter 6, and while Lewis goes to great trouble, as he puts it, to 'control [his] emotions',[12] the scars of his Ghanaian experience cannot help but show through. *Politics in West Africa* is haunted by the ghosts of West Africans, and in particular Ghanaians, who had been incarcerated, or worse, during the period of Africa's false start in the early years of independence. As Lewis emphasized, 'many West Africans have resisted the single-party state, and been killed or jailed or exiled for doing so: let us not forget them' (Lewis 1965b: 36). In many ways, the book is a search for Africa's lost political freedom, and for the linkage between this and political stability.

One particular target of Lewis is the single-party system, which has persisted, either in its pure form or more usually in the form of a politics where one party hugely dominates all the others, through to the present day in many African countries; and indeed, as Lewis reminds us (ibid.: 34) in many others as well, such as Russia and Mexico. In his book, Lewis denied that the single party was an inevitable development from the struggle for independence; rather, he argued, the single party was usually created *after* independence, often by force. The single party does not, in Lewis's view, provide a framework for stable government, though he is careful to pay tribute to decent and honourable exceptions to this rule, such as Julius Nyerere of Tanzania. It fails, according to Lewis, because it cannot effectively manage the tensions created by economic development – and if those tensions are contained, this is often done by brutal means, as in Ghana at the time Lewis was writing.[13] 'The case for democracy,' he argues (ibid.: 44), 'is not that it prevents tension, but that open discussion creates a healthier society than is achieved by suppression'. This constitutional resolution of tensions cannot, however, be created within existing structures, he believes, in the plural societies that are characteristic of Africa; and 'anybody who has seen what a mess party politics can make of a plural society must find himself hankering after a primitive kind of democracy, in which people elect their representatives without the aid of parties, and run their affairs much as other democratic institutions are run' (Lewis 1965b: 38). In pursuit of this rather abstract ideal, Lewis flirts in his final chapter with ideas about a number of standard institutions for making politics fairer, including proportional representation, coalitions and federalism.

'Too much politics is the curse of West Africa' (Lewis 1965b: 36), we are told; this is a familiar Lewis theme, and had indeed had been sketched out as a more general narrative in *The Theory of Economic Growth,* which had described most governments as 'corrupt and inefficient' (Lewis 1965b: 28). Nkrumah's Ghana is often brought in as an illustration of this point, on one occasion to castigate Nkrumah himself, whose famous instruction to 'Seek ye first the political kingdom, and all other things will be added unto you' is dismissed as 'an adolescent attitude to politics' (Lewis 1965b: 78). But most of Lewis's allusions to his recent Ghanaian experience, as he searches for the key to what went wrong, are much more subtle and sublimated. He reminds us that the Ghana Convention People's Party (CPP) (unlike its counterparts in Mali and Guinea) 'does not really try to keep in touch with the rank and file ... their job is to keep the populace in line, rather than to stimulate discussion and transmit opinion upwards' (ibid.: 23), therefore, the views of the people, and in particular poor and underprivileged people, are not transmitted to political leaders as they would be in classical democracy. The CPP, we are told, 'is torn in two, between Marxist and non-Marxist factions, who hate each other, and alternate in Nkrumah's favour' (ibid.: 40); one is reminded of the final tussle over subsidy allocation between Kojo Botsio and K. A. Gbedemah in November 1958, won by the former, which shortly preceded Lewis's departure from Ghana a month later. There is coded criticism of the increasingly interventionist attitude of governments towards foreign capital (ibid.: 61) – and its counterpart, using foreign interference as a scapegoat to excuse all abuse of domestic policy – but aimed mainly at Guinea rather than at Ghana. Nkrumah's abortive attempt to raise cocoa taxes in 1954 – which hit the Ashanti region hardest, and was abandoned after violent protests – is used as an argument that 'a country which has very wide geographical differences can live together at peace only in a federal framework' (ibid.: 53), a conclusion that reads movingly in the light of Lewis's recent travails with a federal framework in his native West Indies.

All these remarks are valid illustrations of, and valid attempts to learn from, the anti-democratic tendencies he had observed in Ghana; they are also part of the process by which Lewis tries to understand his failure to intervene successfully in the policy-making process in that country seven years previously. Lewis, however, is searching for much more than an autopsy of what went wrong in that one country. He is also searching, as a person of African descent, for an understanding of whether there is anything in African political systems that makes them inherently anti-democratic. As the quality of African democracy deteriorated further through the 1970s, specifically in Ghana as well as many other places, the power of Lewis's critique grew. Since the 1990s, there has been a resurgence of African democracy, much of it, however, as in Uganda and South Africa, contained within the dominant-party model that Lewis despised. However, he would draw ironic comfort from the fact that the country which served as the original inspiration for his thesis, Ghana, is now celebrated around the world as an exemplar of mature and good-natured two-party democracy, and in 2011 reported an economic growth rate of 11 per cent, the highest in the world.

It must have been a relief for Lewis, after the turbulence of the previous six years, to get back into a writing groove. Indeed, having published little since *The Theory of Economic Growth* in 1955, he was to produce three more books in the next three years. The first of these, *Development Planning*, followed immediately, in 1966.

Its antecedents go all the way back to the war years, during which both Lewis and Durbin had produced Fabian tracts on how democratic-socialist planning should be done[14] (called *The Principles of Economic Planning* and *Problems of Economic Planning*, respectively). However, since that time, there had been only short periods when he was not critiquing or producing a plan of some kind. Lewis's key contribution to the Colonial Economic Advisory Committee in 1944, also with Durbin, was based on the proposition that colonial development required rational planning of public expenditure and other resources. Between 1947 and 1951, on the Colonial Economic Development Council, he had been reviewing the development plans produced by the British colonies, and finding nearly all of them unsatisfactory, as discussed in Chapter 3 above. In 1952, he had produced a development plan for British Guiana, and in 24 hours, if his account is to be believed, on 16/17 January 1962 he had thrown together an outline ten-year development plan for the entire Eastern Caribbean. Meanwhile, in 1958, he had tried to persuade Nkrumah to make the Ghanaian five-year plan into a rational document, and failed. As in the case of *Politics in West Africa*, just discussed, he had mused on what had gone wrong, in a document called *On Making a Development Plan*, the text of a speech made in 1959,[15] just after his departure from Ghana. Ghana, he reminded his audience, 'had spent heaps on capital investment, but [its] policies were bad'.

Therefore,

> Policy is as important as capital investment ... Ghana would have done better if it had spent less and had better policies. The more important part of development planning consists of getting economic institutions and economic policies right for private sectors.[16]

Given time to reflect in Princeton, it was natural for him to bring together his thoughts about planning in one coherent story: as he now did. One factor favouring this was that there was now a demand for the product, in the shape of Lewis's postgraduate students, all of whom needed references on planning, and to whom he wanted to give something practical, simple and usable, rather than the forbidding mathematical tracts by which the literature was already dominated.

Lewis's teaching programme emerged gradually by experimentation: at one stage, he taught the introductory course, 102 Economics, to an audience of several hundred students, but he soon escaped, with relief, from this fate.[17] He developed three courses at the Woodrow Wilson School: 531 Economic Growth in Developing Areas; 566 Modern Economic History; and 570 Economic Development. The first two of these ran from the autumn of 1965, with an interruption during Lewis's three-year secondment to the Caribbean Development Bank, but Economic Development did not start until 1974. In Economic Growth in Developing Areas, and Economic Development, which were large classes, assessment was by examination, but in Modern Economic History, classes were quite small, around 30, and this enabled Lewis to require every student taking the course for credit to not only write an extended essay, but also to present a paper on that essay to the entire group[18]. Often, a teaching assistant or assistant professor would comment on the paper alongside, or even in place of, Lewis. This is not easily possible in universities less well-resourced than Princeton, and for those students who wanted to go on to do research, or simply to gain practice in making presentations before an audience, it was ideal preparation. It also, as we shall see, provided Lewis with valuable raw material for his research. The style of Lewis's lecture handouts is quite combative, and on issues where he had clashed with the literature, such as the existence of surplus labour, his students must have enjoyed the delicacy of his put-downs. Through the 1960s and 1970s, a succession of right-wing economists, including Bent Hansen,[19] Dale Jorgensen[20] and Lewis's former fellow-committee member in the inaugural UN report, *Measures for the Economic Development of Underdeveloped Countries* (1951), Theodore Schultz,[21] attempted to prove that surplus labour in developing countries, in the sense of low-productivity people who were paid more than their marginal product, or the value of their contribution to the economy, did not and could not exist. But Lewis, with support from several allies, including A. K. Sen, gave as good as he got, and delighted in taking the debate into the lecture room. A student handout demolishing a paper on this theme by Morton Paglin, one of many to attempt to show that surplus labour in India did not exist, reworked Paglin's own data and concluded with the words, 'Paglin's data therefore contained, hidden from him, the exact opposite of what he thought he had proved.'[22]

There was no course purely about development policy or planning, but the subject was on the syllabus of Lewis's course Economic Growth in Developing Areas, and his later course Economic Development. The lecture notes for parts 6 and 7, the planning part, of Economic Growth in Developing Areas, swell to an enormous size in 1965 as Lewis's next book *Development Planning* (1966) is being piloted, and then shrink back to normal size later.[23] *Development Planning* was able to give these courses a real-world feel: Princeton was not short of well-connected faculty members, but for students to be able to rub shoulders with someone who had made actual plans and negotiated with actual prime ministers in actual developing countries gave the programme as a whole, and the students in particular, an enormous competitive boost. Lewis meanwhile was able to refine the course by bouncing ideas off his students. He was delighted to discover that the idea of a three o'clock tea ceremony, which he and Devons had already pioneered at Manchester, was already embedded in the institutional norms of Princeton, and hastened, in conjunction with Gersovitz, to establish such a ritual for the Research Program in Development Studies in the Woodrow Wilson School. Was it, I asked Henry Bienen, who participated in these events, a similar event to the Fine Hall teas, made famous in Sylvia Nasar's *A Beautiful Mind,* in which attendance was mandatory and the best mathematics ideas of the time were born? No, he replied, it was less formal, but the model was similar.[24]

Development Planning picks up on and develops the theme of Lewis's American Society for Public Administration lecture: in a democratic environment, the essence of planning consists of selecting and incentivizing good policies. The book is in three parts, of which the first states what the key policy priorities are, the second assembles them into an essay on national economic strategy, and the third presents the strategy as an arithmetical exercise that enables a real plan to be constructed.

In the first part, we are given another characteristic Lewis 'bare essentials' shopping list. Eight of the elements of development policy that Lewis sees as especially important are:

1. Promoting an increase in saving, both private and public.
2. Provision of adequate infrastructure (water, power, transport and communications), whether by public or private agencies.

3. Investigation of development potential; surveys of natural resources; scientific research; market research.
4. Helping to create more and better markets, including commodity markets, security exchanges, banking, insurance and credit facilities.
5. Seeking out and assisting potential entrepreneurs, both domestic and foreign.
6. Promoting better utilization of resources, both by offering inducements and by operating controls against misuse.
7. Improving the legal framework of economic activity, especially laws related to land tenure, corporations and commercial transactions.
8. Provision of specialized training facilities, as well as adequate general education, thereby ensuring necessary skills.

The quality of a Development Plan should be tested, mainly by examining what is proposed under each of these heads.[25] Readers will have no difficulty in discerning all of Lewis's core policy action principles from Chapter 3 (selective industrialization, supporting smallholder agriculture, remedying the deficiencies of the market system in LDCs, and non-formal education) as the last four of these eight priorities.

The second part of his book relates these policy priorities to the key balances that have to be satisfied (in particular, in terms of paying for imports, financing public expenditure, and meeting requirements for skilled labour) to sustain the growth of the economy. The analysis makes an attempt to be value-free, and there is no reference to socialism of the kind that appears in *The Principles of Economic Planning* (1949c), or any other 'ism'. For Lewis, fascinated by political argument as he was, this must have been a big sacrifice. However, severe inequality of income is presented, not as a moral evil which must be combated, but rather in pragmatic terms as something which, if not counteracted, will cause political instability.[26] The discussion of 'growth without employment creation' in Jamaica[27] anticipates Chenery's unveiling of this problem as a global issue in the early 1970s,[28] and the subsequent McNamara 'redistribution with growth' initiative: the first global poverty reduction programme. Indeed, as Lewis notes, a good number of his eight core policy issues listed above can be recast as, to use modern terminology, pro-poor policies. One such is the technology dimension of resource utilization (issue 6 in the list above). As Lewis notes:

The big waste of capital in underdeveloped countries has tended to be not in the mechanical processes for transforming raw material into manufactured products, since these new processes have usually also improved the product and reduced the wastage of raw materials. The waste has come mainly in substituting capital for labour in moving things about; in the handling of materials inside the factory; in packaging; in moving earth; and in building and construction. The bulldozer, the conveyor belt and the crane usually achieve nothing that labour could not do equally well. They spend scarce foreign exchange solely in order to produce unemployment.[29]

This is the essence of the argument for intermediate technology – there already in the mid-1960s. It is in passages such as this that *Development Planning* rises above the level of the technical manual, which is all that it claims to be. However hard Lewis tries to keep the issue dry and technical, though, political economy, entertainingly illustrated, cannot avoid forcing itself in. Development planning as a discipline has now fallen on hard times, and the five-year plan, revered by many students of development through most of Lewis's professional life, is now the subject of mockery and pub jokes. But the need for rational planning of scarce resources, now rebadged as budgeting or 'policy frameworks', has never gone away.

Whereas, at Manchester, Lewis's most significant friendships and influences had been outside of the Economics Department, it was otherwise in Princeton. The most important of his friends were William Baumol and his wife Hilda, whom he had first got to know in 1947 when Baumol was a junior lecturer at the LSE, and who claim to have prepared for the Lewises the first home-cooked meal they were ever given in London.[30] Baumol and his wife had children of similar age to Lewis's two girls, and when Lewis's work took him abroad it was the Baumols who looked after their children and took them to Sunday school – and they did this so well that, when the Lewises returned, their children complained at being forced to go to Sunday school with them rather than the Baumols.[31] Baumol was a micro-economist of astonishingly wide sympathies, one of which, as in the case of Lewis, was the arts and the economics of the arts.[32] Baumol happily overviewed Lewis' *Development Planning* – casting an especially beady eye on the technical bits related to optimization and linear programming, on which he was expert – and was later also to act as a sounding-board for *Growth and Fluctuations* (1978a). In return, when Baumol submitted research proposals to the National Science Foundation on the economics of the arts, Lewis was nominated as referee.

Mark Gersovitz was one of the young assistant professors the Princeton faculty was able to attract to bolster the university's development economics standing through the generosity of the Robertson donation. Like Lewis, he was aware that markets for crucial factors of production, such as labour and capital, especially in developing countries, do not work in an orthodox way to make everyone better off; he had been fascinated by Lewis's illustration of this in 'Economic Development with Unlimited Supplies of Labour' (1954). But macro problems also attracted him, and he became a pioneer in the development of bargaining models between creditors and debtors. His first working papers for the Research Program on Development Studies illustrate this: they were on two-gap models and on urban bias. Like Baumol, he was Jewish; as at Manchester, Lewis did not find it easy to become on intimate terms with WASPs. Gersovitz arrived late in Lewis's Princeton career, in 1976, but at a crucial time, when, as we shall see, Lewis's spirits and productivity were low. Thirty-five years younger than Lewis, Gersovitz was set the task of teaching classes to complement Lewis's lectures on Economic Development. The combination worked – the older man gave the younger one, in Gersovitz's words, 'understanding of what it means to be a scholar and to understand the world as a social scientist'[33] and the younger man gave the older one, and the seminar group, energy. The two men became devoted friends, accompanying each other to the Philadelphia museums and the Metropolitan Opera as well as 'having a good time when we taught together'.[34] A few years later, when Lewis won the Nobel Prize, Gersovitz was one of the main people whom he asked to comments on drafts of his prize lecture.

Gustav Ranis moved to Yale in 1961 (and has remained there ever since), and in that year, with John Fei, he converted 'Unlimited Supplies of Labour' (Lewis 1954) into a mathematical model which was published in the *American Economic Review* in 1961. Though nervous of being formalized in this way, Lewis forgave Ranis, and was happy to spend his sabbatical in Yale a few years later. Both men were keen economic historians – a somewhat endangered species in Princeton, and Ranis had a huge knowledge of the economic history of Japan, Taiwan and the Far East, on which Lewis drew gratefully. In 1978, Ranis was one of those who successfully nominated Lewis for the Nobel Prize.[35]

It is also important to mention two non-economists who became friends of Lewis and contributed to the Research Program. Robert Tignor, a historian of Africa and the Middle East, arrived from Yale in the early 1960s, and immediately became valuable to Lewis through his knowledge of West Africa, which Lewis was able to draw on as he contemplated his leap into a new discipline in *Politics in West Africa* (1965b); he was to become Lewis's first biographer. Henry Bienen was a political scientist whose main work was also on Africa, in particular on Tanzania. Lewis hired him into the Princeton faculty in 1966, after an interview that began badly because Lewis was suspicious of political scientists.[36] Having survived this experience and learnt to appreciate Lewis's 'devilish sense of humour', he and Lewis became good friends and, between them, helped to convert the development research effort into a Research Program in Development Studies. Much of Bienen's work anticipates research areas that have become important interdisciplinary themes of the twenty-first century, including conflict. An excellent administrator, he moved on from Princeton to become president of Northwestern University.

These people, in particular, gave Lewis a much more secure social environment than he had enjoyed in Manchester. Can it really be that he escaped the traditional academic infighting completely? Not entirely, as we shall see. But things were certainly better. There was one important structural reason for this: Lewis at Princeton had no administrative responsibilities and no need to involve himself in power games. This took a great deal of pressure off him.

As mentioned above, Lewis was determined not to let his life be invaded by the demands of consultancy, which he feared would undermine his equanimity and his recently rediscovered research productivity. He found time, however, to advise the University of the West Indies on things he enjoyed, such as music and the arts – awarding a prize of £20 to Gerald St. C. Rose in 1967 for his essay on Mozart's piano concertos, and a prize of £10 to Cyril Hamblin for his essay on the novels of C. P. Snow,[37] and doing his best, as we recall from Chapter 7, to make sure that West Indian culture was suitably enlightened by the Western mainstream.[38] He was still keenly interested in the problems of people suffering from discrimination and, as we shall see, expressed views on how to help them, as discussed below. Now, however, he never became involved in direct action on their behalf, as he had done both in Manchester and during the period of his developing-country advisory work discussed in previous chapters.

His daughters were now growing up, and reaching the point where Lewis, himself a teacher and the son of a teacher, felt he needed to do some advocacy work on their behalf. In September 1966, on behalf of his 15-year-old daughter Elizabeth, he enlisted the help of one of his colleagues in Princeton's education department to try to persuade Princeton High School's classification of her as 'in the 59th percentile' (that is, below the average grade). He wrote a three-page letter to Professor Robert Lively, stressing that 'if she is not within the top

40 per cent of her class most colleges will not consider her' and insisting that the school's classification of Elizabeth as being no. 149 out of 367 is 'based on an elementary statistical error', which he then goes on to expose at length:

> Elizabeth does not attend any class where she is measured against 367 children. The average class has, presumably, about 30 children, and she is marked only in relation to that particular class. The only scientific foundation for adding the marks of different classes would be the assumption that the distribution of the children's ability was the same in each class. But we know that there is not a random distribution: the average intellectual capacity of the children is much higher in some classes than in others. To add together non-random distributions is a violation of statistical theory and common sense for which any sophomore would be failed.
>
> I am amazed that an educational institution should commit such a vulgar scientific error, which is about as scandalous as a bishop praying to the devil. But it is also no laughing matter, since it libels a large number of intelligent children whose careers are thereby damaged forever.[39]

The tone of the letter becomes so savage (for example, the suggestion that Elizabeth is not in the top 40 per cent of her class is, in this same letter, described as a 'lie') that, while the word 'discrimination' is never mentioned, one suspects that is what Lewis suspects. The Professor of Education's reply is not recorded: but at least the story has a happy ending. Elizabeth did get into college, indeed into Columbia University, and afterwards took an MSc in information technology.

Later, Lewis had to deploy his artillery in support of his elder daughter, Barbara. After she had failed to get into the LSE, her first choice, the universities of Exeter, Warwick, Cambridge (Newnham College) and Oxford (Somerville and Lady Margaret Hall) were all bombarded with letters explaining that her academic performance did not do her justice, and begging for an interview to be granted.[40] Eventually this strategy worked, and Barbara got into Lady Margaret Hall, Oxford.

8.3   Global economic history, 1967–78

By 1966, Lewis had tidied up his desk. In completing his African politics book and his development planning book, he had tied up some of the loose ends, and resolved some of the anxieties, that had been left unsorted following his many collisions between the worlds of scholarship and action in the 1950s and early 1960s. He was ready for something new; but the something new he chose was a little unexpected. Rather than build on his research on growth, or on labour markets, or even on recent development policy, he dived back into history; and this time, not the economic history of the inter-war period he had so innovatively explored in *Economic Survey 1919–1939* (Lewis 1949a) but the preceding period from 1870 to 1913. This was the time when globalization increased in speed because of dramatic reductions in shipping costs, and this, in Lewis's view, was also the time when the divide between the worlds of North and South, and rich and poor, opened up. But why did he shy away from areas where he could continue to make a direct difference to policy? His own account gives little away: he simply notes that the question of why some developing countries gained a massive benefit from the pre-First World War boom, and others little or none, has been little researched, and had always fascinated him. As we recall, though, he had wanted to write the economic history of Jamaica even when he was at the LSE (see Chapter 3 above), a job that was eventually taken over by Gisela Eisner. As Ranis says, 'he was always fascinated by initial conditions'.[41] We can also speculate that Lewis, having been made by his recent experiences somewhat risk-averse, now liked the idea of inhabiting the world of archival research rather than policy: a world in which those who disagreed with him would not be shouting at him, ringing him up late at night and publishing abusive articles about him in the newspapers.

There was plenty of material close to hand that he could pick up on, even on his own desk. In 1952, as described in Chapter 4, he had published an extraordinary piece in *The Manchester School* computing the relationship between global production and trade, which, unlike any other piece published by Lewis, had used the methods of econometrics, or statistical estimation of economic relationships, to explain the process of growth in world trade and how different country groups had responded to it.[42] At the time, aggregative data, let alone econometric analysis, of global trade patterns was almost unknown, and the paper ranks among Lewis's great innovations, as does his later paper (with P. J. O'Leary) of 1955,[43] which examines global trade cycles and the correlation between the business cycles of different countries. While this analysis was global, the part of it relating to developing countries was limited by the fact that, for those countries, only trade data, and not production (let alone national income or well-being) data, existed for developing countries. To answer Lewis's question of how the process of continuous economic growth, which 'began in England and (then) spread during the first half of the nineteenth century to the United States, France, Belgium and Germany, in that order, and thereafter set out to conquer the whole world'[44] had impacted on different countries of the developing world, it would be necessary to generate such data on developing countries' economic structures and policies. This was the nettle he now determined to grasp.

The subject was beginning to be controversial. At the end of the 1960s and through the 1970s, the literature was full of theories of Marxist inspiration, suggesting that the growth of rich countries actually impoverished the poor.[45] Whereas Lewis was clearly unsympathetic to this proposition, it was one that everyone in the 1970s was forced to confront face-to-face. The tide of research results was running in the direction of studies that seemed to show that the rich countries made the poor worse off, and that this was the consequence of colonialism and the perpetuation of colonial relationships after independence. In Princeton and every other university with a development studies programme, students were asking: Is this true? And what are you (the industrialized countries) going to do about it?[46] Some of the more reflective were also asking: What is the evidence for this proposition? How does the impact of global growth on developing countries vary between different developing countries – between South Korea, Brazil, Botswana and the Democratic Republic of the Congo, say? Lewis' contribution was to seek to answer the last of these questions, but within a strictly defined compass of enquiry. As he put it ten years later, in *Growth and Fluctuations*:

> We are not writing general economic history: our focus is on rates of growth and their interactions. Even this is further restricted, since what we are seeking is the causes of growth rather than its consequences. We are taking from history only that part which seems necessary to explain core–periphery economic relations from 1870 to 1913.[47]

As early as 1967, Lewis had been determined to explore this approach, and he did so with the help of his graduate students. He had always lectured only on the first three or four weeks of his graduate courses, devolving the remaining weeks to his students and teaching assistants to lead. In the spring semester of 1967–8 he took this idea further. He invited his graduate students on course Public Affairs 531 *Economic Growth in Developing Areas* – funnily enough, not his economic history course *Modern Economic History 1870–1914* – to write extended essays for assessment which addressed the very question he wanted to research: why did some developing countries latch on to global growth and get carried on to fortune and others did not? The prospectus for this course survives. Lewis tells his students:

> Some members of the seminar have expressed interest in the pos- sibility of our collaborating in producing a book. This has three advantages
>
> a. In giving a central focus to our work, it enables each of us to learn from what the others are doing.
> b. It adds permanently to knowledge.
> c. Since each chapter is published under the author's name, collabo- rators have a piece of writing to their permanent credit.
>
> I have therefore thought of a topic. Naturally it is a topic very close to my own current research and writing. But this is merely a suggestion which seminar members may accept or reject as they please.
>
> Members should not be put off by the dates. The problems of development are essentially the same in 1967 as they were in 1880. It is also quite erroneous to think that this part of the world was stag- nating in this period: on the contrary, for most this is when growth began ...
>
> Just as *R. norvegicus* drove out *R. rattus,* so also the economists have driven the economic historians out of this period. We are providing it with a statistical framework (annual figures of world production, trade, prices, investment, etc.) and painting its development in terms of economic theory rather than in the old historical terms.[48]

As the seminar essays evolved, they threw up some extraordinary stories of development carried out by indigenous people with no help from Europe or America. Lewis's imagination is not normally thought of as poetic, but he had a strong sense of the miraculous, as conveyed in these anecdotes of low-tech export booms uncovered by his students on Economics 531:

> In Burma the flat, wet lands of the Irrawaddy delta were largely unoc- cupied as late as 1870, when the rising demand for rice began to make itself felt. The British Crown claimed ownership of the empty lands, but was willing to sell at nominal prices to small settlers. So Burmese moved down from Upper Burma, squatted and cultivated, and by 1913

were exporting 2.5 million tons of rice from what in 1870 had [been] little more than swamp. The Gold Coast story is equally remarkable. The land suitable for cocoa was covered by apparently useless forest. So the Akwapim farmers ... moved down from the hills, bought it, cut [down] the trees and planted cocoa. The government was asked neither for roads nor for titles, and was indeed hardly aware that the foundations of what by 1913 was already the world's largest cocoa industry were being laid under its nose.[49]

Lewis was so pleased with these case-study revelations that he repeated them, word for word, in *Growth and Fluctuations* ten years later.[50] Twelve of these essays, covering three countries in Latin America, four countries in Asia and five in Africa, he later selected to be published in 1970 under the title, *Tropical Development 1880–1913* (Lewis 1970a). These already throw light on some of the comparative questions that need to be answered in order to throw light on the central question: Why does an entrepreneurial class, capable of implementing industrialization, emerge in Colombia, Brazil, India and Sri Lanka, and only there? Why is state funding of education adequate only in Sri Lanka, and inadequate elsewhere? How did Burma and Ghana manage to achieve a primary commodity export boom in the last quarter of the nineteenth century on the basis of indigenous production without at any point calling on the colonial state to provide them with institutional support, such as roads and land titles? Perhaps most emotively, how did differences in colonial policy – for example, between 'colonies of settlement' where Europeans were allowed to occupy the land and 'peasant export colonies' where they were not, impact on the outcome, and had these inherited differences been reduced or magnified by the elites who had succeeded them? Lewis's Economics 531 class gathered relevant case-study material bearing on all these questions, and associated datasets for each of the twelve countries, to the point that external research funding was not required for the more challenging, developing-country end of the project. Seldom has voluntary labour been mobilized so effectively for the production of development research. It is wonderful to observe Lewis's enthusiasm as he perceives, and then expounds, the mutual benefits he and the class members will derive from the book. Research in Manchester, where Lewis's teaching also had been mainly at postgraduate level, had not been like this: there he had treated his students in the traditional way, as a constraint subject to which his research needed to be optimized. Here, he suddenly realized, they could fulfil a vital missing link in his research.

This path-breaking endeavour – of which Lewis later wrote, 'It nearly killed us, but the students thought it a wonderful experience'[51] – was the first of a number of dry runs for what was to become Lewis's last great research enterprise, culminating ten years later in *Growth and Fluctuations*. Some of the dry runs, such as this one, are empirical in orientation, designed to gather materials, and others are more theoretical, such as Lewis's Wicksell Lectures of 1969, which examine how the volume of trade and the terms of trade have reacted to industrial growth, and his Janeway Lectures of 1977: *The Evolution of the International Economic Order*. Both of them return to the theme of the second part of 'Economic Development with Unlimited Supplies of Labour' (1954): in an open economy, what determines the growth rate and the distribution of income in developing countries, and what are the implications for optimal trade policy? In the Wicksell lectures, the story about the determinants of the terms of trade between steel and coffee from the second part of 'Unlimited Supplies of Labour' is revisited, and we are reminded of the disconnect between the fast growth of tropical trade in the last quarter of the nineteenth century and the slow growth of tropical living standards.[52] One reason for this, highlighted in both the Wicksell and the Janeway lectures, is the decline in the income terms of trade of primary producers. Against this problem, Lewis sketches out various defences. One of them is his most obsessive policy theme: poor tropical countries, especially those that have not gone through a green revolution, need to increase their productivity in the production of food crops;[53] but there is no discussion in this context of the green revolution by which this might be achieved, or even its agricultural extension component, 'mass education', as was done so vividly in the 1950s. Another option, of course, is to escape from the terms-of-trade problem by moving into export-based industrialization on the South Korean or Taiwanese model. However, while the possibility of industrialization in tropical countries is explored in Lewis's second Wicksell lecture, the idea of using protection to achieve that industrialization, emphasized in 'Unlimited Supplies of Labour', is no longer discussed, and regional economic co-operation is the only policy issue considered – in an abstract mode that contains not even an echo of Lewis's adventures in the Caribbean only seven years previously. The excitements and frustrations of practical development policy no longer interest Lewis as they once did.

The late 1960s were the time when Lewis came closest to recapturing the state of intellectual euphoria he had achieved in the early and middle 1950s. He did not, as he once did, try to intermesh large amounts of consultancy and quasi-social work with his writing; but he did broaden out in a number of ways from his main global history theme. One of the most interesting of these ventures was his Aggrey–Fraser–Guggisberg lectures on education, growth and planning, given at the University of Ghana at Legon in 1968, at a time when it seemed as though Ghana might return to the pattern of humane and democratic development that had tempted Lewis to go there ten years before. The second lecture was on the economics of education, and is noteworthy not only for Lewis's attempt to come to terms with post-Nkrumah Ghana, but also for his return to the theme of mass education, the theme that had first provided him with a political platform via Creech Jones in the 1940s. By then, though, Lewis's early passion for mass education with a focus on agriculture has become diluted:

> Primary education is the difficult level. Agricultural productivity would grow much faster if all farmers were literate. But sending farmers' sons to school doesn't necessarily produce literate farmers. At present it tends rather to produce a drift into unemployment in the towns. Rising unemployment is a major problem throughout Africa.[54]

So Lewis began to focus on secondary education:

> The chief need now in Africa is a lot more secondary schools. The number of jobs requiring a university graduate in science, engineering and the other professions is very small. Most other jobs can be done nearly as well by a secondary school graduate as by a Bachelor of Arts, at a fraction of the cost. Also the secondary school is the gateway to other jobs for which there is special training – secretaries, nurses, elementary school teachers, agricultural assistants, medical technicians and so on.[55]

But the development of the argument is perfunctory. Already, as in some of his lectures in Princeton, Lewis is firing only on two cylinders.

Some while later, in 1975, Edward Shils, Professor of Sociology at Chicago, invited him to revisit the education chapter of *The Theory of Economic Growth* (1955). However, by then, Lewis's passion for education had been overlaid by anxieties about the way the subject was moving; so he temporized: 'I have no hope of mastering the literature, which is now enormous,' he protested. Four years later, Shils still did not have his chapter, but he persisted. By now, Lewis's excuse was that

'Education has become an econometrician's plaything, which is rather outside my interests.'[56]

More radically, just before going to the Caribbean Development Bank, in December 1970, Lewis ventured back into his Fabian past, and delivered a lecture at the LSE entitled *Socialism and Economic Growth* (1971a). He was aware that thinking about socialist philosophy, which had been so important to his work of the 1940s and 1950s, had left scarcely a dent on his work of the 1960s; and natural as it is to use the language of socialism more in Britain than in America, Lewis clearly felt moved by more than just nostalgia when he returned to the LSE.

The job he tried to do was to reconcile socialism with two of the key determinants of growth to which socialists have traditionally been hostile: namely inequality of wage income and private ownership of property. At the beginning of the 1970s, just as inflation had revealed itself as a deeply-embedded problem and just as alarm calls were beginning to go out calling for wages to be restrained one way or another, Lewis prophetically predicted 'it is merely a matter of time before the unions are deprived of their collective bargaining functions in Western Europe and North America'.[57] Without wasting any time on solutions such as incomes policy being widely advocated by right-wing socialists at the time, including the Fabian Society, he continued grimly:

> The decade of the 1970s seems likely to be the decade of the backlash – against blacks, against students and against militant unionism – and the social democratic governments, backed by popular resentment against the militants, will be as active in clipping their wings as will governments of more conservative bent.[58]

So what can be done? Lewis invoked two of his heroes, John Stuart Mill and the much-lamented Hugh Gaitskell, with whom he had worked as a Fabian policy adviser in the 1950s (see Chapter 5), and advocated a mixture of public ownership with private management, and a tax policy aimed at the maximization of savings – what would be called now an 'asset-based tax and welfare policy'[59] as the right principles for a socialist welfare policy. Most of the discussion was about the UK, but, in a barely-concealed blast at Nkrumah, he shifted the discussion in his coda to the developing countries where 'most Afro-Asian political parties in power style themselves socialist, but they are necessarily even further from socialism than the parties in Europe'. They too are told to focus on incentivizing public saving.

In addition to his academic work on development, Lewis involved himself, as he had in Manchester, in civil rights work. During the late 1960s a tide of protest, initially in support of civil rights and later against the war in Vietnam, gradually spread across US campuses to encompass, in the words of a famous banner taken on a march to Washington in May 1968, 'EVEN PRINCETON'.[60] There were riots on the Princeton campus in 1968 and again in 1970, after President Nixon sent US troops into Cambodia. On 4 May 1970 a mass meeting endorsed a 'strike against the war', and the building of the Institute for Defence Analysis was surrounded by angry student protesters, who threw bottles at police sent in to suppress the riot. The university's president declared a state of emergency, and the protesters backed off only after several hours of tense negotiations. In this atmosphere, even Lewis was persuaded to emerge a little distance from his ivory tower.

However, much as he welcomed the gradual integration of female and black students on to the Princeton campus at this time, he resisted the introduction of specialist 'black studies' academic programmes, but he was persuaded to write an article on black power for Princeton's alumni magazine in the summer of 1969. In this article, Lewis identified the root of black separatism as being in the urban neighbourhood in the evenings, and the workplace, any workplace, as a factor that counteracts this separatism in the daytime. Returning to his preoccupation with mass education, he stressed that the battlefront is not really universities at all but 'conquering the middle ... getting into skilled posts, foremen's posts, supervisory and white collar jobs through better use of apprenticeships, the high schools and technical colleges'.[61] Every black student, he continued, should learn some Afro-American history, but in the high school or even earlier – 'maybe even around the age of ten; and let the clever whites go to college to read black novels, to learn Swahili and to record the exploits of Negroes of the past; they are the ones to whom this will come as an eye-opener. This, by the way, is very much what happens in African universities'[62] – notably the ones where Lewis had advised, such as Legon and Ibadan. The community is protectionist; the wider world is free-market; and in this context, it is very clear which one was preferable as a means of black advancement. On this issue, Lewis very much went back to his LSE roots.

Given this perspective, Lewis was never going to take an interest in university-level black studies as a way of advancing the black American community. But the Ford Foundation tried. McGeorge Bundy, its president, attempted to persuade him, the first black professor to have been appointed at a UK university and someone who had worked actively against community-level discrimination, to become involved in the design of a pilot programme of this type at Princeton, which was being pioneered in any case by the Foundation. His apologetic reply was that 'experience [that is of being discriminated against] may be a handicap, just as no sensible doctor doctors himself, and no sensible lawyer handles his own case'.[63] He declined to become actively involved in designing such courses, but offered some general advisory principles: it was important to have both white and black students in classes, because white students 'are not dominated by the black militants, who discourage awkward questions and frank answers'; the Foundation's decision to focus on undergraduate rather than postgraduate teaching was to be regretted, because a black university strong enough to attract good white students would be a major fillip to black education and black pride; and black studies should not be a major degree subject but simply, as Lewis put it, a 'general distribution' subject available to students of all degrees.[64]

The following year, he accepted an invitation from Allen Wallis, president of the University of Rochester, and a personal friend of his, to visit the black students on his campus and to advise on how to promote their academic welfare. Lewis spent an afternoon talking to them over lunch, and afterwards in their dormitories. The discussion became sidetracked into a debate about academic fees, but in addition Lewis sensed that Rochester had been backward in not appointing enough black administrative staff to be able to deal with their grievances one-to-one. He worried at the impression the black Rochester students had gained, that the white students were hostile to them,feared that 'the place might divide into separate racial camps as the number of black students declines',[65] and advocated a deliberate attempt to bring blacks into the existing extracurricular activities such as debating, music and drama. But at no point do we find Lewis while in the USA attempting the kind of strenuous interventions on behalf of the black community's welfare that he had in Moss Side. To our knowledge he did have one earnest interchange with a black student, Vernon Dixon, who had asked for his comments on an essay on the theme of cultural pluralism and to whom Lewis replied with a six-page letter, denying Dixon's assertion that American blacks shared a common culture and insisted that all they shared was 'negritude', a reaction of solidarity in the face of persecution;[66] but this is a purely academic intervention and not an action-oriented one. Indeed, most of Lewis's time after 1963 was spent either in the pleasant rural atmosphere of Princeton, or, after the early 1970s, in the equally pleasant atmosphere of the Caribbean, and nowhere near inner cities. He seldom went to New York City (less than an hour away by train), relatively seldom to Washington, and he returned rapidly if he ever had to go to either place.

It is common to compare women's struggles for equal rights with those of black people; and, as we have seen, Lewis took particular trouble, especially in his *Report on the Industrialisation of the Gold Coast* (Gold Coast Government 1953a) and in 'Unlimited Supplies of Labour' (Lewis 1954), to highlight women's roles in development, well before the publication of Ester Boserup's *Woman's Role in Economic Development* (1965).

Indeed Lewis's 'Autobiographical Account', paying tribute to his mother who had brought up five children on her own, emphasizes that 'As a youngster in school I would hear other boys talking about the superiority of men over women; I used to think they must be crazy.' But these are passing references: only once, however, did he allow himself a full-length discussion of women's economic role. But this one exception – an unpublished talk to Rosary College in Illinois in 1970 – is an extraordinary one. It begins: 'When I was 16 years old I wanted to be an engineer. So when my elder daughter at age 16 announced that she wanted to be an engineer, I knew for certain that she was my daughter, although the proposition had never really been in doubt'.[67] As Lewis illustrates, while the proportion of women in the labour force has risen very sharply in recent years, women's share of the better-paid jobs (in essence, the professions) has diminished. And this, he argues, is because educated women have in such numbers treated marriage as a substitute for, rather than a complement to, professional advancement. The proportion of American women who marry, and therefore are vulnerable to this distraction, is one of the highest in the world, Lewis argues: 'as I always warn my male students, American women love marriage, and should not be trifled with because they mean business'.[68] Thus, in this case, the real problem is not male prejudice, which has diminished over time, but that 'women have stymied their own progress by going into a sort of romantic coma, in which they have put more emphasis on the sexual side of their lives and rather less on their intellectual capacity'. So the message is 'do not quit and do not drop out'; but embedded in this little talk is a model of why women do drop out, underlying which is a flashback to Lewis's early Manchester years, containing in turn allusions to his childhood:

> To be a young widow involves a terrible economic struggle. I found this out when I was living in Manchester, England, and my wife went home to the West Indies to have our first child – that same engineer to

whom I have already referred. I advertised in *The Manchester Guardian* for a housekeeper, and received about 50 replies. About ten came from young ladies who misunderstood the meaning of the word 'house-keeper'. They began 'My eyes are blue and I am slim and pretty'. Those letters I threw away. Most of the other 40 letters were from widows with young children, and they were pathetic. To be left a widow with three children at age 30 is about the worst thing that can happen to you, for you cannot work and look after three small children at the same time. This is a sure road to poverty, exhaustion and misery. I have constantly warned my own daughters to prepare themselves lest this should happen to them.[69]

With this one intervention – only a talk to a further education college – Lewis emerges alongside his original inspiration, John Stuart Mill, as one of those economists to have thought most deeply about women's economic roles.

Just at the time when his work on his late nineteenth-century project was beginning to gather momentum, Lewis abruptly interrupted it for various purposes. But even allowing for this, the economic history project was to be a very long-drawn-out process. *Growth and Fluctuations* took eleven years (1967–78) to produce, whereas *The Theory of Economic Growth*, Lewis's only other book of a similar size, was finished in two years in the midst of being head of department, doing multiple consultancies both at home and abroad, advising the Labour Party, and raising two very small children, and none of this applied at Princeton. The evidence points to the Wicksell Lectures (or possibly the LSE lecture in 1970) marking the peak of a euphoric late-1960s phase in which, after the agonies of Ghana and the West Indies, he recovered his good humour and research momentum, and his teaching acquired an unprecedented vitality. But then something forced Lewis to slow down. Certainly there was the interruption caused by the secondment to the Caribbean Development Bank, which took up much of the period 1971–3. And, certainly, he experienced periods of ill-health at this time. But the evidence is also that Lewis was losing the hunger to create and innovate.

On returning from the Caribbean Development Bank in 1973, he had difficulty in adapting back to Princeton. By contrast with his situation in Manchester, where he had been head of department and dean of faculty, Lewis now had no administrative responsibilities, nor did he play any significant part in securing research grants. Initially this was a relief to him, but when he discovered that as a consequence he was forced to work, on his return from Barbados in late 1973, in an office away from the main building, The Elm Club (see Figure 8.1), where the main group of economists was based, without a secretary to protect him from incoming phone calls, he was outraged. He wrote to the Dean, John P. Lewis:

Dear John:

I arrived back from India yesterday, and found your letter of October 26.

I have been expecting to be at Elm Club. This dispersal of economists is bad for Princeton's Economics Department, since we miss the opportunities of teaching and stimulating each other which flow from casual day to day contact, but I suppose it can't be helped. What one needs, I suppose, is an extra cubby hole, however small, in the Economics Department itself, so that one would be encouraged

Figure 8.1   The Elm Club, Princeton University
Source: Author photograph.

to spend more time with one's colleagues. At my last full departmental meeting of the economists I found to my horror that I did not know the names of about a third of the members of the department.

The Dean replied:

lone-wolf professors who are not presiding over some kind of program or another are, regardless of seniority and distinction, not supposed to have buttons on their phones and, therefore, secretarial screening of incoming calls ... [This] is one of the set of economizing measures that eager new middle managers in the University have been charged with implementing aggressively, which they do with good aggregate budgetary effect.

A better longer-term solution would be this: You ought anyway to have and ought fairly readily to be able to get some continuing personal outside research funding that would support a full- or majority-time research assistant. Then that person could be officed adjacent to or near you, could have an extension of your phone and cover same ... Why don't you work on that? Maybe some of the rest of us can help.[70]

Lewis felt particularly affronted at being invited to go and chase research grants,[71] and went into a bit of a sulk. He continued to protest, without success,[72] at not being allowed a direct line.

In addition, one of the strongest pillars of Lewis's research, the idea that growth was the key to development, came to be challenged. At the beginning of the 1970s, Albert Fishlow of the University of California at Berkeley had published a paper on Brazil showing that, in spite of gross domestic product (GDP) growth rates averaging over 7 per cent during the 1960s, the standard of living of the lowest deciles had not improved, and that the already high level of inequality was deteriorating (Fishlow 1972: 391, 399). Even worse, famine, which was widely thought to have been wiped out (this was in ignorance of the appalling Chinese famine of the early 1960s) had recurred in Ethiopia and in Bangladesh. This inconvenient fact destroyed the simple linkage between investment, labour market expansion and poverty reduction underlying the Lewis model, and replaced it with a vision of polarization of wealth between haves and have-nots, putting at risk the stability of both north and south. Of the main international finance institutions, it was the World Bank, under its new president, Robert McNamara, that was quickest on its feet to respond to the challenge. His newly-appointed chief economist, Hollis Chenery of Harvard University, signalled the need for a reorientation of development policy:

> It is now clear that little more than a decade of rapid growth in underdeveloped countries has been of little benefit to perhaps a third of their population. Although the average per capita income of the Third World has increased by 50 per cent since 1960, this growth has been very unequally distributed between countries, regions within countries, and socio-economic groups. Paradoxically, while growth policies have succeeded beyond the expectations of the first development decade, the very idea of aggregate growth as a social objective has increasingly been called into question.[73]

At the annual joint meeting of the World Bank and the IMF in 1973, the Bank committed itself to a reorientation of its development policy effort towards greater equity and the objective of a world without poverty. In terms of models, there was an awareness that Latin America, the source of Fishlow's original alarming findings, was a bad model for inclusive development, and that East Asia was a much better one (a theme that Lewis had plugged repeatedly, especially in his *Report on the Industrialisation of the Gold Coast* (Gold Coast Government 1953a)). In rural areas where poverty was most severe, the Bank reoriented its lending portfolio towards agriculture, and especially towards increasing smallholder agricultural productivity – historically, of course, one of Lewis' main preoccupations – an area the Bank had previously treated as being off-limits because it was not bankable. And in urban areas, it acknowledged for the first time the need to give support not only for the building of new modern housing, but also for the assistance of the millions of people in shantytowns on the fringes of the cities – a group that new research in the early 1970s gave the name of 'the informal sector' (Hart 1973; Weeks 1973; ILO 1974). These new ideas were welcomed and emulated by most of the major donors, and eventually the UN system also began to catch up with them, more in terms of slogans (such as 'basic needs') than in terms of operational interventions; but it did, importantly, realize that to accommodate the new focus on well-being rather than simply on growth, it was necessary to have supplementary measures of well-being that supplemented standard income and output measures, resulting in the production of the UN's *Human Development Reports*.

Lewis, so quick to catch on to a significant development trend in the 1950s and early 1960s, was slow to become involved with these new directions in development policy. He was later to observe rather sneeringly to his colleague John P. Lewis, who had sent a draft research proposal on the same theme around the development group of the Woodrow Wilson School for comment:

> Growth theorists – Nurkse, Rostow, Hirschmann – taught us 30 years ago that growth occurs not all over the economy at the same time but in small leading sectors ... So a few people in a few sectors get rich while the rest of the population remains as before ... I expect Bob McNamara to discover with surprise that the masses in the LDCs were unaffected by a 5 per cent p.a. growth rate between 1960 and 1970; but the Woodrow Wilson school too?[74]

But this misses the point of the McNamara initiative, which is that, if inequality and poverty are increasing for whatever reason, something needs to be done about it. There is a very inconsequential correspondence between Chenery and Lewis while the McNamara initiative was taking shape; but here again the relationship did not gell, possibly, Ranis surmises, because Chenery 'was too much of a modeller for Lewis to be comfortable with'.[75] As a result, Lewis missed out on the opportunity to contribute, both as a writer and as a policy activist, to the Bank's new pro-poor initiatives until the end of the decade. By this time the whole pro-poor, pro-smallholder agriculture thrust of the World Bank, and indeed most of the donors, was nearing its end, and was about to be replaced by a quite new ideology and a quite new policy framework.

Finally, in October 1978, Lewis was given the opportunity to work with the World Bank but as an adviser, not on operations, but on research policy. He was invited to take part in an inquiry into the Bank's research, as part of a panel that included Bela Balassa, of Johns Hopkins University, Baltimore, and T. N. Srinivasan (at that time working in the Development Research Center of the World Bank, and now, at the time of writing, at Yale). The panel's remit was quite wide: according to Chenery, 'Mr McNamara wants an indication of the role the Bank should play in research. Besides this, he also wanted an indication of the major fields in which knowledge deficiencies severely hampered development efforts'.[76] There is no mention in the papers of the Bank's poverty focus, which at that time was increasingly under attack from the New Right both inside and outside the Bank. Lewis was asked to specialize in the area of income distribution and employment. The panel of experts held two meetings, in late 1978 and mid-1979. To the second of these Lewis presented a report co-authored with a Bank economist,

Suman Bery, the main thrust of which was that the Bank should work out more precisely the jobs it did best and focus its work on these areas of comparative advantage;[77] that it should make sure that research was properly linked with Bank country operational work; and that more of its research should be devolved to researchers in developing countries, an issue that still, 35 years later, is heavily debated.

The Bery/Lewis report was received less than enthusiastically by the panel, and Lewis, a master of precise exposition, must have been particularly irritated by Srinivasan's description of it as 'rather fuzzy'.[78] In particular, Srinivasan suggested that research capacity in developing countries, to whom Lewis had asked for work to be devolved, was in many cases falling apart, and not able to bear the load Lewis wanted to put on it. If this was true of India, the source of most of Srinivasan's examples, it was ten times truer in Africa, and even in the West Indies; and the irony is that the Lewis of 15 years before could have told them that. He could have told them that the *Economic Bulletin of Ghana* was no longer being published, that field trials on many agricultural research stations were already being abandoned or curtailed – a situation that was to deteriorate further under structural adjustment in the 1980s – and that the extension workers, there and in many African countries, were no longer going out in the field, because the funds to pay them were not there. But the Lewis of 1978, having retreated from field work and 'making people do what they do not want to do', either was not aware of this or, if he was, he simply left the point to others to make.

One senses – and there is no direct evidence on this – that, while half of him was very glad to have retreated from the battlefield and no longer be doing sharp-end operational jobs such as the one he did for Nkrumah (and could have done for McNamara's operational divisions), another part still longed for them. The Lewis/Bery report does not read like Lewis's style: it reads like something you or I or anyone might have written. The razor-sharp edge of the *Report on the Industrialisation of the Gold Coast* (Gold Coast Government 1953a), or of the ten-year development plan Lewis wrote in 24 hours for the Federation of the 'Little Eight' (pp. 201–2 above), or of the increasingly impassioned letters he wrote to Nkrumah in 1958, are all missing. It reads like a piece written to help pay the bills, not something written out of passion. And if it is surprising that Lewis did not engage with the McNamara World Bank, it is even more surprising that he did not engage, at a time when the thrust of policy was becoming more inclusive, with the UN system, which in 1951 had given him the opportunity to write the report that first gave him a global reputation.

Lewis therefore spent much of the 1970s out of the mainstream – initially trapped in the Caribbean, where his influence was strictly local rather than global, not well acclimatized to Princeton when he returned there,[79] and disconnected from some major new trends in development policy. Gradually, though, towards the end of the decade, he fought his way back. At Princeton, Gersovitz's arrival in 1976 was important in reviving Lewis's joy in teaching. The momentum of his work on global growth and fluctuations gradually revived, under the stimulus of the invitation to deliver the Janeway Lectures, *The Evolution of the International Economic Order* (1978b), at Princeton in 1977. The Janeway lecture series 'in historical economics in honour of Joseph Schumpeter' was, according to John P. Lewis, 'jointly designed by you [Arthur Lewis], Bill Bowen [the President of Princeton], Dick Quandt and me at Prospect House [the faculty club] one day in 1970',[80] and Lewis used the lectures to help design one of the key stepping-stones he needed to complete the story of *Growth and Fluctuations* (1978a) – namely the adverse factoral (income) terms of trade for the products of the developing countries, and their consequent dependence on the industrialized world and its financing for their own growth impulse. These adverse terms of trade in turn were caused by, in Lewis's view, the failure to achieve a technological revolution in food crop production[81] – indeed, at this point Lewis hardens his position and claims that this is the *only* way in which developing countries have the power to turn the factoral terms of trade in their favour.[82] Adverse terms of trade, and not the influence of colonialism, apparently emerge as the main reason why tropical countries did not convert their rapid growth of exports at the end of the nineteenth century into the kind of industrial growth that was being achieved at the time in Germany, Russia and Japan – and even more significantly in Australia, which, unlike the others, exported mainly raw materials.[83]

Even so, it took the whole of the 1970s, and a great deal of tinkering with the structure at the behest of Baumol and others,[84] to convert the building-blocks of Lewis's big story on international economic relationships before 1900 – *Aspects of Tropical Trade* (1969c), *Tropical Development* (1970a) and *The Evolution of the International Economic Order* (1978b) – into *Growth and Fluctuations 1870–1913*, the apex of the entire pyramid, which finally appeared in 1978. *Growth and Fluctuations* is the river into which all Lewis's previous international economic history flows – the groundbreaking 1952 and 1955 papers in *The Manchester School*, the country case-studies of *Tropical Development*, the more theoretical perspectives of the Wicksell and Janeway lectures, and a good deal of empirical material that could not be fitted into any of these, including a triumphant mention for Gisela Eisner's 150-year span economic history of Jamaica. The book's structure is a little strange, in the sense that its core theme is the response of over a hundred tropical developing countries, during the last quarter of the nineteenth century, to a stimulus (the growth of global production and trade); and yet Lewis's discussion of that response is compressed into one chapter (Chapter 8), comprising only 30 of the 245 pages, that 30 pages being encased in the remaining 200-plus pages documenting the stimulus, namely the global growth process and its ups and downs (there is also an epilogue on the period after the main story ends, which conjures up both the subject matter and the approach of *Economic Survey 1919–1939* (1949a)). But the response, of course, is the heart of the matter, so let us begin there and work backwards.

As Lewis brilliantly illustrates, the impact of the world economy on the global South, as it is now known, is no simple matter, and ramifies into many different components, some of which had been illuminated by his graduate students ten years before in *Tropical Development* (1970a). The tree diagram shown in Figure 8.2 captures only some of the major components of the impact, and omits a number of feedbacks.

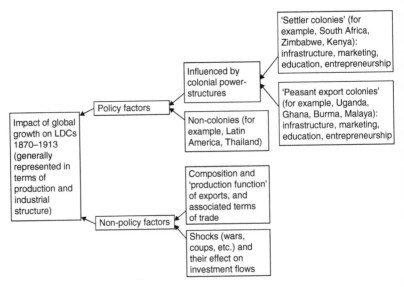

Figure 8.2 Elements in the impact of global growth on the 'South', 1870–1913, as portrayed by Lewis (1978)

In Chapter 8 of his book, Lewis tells the comparative stories of the impact of the centre on the periphery, using the categorizations in the diagram as major building blocks. As Lewis notes (see the right-hand side of the diagram), the impact of colonialism is too complex to capture even by distinguishing between the policies of different colonizing powers, because 'the same power [often] pursued different policies in different colonies – the most spectacular example being the diametrically opposed policies of Britain in Kenya and neighbouring Uganda ' (Lewis 1978a: 32). The elements in development neglected most critically by policy-makers, in his opinion, echoing two of Lewis's most abiding themes, are education (ibid.: 218) and industrial entrepreneurship (ibid.: 215): across most of the developing world most administrations , apart from Brazil, simply did not learn the obvious lessons from labour-abundant 'late industrializers' such as Japan. Some themes from 'Economic Development with Unlimited Supplies of Labour' (1954) are picked up and reincorporated here, notably the tendency for wages not to rise above the subsistence level, if there is surplus labour, even where productivity is rising fast (Lewis 1978a: 158) , and the implications of this for the distribution of income.[85]

His conclusion concerning the most emotive actor in the story, the impact of colonization, is sober: 'In general, it is not possible to say how much difference colonial status made to the rate of industrial growth' (ibid.: 213). But then he qualifies this remark, returning to the entrepreneurship theme:

> Probably the most important negative effect of the colonial system was to hinder the development of a native industrializing cadre. The backwardness of the less developed countries of 1870 could be changed only by people prepared to alter certain customs, laws and institutions, and to shift the balance of political and economic power away from the old landowning and aristocratic classes. But the imperial powers for the most part allied themselves with the existing power blocs. They were especially hostile to educated young people, whom, by means of a colour bar, they usually kept out of positions where administrative experience might be gained, whether in the public service or in private business. Such people, they then said, could not be employed in superior positions because they lacked managerial experience, as well as the kind of cultural background in which managerial competence flourishes. One result of this was to divert into long and bitter anti-colonial struggles much brilliant talent that could have been used creatively in development sectors.

Another result was to implant a sense of inferiority, which still today prevents some leaders of newly independent countries from achieving their full potential.[86]

The process analysed here, of course, had a personal resonance for Lewis: 40 years previously in St Lucia, he had been one of those 'young people ... kept out of positions where administrative experience might be gained'. So, governance, and the effect of colonization on it, is one part of the reason why tropical growth did not convert into industrialization; and another, as we have seen in the Janeway Lectures, is the declining factoral terms of trade of the tropical countries *vis-à-vis* the industrialized countries, behind which lies Lewis's familiar *leitmotiv* – their failure to achieve a revolution in food crop productivity.[87] Once we go back up the causal chain in search of an explanation of why this revolution has not happened, we are presented with an expanded version of the political economy of class conflict that crept into 'Unlimited Supplies of Labour' only as an aside – for example, when illustrating rural capitalists' incentive to block pro-poor policies that would raise real wages, such as agricultural extension.[88] Therefore, in a defiant rebuttal of the econometric approach, we are told:

> The study of economic development is therefore as much a task for the political historian, with his interest in individual personalities and the behaviour of conflicting groups, as it is for the economist with his concentration on markets, prices and profitability. After one has studied trends and opportunities, the response of any particular country cannot be fully understood without the detailed analysis of its particular circumstances. Attempts at putting economic history into a set of dynamic equations are doomed to failure.[89]

To us, *Growth and Fluctuations* does not have the white-hot inspiration of Lewis's masterpieces of the 1950s: not only 'Economic Development with Unlimited Supplies of Labour', but also *Theory of Economic Growth*, his 1952 *Manchester School* article which yielded some of the raw material for *Growth and Fluctuations*, and – in some ways more remarkable than any of them – his unpublished 1948 pamphlet on *Colonial Development*. However, in many ways, it is broader in scope than any of these masterpieces. Unlike them, it looks at the whole developing world as just a part of the world economy: as Ronald Findlay was later to write, 'one of the main strengths of his work on development economics is that he has never considered the problems of the less developed countries in isolation but always in the context of a single interdependent system'.[90] Unlike all of them except the 1952 *Manchester School* article, it generates new datasets, which Lewis proudly segregated in appendices. And it exceeds all of them in its ambition to combine economics, political theory and history. At least in intention, it aspires to be a metaphor for growth at all times and places and not just the nineteenth century, as his playful document selling the initial idea to the students had made plain ten years before. At least in intention, this is Lewis's Ninth Symphony: bringing back themes from all his previous works, developing them, and combining them in one final triumphant restatement. Who but Lewis could have written the following passage, from the scene-setting Introduction to *Growth and Fluctuations*? (Notice in particular his further sideswipe at quantitative methods, and his mournful and forward-looking[91] allusion to the 'temporary glamour of the Keynesian system', both compressed into one short final sentence.)

> From 1870 onwards organized hostility to 'pure' capitalism or to the unregulated market economy mounted steadily. This was not confined to the workers with their trade unions and burgeoning political institutions, nor to the farmers. The industrialists abandoned free trade ... and began a movement towards associations, cartels, mergers, combines and trusts, of which the celebrated 'multinational company' is only the latest phase. The middle classes also moved leftwards, tasting Fabianism, Populism and Social Democracy. The welfare state was spawned, fathered by of all people the German chancellor Bismarck. The trend was compounded by the economists' abandonment of Malthusian political economy, whose more dismal adherents had taught that attempts to raise working-class standards were doomed to frustration. By 1880 the economists' long march into algebra had begun, and with it, until the temporary glamour of the Keynesian system, disappeared their intellectual prestige.[92]

All the indications are indeed that in the late 1970s this mournful tone had become the main tenor of every part of Lewis's life –though he still, certainly, had some good moments. Materially, he was more than comfortable,[93] and he had good reason to be proud of *Growth and Fluctuations*. But, while the move to academia, and in the winter to the

Caribbean, had been good for his health, it was beginning to get worse again by the end of the decade.[94] Despite many of his graduate students being in awe of his achievements, not all were, and some were openly exasperated, as he must have noticed, by his habit of kicking off the first three lectures of a course and leaving the rest to students or graduate assistants to lead; some of his students in the 1970s, such as Michael Hodd and Thomas Warke, felt that, by then, some of his lectures were not clear.[95] In addition, he felt neglected by the profession and by the world. When belatedly noticed by the World Bank, he had been treated condescendingly by them, as we saw above. The sniping of the Chicago School, in the person of Harry Johnson, which had been going on ever since the early 1950s (see Chapters 4 and 7 above), still continued, even though Johnson now disdained to attack Lewis in person and did so by proxy through an attack on applications of Keynesian economics to development, which condemned 'the notion that there exists masses of "disguised unemployed" people, [which] leads easily into the idea that "development" involves merely the mobilisation and transfer of these resources into ... investment or industrial production at an obvious and virtually costless economic gain'.[96] As we saw above, a range of empirical economists had joined this chorus during Lewis's Princeton years, and continued to attack his credentials, in print by means of critiques of the surplus-labour assumption,[97] and on the grapevine through insinuations that anyone who still chose to argue his story without the standard mathematical and econometric apparatus could not be treated as credible.

How much these critiques penetrated into the Princeton common room is a matter on which opinion is divided. His staunch friends, such as William Baumol, maintain that his unorthodox habit of expressing himself in simple prose (rather than mathematics) was accepted as the unorthodoxy of someone who was clearly a star,[98] but there were others, such as his future colleague Paul Krugman, who took a different view, and who was to publish dismissive put-downs of 'the Lewis model' which were in fact a critique of the quite different Rosenstein-Rodan model.[99] Lewis was by then 63, knew that he was slowing down physically, and suffering from the doubts that many people of that age have about their memory and reasoning abilities. Indeed, for some time he had been trying to move his life into a pattern that involved not only less arduous consultancy, but also less academic work.

As early as 1966, aged 51 and only three years into his Princeton job, he had begun planning for his retirement. He wrote about a plot of land, not to the estate agent, but directly to the prime minister of Barbados,

Errol Barrow, with whom he had worked with to set up the Federation of the Eight four years previously:

My dear Premier

This refers to conversations about planning a plot of land on which to build a house in the new Cave Hill development. Mr Leonard St Hill showed me last week the exact spot I would like to have. It is at the southern end of the area marked '3' in the Basic Plan, a mound right next to the spot reserved for a church, and bordering the existing road. I understand that about half an acre could be made available to me.

I should be grateful if you would do whatever is necessary to have this spot committed to me as soon as possible. I am willing to pay the whole or part of the purchase price on demand.[100]

In the event, Lewis first acquired, in 1969,[101] a property – Blue Waters in Antigua (which he was to rent out throughout his period with the Caribbean Development Bank, even though his job was in Barbados). However, it was Barbados that he had in mind to make his permanent home, and this eventually materialized in 1975 at Wanstead Heights, after many setbacks.

Immediately after the secondment to the Caribbean Development Bank, he began a pattern, which he maintained for the rest of his life, of spending his winters in the Caribbean. By 15 December 1975 he was 'getting ready for [my] annual migration away from the cold'.[102]

In 1974, at the age of 59, he wrote: 'We have settled back in Princeton ... and it is very pleasant to be back in academic life. I would like to retire, but thanks to inflation, the pension is too small, so I have another six years to go.'[103] A year later, he was looking forward to 'putting [my] feet up and reading nineteenth century novels'.[104]

This was a time at which development economics was changing, away from the idea that developing countries' governments needed to diversify away from primary commodity dependence through import-substituting industrialization with the help of development plans.[105] Even the broader and more equity-focused view of development that had been introduced into donors' aid programmes by McNamara, Chenery and the recently-initiated UN *Human Development Reports* came under threat, as those donors, in an environment of stagflation, prepared for the crash to come. Well before it arrived in 1980, however, the tide of development thinking was changing, towards more emphasis on smaller government and on free markets, and on combating abuses of governance such as corruption (Anne Krueger's 'The Political Economy of the Rent-Seeking Society', published in the *American Economic Review* in 1974, pointed the way). Development planning was abandoned, and even development economics, which Lewis had helped to invent, was beginning to come under threat from Lewis's old nemesis, Peter Bauer, and from other influential agents of what has been called the 'counter-revolution' in development studies at that time.[106]

8.4   The Nobel Prize, 1979

And then Lewis learnt, in early October 1979, that he had been awarded the Nobel Prize. As the account published by the Woodrow Wilson School has it:

> The notifying phone call came at 6:45am on Tuesday, October 16. Lewis' wife Gladys was already up making tea at the time, and she was somewhat surprised to find herself talking to a Swedish reporter who said he had important news for her husband. She tried to reason with the man, but he assured her the message was worth a few minutes of her husband's sleep. 'I handed him the phone and went out of the room,' she recalls. 'When I came back in I heard him say "Schultz", and I pricked up my ears and thought, 'This has something to do with economics'. Then he said, 'What is the citation?' I began to think, 'Oh, my goodness'.[107]

He phoned Baumol with the news, and told him, in a calm and puzzled tone that barely betrayed any excitement, that he was 'surprised' to be awarded the prize for work he had done over 20 years before[108] (on 'Unlimited Supplies of Labour' and *The Theory of Economic Growth*). Baumol wrote Lewis a jocular note of congratulation, addressing him as 'Sir Arthur Lewis', to which Lewis replied, 'What have I done to offend you?'[109] Gersovitz, on the Princeton campus, heard the news from one of the research students in economics and 'immediately ordered himself an enormous breakfast'.[110] This, the first Nobel award to be made for development economics, was shared between Lewis and Theodore Schultz, who had been co-panellists on the United Nations' *Measures for the Economic Development of Underdeveloped Countries* in 1951. The two men had grown apart somewhat over the years, and in particular had clashed over the surplus labour issue,[111] but continued to share considerable mutual respect, as well as a common passion for mass education. Apart from Lewis's supporters in Princeton, John P. Lewis and Donald

Stokes,[112] other development economics buddies, in particular Jagdish Bhagwati,[113] emerged to explain to Lewis that they had recommended him for the award. Tributes also came from many others, including the previous Nobel Prize winner, Herbert Simon, who commended Lewis for entering areas 'which although of the greatest theoretical and practical importance have been outside the narrow main stream';[114] from the director of economics at the Eastern Electricity Board in Ipswich, UK, who had debated the economics of two-part tariffs with him 30 years previously;[115] and from others of an innovatory turn of mind, including Nirmal Kumar Sethia, who styled himself as 'Inventor of Magnetic Chain, Flexible Car, Cardboard Cassette, Master Bonding Liquid' of Satna, Madhya Pradesh.[116]

The award was presented to Lewis in Stockholm on 10 December 1979. In his Nobel lecture, greatly indebted in particular to the assistance of Gersovitz, he linked together his economic history and economic growth interests to analyse 'The Slowing Down of the Engine of Growth'. The great global boom of 1950–73, Lewis explained, had already slowed and was unrepeatable: the backlog of innovations following the Depression and the Second World War had been exhausted, surplus labour reserves in and around Western Europe had been exhausted, and the world was running into shortages of raw materials. He then developed the model he had used in *Growth and Fluctuations* to explore the reasons why, even if global growth was slowing, developing countries might be able to resist this trend, paying particular attention to regional economic co-operation, his ordeals in the West Indies notwithstanding.

Among the many letters of congratulation, two from people who had been Lewis's colleagues at the LSE, 40 years before, stand out. Sir John Hicks alluded none too subtly to the extent to which Lewis and Schultz, colleagues on the UN's *Measures for the Economic Development...* mission of 1951, had grown apart:

Dear Arthur,
I am very glad to see that you are joining us. We are a motley collection, made more motley by the current practice of balancing – Myrdal–Hayek being the choice example, but Lewis–Schultz does seem to be a bit of another. I began to suspect that there was something of it in Hicks–Arrow, but that would have been more subtle.[117]

I see you have said that it was odd to be honoured for work which you did twenty years ago. I felt that, perhaps even more strongly, for it was my own more recent work, which has been quite anti-General Equilibrium, for which I would have preferred to be honoured.

If you are going to be in the Bahamas next March, we may perhaps pay you another visit. For I have just had an invitation to a conference in the Bahamas – so far only over the telephone, so I don't know any details. But if it comes off, we shall not resist the opportunity to come again to the Caribbean (poor Caribbean – I am afraid it is having a rough time[118]) and if you are there we shall look you up.

...

Best wishes and congratulations
John[119]

A year later, Lord Robbins, then aged 82, joined the chorus with a letter which we reproduce in full:

Dear Arthur
This a disgracefully belated note to convey the warmest congratulations on your Nobel prize. I was away when it was announced – indeed I only heard of it later in an accidental conversation with a friend – and nowadays, although I keep about me all sorts of practical enterprises, I tend to be a very bad correspondent where intimate letters are involved. But I am truly ashamed of not having taken up my pen in this connection before; for the news gave me tremendous delight and made me think well of the advisers to the Nobel Foundation. It is good to think that excellence such as yours, applied to so many parts of our subject too often neglected, has been recognised in this way.

It seems a long time since we met and I very much hope that you will pass this way soon so as to give your many friends in London the opportunity of expressing their happiness at your honour in personal contact. I still lecture twice a week at LSE in the Michaelmas and Lent terms on the *History of Economic Thought* – a subject which affords almost limitless opportunities for wide miscellaneous reading [and] is peculiarly congenial at my age. But I don't know so much of the Economics Department – it has become so enormous that I sometimes doubt whether they all know each other.[120]

As you probably have heard, the government here has introduced the *most highly distasteful*[121] regulations regarding fees to be charged to students from abroad which hits LSE very hard, since so much of our characteristic atmosphere derives from our truly international character. However Ralf Dahrendorf, in many ways the best

Director in my recollection, is making heroic efforts to overcome the difficulty by an appeal for special funds and, although it will be difficult, I suspect that in one way or another he will succeed.
Please give Iris' and my love to Grace[122]
Affectionately, Lionel

Both Hicks and Robbins, here, are paying tribute not only to Lewis, but also to the LSE's liberal tradition. By mixing in his insights from the developing world, Lewis took that framework into places with which they had initial difficulty in identifying, in particular Lewis's insistence that the traditional-sector wage does not equate to the marginal product. But both were sympathetic to Lewis's long-term, classical approach to development, and both understood that if microeconomics was to progress it could no longer, least of all in developing countries, be via repeating the standard assumptions of perfect knowledge and instantaneous adjustment of markets. By illustrating how labour and capital markets fail to adjust in developing countries, Lewis helped to open the door for Akerlof's asymmetric-information model of market adjustment; by insisting that income distribution as well as the behaviour of commodity markets is relevant to well-being, the Lewis model also contributed to the perspective that became Sen's analysis of famine; and by emphasizing, in his reciprocal, 'sharing' assumptions for the traditional sector, non-market allocation mechanisms, he paves the way for Elinor Ostrom's work on collaborative solutions to local-level governance problems. All of these ground-breaking ideas stem from Lewis's rough-cut empirical insight of 1948 that 'outside the study and the classroom, prices bear no relation to marginal productivity ... prices are therefore a false guide to the real economic situation, and policy must therefore be in defiance of prices if the true economic situation is to be met.'[123] Between them, they have helped to pull development economics out of the 'cul-de-sac' where Lewis glumly saw it as being trapped.

8.5 Winding down, 1980–4

The glow of being awarded the Nobel Prize faded quite quickly for Lewis. The early 1980s were a bad time for development: the worst recession, and the first global recession, since the Second World War, with the worst effects falling on the poorest developing countries, who, on turning to the aid donors, found that the latter's budgets had been cut by right-wing regimes – Reagan in America, Thatcher in Britain, Kohl in

Germany – who had now come to power. Angus Deaton, who arrived in Princeton as Lewis prepared to leave, recalls 'his great sadness that no one ... in economics seemed to care much about why world poverty was as pervasive as it was'.[124]

Lewis made no contribution as writer, nor was he invited to make one as a practitioner, to the great development policy innovations of the 1980s – new growth theory and supply-side economics – even though he was important in bringing about both advances.[125] He maintained very little communication with former contacts in either London or Manchester, though Gluckman kept writing to see if they might coincide on one of his American trips. Lewis seemed to have lost the desire to explore, and warned an enquirer from the United States Agency for International Development (USAID), 'I am no longer able to go on long journeys without my wife, both in her interest and mine.'[126] But Lewis was invited to be president of the American Economic Association in 1982, and out of that came one very poignant contact with the past:

> Dear Sir Arthur
> It was such a pleasure to meet you at the Denver meetings last year, although you may have forgotten me by now because I have taken so long to follow through! I am Evan Durbin's daughter and for the past five years I have been doing research on the economists of the NFRB and their contribution to Labour Party policy in the thirties. I am halfway through a book which Routledge, Kegan and Paul are going to publish next year. I enclose the introduction and synopsis of the book and the paper which I gave in Denver. As you can see I have already taken your name in vain and I do hope that I may come and talk to you soon.
>
> Meanwhile I am also trying to arrange a session to mark the centenary of Keynes' birth (January 1882)[127] at the December 1982 [American Economic Association] meeting in New York. I called Will Baumol last week to find out whom to contact and was so delighted when I found it was you! The person I would most like to speak with is James Meade...
> I do look forward to hearing from you and meeting you properly.
> Yours sincerely,
> Elizabeth Durbin
> P.S. I found a super photograph of Evan in the Fabian papers which had a blurry picture of you in the background and I want to use in the book. I am in the process of getting the negative copies.

Lewis replied kindly and warmly, without unwinding completely – or agreeing to involve himself in the search for money to fund Meade's trip. But he did invite Elizabeth to come over for lunch one day the following term.[128]

As we have stressed, Lewis after the 1960s was very selective about taking on consultancies. But he did allow himself, at the beginning of the 1980s when the glow of the Nobel Prize was beginning to fade, to accept a request from the Rockefeller Foundation to undertake an analysis of racial differences in earnings and unemployment in the USA. Formally, this was new territory for Lewis, who had always been interested in racial discrimination, and fought it long before in Manchester; but he had never previously done research on North America, and had written only a small burst of magazine articles and talks on college campuses (see pp. 232–5 above) around the time of the civil rights demonstrations of the early 1970s. However, for the first black professor to work in Europe, the theme was something of a homecoming, analytically as well as personally. At root, the 'Lewis model' of 1954 is simply a supply-and-demand model of the labour market, and the supply and demand for black professional-grade labour (in particular, the fact that black unemployment at the time was twice the level of white unemployment) is what Lewis now proceeded to analyse. He reviewed the various obstacles facing upwardly mobile black people, including the activities of trade unions, the need to pass tests that are 'irrelevant, culture-bound or specially designed to trap black candidates, the need to extract references from a person whose recommendation carries weight, and the cost of financing a learning period in one's first job'.[129] As he notes, part of the problem is locational: the places where black people are concentrated, especially in the inner cities, are far from the places where rapidly-growing middle employment is concentrated (this was in the early dawn of Silicon Valley). At the point where he draws attention to black unemployment rates in the 16–19 age group (frighteningly high at that time, in the early 1980s global recession, and at the time of writing, once again very similar) he flirts with but does not pursue the idea that a reformulation of welfare policies, such as indeed did occur under the Clinton administration ten years later, might have a part to play.[130] Among his recommendations, four are particularly interesting: (1) overcome the legal obstacles to black middle-class advancement by expanding the capacity of organizations such as the NAACP (National Association for American Coloured People);[131] (2) improve the state-funded schools attended mainly by blacks; (3) help black people, through local housing policies, to move to the suburbs where the new industries are; and (4) revitalize inner cities to the point that modern industries return.[132] The paper ends with a plea for black leaders 'to reject the current policy of maintaining a high level of unemployment as a supposed weapon to control inflation',[133] the policy which was at the time being implemented by the Reagan administration in the USA, as well as by the governments of Great Britain, Germany and other industrialized countries in an attempt to get the macro economy back under control. The macro-economic part of these recommendations was, of course, not accepted by government, but the educational and housing components, together with welfare-to-work, were to experience more success in improving black living standards after the advent of the Clinton administration in 1992.

This is in essence a think-piece, with little empirical analysis, which resists the temptation to draw on Lewis's experience and previous theoretical analysis of black labour markets in the UK and developing countries. The policy recommendations, sensible as they are, give no impression of having been bounced off practitioners – for example, in the NAACP or in federal departments of education and housing, as Lewis would routinely have done before the 1960s.

In April 1982, Lewis expanded his Rockefeller Foundation paper into the W. E. B. DuBois lectures at Harvard University, given in honour of the nineteenth-century pioneer black educator and opponent of racial discrimination, and was then persuaded by Harvard University Press to publish these lectures as a book – his last book, which appeared three years later, in 1985, under the title *Racial Conflict and Economic Development*. This was an error. The chapters added to the Rockefeller paper to make up the book, mainly casual observations on developing-country labour markets and on global inequality, do not add to the tight argument of the Rockefeller paper and indeed blur it considerably. Unlike anything else by Lewis, published or not, it is not clear what is the central message, and the book's narrative, meandering around no coherent story, is indeed so muddled as to open up the unresolvable question of whether Lewis was beginning to suffer some loss of mental capacity at this time.

Where Lewis continued, of course, to be deeply embedded in social networks was the West Indies, where he now spent every winter, which calmed him and wound him up in equal measure. From the University of the West Indies, whose imminent break-up Lewis had repeatedly feared in the 1960s, came the news that his deputy Philip Sherlock, now Sir Philip, had made a good fist of holding the university together.

Lewis was warm in his congratulations: 'What a lot you have achieved in helping 45 schools to learn from one another. It is very satisfying to create useful institutions in which others can flourish.'[134]

However, Lewis's occasional waspishness, especially when he was dealing with Trinidadians and Jamaicans, also came to the fore again at this time. One correspondent, searching for a tribute to the recently deceased Eric Williams, wrote in May 1981: 'Since Eric Williams' death I have been thinking how great his contribution to Caribbean history was ... you set Gisela Eisner on her way with one of the most useful pieces of research we have.' Lewis, still smarting from his clashes of 20 years before, retorted: 'As far as I know Eric's only scholarly output was the book on Capitalism and Slavery. The rest was flawed by its political motivation and style.'[135]

His other habitual sparring partner, M. G. (Mike) Smith, in congratulating Lewis on his Nobel Prize, also swallowed the various slings and arrows he had exchanged with Lewis over the years and invited him to become principal of an inter-university school for advanced graduate work in the social sciences, established by the universities of Guyana, Suriname and the University of the West Indies, and co-funded by the United Nations Educational, Scientific and Cultural Organization (UNESCO) and the United Nations Development Programme (UNDP).[136] But Lewis, by then preparing seriously for retirement, had no difficulty in declining this offer.

Eventually, in July 1983, Lewis officially retired from Princeton, and at his farewell reception a Festschrift edited by Gersovitz (with support from Diaz-Alejandro, Ranis and Rosenzweig) was handed to him. His speech of thanks to President Bowen, Dean Stokes and the assembled gathering began, 'I always seem to be just about to retire from Princeton and coming back again – so don't be surprised if you see me hanging around here in a few months' time.' He then told three not (from the viewpoint of the current authors) desperately funny anecdotes, one about the Iranian Ambassador, one about the Pope and one about Simon Kuznets, whose first question to everyone, we learn, was 'And what are you working on?' Lewis added, 'Ever since I turned 60 I have been annoyed by people who ask me "and what are you doing now?" – many of them people whom I am meeting for the first time.'

The question [Lewis added] seems to survive even beyond retirement. When I tell people I'm retiring they say And what are you going to do, and I say, 'Nothing'. And they say Ho Ho Ho I'm sure you will take on some new assignment. And I think: Well, I've been a Puritan all my life while the other chaps were having a good time lying on the beach and going to the races and what not – let me try that way for a change.[137]

Lewis did not, indeed, fulfil his promise of spending his retirement reading nineteenth-century novels, lying on the beach and what not. The Lewises did not give up their Princeton house, and each May until at least 1987, they migrated north with the swallows, and Arthur Lewis continued not only to 'hang around' but also to give classes on development.[138] It is clear that, in spite of his disclaimers, he really wanted to be still appreciated as a lecturer. As we have seen, opinion is divided on the quality of the lecture experience Lewis provided, but for many in the Woodrow Wilson School, being able to get this legendary figure into conversation with the graduate students on any terms was worth any quirks in his delivery.

In the West Indies, Lewis had indeed become an icon since the award of the Nobel Prize. He was lionized in newspaper articles, books, the creation of a Sir Arthur Lewis Institute for Social and Economic Studies (SALISES) in Barbados, and even the creation of a comic-strip biography in a series of *Caribbean Heroes* (see Figure 8.3). Though very much wanting to slow down further and avoid the limelight, Lewis for a time did his best to deal graciously with the demands for public appearances. Though his personal regard for Eric Williams (who died in 1981) had fallen, he agreed, in August 1983, to give an inaugural Eric Williams Memorial Lecture entitled 'Outlook for Development'. Alongside his race relations book for Harvard University Press, this is the last writing we have by Lewis for a public audience. He reverts to a theme he had first proposed in *Colonial Development* 40 years earlier: 'instead of making more jobs in the towns, make more jobs in the villages'.[139] He drew attention to the fact that economic performance in the global South, rapidly diversifying even when he was writing *Growth and Fluctuations*, now spanned the range 'from zero to beyond all previous experience'.[140] Presciently, he showed that in many of the 'zero' – or as they would now be called, 'bottom billion' – cases, failure to develop is a result not of bad policy or even of low agricultural productivity, but 'their trouble is internal war or marked political insecurity, such that their nationals are trying to get their money out, rather than invest it at home – countries such as Upper Volta [Burkina Faso], Zaire [DRC], Uganda, Chile or Burma'.[141]

Figure 8.3 Strip cartoon of a scene from the life of Sir Arthur Lewis, 1987

Source: Guy Ellis and Lisa Bhajan, *Sir Arthur Lewis*, school textbook published in series *National Heritage Series of Caribbean Heroes*, by Inprint Publishing, 1987. In Lewis Archive, Princeton, Box 1/8. Reproduced by kind permission of the Lewis Archive, Princeton University.

Later, he reminded his fellow West Indians for a final time, with characteristic mockery, that they cannot go on blaming their problems on the colonial or post-colonial legacy. This is close enough to vintage Lewis to provide a worthy finale to his published work:

> Even after the imperial powers had gone away – especially Britain and France – it was still a shock to leaders of tropical thought to find that other tropical countries were indeed industrialising successfully.
>
> As one moved from country to country people said: yes it can be done in Singapore because that is a small place; or it can be done in Brazil because that is a large place; it can be done in Mexico because they are Catholics; or in Pakistan[142] because they are Muslims – but there were always reasons why it couldn't be done here. To discover that it could be could be done here had many of the symptoms of being born again.[143]

Here, as in *Racial Conflict and Economic Development*, Lewis maintained his global outlook and his insistence that all branches of knowledge must work together to achieve development. In the latter publication, on the last page of his last book – and these may very nearly be his last published words– he wrote, 'In the end, economics is not enough.'[144] True; and the awareness of this is a large part of what makes Lewis's contributions to development distinctive.

8.6   Last years, 1984–91

After his retirement, Lewis no longer did any research or consultancy travel. However, he was willing, in the right season[145] and for any tempting excuse, such as the award of an honorary degree, to go to places in Europe that he and Gladys liked. He continued to migrate up to Princeton each year in the late spring to lecture as required and to catch up with the gossip. He continued, also, to correspond at some length with his friends – more now, especially after the publication of *Racial Conflict and Economic Development*, about black economics than about development.[146] Finally, he continued to be a member of various Caribbean bodies – in particular, as chairman of the Caribbean Medical Council of the Commonwealth Secretariat,[147] which involved him in conferences. Ranis and several other North American friends took up his invitation to escape from the cold and luxuriate in the Caribbean sunshine, with Gladys driving them around the winding roads of Barbados.[148] Lewis's fondness for Barbados strengthened in proportion to its weakening towards most of the other islands: he had never been comfortable in Jamaica, nor in Trinidad since the Eric Williams debacle of 1962, and now he showed increasing reluctance to visit even his birthplace, St Lucia,[149] even though his brother, Alan (later to become Sir Alan, the Chancellor of the University of the West Indies) was the governor there. Living in Barbados barely a mile from the UWI campus, he would complain 'Why don't any of my staff (on the Mona campus) come and see me?',[150] but this was partly self-pity: several of them did, in particular Richard Allsopp, a senior administrator on the campus whom Lewis had brought over from Guyana in 1961 and who as a spare-time activity had become the finest lexicographer in the Caribbean and author of a *Dictionary of Caribbean English Usage*. His other friends, in particular Neville Nicholls, the third president (after Lewis and Demas) of the Caribbean Development Bank, were also on the island. Lewis's appetite for discovery, once insatiable, eroded over time from the 1960s onwards.

In 1985, the University of Aix-en-Provence offered Lewis an honorary degree, which he very much wanted to accept in person. In correspondence with the university's Rector, he apologizes for his ability to correspond only in English and not in the 'exquisite' French language,[151] and emphasizes how much he is hoping to travel with Gladys to Provence. Arrangements were made for him to receive the degree in June 1987. However, during the winter of 1986/7, he suffered a stroke: 'My health deteriorated all through the winter. It is improving but I am still unsteady of leg and speech,' he reported to the Rector.[152] His doctors eventually refused him permission to travel. Consequently, his hoped-for last visit to Europe did not materialize.

However, he continued to make appearances on the development stage as an occasional lecturer. His Princeton colleagues even tried to get him involved in lecturing on controversial new topics, such as structural adjustment and supply-side economics, in relation to his old stamping-ground, Ghana. On 17 October 17 1988, Lewis was invited to contribute to course PA575A, Economic Policy Making in Africa. The instructor explained: 'The group's final project is to design a structural adjustment package for Africa that is better than the World Bank's. Given your long association with Ghana could you meet informally with the class to share some of your reflections on the evolution of Ghana?'[153] This Lewis willingly did. To our knowledge, this was his last lecturing assignment. His final publication, written for the *Handbook of Development Economics* (Lewis 1988) investigates 'how much of the development theory of today is to be found in the writings of the eighteenth century' [David Hume,

James Steuart and Adam Smith], and looks back into a more remote past even than the one he had examined in *Growth and Fluctuations*. He suffered a further stroke in the winter of 1989/90 and did not teach at Princeton the following spring. He died at his home in Barbados on the morning of 15 June 1991. His funeral on the island of St Lucia was attended by friends and admirers from every continent, and a moving address was given by Lewis's loyal friend Richard Allsopp. But the cathedral was far from full, and the two benches reserved for government staff remained empty.

9

'The fundamental cure for poverty is not money but knowledge': Lewis's Legacy

Lewis's achievements were extraordinary, but they emerged from a haphazard rather than a planned process, and indeed his career can best be seen as a series of improvisations. Having planned to be an engineer, he became an economist. Having made a success of being an industrial economist, he was then overtaken by the challenge of constructing what at first he called colonial economics and then development economics. Having made a success of development economics, he felt an obligation to give something practical back to the Afro-Caribbean communities in Manchester, Ghana and the West Indies who were not fortunate enough to have the opportunities he had had, and in attempting to do so he got his fingers burnt more than once. Retreating from these bruising experiences, he did not return to development economics, but rather expanded his work on global economic history; in so doing, however, he did not scale the heights he had in the 1950s but was forced to settle for something more modest. The award of the Nobel Prize in 1979 took him by surprise when he thought he had been forgotten, and gave his career an appearance of inevitability that the reality completely lacks.

While Lewis's work on industrial economics at the LSE gave him the necessary platform, it is a Fabian Society pamphlet written at the age of 24, before the Second World War, *Labour in the West Indies* (Lewis, 1939) that gave him his vocation. This extraordinary manifesto, and in particular the lengthy policy programme contained in its coda, contains nearly all of the ideas about development that were to make him famous. Just as important, it embodies Lewis's determination to act on those ideas. Having explained the concept of a poverty trap, or vicious circle of poverty, as it applies in the West Indies, he then added the words, 'But there is no vicious circle for men of determination.'[1] These words provide the key to the first half of Lewis's life. At the same time as he was elaborating and formalizing his picture of what kept poor people poor, he was working with his bare hands, both in Britain and in the developing world, to change that state of poverty and oppression.

Partly as a consequence of this contact with the real world, his picture of the developing world and how it needed to be reformed becomes, during the 1940s and 1950s, progressively more globally-oriented and less radical. The word 'revolution' is in fact mentioned once, in *Labour in the West Indies,* as a description of what the developing countries of the West Indies need to do in order to realize their potential, and then disappears from his vocabulary. In *Colonial Economic Development* (1944), and more fully in *Colonial Development* (1948), Lewis breaks with neo-classical economics, and rejects 'the economics of marginal utility' in favour of 'the economics of laws, institutions, tenures, nationality, race, religion, ideology and kindred determinants of economic equity and of the rate of economic progress which were banished from the economic textbooks and seminars as disreputable topics over seventy years ago'.[2] But these pamphlets were never published; and by the time Lewis's view of the development process reached its definitive form, in 'Unlimited Supplies of Labour' (1954) and *The Theory of Economic Growth* (1955), the revolutionary language has gone, and marginal utility has bedded down comfortably alongside the institutional factors that determine the wealth of nations. Indeed, the apex of the whole pyramid, the open-economy section of 'Unlimited Supplies of Labour' and its formalization of the case for industrialization achieved through protection, rests on marginal-utility principles. Lewis had realized that, to explain market imperfection, in the labour market and elsewhere, the principle of marginal utility does not need to be thrown away but only the 'limitations of the special case', to quote Seers' (1963) famous phrase, recognized. Much of microeconomics since the 1940s has consisted of a coming to terms with this extension of basic motivational principles to economies that do not 'behave', but it was Lewis, with Rosenstein-Rodan, who in the mid-1940s set the ball rolling.

Embedded in Lewis's view of development are four propositions, which underlie not just his published work on development but also all of his policy advocacy work. The first of these has already been introduced, namely the idea that free markets and laissez-faire cannot be expected to work in proportion as economies are poor. The second is the idea that, in the face of declining income terms of trade, poor countries must not accept the international division of labour implied by current 'static' comparative advantage, but must work to transform their economies from primary production towards export-based industry and services, which implies a need for infant-industry protection and other purposive state interventions. The third is that energetic steps need to be taken to increase agricultural productivity in poor countries, partly to achieve industrialization in a viable manner and partly to increase the well-being of the smallholder populations themselves. The fourth is that, partly as a means of increasing agricultural productivity, and partly as a means of increasing the productivity of the economy as a whole, education needs to be extended from the children of the elite to the mass of the population. All of these propositions were first encountered in our second chapter, as building-blocks in Lewis's 1944 essay with Durbin, *Colonial Economic Development*. While each of the four propositions has been the basis of much empirical literature, Lewis never tested the factual content of this literature, nor did he seek to establish any of the propositions empirically; in this, he resembles his revered classical economists. Rather, in Lewis's hands, the propositions are *a priori* axioms: part of the bone-structure that makes his analysis distinctive and holds it together, rather than part of a story backed by verified data. Therefore, the bone-structure of Lewis's analysis appears out in the open, as it were, much more in his unpublished works and consultancy reports than in the publications for which he is well known.

This consultancy and advocacy work, however, is also an essential part of Lewis's legacy. From 1939 to 1963, as a 'man of determination', he sought to break the vicious circle of poverty, not only in a generalized way by publishing his work, but also by throwing himself into the defence of specific oppressed and marginalized groups: West Indian workers at the outset, in *Labour in the West Indies* (1939); Afro-Caribbean people in Moss Side, Manchester, between 1951 and 1955; Ghanaians, with an increasing emphasis on the neglected majority outside Accra, from 1952 to 1958; and West Indians once again at the climax of his activism between 1959 and 1963. In all of this advocacy work, the mass education principle is clearly observable, and often also, where his remit is broad, the selective industrialization and agricultural productivity principles. Few things in Lewis's life are more moving than his tireless attempts in 1960–2 to escape from his vice-chancellor's chair and broaden the base of West Indian agriculture – for example, by appealing to Israel to send over specialists to provide expertise in dryland citrus cultivation.[3] At that time he still saw the main purpose of his work as being to engage directly in the development process, in particular through mass education.

Not for much longer, however. Much of Lewis's advocacy work, as we related in Chapters 3, 6 and 7, did not go well, and after 1962–3 he tired of taking up arms against a sea of troubles. It is not correct, as we argued in Chapter 8, to see Lewis's Princeton years, from 1963 onwards, as purely a retreat into an ivory tower, and he continued to engage with many of his publics – Ghana in the Aggrey-Fraser-Guggisberg lectures of 1968, discriminated-against black people on the Princeton campus in 1969, and more broadly in his work for Rockefeller in the early 1980s, and the West Indies in response to numerous isolated appeals. But after 1963, when he was still only 48, his behaviour changed in many ways. He ceased to wander around the world in search of new discoveries and challenges; he stopped trying to 'get people to do what they do not want to do'; he gave up even being proactive in economic policy-making. The big development controversies of the 1970s and 1980s, on inequality, pro-poor development, state versus market, and even the revival of growth theory in empirical form, passed him by. Rather, he becomes proactive in global economic history, of which he had been one of the initiators in the shape of *Economic Survey, 1919–1939* (1949a), which he had mentioned to the Director of LSE as wanting to focus on as early as 1946,[4] which he had returned to at times in his Manchester years, but from which he had then become deflected repeatedly in the interests of 'making a difference'. Now tired of all that, he could begin to take a run at this issue. Beginning from a wish to understand the historical reasons why different tropical countries, after the boom of the last quarter of the nineteenth century, had achieved so differently, Lewis found himself, in the sequence of books that climaxed with *Growth and Fluctuations* in 1978 (Lewis, 1978a), unable to produce a soundbite that explained this, and in particular exasperated his more radical constituencies by refusing to say that it was the nature of colonial policies that made the difference. Inasmuch as there was a clear message about what did make the difference, it related to two things, intimately related to Lewis's early experience: the quality of institutions; and the diffusion of knowledge. We are back with Lewis's old and trusted friend, mass education.

We make the claim here that there are three areas in particular in which Lewis deserves a permanent place in the history of economic development: the explanation of growth processes; the formulation of economic development strategies; and the implementation of economic strategies which 'change the world'.

The explanation of growth processes

The idea that missing or malfunctioning factor markets are a major cause of underdevelopment is a key building block, some might say the most important one, in present-day development economics. It continues to stimulate controversy some 70 years on – for example, between Jeffrey Sachs (2005) who argues that the way to overcome those missing markets is to increase the volume of overseas aid, and William Easterly (2006), who argues that the way forward is to encourage the efforts of innovators in the private and non-governmental organization (NGO) sectors. Whether people are still caught, because of these missing markets, in a poverty trap of poor health, low productivity and low income – a question that Lewis originated in his *Labour in the West Indies* paper of 1939 – has recently been reinvestigated by the MIT economists Abhijit Banerjee and Esther Duflo (2011), one of whose five key lessons is: 'There are good reasons that some markets are missing for the poor, or that the poor face unfavourable prices in them.'[5] Banerjee and Duflo then show that the reasons relate not only to the availability of medicines but on the information available to sufferers, and consequently their response to the subsidies and other incentives that are given to assist them to buy medicines (Banerjee and Duflo 2011, esp. ch. 3). But the idea that development required action which sometimes overrode the signals of the market originated with Lewis, and specifically with Lewis's and Durbin's *Colonial Economic Development* 1944 paper, which Lewis then developed into the ground-breaking proposition that

> outside the study and the classroom, wages bear no relation to marginal productivity. Prices are therefore a false guide to the real economic situation, and policy must be in defiance of prices if the true economic situation is to be met. Industries ought to be established even though their costs of production may greatly exceed the money costs of imports.[6]

... and thence to the idea that, if labour was overpriced, investment, the key to growth, would be insufficient in labour-surplus economies if simply left to the market to determine. Lewis's idea that the quality of microeconomic policy determines growth performance is central to all modern analysis of growth, even though he has not been given proper credit for it in most of the growth literature.[7] Much of what is known about development now is owed to Lewis's writings of 60 or more years ago.[8]

The formulation of economic development strategies

As the above quotation implies, the application of static comparative-advantage principles will discourage low-income, natural-resource-dependent economies from diversifying into industrialization. Lewis had been aware instinctively of the constraint this imposed on the West Indian islands since his *Labour in the West Indies* of 1939, and in the second part of 'Unlimited Supplies of Labour' (1954) he developed the idea into a formal statement of the case for infant-industry protection. This was at the time, and remains, a high water-mark, charting an admirable middle way between the disasters caused by unselective import-substituting industrialization on the one hand (to which Nkrumah, among other Lewis advisees, fell victim) and the disasters caused by unthinking laissez-faire on the other – to which the World Bank in its turn fell victim in the 1980s and 1990s in its recommendations for Africa (World Bank, 1981, 1989, 1994), insisting on 'getting the prices right' (that is, removing all controls) in Africa,[9] even though Lewis had shown, in the quotation above, that some of the prices were wrong all the time, and that no country had made the transition to being an exporter of manufactures without judicious state intervention. Eventually, in the mid-2000s, the World Bank, or at least its chief economist (Lin, 2009, 2011; Lin and Monga, 2011) has acknowledged the importance of state-interventionist strategies, especially in the Far East, for achieving structural change in low-income economies, though these 'new Bank' proposals put more emphasis on intervention through export subsidy and tax incentives, and hesitate to offer the unfashionable word 'protectionism'. That, however, was just window-dressing: it would be right to acknowledge the influence of Lewis's ground-breaking analysis of 1954, as well as the influence of more recent Far Eastern experience, in establishing the importance of transformative trade-and-investment strategies for low-income countries.

The implementation of ideas which 'change the world'

Lewis's significance is not, we maintain, defined just by his writings, but also by his actions. More than most development economists, Lewis got into the field and for eighteen crucial years – 1944 to 1962 – had the desire and the ability to convert his ideas about the policies and institutions required for equitable development into practical recommendations for the design and reform of those institutions. The mass education campaigns of the Colonial Office in 1948–9, the South Hulme and Moss Side evening centres of 1953 onwards, even Lewis's initiatives to extend the reach and cut the cost of the University of the West Indies in 1960 and 1961 via night schools: all these are innovative actions of Lewis's in the field of development practice, rather than the development theory for which he is best known. That Lewis during these years did not retreat into his ivory tower but was willing to put his own ideas into practice in the interests of the poor populations of developing countries, in spite of the risks and frustrations involved, is one of his most admirable, even quixotic, features. However, as we saw in Chapter 6, Lewis rather often came unstuck in the course of making the traverse from theory to practice, and after 1963 the desire and even the energy to tilt at windmills desert him.

At this point, Lewis's achievements intersect fascinatingly with his personal and social life. Personal relationships were very important to Lewis, but he was from the beginning an independent and a non-conformist, and, as we have seen, from an early age not the most trusting or diplomatic of people. His writings, with three exceptions from among over a hundred works,[10] are all sole-authored, and when he found himself a member of a team, as with the UN mission on *Measures for the Economic Development of Underdeveloped Countries* in 1950, he quickly took over the leadership. When the barriers did come down, it was typically in relation to people of a different status from him – such as, at the beginning, Arnold Plant, who was something of a father figure to him, and towards the end, Gersovitz, to whom he was a bit of a father figure himself.[11] He was a black man who revered women (beginning with his mother), but few of his close and enduring friendships outside his family were with black people[12] or women (Hilda Baumol being an important exception). With some women who were admiring and well-disposed toward him – Rita Hinden being a notable case – he could be very savage. As a West Indian who tried to stay aloof from, and then was dragged into, the quicksand of West Indian politics, his relationships with his fellow West Indians were often edgy, and sometimes went beyond edginess into malice, even gratuitous malice, as in the case of Grantley Adams, cited in Chapter 7, when it was Lewis who had won the argument and who could therefore afford to be generous. In Lewis's defence, it can be said that the malice was almost always directed at influential people who could look after themselves, such as Adams, Williams, M. G. Smith and Margery Perham, whereas he supported the weak and needy with many acts of kindness that he took great trouble to keep private.

In only three cases, so far as is known, did he form a close friendship with a person of his own age. The first, cruelly interrupted after only a few years, was with Evan Durbin; the second was with Max Gluckman and his wife Mary; and the third and longest-lasting was with Baumol and his wife Hilda. Lewis's alliance with Durbin was a major reason why his main practical achievement – his conversion of Creech Jones' mass education ideas into a Colonial Office-wide development programme – came into being in 1948–9. His friendship with the Gluckman family was also instrumental in developing the idea of the South Hulme evening centre into concrete form in 1953. And while the reasons for his frequent unhappy experiences as a practitioner are complex, as we saw in Chapters 6 and 7, a part of Lewis's inability to break through into influencing policy, from the CDC in 1953 to Nkrumah's Ghana in 1958 to the Agony of the Eight in 1962–3, was often simple intellectual isolation – the absence of a trusted friend to support him in mediating with the power-brokers, in making the hazardous transition from ideas to practice.

Had he so chosen, Lewis might have learnt from this experience that he needed to put more effort into networking and into making relationships that might protect him against upset. In fact, he did the opposite, and after 1963 he explored less, travelled less, and in his Princeton period retreated increasingly into a tight circle of family and known and trusted friends – with only a few individuals allowed to break through the barrier, typically young people who presented no threat to him, such as Gersovitz and Deaton. Venturing less into the wider world, he found that the wider world came less often to him, and asked him less often to solve its problems, and even the splendid festivities that marked the award of the Nobel Prize were soon over. At this time, the beginning of the 1980s, he professed, as we have seen, a desire to retire from the world and read nineteenth-century novels, but his actions belied his words. He could see, and wanted to resist, the risk of being caught up in one of the 'vicious circles' he had done so much to warn against, and every spring from 1981 to 1988, by which time he was 73, he offered himself to the Princeton faculty, and was gladly taken on,[13] as an occasional part-time lecturer.

Towards the end of his life, Lewis increasingly professed the Tolstoyan belief that enlightenment should be learnt not from the powerful and the highly educated, but from the humble, and specifically that the answers to big problems, in development as elsewhere, should not be sought mainly from intellectuals in universities, but rather from those who possessed wisdom, rather than intelligence – the gift of relating to the mass of people and in particular the downtrodden and the oppressed. Writing just after Lewis's death, *The Guardian* columnist,

W. J. Weatherby, who had interviewed him many times for the paper, emphasized how much Lewis had learnt from non-intellectuals, including in particular one of the Catholic priests with whom he had worked in Moss Side in the 1950s,[14] probably Brother Bernard of Community House. His appreciation concluded, 'Like those in Manchester, his American students found that his economics courses put more emphasis on ideas than mere statistics and he liked to relate everything to human beings. "Was that the lesson you learned that time in Moss Side?" I asked him at our last meeting [after he had retired from Princeton]. "It helped me to get things straight," he said. "The effects of independence at home completed the lesson. I try to pass it on to my students – that economics concerns life more than numbers."'[15]

Notes

Preface and Acknowledgements

1. R. Skidelsky, 'Introduction', *John Maynard Keynes, Vol. 3: Fighting for Britain 1937–1946* (Macmillan Papermac, 2000), p. xxii.

1 The Caribbean in Turmoil: Prologue to a Biography

1. Lewis Archive, Princeton, Box 1/10; 'Autobiographical Account' by Sir Arthur Lewis, prepared for Nobel Prize Committee, December 1979, p. 4.
2. Lewis (1939), p. 5. In the 1920s, the white population in St Lucia and on average across the islands, was relatively low, at about 3 per cent of the population. The proportion was higher than this on islands completely dominated by sugar cultivation, such as Barbados.
3. Lewis (1939), p. 7. On the significance of colour gradations in the social and power structures of the West Indies, see 'The Light and the Dark', ch.4 in James (1963) and Tignor (2005) notes: 'In place of the rigid two-tiered racial system, there had appeared a coloured middle class ... usually light skinned, well educated, professional and urban ... To this generation, Lewis ... belonged' (p.11).
4. Lewis (1939), p. 5.
5. Lewis (1939), p. 9.
6. The total value of exports from St Lucia fell from £421,000 (£8.10 per capita) to £207,000 (£3.91) between 1920 and 1925, and to £143,000 (£2.65) by 1930 (Armitage-Smith, 1931, p. 62).
7. These data derive from Sir Sydney Armitage-Smith's financial mission to the Leeward Islands and St Lucia in the depths of the depression in 1931 – undertaken while Lewis was serving time in the Agricultural Department office waiting to sit his scholarship exam. Sir Sydney reported (Armitage-Smith, 1931, p. 72) that 'there are only two trained teachers, the rest being ex-pupil teachers who have received a certificate from the Governor in Council which represents merely a licence to teach, these certificates being graded first, second or third class according to the marks earned in an examination (80%, 60% or 33%.)'. The Lewises were certificated teachers in the primary school system. They were staunch Anglicans. The two trained secondary school teachers in St Lucia were at the Roman Catholic St Mary's College in Castries. Recruitment for these posts was normally via a London-based teacher-training college. One post was for a headmaster and one for a science teacher, who by the 1930s had in addition been given responsibility for agricultural extension, 'imparting agricultural instruction and following up the planting material supplied by the Government Nurseries' (Armitage-Smith, 1931, p. 106). Armitage-Smith added: 'the best hope for the financial salvation of St Lucia lies in the acceleration of this planting' (Armitage-Smith, 1931, p. 107).

8. The mission to the Eastern Caribbean islands led by Sir Sydney Armitage-Smith (Armitage-Smith, 1931, p. 71) recorded that 'St Lucia is the [Caribbean] island where the English language is least widely spoken and understood' and that 'the educational standard of the Primary Schools is lower in St Lucia than in any of the other islands which I was instructed to visit'.

9. Lewis Archives, Princeton, Box 1/10: 'Autobiographical Account' by Sir Arthur Lewis, p. 1.

10. Marcus Garvey (1867–1940) was a Jamaican publisher, entrepreneur and orator, and an enthusiastic proponent of the interests of black peoples, both in the West Indies and globally. In this cause he founded, in 1914, the Universal Negro Improvement Association. He established a Negro Factories Corporation with the intention that black entrepreneurs should be able to manufacture every marketable commodity in the West Indies, the United States and Africa, and attempted to develop Liberia as a permanent home for black people in Africa.

11. W. Arthur Lewis, 'The Economic Status of Women', Commencement address, Rosary College, Illinois, May 1970. (Lewis Papers, Princeton, Box 39/8, p. 1.)

12. Lalljie (1997) page 31.

13. Lewis engaged in 1952 in a dialogue with the Manchester industrialist Lord Simon of Wythenshawe about the quality of BBC music broadcasting; see Chapter 5.

14. Lewis described this adolescent part of his life as follows:
    '[From the age of eleven onwards] I was always in the company of boys two or three years older than myself. They flexed their muscles, but I had nothing to show. They played cricket in the first eleven, whereas I was in the fourth eleven. I acquired an acute inferiority complex with regard to my physique. I also learned that your acceptance into the group is not a matter of academic performance only: you must meet their criteria as well as your own.' (Lewis Archive, Princeton, Box 5/1: Autobiographical Account, reprinted in Breit and Spencer (1986).

15. Conversation with Andrew Downes (Professor of Economics, UWI), Manchester, 6 July 2004.

16. The prices of most of the primary exports of the West Indies, with the exception of bananas, were approximately halved between 1921 and 1939 (Moyne, 1945).

17. The writer Austin Clarke was brought up in Bridgetown, Barbados. Though a talented boy who passed the highly competitive examination for Combermere College in Barbados, he did not go on to take up an overseas scholarship. His mother, while ambitious for her son, lacked the status and education of Ida Lewis. She was a sugar cane worker.

18. Lewis Archive, Princeton, Box 1/10: 'Autobiographical Account' by Sir Arthur Lewis, prepared for Nobel Prize Committee, December 1979, p. 2.

19. When invited in 1984 by William Darity, a black economist of some distinction at the University of Tulsa, to collaborate with him in writing his (Lewis's) intellectual biography, Lewis replied baldly, 'I am not willing to do so', Lewis Archive, Princeton, Box 4/5: Lewis to Darity, 1 November 1984.

2   'Marvellous intellectual feasts': The LSE Years, 1933–48

* The authors are grateful to reproduce the paper 'Marvellous Intellectual Feasts: Arthur Lewis at the London School of Economics 1933–48', *History of Political Economy*, vol.45, issue 2, pp. 187–221. Copyright 2013, Duke University Press. Reproduced by permission of Duke University Press.
1. Tignor (2005), p. 35.
2. Autobiographical Account in Breit and Spencer (1986).
3. Heinz Arndt had arrived at the LSE as a postgraduate student via Lincoln College, Oxford. His father, Fritz Arndt, was a prominent academic dismissed from the University of Breslau in 1933. The family had been helped to escape from Nazi Germany in the early 1930s through the efforts of the Academic Assistance Council founded by William Beveridge in 1933. The Council was instrumental in Fritz Arndt's appointment to the Department of Organic Chemistry at Oxford. In 1948, when Lewis had left the LSE for Manchester, the young Heinz Arndt drew on their LSE friendship for advice regarding his own application for a Readership in international trade that was being advertised at the University of Manchester. Lewis encouraged Arndt to apply but warned that his application was likely to encounter problems because he did not have the support of Professors John Jewkes and John Hicks, both of whom had recently vacated Chairs at Manchester. The episode is related in the biography of Arndt by Coleman *et al.* (2007).
4. Lewis, Autobiographical Account in Breit and Spencer (1986) p. 2.
5. Ronald Coase had also entered the LSE (in 1929) to study for the B.Com. degree. In his Nobel speech (1991) he related how, in 1931, he 'had a great stroke of luck. Arnold Plant was appointed Professor of Commerce ... He was a wonderful teacher. I began to attend his seminar ... It was a revelation.'
6. Information on the career of Arnold Plant is from Ronald Coase, 'Professor Arnold Plant: His Ideas and Influence" in M. A. Anderson (ed.), *The Unfinished Agenda: Essays in Honour of Arthur Seldon* (London: Institute of Economic Affairs,1986).
7. From Plant (1974). The book was given a favourable review by Ronald Coase (1977).
8. Plant (1965).
9. Lewis had a lifelong attachment to the nineteenth century, and in 1951 wrote an article in *The Manchester Guardian* to explain how much pleasanter the mid-nineteenth century, with its spirit of enterprise, its low unemployment and its low inflation, was than the mid-twentieth century. Much later, while on the verge of retiring from Princeton and already declining invitations to write books and papers, he said that the main thing he wanted to do in his retirement was to read nineteenth-century novels (see Chapter 8).
10. Mill (1994[1847]), p. 16. The quotation, relevant to Lewis's own writings on social democracy and socialism, continues: 'these (social institutions and policies) being supposed, the question of Socialism is not, as generally stated by Socialists, a question of flying to the sole refuge against the evils which now bear down humanity; but a mere question of comparative advantages, which futurity must determine'.
11. The story of the CSRRC is told in Mills (2002).
12. Lewis, Autobiographical Account in Breit and Spencer (1986), p. 3.

13. Sociology was a discipline favoured by women students at the LSE. During the Cambridge years the sociology department grew rapidly. Judith Hart, later Minister of Overseas Development in the Wilson government, was an LSE sociology undergraduate at Cambridge and Secretary of the Cambridge University Labour Club during the LSE wartime evacuation.
14. Interviewed in Montreal by telephone, October 2006.
15. The female students from Bedford College were formally assigned to Newnham but they seem to have had a particularly bleak time, being 'offered to Cambridge householders as an alternative to evacuated school children and their mothers'; Cambridge University Archives, Accommodation London Colleges, 1940.
16. LSE Archives: Letter to Lewis from Hailey at the Colonial Office, September 1941.
17. LSE Archives: Letter from Carr-Saunders to Hailey, October 1941.
18. LSE Archives: Letter from Hailey to Lewis, October 1941.
19. Letter from Paul Cadbury to Carr-Saunders, December 1941. Lewis travelled to Birmingham on a number of occasions in connection with research on the Cadbury cocoa plantations.
20. Memo from Lewis to Carr-Saunders, November 1941. Carr-Saunders replied fairly brusquely that 3 guineas could be charged to the project. The School appears to have had great difficulty in getting research expenses out of the Colonial Office.
21. Tignor (2005, p. 36). A brief quotation can convey the flavour of Lewis's review: 'The book is not merely smug and self-satisfied: it reeks of that self-conceit which typifies the colonial Englishman and which is doing more than anything else to poison the relations between the races.'
22. LSE Archives: Letter from Richenda Scott to Carr-Saunders, October 1941.
23. Lewis (1942b), pp.15–16.
24. Ibid., p. 15.
25. The three papers are Lewis (1941); ; (1942); and (1946).
26. Dr McShine was an Island Scholar from Trinidad, educated there at the prestigious Queen's Royal College. In the Preface, Lewis also acknowledges help from two head teachers in the south of England, and Arnold Plant and Lionel Robbins, 'who have taught me all the economics I know'.
27. The full anecdote is worth repeating. It goes: 'I dropped industrial economics in 1945 to teach another subject not of my own choosing, namely a survey of the world economy between the world wars. This came about in the following way. The Acting Chairman of the Economics Department in 1945 was Friedrich Hayek. One day he said to me: 'We fill our students up with trade cycle theory and explanations of the Great Depression, but the entering class was born in 1927, cannot remember the depression, and has no idea what we are talking about. Why don't you give a course of lectures on what happened between the wars?' 'The answer to your question,' I said, 'is very easy. It is that I myself have no idea what happened between the wars.' 'Well,' said Hayek, 'the best way to learn a subject is to teach it.' From 'Autobiographical Account', in Breit and Spencer (1986), p. 6.
28. Lewis (1949a), p. 9.
29. Harold Wilson drew on his experiences as a temporary civil servant to produce a book *New Deal for Coal*, which, according to his biographer Ben

Pimlott, 'had the character of a Fabian blueprint'. It was published on the day of the 1945 election. In it, Wilson rejected the populist workers' control approach to nationalization, in favour of control by 'men chosen for their ability and technical competence'. Socialism was equated with modernization. Nationalization was recommended not for doctrinal reasons but on the grounds of efficiency' (Pimlott, 1992, p. 88).

30. The quote is from an article written by the celebrated owner/editor, C. P. Scott, to mark the centenary in 1921 of *The Manchester Guardian*. The quote, which goes on to say 'the voice of opponents no less than that of friends has a right to be heard' has often been taken as a statement of the values of a free press.

31. Lewis (1944). Reprinted in Emmanuel (1994).

32. Minutes of the Colonial Development course, University of Cambridge.

3   The Colonial Office and the Genesis of Development Economics

1. Lewis wrote an obituary when Padmore died in London in 1959. Padmore had come to London that year for medical treatment. Like Lewis, he had briefly been an adviser to Nkrumah in post-independence Ghana.

2. The Fabian Colonial Bureau's main functions were to provide an information service and a source of policy ideas about the British colonies, and in addition to make contact with political activists and opinion-formers within the Colonies. A short account of the origins of the Fabian Colonial Bureau is provided at Rhodes House, Oxford: Fabian Colonial Bureau archive, List 1, Introduction to the Collection.

3. See Mine (2004).

4. Hinden (1941) (also at Rhodes House, Oxford: 600.14 r.13). For a discussion of Hinden's pioneering work in setting up the Bureau, see Rhodes House, Oxford: Mss.Brit.Emp.s.365, Papers of the Fabian Colonial Bureau, catalogue, list 1, 'Introduction to the Collection'.

5. Rhodes House, Oxford, Fabian Colonial Bureau papers: FCB 5/6, Lewis to Rita Hinden, 15 December 1948.

6. The evidence we have (which is indirect) suggests that Lewis failed to appreciate properly Hinden's networking skills, her enthusiasm and most notably her knowledge of Africa, and typecast her as a naïve chatterbox. See the later (1957) exchange between Lewis and Hinden, in Chapter 6, p. 161, notes 33–4.

7. Lewis (1939), p. 9.

8. Ibid., p. 33.

9. Moyne (1945), p. 426.

10. Lewis Papers, Princeton, Box 4/5: 'Puerto Rican Notebook by W. Arthur Lewis' appended to correspondence between Lewis and Charles Davey, Assistant Editor of *The Observer*, 7 June 1940, p. 1.

11. Lewis's written evidence to the Moyne Commission is contained in the National Archives, Kew: CO 318/445/47, 29 May 1940.

12. The concept of mass education was used over the years by Creech Jones, the Labour Party and the Colonial Office in several different ways. Sometimes it was used to mean adult education; sometimes non-formal education; sometimes 'applied' education, such as agricultural extension; and sometimes, as

in this 1943 report and often in Colonial Office parlance, it is used to refer to all education, with an emphasis on extending it to the illiterate.

13. Rhodes House, Oxford, Fabian Colonial Bureau archives: FCB 68/1, Minutes of the 94th Meeting of the Advisory Committee on Education in the Colonies, 18 May 1939.

14. Rhodes House, Oxford, Mss. Brit.Emp.s.365: Fabian Colonial Bureau Papers, Box 46/1, folio 10.

15. UK Colonial Office (1943). Rhodes House, Oxford: Creech Jones Papers (Mss. Afr. s.332).

16. Ibid., p. 5.

17. See, for example, Nafziger and Auvinen (2002) and Collier and Hoeffler (2004).

18. UK Colonial Office (1943), p. 26, para. 61.

19. Ibid., Annex, paras 8 (on Indonesian Desa system) and 167–179.

20. Ibid., p. 10, para 16.

21. The Fabian Colonial Bureau advisory committee was a think tank of many talents: others elected to the committee at that time included the biologist Sir Julian Huxley; the Oxford political science academic Margery Perham; and Leonard Woolf, the socialist political editor and husband of the writer Virginia Woolf, with Creech Jones acting as chairman. Rhodes House, Oxford: Mss. Brit. Emp. s.365, Papers of the Fabian Colonial Bureau, catalogue, list 1, 'Introduction to the Collection'.

22. Because of having no developing-country experience, he was nervous about what he might be able to contribute to the CEAC. To the Secretary of State, on accepting the appointment, he expressed the fear that 'I shall not be able to contribute anything of any great value to the discussions of the Committee'. National Archives, Kew: CO 852/510/29, Durbin to Stanley, 18 October 1943.

23. See Skidelsky (1992), pp. 455, 603, which contains an explicit discussion of Durbin's take on Keynes, and the account of the evolution of democratic socialism in the 1930s by Durbin's daughter Elizabeth (Elizabeth Durbin, 1985). Lewis's remark about the savings rate is in Lewis (1955), pp. 225–6.

24. Lewis (1955), pp. 225–6 .

25. Meade (1950), pp. 117–22.

26. Craig (1977). Susan Craig advises that 'Lewis must not be seen simply as a lone visionary, a consultant-at-large. He was, in fact, the leading ideologue of his class and of imperialism, at the crucial period in the formation of the modern Caribbean', p.77.

27. The Colonial Office dealt with most, but not all, of the poor developing countries in the British colonial empire, most of them in Africa, southeast Asia and the West Indies. However, it did not deal with India and Pakistan – at that time, four years short of full independence – which came under a separate India Office.

28. These 'unofficial' members of the Committee varied greatly in their commitment and expertise. Some were complete dinosaurs, sceptical of the entire notion that development was a good idea – notoriously Sir John Hay, who at Lewis's last meeting complained that 'there was no indication in the memorandum[the Durbin–Lewis Memorandum on colonial economic development] of what might be the views of the people on whom this progress was to be imposed. There were some people within our protectorates

whose conception of progress differed fundamentally from ours and who thought they were wiser than we. It might be that many of the ideas in the memorandum were not acceptable to the people we were so anxious to help and they might think that all this material progress was not for their welfare'. National Archives, Kew: CO 990/1, Minutes of the eighth meeting of the Colonial Economic Advisory Committee, 31 October 1944.

29. Caine's research was principally on international commodity price fluctuations and the possibility of controlling them by means of stabilization arrangements such as buffer stocks – an issue which had caused great distress to developing countries during the inter-war depression, and had already been a research priority for several years in the applied economics of development. Clauson's was on international monetary arrangements, and specifically on colonial currencies. Noel Lee, a former professor of commerce on secondment to the Colonial Office, reported on the latter paper to Clauson: 'It gives me precisely the accurate and lucid account that I sorely needed and I am most grateful. I am not surprised that Keynes leaped at it for the Journal [*Economic Journal*]'. National Archives, Kew: CO 852/587/4, Noel Lee to Gerald Clauson, 1 July 1944.

30. The words 'really competent' are those of Sydney Caine, who wanted, but of course did not get, an insider for the job of Secretary: 'Either we should get a good young economist with some experience of administration from one of the other Departments, or we should put on to the job a really good principal of our own.' National Archives, Kew: CO 852/510/29, Sydney Caine to Sir George Gater, 23 April 1943.

31. In December 1939, the Director of the LSE, A. M. Carr-Saunders, had written to the Secretary:
I discussed with Mr Lewis his work at the Ministry of Information. I said (a) that two full days away from academic work in a week must react disadvantageously upon his teaching and research; (b) that if continued it would be necessary to give him leave of absence for those days and to adjust financial arrangements accordingly. I suggested that the best course would be for him to reduce his work to one day, and I said that if he did so, what he earned for the day could be retained by him. The Secretary retaliated, 'He has not fulfilled this condition for November; ought he not therefore to pay the whole of his earnings to the School for that month?' The Director answered: 'The past can be allowed to bury itself. It constitutes no precedent.' London School of Economics Archives: Lewis staff file, Notes by Director to and from Secretary, LSE, 5 December 1939.

32. This debate on the role of the CEAC is documented in Tignor (2005), pp. 58–9.

33. In the TV programme *Yes Minister*, popular with viewers in Britain and elsewhere in the 1980s and 1990s, Sir Humphrey Appleby is the Permanent Secretary (chief civil servant) whose duty is, of course, to execute the wishes of his minister. Even if his own views are in conflict with his minister's (as was the case between Sydney Caine and Oliver Stanley in 1943) he therefore, in response to any instruction from the minister, replies 'Yes, Minister'. This does not, of course, preclude Sir Humphrey from working over the long term to get his own way by other means.

34. National Archives, Kew: CO 990/2, *Report on Agricultural Production* by Sir Alan Pim.

35. National Archives, Kew: CO 990/2, *Development Problems in West Africa*: report by (Prof.) Noel Hall. (Professor Hall was a former professor of commerce seconded to the Colonial Office. He objected to his professorial title being used on CEAC documents, claiming that he had disposed of it 'in the dim ages of long ago' (ibid.)).

36. National Archives, Kew: CO 852/587/8, CEAC Report on Colonial Economic Research published September 1946.

37. Rosenstein-Rodan (1943); reprinted in Agarwala and Singh (1963), ch. 11. Before moving to the LSE, Durbin had worked alongside Rosenstein-Rodan at UCL and both of them 'felt much more at home in the Wednesday seminar run by Gaitskell and Rosenstein-Rodan. Rosenstein-Rodan recalls that their "pink" seminar was held in direct and conscious contrast to the activities in the "Grand Seminar" at the LSE. The atmosphere was pro-planning and Marxists and other left-wingers such as [Michal] Kalecki were invited to speak', Elizabeth Durbin (1985, p.108).

38. P. Rosenstein-Rodan (1985).

39. LSE Archives: Lewis personal file: Lewis to Miss Evans, 20 March 1944. Miss Evans was the school secretary. Lewis wrote from Woolwich Memorial Hospital to update her on his medical problems.

40. National Archives, Kew: CO 990/2, Colonial Economic Advisory Council, CEAC (Agenda) (44) 7, 23 June 1944, Memorandum on 'Colonial Economic Development' by W. A. Lewis in consultation with E. F. M. Durbin, para. 3.

41. National Archives, Kew: CO 990/2 , Colonial Economic Advisory Council, CEAC (Agenda) (44) 7, 23 June 1944, Memorandum 'Colonial Economic Development' by W. A. Lewis in consultation with E. F. M. Durbin, para. 27.

42. Lewis with Durbin (1944), p. 4, para. 13.

43. National Archives, Kew: CO 990/2, Colonial Economic Advisory Council, CEAC (Agenda) (44) 7, 23 June 1944, Memorandum on 'Colonial Economic Development' by W. A. Lewis with E. F. M. Durbin, para. 14. Emphasis in original.

44. National Archives, Kew: CO 990/2, Colonial Economic Advisory Council, CEAC (Agenda) (44) 7, 23 June 1944, Memorandum on 'Colonial Economic Development' by W. A. Lewis with E. F. M. Durbin, para. 11.

45. Education, being dealt with by a separate Colonial Office committee, was not formally referred to the CEAC, but through the Fabian Society, as well as through his previous experience of the Colonial Office, Lewis knew what was in the wind.

46. National Archives, Kew: CO 990/2, Colonial Economic Advisory Council, CEAC (Agenda) (44) 7, 23 June 1944, memorandum on 'Colonial Economic Development' by W. A. Lewis with E. F. M. Durbin, para. 25.

47. Ibid.

48. Though it was agreed, under Creech Jones' impetus, on the need to make mass education a key policy priority, the Labour Party was more divided on other development issues. One indication of its approach to colonial policy is given by the Labour Party's document 'Colonial Economic Policy During the War' (Labour Party, 1941). The author(s) are not listed but almost certainly Rita Hinden is one of them. The emphasis of the document is on commodity price stabilization and labour-intensive public works, but also on the 'provision of advisers ... to help in the founding of new enterprises'.

Only the last of these is perceptible as an influence on the Lewis–Durbin paper. Oddly, mass education is not mentioned.

49. Noel Hall's report, 'Post-War Economic Readjustment' (1944), based on his six-month visit to West Africa in the first half of 1944, ranges across the whole field of development policy, and is the only CEAC document apart from the Lewis/Durbin memorandum, discussed below, to attempt to do so. Towards the end he writes:

> The productive potential of the West African, e.g. in a variety of crafts in the armed services, is much higher than has commonly been sup- posed ... It has shown that we ought to have a positive policy for indus- trialization ... I should be prepared to recommend that we should be prepared to make largely [the word 'purely' has been crossed out here in favour of 'largely'] arbitrary assumptions about the fields in which local industry may expect to be successful, and, for a period of years, try direct action to carry out experiments in those selected fields.

The part of this passage from 'I should be prepared' to the end has been sidelined by Lewis, who has written in pencil in the margin: 'Hurrah: properly planned development is essential, in contradistinction to the pro- posals of the Industry sub-committee' (W. A. Lewis).
50. See passage keyed by Note 28 above.
51. National Archives, Kew: CO 990/2, Colonial Economic Advisory Council, CEAC (Agenda) (44) 7, 23 June 1944, memorandum on 'Colonial Economic Development' by W. A. Lewis with E. F. M. Durbin, para. 10.
52. Ibid., para. 3.
53. The financial implications of the Lewis–Durbin proposal are, as the authors concede, glossed over rather than fully analysed, even while acknowledg- ing that 'the policy here outlined will cost a lot of money'. It is, however, acknowledged that the amount of money required might prove to be more than was available from Britain's Colonial Development and Welfare Fund. In such a case, 'it will therefore be necessary to seek assistance from other sources: from the proposed international investment authority for the development of backward countries, if it materialises, or if not, from the United States of America'. Presumably the 'proposed international investment authority for the development of backward countries' refers to the (at that time still embryonic) World Bank: the Lewis–Durbin paper was written at the same time as the Bretton Woods conference, and the World Bank was not ratified until February 1946.
54. National Archives, Kew: CO 990/2, Colonial Economic Advisory Council, CEAC (44) 38, Memorandum on Colonial Economic Development by the Agenda sub-committee to Secretary of State, 14 September 1944.
55. For the replies, see National Archives, Kew: CO 990/1: Answers to Memorandum from the Economic Advisory Committee CEAC (44) 46, appended to Minutes of the ninth meeting of the Committee, 19 December 1944.
56. Tignor (2005), p. 65.
57. National Archives, Kew: CO/852/586/7: Letter from Durbin and reply from Oliver Stanley.
58. Lewis Archive, Princeton, Box 26/11: Note by Lewis to file, 30 November 1944, para. 11.
59. National Archives, Kew: CO/852/586/9, Memorandum from Sydney Caine to Sir George Gater, December 1944.

60. The Economic Division of the Colonial Office was formed in 1942. Initially it did not discuss 'economic development'. Its main concern was the imperial preference system and international commodity agreements. The operations of the Economic Division are described in Lee and Petter (1982).
61. National Archives, Kew: CO/588/2, August 1943, Memorandum from Sydney Caine.
62. Lewis's letter to Miss Evans in the LSE Personnel Department (LSE Archives, Lewis Staff File) of 20 March 1944 concludes that, following his sick leave, 'I hope to be on duty fresh as a daisy when term begins.' If 'when term begins' meant anything other than autumn (September/October) 1944, Lewis would surely have said so.
63. 'I feel that most of my time here is wasted', LSE Archives: Lewis Staff File, Lewis to Carr-Saunders, 31 December 1944.
64. National Archives, Kew: CO/58610, Actions taken on Reports submitted before the end of 1944.
65. The Foreign Secretary Discussed the role of colonial development and welfare in foreign policy in the article 'United Europe as Organism to Preserve Peace', *The Times*, 26 January 1949, Rhodes House, Oxford: MSS. Brit. Emp. s.332, Creech Jones Papers, ACJ 44/1, folio 61.
66. CO/991/1, First Minutes of the Colonial Economic and Development Council, October 1946.
67. Phyllis Deane describes in her memoir how the shortage of academics because of military conscription had brought her as a young graduate to London from Glasgow University. She had been recommended for the NIESR post in London as an ex-pupil of Alec Cairncross, who was then serving as economic adviser in the Cabinet Office. Phyllis Deane documented her experiences in a note: 'The NIESR: Memoirs of a Survivor' (1959).
68. See, in particular, Hinden *et al.* (1942).
69. As Parliamentary Secretary to the Chancellor, Hugh Dalton, from 1945 to 1947, and then as Parliamentary Secretary, Ministry of Works, from 1947 until his untimely death in September 1948.
70. In Rhodes House, Oxford: Mss. Brit. Emp. s.332: Arthur Creech Jones papers, Box 44/4 (Colonial Development and Welfare II), file 4, 'Price policy', Creech Jones discusses in the light of Lewis's views in *Overhead Costs* how colonial corporations such as the Colonial Development Corporation (CDC) and Overseas Food Corporation (OFC) should charge for their services, and in particular how they should allow for external costs and benefits of such interventions.
71. Not only of a left-wing disposition – Sydney Caine used the phrase repeatedly in his papers for the CEAC.
72. 'The Ten Year Plans put forward by nearly all the colonial governments constitute a waste of public money'. National Archives, Kew: CO 852/941/3, Colonial Economic and Development Council, Principles of Economic Planning: Memorandum by Professor Lewis, CEDC (48) 1, 11 April 1948, p. 5.
73. Ibid., p. 4.
74. Ibid., title page.
75. Ibid., p. 5.
76. Ibid., pp. 4 and 6.

77. Some Colonial Office staff commented quite reasonably that infrastructural expenditure financed out of the colonial development and welfare budget could be seen as a key development priority and were not a waste of money. See, for example, memoranda by Cohen appearing as appendices to National Archives, Kew: CO 852/941/3, Colonial Economic and Development Council, *Principles of Development Planning: Memorandum by Professor Lewis*, CEDC (48) 1, 11 April 1948.
78. Cohen, comment on Lewis's *Principles of Development Planning*, Appendix to National Archives, Kew: CO 852/941/3, Colonial Economic and Development Council: Memorandum by Professor Lewis, CEDC (48) 1, 11 April 1948.
79. Rhodes House, Oxford, Fabian Colonial Bureau papers: FCB 68/2, Report of Sub-Committee on Mass Education and Development Planning, June 1948.
80. For the detail of mass education activities in each colony, see Rhodes House, Oxford: Mss. Brit. Emp. s.332, Arthur Creech Jones papers, Box 34/1, Mass Education (Community Development), January 1950.
81. For the Gold Coast riots, see the account by Austin (1964).
82. The idea of community development went through many metamorphoses after its incarnation in the Creech Jones Colonial Office, re-emerging most recently as an element of the participative, social-capital-infused poverty strategies of the late 1990s and 2000s, see Woolcock (1998); World Bank (2000); and Woolcock and Narayan (2000).
83. 'Colonial Development' (Lewis, 1949e), *Transactions of the Manchester Statistical Society*.
84. National Archives, Kew: CO/990/2 133087, Memorandum on Colonial Agricultural Policy, 1946.
85. National Archives, Kew: CO/990/3, Report on Agricultural Credit in the Colonies, 1946.
86. National Archives, Kew: CO/990/3, Second Report on Agricultural Credit in the Colonies, 1946.
87. National Archives, Kew: CO 999/1, First Minutes of the Colonial Economic Development Council, October 1946.
88. National Archives, Kew: CW, 24, p. 247.
89. National Archives, Kew: CO 852/5881/19260/2/44, November 1944, Draft answers to a Memorandum from CEAC.
90. National Archives, Kew: CO 852/482/2, January 1944, 'Some Aspects of the Flow of Capital into the British Colonies'.
91. Lewis (1949d).
92. National Archives, Kew: CO 852/1348/7, Minutes of thirteenth meeting of the Colonial Economic Development Committee, 10 March 1947.
93. National Archives, Kew: CO 852/1349/2.
94. LSE Archives: Lewis to Carr-Saunders, 20 February 1946.
95. National Archives, Kew: CO 852/1349/2, Summary of Press Comment on CDC Annual Report.
96. The Press comment pointed to what it saw as an internal contradiction in the CDC's terms of reference, which required the Corporation to be profitable and yet not to pursue projects that the private sector was willing to handle unassisted (*The Times*); and to its rigid capital structure, which contained no ordinary shares and thus made the Corporation ill-equipped to bear risks (*The Guardian*).

97. See Hirschman (1958).
98. Rhodes House, Oxford: Arthur Creech Jones Archive (Mss. Brit. Emp. s.332): Box 44, 'CDC Projects: Note by Professor Lewis', 20 December 1952, para. 42.
99. Rhodes House, Oxford: Arthur Creech Jones Archive (Mss. Brit. Emp. s.332): Box 44, 'CDC Projects: Note by Professor Lewis', 20 December 1952, para. 42.
100. Ibid., paras 11 and 12.
101. Ibid., paras 24, 29, 30 and 31. Also in Lewis Papers, Princeton, Box 11. It needs to be emphasized that, impassioned fighter against discrimination though he was, Lewis did not always recognize this when evidence of it was presented to him. In March 1952, a chartered accountant with a City firm, Ray Powell, approached Lewis on behalf of a Nigerian chartered secretary and certified accountant at the CDC, B. O. Aina, who was none the less being paid by the CDC as an unqualified employee. Powell protested to Lewis that this evidence of discrimination gave him 'a nasty feeling of a desperate attempt to victimise and drive away Mr Aina' (Lewis Archives, Princeton: Box 11/1; Powell to Lewis, 31 March 1952). But Lewis, on investigating the case, insisted, in spite of Aina having ten years' business experience (Lewis Archives, Princeton: Box 11/1; Powell to Lewis, 22 May 1952) that the CDC had no case to answer, because Aina, although qualified, was, as far as the CDC was concerned, a trainee lacking in experience.
102. 'Prof. A. Lewis Not Reappointed: Colonial Corporation', *The Manchester Guardian*, 18 May 1953.
103. National Archives, Kew: CO 967/194, Private papers of Sir Thomas Lloyd: Aide-memoire of a conversation with Professor Lewis, 8.5.53.
104. National Archives, Kew: CO 967/194, Private papers of Sir Thomas Lloyd: Aide-memoire of a conversation with Professor Lewis, 8.5.53.
105. Lewis, letter to the Editor of *The Observer*, 24 February 1953.

4 'It takes hard work to be accepted in the academic world': Manchester University, 1948–57

1. LSE Archives: Carr Saunders to Ida Greaves, 30 June 1948.
2. LSE Archives: Correspondence with Eve Evans, School Secretary, October 1948.
3. Dahrendorf (1995), p. 370.
4. Gladys Jacobs, a qualified teacher and school inspector from Grenada, was herself the daughter of a headmaster. The Lewises had two daughters, the first born in 1949 and the second in 1951.
5. In his Lewis biography, Robert Tignor closely documents the progress of Lewis's application to Liverpool using the LSE staff files. Carr-Saunders at the LSE and the Liverpool selection committee strongly supported Lewis, but Liverpool's Vice-Chancellor rejected him on the grounds that there could be problems gaining acceptance for Lewis by the student body and the Liverpool business community (Tignor (2005), pp. 37–9).
6. There is often confusion over the date(s) of Lewis's appointment to a Chair at Manchester. The University of Manchester Calendar records that he was appointed to a Chair in Economics at Manchester on 25 December 1947, but 'resigned' from this appointment in 1949 to take up the Stanley Jevons Chair in Political Economy at Manchester, which he held until 1958.

7. Williams (2005).
8. Ten years later, Polanyi's wife was to write: 'We miss you and Gladys very much and think of you with great affection. I for one will never forget how you pressed me to advise Michael not to wait any longer for the American visa and to take up his work(??) at M/c. University again. We would have been on the dole ever since, if it had not been for your advice.' Lewis Archives, Princeton, Box 11/1: Magda Polanyi to Lewis, 6 November 1957.
9. Leeson and Nixson (2004); Hagemann (2006).
10. Toye (2006).
11. Martin Jay (1973) , for an account of Carl Grunberg and the Frankfurt School.
12. Lewis (1955), p. 6.
13. Lewis Archives, Princeton, Box 9/3,: Martin to Lewis, 10 May 1984, and reply by Lewis, 12 June 1984.
14. Recommending Devons for a research fellowship in 1957, Lewis wrote: 'He is most highly intelligent, with a very critical mind. He and I are perfect mutual foils, for whereas I get a new hunch every week and waste a lot of time chasing hares, he is highly suspicious of any idea for which there is not overwhelming evidence. This keeps his creative output small, but what he does is excellent. It also gives him special value as a member of a team, since the others get much help from trying out their ideas on his critical mind.' Lewis Archives, Princeton, Box 13/4: Lewis to Ralph Tyler (Yale), 20 February 1957.
15. Lewis Papers, Princeton, Box 29: Letter from Lewis to Ely Devons, 21 March 1958.
16. Interview, Gisela Eisner, 5 May 2006.
17. Interview, Gisela Eisner, 5 May 2006.
18. Correspondence between Leah Lomax and the Lewises, 20 June 1959: Lewis Papers, Princeton, Box 2915.
19. Lewis Archive, Princeton, Box 10/1: Lewis to Mars, 27 November 1951, p. 2.
20. Lewis Archive, Princeton: Box 10/1, Lewis to Mars, 27 November 1951, p. 1.
21. Respectively, Mars to Lewis, 1 June 1952 (which is polite and respectful, but at the end moans that Hicks 'got more help from his colleagues than I shall ever get'; and Mars to Lewis, congratulating him on his election to Director of the UN Fund for Economic Development, 17 January 1959. Lewis Archive, Princeton; Box 10/1.
22. Interview, Eisner, 5 May 2006.
23. Gisela Eisner recalls 'very strong words' between Lewis and Coppock around 1954 (interview, Eisner, 5 May 2006). One problem appears to have been that Coppock's early brilliance was in economic theory, 'and the first which he took in finals' according to a later letter by Lewis, 'was spectacular'. However, Lewis continues, 'we could never get him to write anything in economic theory. Instead, he attached himself intellectually to me, who am no economic theorist, and began to potter about with the things I was working on. This was a mistake, since he is not very good at applied economics, and though he has published one or two respectable papers in my field, he could not make an original contribution. I tried hard to disconnect him from me ... [but since the arrival of Harry Johnson and John Johnston] he has now published three excellent papers, and I felt

proud to have had some part in his intellectual history'. Lewis Archives, Princeton, Box 15: Lewis to B. R. Williams (recommending Coppock for a Senior Lectureship at Manchester), 28 November 1960.

24. These national accounts (see Deane 2011 [1953]) were for Northern Rhodesia (now Zambia), which is where Gluckman also worked, at the Rhodes–Livingstone Institute, before moving to Manchester. Phyllis Deane, interview with author, Cambridge, 2 April 2004.

25. See acknowledgement to Devons in Gluckman(1955), p. viii.

26. Lewis Archives, Princeton, Box 6/3: Gluckman to Lewis, 27 June 1958.

27. John Rylands University Library: Introductory materials to Papers of Max Gluckman. Available at: http://archiveshub.ac.uk/gb133glu.

28. *The Manchester Guardian,* 12 and 15 March 1950. Lewis, in his letter, resigned his membership of the Colonial Office's Colonial Economic and Development Council. Gluckman, in his, wrote, 'If it is an attempt to appease the Negrophobes in South Africa, it is bound to fail, and it will discourage the liberal Europeans who do exist in these territories.'

29. Gluckman (1955), p. 2.

30. See John Rylands University Library, Manchester: Gluckman Archive, GLU 4/4, Gluckman to Firth, 3 May 1962.

31. Lewis Archives, Princeton, Box 5/4: Lewis to Eastwood (Colonial Office), 3 April 1950.

32. Even when McNamara arrived at the World Bank in 1967, 'research on development was not a major, ongoing activity of the World Bank' (World Bank, 1983). See also Toye and Toye (2004), pp. 102–3.

33. Toye and Toye (2004), p.103. John Toye has added, in personal correspondence, 'Schultz was Lewis' colleague, but not his ally, on the 1951 UN mission. Schultz had reservations about Lewis' draft and signed it reluctantly.'

34. United Nations, (1951), p. 35, para. 96.

35. Discussion of agricultural productivity is to be found in ibid., p. 21 (paras 55–56). The problems of small family farms are specifically addressed on pp. 26 (para. 75) and 29 (para. 81).

36. Education and training are discussed in ibid., paras 92–95 (pp. 32–4) with the discussion of mass education in para. 94, p. 33. Paras 84 (p. 30), 86 (p. 31) and 163 (pp. 52–3) refer specifically to education in the form of agricultural extension for small farmers; and paras 164–165 on p. 53 discuss training, especially administrative and technical training, at the tertiary level. Education, it must be stressed, was a priority for Theodore Schultz (the only member of the panel from an industrialized country), as well as for Lewis, and it was for his work on human capital that Schultz, jointly with Lewis, was to be awarded the Nobel Prize in 1979.

37. United Nations (1951), ch. VI, para 112.

38. Ibid., ch. XI; see also Toye and Toye (2004), p. 105. For data on the varying proportions of aid allocated to technical assistance, see Mosley (2012), table 2.3, p. 40.

39. United Nations (1951), p. 59, para. 189.

40. Frankel (1952), pp. 301–26. An excellent discussion of Frankel's contributions to development economics is provided by Toye (2009), pp. 171–82, commenting on Frankel, (1952), p. 310.

41. More controversial ... is the emphatic statement (para. 39 of the UN report) that 'economic progress depends to a large extent upon the adoption by *governments* of appropriate administrative and legislative action, both in the public and private sectors ... It seems to me very doubtful whether a history of economic change, of innovation, or of economic growth in different societies supports this optimistic view of the roles and capacities of governments', Frankel (1952), p. 303; emphasis in original.

42. Ibid.; emphasis in original.

43. Toye (2009), pp. 171–82, commenting on Frankel (1952), p. 324.

44. The relevant parts of the letter read: 'I am disturbed by your letter of January 19th [which alleges that Plant is 'violently against me' and later that 'Frankel's QJE outburst I believe is very typical of Plant's thinking'] ... I have not seen him for about two years, and keep far from the Colonial Office crowd, so I am quite in the dark as to their views.

    You suggest that it may be that he dislikes your philosophy with regard to development policy, but I should be surprised if this were a major issue. After all, he appointed me to his staff in 1938, and supported all my subsequent promotions, in spite of our open disagreement on this issue. And he must have known how you felt on those matters in all the years when you were working close together.

    In academic life the answer to all personal criticism is to publish, and thereby to establish one's own reputation. Everything is bound to work out if the Institute publishes good stuff ... Presumably the Institute's grant runs from 1948 to 1955 and, therefore, presumably the Colonial Office will begin discussing it at least by January 1954. [Your] present plan suggests leisurely publication through 1953 and 1954, but I think you would be wise to put things out as soon as possible, instead of thinking in terms of a magazine which appears at regular intervals.' Lewis to D. L. Huggins, 6 February 1953, replying to letter from Huggins to Lewis, 19 January 1953, Lewis Archives, Princeton: Box 7/3.

45. Lewis Archives, Princeton, Box 7/3: Lewis to D. L. Huggins, 6 February 1953.

46. 'It is certain that [Frankel] dislikes the idea of *speeding* up development': Lewis (1953b), p. 268; emphasis in original.

47. Lewis (1953b), pp. 268–9.

48. Ibid., p. 269.

49. Lewis, (1953b)p. 274.

50. Hilgerdt, in thanking Lewis for an offprint of his *Manchester School* article, wrote 'It is a matter of concern to me that figures supplied as provisional and not for publication have now been published and presented as revised, and moreover, that they have been made public without the reservations, qualifications and explanations of methods used in computation that I have intended should accompany the planned publication by the United Nations.' (Lewis Archive, Princeton: Box 7/2, Hilgerdt to Lewis, 13 June 1952). Lewis was forced to undertake not to pass on the Hilgerdt dataset to any other party and to publish a note in the *Manchester School* acknowledging that the data were provisional and unconfirmed.

51. Lewis (1952), pp. 105–37; the estimated equations (calculated by ordinary least squares (OLS), in logs so as to directly derive the response elasticities) are on pp. 111, 120 and 123.

52. The terms of trade, of course, were also preoccupying other United Nations writers at the time – in particular, Raul Prebisch at the Economic Commission for Latin America, and Hans Singer at the main United Nations Secretariat.
53. Lewis Archives, Princeton, Box 7: Lewis to Weintraub, 16 January 1952.
54. Essay by Lewis in G. Meier and D. Seers (1984).
55. *The Principles of Economic Planning* does, however, have a short appendix on planning in under-developed countries, which appears to recommend laissez-faire except where the whole population can be mobilized behind the plan. We are grateful to John Toye for reminding us of this.
56. This draft of the paper (entitled *Colonial Development in British Territories*) can be found in the library of Rhodes House, Oxford (Mss.Brit.Emp.s.350).
57. In his 'signpost paragraph' at the start of the paper, only the first three of these are mentioned: 'The colonies are so poor because they apply so little knowledge to production, use so little capital, and operate on so small a scale. It is these factors that most distinguish their economies from those of wealthier countries'. Lewis (1949e), p. 3.
58. Ibid.
59. Lewis (1949e), pp. 18 and 21. An earlier draft of this material can be found in Lewis, *Colonial Development in British Territories*, Rhodes House, Oxford, Mss.Brit.Emp.s.350, January 1949e, p. 10.
60. Lewis, (1949e), p. 10. After independence, the Indonesian village banks evolved into regional development banks operated by provincial administrations, which still survive – one of the most successful cases globally of government-sponsored micro-finance.
61. '[The large-scale Tanganyika land development schemes, including the 'groundnut scheme' are] among the most highly capitalised undertakings in the world. Well, we can find £25 millions for one of these, or £50 millions for two, but it is an illusion to think that this capital starved country will be able to pursue much colonial development of this kind. The sooner we tear our eyes away from the fascination of big numbers and face squarely how to make existing peasant producers on existing lands produce more, the nearer we shall be to making big strides in development': Lewis (1949e), p. 18.
62. Ibid., pp. 20 and 23–7.
63. Ibid., p. 19.
64. Ibid., p. 10.
65. A possible exception to this proposition is Lewis's embittered and disillusioned interchanges with Kwame Nkrumah in 1958 (see Chapter 6 below).
66. In February 1953, in the letter to Dudley Huggins previously quoted, Lewis describes himself as 'sketching out some ideas for a book on the Theory of Progress', Lewis Archive, Princeton: Lewis to D. L. Huggins, 6 February 1953, Princeton: Box 5/3. Even in November 1950, Lewis had announced that he had 'just spent three months reading the history books, seeking to discover the causes of economic progress and decline – especially decline' ('How Countries Go Down', *The Observer*, 19 November 1950, p. 4). This was, of course, at the time when Lewis was working on the UN report, *Measures for the Economic Development of Underdeveloped Countries*, and it looks, purely from the timing, as though the invitation from the UN to

think on a world scale about short-term development policies made him think also about the historical experience of growth and decline.

67. Other Nobel Prize-winning ideas based on a simple supply-and-demand diagram include Akerlof's model of the market for 'lemons', or bad used cars (1970) which shows that the market will fall apart (the supply and demand curves will move progressively inwards until the point of collapse) in markets where the buyer does not know the quality of what s/he is being sold; and Sen's (1982) analysis of famine in which, for the first time, famine is explained in terms of a rightward shift of the demand curve for food, rather than a leftward shift of the supply curve. Both of these models have analogies with Lewis's model, in that they also explore the idea of market imperfection and its implications for well-being; both, of course, apply a good part of their story to developing countries.

68. Lewis (1954), pp. 139–91, reprinted in Agarwala and Singh (1958), ch. 19, p. 417. Page reference is to the Agarwala and Singh edition.

69. We reproduce here the simple example by which Lewis made his case – because this part of his paper is not so well known as the (closed-economy) first part, because it became the object of criticisms with which we shall engage as we proceed, and because its policy implications are so enormous. Text in square brackets is added to Lewis's original.

'We assume ... two countries [one industrial and one underdeveloped, which] can produce the same things, and trade with each other. A is the country where labour is scarce, B the country where unlimited labour is available in the subsistence [food)] sector. Using the classical framework for the Law of Comparative Costs we write that one day's labour in A produces 3 food or 3 cotton manufactures [and]in B produces 2 food or 1 cotton manufactures. This, of course, gives the wrong answer to the question "who should specialize in which" since we have written the average instead of the marginal products. We can assume that these coincide in A, and also in cotton manufacture in B. Then we should write, in marginal terms, in A produces 3 food or 3 cotton manufactures [and] in B produces 0 food or 1 cotton manufactures.

[The marginal product of labour in food production being assumed zero on account of labour being in surplus in rural areas] B should specialize in cotton manufacture and import food. In practice, however, wages will be 2 food in B and between 3 food and 6 food in A, at which levels it will be 'cheaper' for B to export food and import cotton.

The divergence between the actual and what it ought to be is the most serious difference which the existence of surplus labour makes to the neoclassical theory of international trade. It has caught out many economists, who have wrongly advised underdeveloped countries on the basis of current money costs, instead of lifting the veil to see what lies beneath. It has also caught out many countries which have allowed (or been forced to allow) their industries to be destroyed by cheap foreign imports, with the sole effect of increasing the size of the labour surplus, when the national income would have been increased if the domestic industries had instead been protected against imports. The fault is not that of the Law of Comparative Costs, which remains valid in written in real marginal terms, but of those who have forgotten that money costs are entirely misleading in economies where there is surplus labour at the ruling wage.'

(Lewis (1954), pp. 139–91, p. 185, reprinted in Agarwala and Singh (1958), ch. 19, pp. 443–4.)

70. In 'Unlimited Supplies of Labour' (Agarwala and Singh (1963), p. 408) Lewis vividly characterizes the cultural divide between the two parts of the dual economy as being 'between the few highly westernised, trousered, natives, educated in western universities, speaking western languages, and glorying in Beethoven, Mill, Marx or Einstein, and the great mass of their countrymen who live in quite other worlds'; Mill is the only economist admitted to the pantheon. As he moved away from the radicalism of *Colonial Development* (1949e), Lewis shifted his position increasingly towards Mill's own intellectual orientation – on the right in terms of economics, but socially and redistributively still well to the left of centre.
71. J. S. Mill (1994[1848]), p. 16.
72. Lewis (1955), p. 5.
73. Ibid.
74. Ibid., p. 12.
75. Ibid., p. 8.
76. Ibid., p. 226.
77. Ibid., p. 233.
78. ibid., p. 28.
79. In particular, for fairly obvious reasons, the focus on the small scale that is so important in *Colonial Development* (Lewis 1949e) does not reappear in *Economic Growth*. In the British colonies, and in particular the Caribbean islands from which Lewis came, the 'small country' problem is fundamental, which is much less the case for developing countries as a whole.
80. Lewis (1955), p. 103. This may surprise readers, as Lewis was well aware of Tawney's *Religion and the Rise of Capitalism* (1926), and other works that associated the British Industrial Revolution with the emergence of Nonconformist entrepreneurs. In fact, by page 105 Lewis has retreated to the proposition that 'some religious codes are more compatible with economic growth' than others.
81. Gluckman (1955), p. 2.
82. 'Restrictions on the work women may do are everywhere a barrier to economic growth ... economic growth and a transference of women's work from the household to the market go closely hand in hand. As income per head grows there is an even more rapid growth of such activities as dressmaking, hairdressing and catering, not to speak of the education of the young in schools, which is a substitute for education at home ... To create more paid jobs for women is the surest way simultaneously to raise their status, to reduce their drudgery and to raise the national output ...' Lewis (1955), p. 116.
83. Lewis (1955), p. 128.
84. In particular, the commercialization of agriculture had long been biased, especially under the pressure of colonialism, towards 'the commercial crops which are exported to industrial countries (sugar, cocoa, rubber, tea, etc.) and has almost wholly neglected what is produced for home consumption (yams, cassava, sorghums and the like) despite the fact that in nearly all these economies the manpower and acreage devoted to food production is four or more times as great as that which is devoted to commercial crops', Lewis (1955), p. 188.

85. 'The USA ... has one extension worker to every seven hundred persons gainfully employed in agriculture, and it spends upon agricultural extension and research about three-quarters of one per cent of net agricultural output. The United Kingdom also has a ratio of 1 to 700, but among the poorer countries of the world the only country which spends at this level upon agricultural services is Japan (*it is also the only one which has had spectacular increases in peasant productivity*), Lewis (1955), p. 188; emphasis added.
86. Lewis commends the practice of free medical services and subsidized meals for employees as a way of increasing productivity in developing countries, in a way that seems to anticipate the 'efficiency wage' theories that were produced by the next generation of development economists (Lewis (1955), p. 194, anticipating, for example, Stiglitz (1976), pp. 185–207).
87. Lewis (1955), p. 28.
88. Lewis (1955), p. 408.
89. Lewis (1965b).
90. Lewis (1955), pp. 401, 408.
91. In Ghana and Uganda, until the 1990s, taxes of up to 90 per cent were imposed on exports; Kenya, until the 2000s, and Zimbabwe, from the 1930s to the present, imposed limits on the amount of maize and other food crops that could be bought or sold across district boundaries, in the interests of local self-sufficiency.
92. Much later, Lewis was to write: 'My concern in those days was not with the amount of money paid to urban workers, which I assumed would be linked to the productivity of the small farmers, but rather with the social wage, especially education, health services, water supplies, workmen's compensation, unemployment pay, pensions, and such. This network seemed to me, as a social democrat, to be one of the best products of the past hundred years.' In Meier and Seers (1985), p. 131.
93. Lewis (1955), p. 382.
94. See Mosley (2012), ch. 10.
95. These include (1961); Arrighi (1970), pp.198233, for Zimbabwe; Wilson (1973) for South Africa; and Huff and Caggiano (2007), pp. 33–69 for Burma, Thailand and Malaya.
96. Lewis had written in his autobiographical account (Lewis Archives, Princeton: Box 12, page 16) that 'I had read in the works of John and Barbara Hammond that the industrial revolution had not raised urban wages.' However, the Hammonds' studies (Hammond and Hammond, 1911, 1918 and 1919) are mainly qualitative. Where quantitative data are presented, they never cover the whole of the Industrial Revolution period, but their evidence on the trend of real wages is definitely downwards (for example, page 111 of *The Village Labourer* states that between 1760 and 1813, money wages rose by 60 per cent and the price of wheat by 130 per cent; ch. 6 of *The Town Labourer* on 'The Economic Conditions' also contains data on prices but none on wages.)
97. Phyllis Deane, interview with author, 2 April 2004.
98. Lewis (1955), p. 6.
99. Gisela Eisner (1961), Appendix II, pp. 376–7, and Appendix III, pp. 378–9. Eisner's study aims at a comprehensive economic history of Jamaica, adopting the long-period perspective Lewis had pioneered in *Economic Growth*, but

going far beyond the labour-market focus of 'Unlimited Supplies of Labour': For example, Eisner's ch. 1 computes estimates for the national income of Jamaica between 1830 and 1930.

100. Lewis Archives, Princeton, Box 12: Lewis to Polanyi, 11 January 1951.
101. Schultz (1969).
102. Sen (1966), pp. 425–50.
103. Fei and Ranis (1964).
104. Lewis Archive, Princeton, 1955, box 8/1: Lewis to Johnson, 15 December 1954, and reply by Johnson, 21 December 1954.
105. In addition to the discussion of Lewis's views on smallholder agriculture as expressed in *Colonial Development* and in ch. 3 of *The Theory of Economic Growth*, discussed above, see also his remarks in *Report on the Industrialisation of the Gold Coast* (Gold Coast Government, 1953a), where he argues (in para. 24) that 'the surest way to industrialise the Gold Coast would be to multiply by four or five the resources available to the department for fundamental research into food production'.

5   The Manchester Years: Lewis as Social and Political Activist

1. A combination of fog and smoke from coal fires, which would descend on industrial cities each autumn and often, if there was no wind, get into people's lungs over periods of weeks on end throughout the winter. See *Manchester Evening News*, Letters to the Editor, 20 October 1953, p. 4.
2. An article headed '100,000 Manchester Houses are "Unfit"' went on 'Dr Charles Metcalfe Brown told a public inquiry this afternoon that in his opinion nearly half of the 200,000 houses in Manchester were unfit to live in'; many of them could be improved but 68,000 were beyond repair. *Manchester Evening News*, 10 September 1953, p. 7.
3. This picture of working-class life in the early years of Lord Beveridge's welfare state is taken from an account of the year 1950 by Beveridge's biographer, Nicholas Timmins (Timmins (2001), p. 21).
4. Between the wars, most of the Afro-Caribbean population of Britain lived in the port cities of Cardiff, Liverpool and London ('Coloured People in Britain: Dilemma of Uncertain Status', *The Manchester Guardian*, 12 March 1951). From 1948 onwards, when the *Empire Windrush* brought the first cohort of Caribbean ex-servicemen to Tilbury, there were campaigns in the Caribbean to encourage people to come to Britain, with a (reorganized) British Railways and a (newborn) National Health Service among the most active recruiters; and many of these post-war immigrants went to cities with a fast-growing manufacturing and construction sector, such as Birmingham and Manchester. When Lewis began his campaign for an Afro-Caribbean social centre, there were about 3,000 non-white immigrants in Manchester, about half of these West Indians ('Growing Coloured Community Fends for Itself', *The Manchester Guardian*, 24 March 1953) out of a UK population of 40,000, but by 1958 the Manchester population had risen to 10,000 or about 6 per cent of the national population of 190,000 ('Open Door for Coloured Immigrants', *The Manchester*

Guardian, 20 November 1958 and Manchester City Council, 2012), most of them living in Moss Side. For a study of Moss Side which traces the Manchester Afro-Caribbean communities back to their 1950s roots, see Hudson *et al.* (2007).

5. Just after arriving in Manchester, Lewis forwarded to the Fabian Colonial Bureau the following letter that had appeared in the *Manchester Evening News*:

Ex-Boxer Fights Pit Colour Bar:

Len Johnson, famous Manchester coloured boxer in the 1930s, is campaigning against what a National Coal Board spokesman in Manchester describes as 'a general principle not to employ coloured men in the mines where it can be avoided'.

Johnson, who has formed a society in Manchester to resist all forms of colour bars, today quoted the case of Benjamin Lord, a 24-year-old native of British Honduras, who, he says, last week applied for a job in a Lancashire pit and was turned down. 'Lord had already done a week's work in a pit and had proved satisfactory,' said Johnson. 'I myself went to the labour exchange and was read the typewritten instruction from the Coal Board.' A National Coal Board official in Manchester said: 'The objection came first from the National Union of Mineworkers, as some of their members disliked working with coloured men.'

Lewis asks: 'Can you get the Fabian Colonial Bureau to take up the enclosed at the highest quarters and pursue it relentlessly? What is there to say for socialism if this is to be the joint policy of a socialist Ministry of Labour, a socialised industry and a communistic trade union? The extract is from the *Manchester Evening News* of 28/2/48. I suspect that this is just the right occasion for a great deal of publicity, and a demand for legislation.'

Then, in a PS, he writes:

'Will the Bureau take legal advice on this? It may be that Lord can sue for damages the Minister of Labour, the National Coal Board, and the NUM, who are a conspiracy to deprive him of employment on grounds – racial discrimination – that are contrary to public policy. Many of us would gladly put up the money to take this into the courts, and it may be easier to get the law established this way than to seek Parliamentary time. H. S. Polak, the solicitor to the Imperial Advisory Committee, would gladly advise on this.'

(Rhodes House, Oxford, Fabian Colonial Bureau 5/6, folio 44: Lewis to Edith (surname illegible), Fabian Colonial Bureau.)

On the behaviour of trade union leaders towards West Indians, see Stanley (1998) one of whose informants, Barrington Young, reports: '(The unions) were supposed to be there to protect the rights of workers but instead they encouraged racial discrimination, by being outspoken against black people and ensuring that promotion was unlikely, if not impossible. Also a lot of union men supported the National Front ... Because the "Bosses" were too afraid to cause disruption, they followed the Union.'

Barrington Young, emigrated from Jamaica to Manchester in 1954, as told to Stanley (1998), p. 43.

6. During the 1950s there was a great deal of goodwill towards British immigration policies from emergent West Indian leaders: for example, they were praised explicitly in 1958 by Norman Manley, at the time Chief Minister of Jamaica: 'It was greatly to England's credit that she had refused to establish an official colour bar (whereas) most of the commonwealth had closed its doors to coloured people.' Quoted in *The Manchester Guardian,* 15 July 1955.

7. Data from 'Growing Coloured Community Fends for Itself', *The Manchester Guardian,* 24 March 1953, and 'Open Door for Coloured Immigrants: Demand for Restriction Resisted', *The Manchester Guardian,* 20 November 1958.

8. Lewis Archives, Princeton, Box 9/4: Michael Meredith, Rector of Moss Side, to Lewis, 12 January 1950.

9. Lewis's report on mass education (Lewis, 1948) is an internal Colonial Office document. The key popularizer of the mass education theme in the Colonial Office was Arthur Creech Jones, Colonial Secretary in the Attlee government, who in 1943 had sponsored the publication of a Colonial Office policy document with this title (UK Colonial Office, 1943).

10. Lewis Archives, Princeton, Box 29: N. G. Fisher, Chief Education Officer, Manchester City Council, to Lewis, 12 July 1951.

11. Ibid..

12. The Bishop of Manchester, along with Sir Thomas Barlow, were persuaded by Lewis to be on the organising committee. Lewis Archives, Princeton, Box 29: leaflet *Colonial People in Manchester,* September 1953.

13. Lewis Archives, Princeton, Box 29: Lewis to Sir Thomas Barlow, 26 March 1952.

14. Lewis Archives, Princeton, Box 29: Lewis to Councillor W. A. Downward, 6 March 1952.

15. Greater Manchester County Record Office, Manchester City Council Education Committee minutes: Meetings of the Further Education Sub-Committee, folio 1763, 15 December 1952.

16. In Liverpool, the model Lewis examined was the Stanley House Centre for Coloured People, established in 1942, and in Birmingham the Clifton Institute for Coloured Peoples, established in 1951. Stanley House was essentially a social club with sports and recreational facilities, but in the Clifton Institute the focus was much more educational, with a basic course in English being compulsory, after which the student 'expands his studies to take geography, history, mathematics, and technical shop work', article 'Escaping from the Prison of Illiteracy: Help for Coloured Immigrants', *The Manchester Guardian,* 19 May 1952.

17. 'White workers will not object to working alongside a Coloured man, but they resent taking orders from him, even though he may be a lot more skilled in the trade than the Whites', Lewis Archives, Princeton, Box 29: E. B. Ndem, 'Memorandum' to members of the Organisational Sub-Committee for the South Hulme Evening Centre, p. 2.

18. Lewis Archives, Princeton, Box 29: E. B. Ndem, 'Memorandum' to members of the Organisational Sub-Committee for the South Hulme Evening Centre, p. 2.

19. Ibid., p. 3.

20. Ibid., p. 4. Ndem noted that 'The Olympia Restaurant and Snack Bar in Oxford Road is barred to Coloured. This was ostensibly demonstrated in the presence of an American anthropologist whom I invited to lunch with me' (ibid.).

21. Lewis Archives, Princeton, Box 29: E. B. Ndem, 'Memorandum' to members of the Organisational Sub-Committee for the South Hulme Evening Centre, p. 4. On relations between Afro-Caribbeans and the police, see also the paper by Stanley (1998).

22. Lewis Archives, Princeton, Box 29: E. B. Ndem, 'Memorandum' to members of the Organisational Sub-Committee for the South Hulme Evening Centre, p. 8.

23. Ibid.

24. Lewis Archives, Princeton, Box 29: Lewis to Sir Thomas Barlow, 26 March 1952, p. 2.

25. Princeton University, Lewis Archive, Box 4: Norman Fisher, Chief Education Officer for Manchester, to Lewis, 5 February 1953.

26. 'What we really need is a place which can be a centre for various activities – not only evening classes, but adult classes, visitors from the Citizen's Advice Bureau, Poor Man's Lawyer, religious bodies and so on. Of course this is beyond the scope of the Corporation's finances, but the question is, if we put such a building at the Corporation's disposal, can we have the Institute there? As I suggested in an earlier letter, several of us could put up the rent, in advance, for a building, if you would agree', Lewis Papers, Princeton, Box 29: Lewis to N. G. Fisher, Director of Education, 10 February 1953. There was constant market research to ascertain who might be interested in the Centre, and the idea of it operating in the city's prisons seems to be have been considered and discarded at this stage. Greater Manchester County Record Office: Manchester City Council Education Committee minutes: Meetings of the Further Education Sub-Committee, folio 2868, 20 April 1953.

27. 'Evening centre for coloured people: proposed arrangements', memorandum dated 3 February 1953, Lewis Papers, Princeton, Box 29. On the single typed page detailing the curriculum a hand that is clearly Lewis's has pencilled the words 'Driving and maintenance'. By this point the council was very committed to the centre, and it cancelled 50 classes to free the resources for the centre to be set up. Greater Manchester County Record Office: Manchester City Council Education Committee minutes: Meetings of the Further Education Sub-Committee, folio 1763, 15 December 1952.

28. Lewis Archives, Princeton, Box 29: Norman G. Fisher, Chief Education Officer, to Lewis, 17 February 1953.

29. Greater Manchester County Record Office, Manchester City Council Education Committee minutes: Meetings of the Staff Sub-Committee, folio 896, 4 April 1953.

30. Summarised as case study 34 in Mosley and Ingham (2012).

31. Thanks in particular to the West Indies' spin bowlers, the 1954 Test series against England was won comfortably by the West Indies.

32. Lewis Archives, Princeton, Box 29: Memorandum by Professor Lewis to Race Relations Sub-Committee of Manchester Council for African Affairs, 20 August 1953.

33. Lewis's only sole-supervised PhD student within the Department of Economics was Gisela Eisner, but he also co-supervised various students with Gluckman, including Scarlett Epstein (see letter from Gluckman to Lewis, 1958).
34. Lewis, as will be remembered from Chapter 1, was an enthusiastic amateur musician. He had written in November 1952 to the industrial magnate and university benefactor Lord Simon of Wythenshawe: 'I do not consider the [BBC] Third Programme to be valuable in its present form [at that time it only reached 7 per cent of listeners] ...
    The classical music should be the sort of music that one hears in the concert hall, instead of setting out to be the sort of music one does not hear in the concert hall ... (By the way, one of my biggest grudges against the BBC is that it broadcasts so little classical organ music)', Lewis Archive, Princeton, Box 12/4: Lewis to Lord Simon of Wythenshawe, 21 November 1952.
35. 'Once a senior politician soon to be Prime Minister remarked in amazement and awe to Gladys [Lewis] "Why isn't he marvellous: he even plays with his children!"'. Lalljie (1997), p. 58. The future prime minister in this quotation is Sir Harold Wilson, whose Huyton parliamentary constituency was only about 30 miles from Didsbury (Interview, Robert Lalljie, 18 June 2012).
36. Lewis Archives, Princeton, Box 29: Mary Walsh, matron of Doriscourt Nursing Home, to Lewis, 8 October 1953.
37. As Blackburn later reported, 'Professor Lewis did an astonishing amount of work in preparation for this centre and was mainly responsible for the musical side of the programme', Greater Manchester County Record Office, Manchester City Council Education Committee minutes, 1953–4: Report by E. W. Blackburn to meeting of the Further Education Sub-Committee, folio 1791, 21 December 1953.
38. Greater Manchester County Record Office, Manchester City Council Education Committee minutes 1953–4: Report by E.W. Blackburn to meeting of the Further Education Sub-Committee, folio 1793, 31 December 1953.
39. Greater Manchester County Record Office, Manchester City Council Education Committee minutes: Meetings of the Further Education Sub-Committee.
40. 'City's Coloured Community: Allegations Denied', *The Manchester Guardian*, 9 November 1953.
41. Greater Manchester County Record Office, Manchester City Council Education Committee minutes 1953–4: Meetings of the Further Education Sub-Committee, folio 1792, 31 December 1953.
42. Greater Manchester County Record Office, Manchester City Council Education Committee minutes 1952–3: Meetings of the Further Education Sub-Committee, folio 2868, 20 April 1953.
43. Greater Manchester County Record Office, Manchester City Council Education Committee minutes 1954–5: Report by E. W. Blackburn to meeting of the Further Education Sub-Committee, folio 667, 19 July 1954.
44. In the final class of the spring term in early April 1954, 37 out of 97 students were present. Greater Manchester County Record Office, Manchester City Council Education Committee minutes 1952–3: Report by E. W. Blackburn to meeting of the Further Education Sub-Committee, folio 2868, 20 April 1953.

45. Of the 37 enrolled students, 31 attended classes in English, carpentry and dressmaking, while nine attended classes in 'technical subjects' – engineering, metalwork and car repairs. (The total adds up to more than 37 because some students were attending classes in both areas of study.) Data from Greater Manchester County Record Office, Manchester City Council Education Committee minutes 1952–3: Report by E. W. Blackburn to meeting of the Further Education Sub-Committee, folio 2868, 20 April 1953.
46. Greater Manchester County Record Office, Manchester City Council Education Committee minutes 1953–4: Report by E. W. Blackburn to meeting of the Further Education Sub-Committee, folio 1791, 31 December 1953.
47. Greater Manchester County Record Office, Manchester City Council Education Committee minutes 1954–5: Report by E. W. Blackburn to meeting of the Further Education Sub-Committee, folio 667, 19 July 1954.
48. Ibid.
49. Ibid.
50. Ibid.
51. Ibid.
52. Greater Manchester County Record Office, Manchester City Council Education Committee minutes 1954–5: Minute of meeting of the Further Education Sub-Committee, folio 1960, 20 December 1954.
53. Ibid. Emphasis added.
54. 'Miss Horsbrugh to Open New Centre for Coloured People: Missionary Society Work in Manchester', *The Manchester Guardian,* 13 October 1954. Getting Miss Florence Horsburgh, the Minister of Education, whose parliamentary constituency covered Moss Side, to open the centre was a big coup for St Gerard's (NB: St Gerard's was still operating in 1962; see Stanley (1998), p. 48).
55. Interview, Victor Lawrence (member of committee of Community House 1954–81), Moss Side, 10 October 2012.
56. Lewis Archives, Princeton, Box 29: J. K. Elliott, Chief Education Officer, Manchester Education Committee, to Lewis, 7 April 1955.
57. Lewis Archives, Princeton, Box 5/4: Lewis to J. K. Elliott, 18 April 1955.
58. Lewis Archives, Princeton, Box 29: J. K. Elliott, Chief Education Officer, Manchester Education Committee, to Lewis, 7 April 1955; also Greater Manchester County Record Office, Manchester City Council Education Committee minutes: Minute of meeting of the Further Education Sub-Committee, folio 2880, 21 March 1955.
59. Greater Manchester County Record Office, Manchester City Council Education Committee minutes 1958–9: Minute of meeting of the Further Education Sub-Committee, folio 2805, 16 March 1959. Emphasis added.
60. Summarised as case study 34 in Mosley and Ingham (2012). In this study, Aston Gore was asked:
    'How did you raise the money?'
    'You see it's a fallacy, a myth going about that Black people mistrust one another. It's something deep-rooted, in various elements. We found the money among the members, seventy-odd thousand pounds ... some gave half a crown, some gave seven and six, some gave twenty, some gave more. How many Black people [ever] raised seventy thousand pounds in four years? It was raised. (Ibid.)

61. Beresford Edwards, in his interview (summarised as case study 29 in Mosley and Ingham (2012).) Edwards describes black churches as 'another opium ... an escape from facing up to the realities of black people here'. Victor Lawrence is also the interviewee in case study 21 in Mosley and Ingham (2012)).

62. For a discussion of what has been achieved, with a focus on Birmingham, see Lenton and Mosley (2011), ch. 5; or in more detail, Hussain and Mosley (2012).

63. Labour Party International Department: Report by W. Arthur Lewis to the Commonwealth Sub-Committee of the National Executive, May 1952.

64. W. Arthur Lewis, New Fabian Essays, *Draft Chapter on Overseas Development*, 1953.

65. Rhodes House, Oxford, Arthur Creech Jones papers: ACJ 44/4, May 1952, p. 15.

66. 'Poverty is taken as the test': Rhodes House, Oxford, Arthur Creech Jones papers: ACJ 44/4, May 1952, p. 2, para. 2.

67. Ibid., pp. 1 and 6.

68. Ibid..

69. Ibid., para. 44.

70. Rhodes House, Oxford, Arthur Creech Jones papers: ACJ 44/4, May 1952.

71. See, for example, the critiques of using aid as export subsidy contained in Independent Group on British Aid (1981); and Morrissey *et al.* (1992).

72. Rhodes House, Oxford, Arthur Creech Jones papers: ACJ 44/4, May 1952, para. 48, p. 12. Emphasis added.

73. W. Arthur Lewis, New Fabian Essays, *Draft Chapter on Overseas Development*, p. 21.

74. Biographical details on Hugh Gaitskell taken from Williams (1979). See also Saville (1980), pp. 148–69.

75. Lewis Archives, Princeton: Box 6/2: Letter from Arthur Lewis to Hugh Gaitskell, 22 December 1955.

76. The unsubstantiated theory that Gaitskell was assassinated by the Soviets to make way for Wilson as Labour Party leader surfaced in the 1960s in British intelligence, and emerged again in the 1970s. There were speculative rumours that Wilson's resignation as prime minister in 1976 had been forced on him by the continuing activities of the British security services. See, in particular, Pimlott (1992) for a full discussion of the allegations, which remain cloudy and lacking in any substantial factual basis.

77. Letter from Nicholas Kaldor, King's College, Cambridge, to Hugh Gaitskell, April 1954.

78. Lewis Archives, Princeton: Box 6/2: Letter from W. A. Lewis to Hugh Gaitskell, 7 May 1954.

79. Ibid.

80. Lewis Archives, Princeton: Box 6/2: Gaitskell to Lewis, 14 December,1955.

81. Ibid.

82. Lewis Archives, Princeton: Box 6/2: Lewis to Gaitskell 22 December 1955.

83. An enthusiasm for the US was something else that Lewis had shared with Gaitskell. Gaitskell was described by his biographer as 'an enthusiastic, committed and undeviating supporter of the American alliance'. The Labour leader was a great believer in the US Democratic Party, which he

carried through in practical terms by a willingness to support increased military spending through NATO. None of this, of course, had endeared him to the left of the party.

6   Why Visiting Economists Fail: The Turning Point in Ghana, 1957–8

1. Much of this was to the result of the work of a visionary governor, Sir Gordon Guggisberg, who between 1920 and 1928 implemented policies of investment in infrastructure, health and education which were aimed explicitly at improving the living standards of Africans, and in particular lower-income Africans; for example, public expenditure policies were skewed explicitly towards the poorer northern region of the country. (On Guggisberg's work, see the biography by Wraith, 1967.) As a result, the demographic profile of Ghana from the First World War onwards looks different from that of other tropical African countries: the (under 1 year) infant mortality rate, for example, dips to around 115 per 1,000 by the mid-1920s, whereas in other tropical African countries it was more than double that level (see Bowden and Mosley, 2012). In her *Plan for Africa* (1940), Rita Hinden made a case study out of this remarkable performance, illustrating that 'Government expenditure on all children at school in the Gold Coast is between £3–£4 per head – the highest in any African colony except Zanzibar.' She added that 'the [school] enrolment [had] more than doubled itself in the last twenty years' – in many other African countries it was static at a very low base. At the top end of the system, the Gold Coast, also had an elite further education college, Achimota College, which already had the power, absent from most British colonial colleges, to award external degrees of the University of London (Hinden, 1941), pp. 182–3.
2. Seers and Ross (1952).
3. Seers and Ross (1952), p. 170.
4. Aggrey–Fraser–Guggisberg Memorial Lecture, University of Ghana, 1968. Published as Lewis (1969b).
5. National Archives, Kew, CO 990/2: Colonial Economic Advisory Committee, Industry Sub-Committee, folio 15: *The Analysis of Secondary Industries* by W. A. Lewis and F. V. Meyer.
6. Gold Coast Government (1953a), para. 29.
7. Gold Coast Government (1953a), para. 24. On this theme, see also Ingham (1987), vol. 3, pp. 76–7.
8. Gold Coast Government (1953a): para. 24, drawing on Rhodes House Oxford: Mss. Afr.s. 332: Arthur Creech Jones Papers, Box 34, folio 1: 'The People's Educational Association in Ghana'.
9. Johnson's book (Johnson, 1982) uses Japan, South Korea and Singapore as his exemplars. As presented by Johnson, the essence of a developmental state is a partnership between the state and the private sector to achieve rapid economic growth, with the state providing financial support (and in particular selective, performance-based subsidies) to the private sector, and the private sector being expected in return to co-finance the costs of health, education and social protection. Developmental states are

sometimes characterized as 'hard states', in contrast with the 'soft states', whose softness was seen by Gunnar Myrdal (1967) as a cause of poor developmental performance in South Asia. In the 2000s, the president and finance minister of South Africa openly sought to identify a 'developmental state' as a model for where they seek to be (this idea is also embedded in the Latin-American idea of *neodesarrollismo*, or neo-developmentalism, which became popular in the 2000s in the wake of the East Asian crisis).

10. Among the vulnerable groups Lewis sought to include, note in particular the case of women: 'It is permanently the case that the economy would gain if women were more widely employed in every occupation other than petty trading' (Gold Coast Government, 1953a, para. 225).

11. National Archives, Kew: CO 554/202/66472: response by Colonial Office to Lewis Report (Lewis 1953a).

12. Lewis Papers, Princeton, Box 6/2: Gbedemah to Lewis, March 1953.

13. The Gold Coast must rely to a large extent on foreign enterprise, and the government is anxious to give it every encouragement' (Gold Coast, *Legislative Assembly Debates*, 17 February 1954, pp. 1082–3).

14. Private communication in the mid-1980s from the late Jonathan Frimpong Ansah.

15. Nkrumah (1957).

16. Killick (1978), p. 45.

17. Ibid., p. 46. The quotation is from Nkrumah (1961), p. 28.

18. Lewis Papers, Princeton, Box 10/2: Lewis to Nkrumah, 18 March 1957. We therefore disagree with Robert Tignor's view that 'the year 1955 marked the apex of Lewis' enthusiasm for the scheme' (2005, p. 202): in our view it came two, maybe even three, years later.

19. Lewis Papers, Princeton, Box 10/2: Lewis to Nkrumah, 18 March 1957; and Eugene R. Black, president, World Bank, to Nkrumah, 15 March 1957.

20. Lewis Papers, Princeton: Box 10/2, postscript to letter, Nkrumah to Lewis, 2 April 1957.

21. Lewis Papers, Princeton, Box 10/2: Nkrumah to Lewis, 4 November 1957.

22. Ghana National Assembly: *Debates,* July 7 1958.

23. Lewis Archives, Princeton, Box 10/5: Lewis to David Owen (Executive Chairman, Technical Assistance Board, United Nations), 3 February 1958. Emphasis added.

24. See passage keyed by note (23) above.

25. '(When I threatened to resign) Mr Gbedemah commended me and [said] that he himself had been on the verge of resignation for some time (he has often told me this)', Lewis Papers, Princeton: Box 8/2, Lewis to Hugh Keenlyside, Director-General of Technical Assistance, United Nations, New York.

26. Lewis Papers, Princeton, Box 10/2: Lewis to Nkrumah, 1 August 1958.

27. Lewis Papers, Princeton, Box 8/2: Lewis to Hugh Keenlyside, Director-General of Technical Assistance, United Nations, New York.

28. Lewis Papers, Princeton, Box 10/2: Lewis to Nkrumah, 1 November 1958. Italics in original. E.A. stands for Economic Adviser: K.N. is Kwame Nkrumah; and Eric Taylor is an expatriate engineering adviser.

29. Lewis Papers, Princeton, Box 8/2: Lewis to Hugh Keenlyside, Director-General of Technical Assistance, United Nations, New York. 'Destooling' = removal of chiefs from their position of authority.

30. Lewis Archive, Princeton, Box 10/2: Lewis to Nkrumah, 18 December 1958.
31. Lewis Archive, Princeton, Box 10/2: Nkrumah to Lewis, 19 December 1958.
32. *Evening News* (Accra), 30 September 1961.
33. Lewis Papers, Princeton, Box 7/2: Rita Hinden to Lewis, 21 May 1958. This was a bare four months before Lewis was to describe Krobo Edusei as 'of worldwide fame for the ease with which he imprisons or deports'.
34. Lewis Papers, Princeton, Box 7/2: Lewis to Rita Hinden, 24 May 1958.
35. Seers (1962), p. 326.
36. This is a criticism particularly often encountered, even now, in relation to visiting economists requesting reform packages in return for loans from the World Bank, IMF or other international financial agencies. The literature that has emerged since the 1990s emphasizing the importance of recipient country 'ownership' of reform packages is an attempt to respond to the criticism.
37. On this issue, Seers wrote: 'Some peripatetic economists prescribe the same medicine for all countries, whatever the symptoms. (In the medical profession, to do this is considered quackery.)' Seers (1962), p. 326. While Seers did not define the case he had in mind, it is fairly clear that he is referring to the quantity theory of money, and to the IMF's practice of invariably prescribing fiscal and monetary deflation as a remedy for the inflation and debt problems of Latin America, using the 'Polak model' which, at the time Seers was writing, had already been a standard tool that the Fund used routinely to calculate the degree of fiscal and monetary deflation required to correct a macro-economic disequilibrium in any country.
38. Bianchi (2011), p. 223.
39. Bianchi (2011), p. 229.
40. In Hirschman (1984).
41. See Bianchi (2011), pp. 217–42.
42. Hirschman (1963), p.177.
43. Seers (1962), p. 338.
44. See Lewis Papers, Princeton, Box 2/3: Letters by Lewis to and from George Abbott.
45. Meier (1993), pp. 381–9.
46. Kanbur (2001), pp. 1083–94.
47. Seers (1962), p. 325.
48. For a number of cases of this, see Mosley *et al.* (2012). One particular case, with a number of resonances to the role Gbedemah attempted and failed to carry through in Ghana, is that in Uganda in the late 1980s, seeking to reconstruct out of conflict with donor assistance, the policy dialogue became deadlocked because President Museveni was not willing to concede to donors either on the principle of flexible exchange rates, or on export taxation of coffee, or on the need for a poverty reduction strategy. Luckily, there existed an intermediary (Emanuel Tumusime-Mutabile, Permanent Secretary of the Ministry of Finance, and now Governor of the Bank of Uganda) who held the confidence of both president and donors, and who was able to persuade the president to leave the donors to him, and to concentrate on the rest of his agenda. By this means, a poverty strategy was constructed by Tumusime-Mutabile and the donors with the president's agreement, on the grounds that that was the key to securing long-term

programme finance, and the financial padlock previously imposed by the donors was removed. By contrast, Kenya and Malawi, in the late 1980s and early 1990s, were countries with about the same degree of policy imperfection (that is, slippage on World Bank and IMF conditions) as Uganda, but unlike Uganda did not have an intermediary such as Tumusime-Mutabile who could sell to the donors the proposition that, on core issues, the government's strategy was in line with the donors' conditionality. See Mosley *et al.* (2012) ch. 5.

49. Perkins and Roemer (1991).

7 Disenchantment in the Caribbean, 1958–63

1. Lewis (1960).
2. Interestingly, on the question of whether Lewis had intended initially to research the Caribbean for his doctoral thesis, Mark Figueroa has drawn our attention to an article in the Caribbean periodical *Jamaica Arise* (August 1947) suggesting that Lewis did spend part of the time after graduation on his travelling scholarship, researching labour conditions in the Caribbean.
3. A brief contemporary account of the disturbances in the British West Indies can be found in the preface to the second edition (1938) of W. M. Macmillan's book *Warning from the West Indies*. Strikes and other serious upheavals began in the early 1930s in St Vincent, St Lucia and Barbados. By 1937 the unrest had spread to all the islands, including Jamaica, where there were violent demonstrations by unemployed ex-servicemen and riots on the sugar estates. There were further strikes in St Lucia in the sugar industry, and dock strikes in British Guiana and Trinidad.
4. Lewis, autobiographical account in Breit and Spencer (1986).
5. We are grateful to Yoichi Mine for drawing our attention to this letter in the Creech Jones papers in the Bodleian Library. See also Mine (2004).
6. Craig (1977).
7. The quotes are from Hintzen (1991).
8. 'It is difficult to find a text written by Caribbean researchers, devoted to the ideas of Lewis, which does not have as its central feature criticisms of Lewis's economic prescriptions and questions about his authenticity as a genuine Caribbean thinker. In such works, Lewis's reflections on West Indian identity in particular, but his wider economic ideas as well, are often branded as reactionary or pro-European', extract from Joseph (2009). Tennyson Joseph's statement that anti-Lewis sentiments are still widespread among present-day intellectuals in the Caribbean has been challenged by Caribbean scholar Mark Figueroa. Nor was Joseph's view supported in our own interviews with academics and policy-makers in the Caribbean, where there appeared to be a growing belief in the soundness of many of Lewis's ideas.
9. C. L. R. James was encouraged to travel to London to write, by Learie Constantine, the first West Indian to play cricket at a professional level in Britain. The story is told by James in his autobiography (James, [1963]).
10. James [1963], p. 59.

11. James (2009 [1963]), p. 250.
12. Naipaul (1962).
13. Minutes of the Moyne Commission, [Lewis's] Memorandum on Social Welfare in the British West Indies, Serial Number 45.
14. LaGuerre (1991).
15. Lewis (1944), reprinted in Emmanuel (1994).
16. Lewis (1994).
17. Lewis (1959).
18. Lewis (1944).
19. An example of this blunt and forthright tendency can be found in the final paragraph of Lewis's Report on the British Guiana Plan: 'The writer of the Colonial Office memorandum says that this is a good plan, and in particular that the agricultural part is satisfactory, but it is obvious that he does not really believe this since his remarks all question whether the plan will really have much effect on the national income' (Lewis, 1948, para. 20), Colonial Development Council, British Guiana Ten Year Development Plan. Comments by Professor Lewis, August 1948.
20. Letter to Dr D. Huggins, University College, Mona, Jamaica from Arthur Lewis, January 1954. Lewis collection, Mudd Library, Princeton.
21. The letter from Dudley Huggins (1953) also reports increasing hostility to Lewis's industrialization strategy at international conferences including those sponsored by the World Bank (Lewis Archives, Princeton: Box 7/4).
22. Moggridge (2007)
23. Lewis (1965c).
24. Copies of the resignation letter are on file in the Archives in UWI, at Mona, Jamaica, and in the Lewis collection in the Mudd Library at Princeton.
25. UWI Archives, Mona, Jamaica: W. A. Lewis Personal Files.
26. Private communication from Mark Figueroa.
27. The two letters from Norman Manley to Lewis can be found in the Lewis papers in the Mudd Library at Princeton (Box 9/3).
28. University of the West Indies: Memorandum for the Conference on the Common Services (1962).
29. Letter from W. A. Lewis (Principal) to Professor Bras (Senate), 15 March 1962.
30. Letter from the Principal to Deans, 29 November 1961. Principal's copy in the Lewis papers in the Mudd Library, Princeton.
31. Lewis (1960).
32. King (2000). Like Lewis, Walcott was born in St Lucia and educated at St Mary's College.
33. Lewis (1960). See also Lewis (1971b).
34. Lewis Archives, Princeton, Box 32/7: Minutes of the Meeting of the Board of Governors of the Jamaica School of Music held on 21 February 1961.
35. Lewis Archives, Princeton, Box 32/7: Correspondence between Norman Manley and Charles Napper of Fletcher, Napper and Co., London solicitors, 8 November 1960; and letter, Napper to Lewis, 8 March 1961.
36. Lewis Archives, Princeton, Box 32/7: Minutes of the Meeting of the Board of Governors of the Jamaica School of Music held on 21 February 1961.
37. Lewis Archives, Princeton, Box 19/5: Correspondence between Lewis and Dean of the Faculty of Agriculture, University of the West Indies.

38. An example of this genre is a nine-page note of a lecture, 'Agricultural Development', given to the Faculty of Agriculture of what was then the Barbados campus of the University of the West Indies (Lewis Archives, Princeton, Box 19/5: 'Lewis' Writings, 1961–62'). This paper rehearses Lewis's familiar themes of the need for agricultural programmes to orientate themselves towards small and undercapitalized farmers, and the need for a wide extension network (p. 6), and alludes to the low political status of agriculture in most LDC governments as a reason for the lack of urgency in the vital field of agricultural development (p. 5).

Towards the end of his time at UWI, in October 1962, Lewis attended a conference on Economic Growth and Investment in Agriculture on the Mona campus for which he did not produce a paper, but his remarks were transcribed (Lewis Archives, Princeton, Box 19/5: 'Lewis' Writings, 1961–62'). His remarks extend his proposition about the high costs of UWI to African universities: 'it is actually cheaper if you count all the resources for an African student to send him to London than it is for him to be trained at Ibadan or Achimota' … thus 'the poorest countries are carrying the highest costs'. His recommendation is that aid donors should pay a higher share of the costs of tertiary education in low-income Commonwealth countries. The mass education theme takes a back seat at this point, as it does in Lewis's 1969 Aggrey–Fraser–Guggisberg lectures on the economics of education (see Chapter 8 below).

39. See Figueroa (2008).

40. Beckford (1984).

41. Girvan and Jefferson (1971).

42. Typescript of his address to the SALISES (Sir Arthur Lewis Institute of Social and Economic Studies) Conference, Kingston, Jamaica, March 2005, supplied by Norman Girvan to the authors.

43. Figueroa (1994).

44. Lewis Archives, Princeton, Box 18: 'West Indies Federation', January 1962.

45. Lewis Archives, Princeton, Box 8/5: Lewis to Carl La Corbiniere (Deputy Prime Minister, Trinidad), 6 February 1961.

46. Lewis Papers, Princeton, Box 14: Williams to Lewis, 27 March 1950.

47. 'Professor Lewis was probably the only man who could do this. He is universally respected and is known to have no political bias and above all is liked by Dr Williams and can gain access to him, which is not easy except for a favoured few', National Archives, Kew, CO 1031/3374: Colonial Office Brief for Secretary of State's visit to the West Indies, 8/1/62.

48. Lewis Archives, Princeton, Box 12/6: Lewis to Philip Sherlock, 22 September 1961.

49. 'I was particularly impressed with the thought of the West Indies becoming like Sweden and Switzerland a reservoir for people to help in trouble spots of the world – an obvious idea when one thinks of it, but I just had not done so', Lewis Archives, Princeton, 19 July 1961, Box 3/1: Lewis to Kenneth Blackburne, King's House, Jamaica.

50. This is at National Archives, Kew, CO 1031/3374: Colonial Office Brief for Secretary of State's visit to the West Indies.

51. From the context here, Lewis appears to mean 'attach itself to' or 'leave within a new unitary state'.

52. The rhetoric and tone of this appeal was almost identical to the way he had addressed Nkrumah three years before: 'I plead first on behalf of the common people of Ghana, who love you, and who will trustfully accept whatever you give them, whether it is an international conference hall or water supplies', Lewis Archives, Princeton, Box 10/2: Lewis to Nkrumah, 1 August 1958.

53. Lewis Archive, Princeton, Box 19/2: Memorandum by Lewis, 'Williams and the Eight'. Passages in parentheses are paraphrases by the author. Capitals in the final line are Lewis's.

54. Lewis Archive, Princeton, Box 19/2: Lewis, 'Efforts to Organise Eight', undated, probably March 1962.

55. The outline constitution is in Lewis Archive, Princeton, Box 16/2: 'Eastern Caribbean Federation: Note by Professor Lewis', 17 January 1962. The timetable is also in Box 19/2: 'Efforts to Organise Eight', undated, probably March 1962.

56. This document is with Lewis Papers, Princeton, Box 16/2: 'An Eastern Caribbean Federation: Further Notes by Professor Lewis', undated, probably early February 1962.

57. Lewis Papers, Princeton, Box 16/2: 'An Eastern Caribbean Federation: Further Notes by Professor Lewis', p. 2. Aid dependence (as a proportion of GNP) in the Windward and Leeward Islands at that time was around 14 per cent, which is approximately what it is for the average of the poorest African countries today.

58. It is now commonplace to argue that excessive aid may disincentivize tax collection (see further discussion in Chapter 5 above).

59. 'The Parliamentary Under-Secretary of State said he would like to know whether the aim of the tariff would be to protect revenue or to encourage industry. Dr Lewis replied that the feeling of Ministers was that tariffs should stimulate development of light industry in the area. Industries would be set up not just on a scale for a market of 700,000 but for export – for example, the Antigua oil refinery', Lewis Archive, Princeton, Box 16/2: Minutes of East Caribbean Federation conference, London, 9 May 1962, second session, p. 7.

60. Ibid., pp. 2/3.

61. Ibid., p. 2.

62. Ibid., p. 5.

63. Lewis archive, Princeton: Box 16/2, Statement by Errol Barrow, Chief Minister of Barbados, at East Caribbean Federation conference, London, 9 May 1962.

64. Lewis looked to his allies Errol Barrow, prime minister of Barbados, and Vere Bird, prime minister of Antigua, to bring the others round to his fiscal proposals.

65. The words of Mr Gairy, prime minister of Grenada.

66. Lewis (1965a), p. 23.

67. Ibid., pp. 36, 39. Uppercase in original.

68. Lewis Archive, Princeton, Box 1: Lewis to Princess Alice, Chancellor of the University of the West Indies, 19 July 1962.

69. Letter from Lewis to Lord Hailes, 21 June 1962, in Lewis collection, Mudd Library, Princeton.

70. Recorded in Lewis's personal files in the UWI Archives at Mona, October 1961.

71. Lewis, 1965a). See also Lewis (1968).
72. Lewis's response is in the Lewis collection in the Mudd Library at Princeton.
73. We are grateful to the editors of the *Journal of East Caribbean Studies* for permission to quote freely from Ingham and Figueroa (2009).
74. 'Jamaica's Economic Problems: A Series of Seven Articles' *The Daily Gleaner*, Editor D. C. Stokes, 1964. Reprinted in Emmanuel (1994), Vol. 2.
75. Lewis file, Letters 1971–73, Caribbean Development Bank Archives.

8 Princeton and Retirement, 1963–91

1. Fitzgerald in 1913 described Princeton as being 'lazy and good-looking and aristocratic – you know, like a spring day', and Fitzgerald's biographer, Matthew Bruccoli, describes Princeton as 'the Southerner's Ivy League college' (Bruccoli, 1981, p. 44). Our thanks to Nicholas Mosley for uncovering this reference.
2. Fitzgerald (2000), p. 36.
3. Oberdorfer (1995), p. 11.
4. Ibid. p. 150. The black proportion of the postgraduate population is almost certainly higher than this.
5. See Sternlieb *et al.* (1971), ch. 1.
6. See Einthoven and Smagorinsky (1992), p. 3. This booklet contains photographs of many of them. Fitzgerald composed a competition-winning football song in celebration of the Princeton Tigers, one line of which goes 'Eli, Eli, all your hopes are dead, for the tiger's growling in his lair'. (Bruccoli, 1981, p. 70. 'Eli' means Elihu Yale, after whom Yale University is named.)
7. For example, Lewis's discussion of caste in *The Theory of Economic Growth*, beginning on p. 45 and running throughout the book, where over-population is given as a major reason why employers may restrict employment to people of their own caste and social status.
8. 'World University Rankings 2011–2012', *The Times Higher Education Supplement*, 6 October 2011.
9. Einstein eventually moved from the University to the Institute of Advanced Study.
10. John Nash, after whom the Nash bargaining equilibrium is named, received his graduate training, and in 1950 his Ph.D., not in Princeton's Department of Economics, but in the Department of Mathematics. In 1959 he was hospitalized, probably suffering from paranoid schizophrenia, resigned his tenured post at the Massachusetts Institute of Technology (MIT), and wrote little for the following 30 years. After 1990, his productivity began to return and, jointly with John Harsanyi and Reinhard Selten, was awarded the Nobel Prize for Economics in 1994. Some of the information about Princeton local colour found in this book is heavily indebted to the classic biography of Nash by Sylvia Nasar (Nasar, 1998).
11. As William Baumol put it: 'The development part of the Princeton economics department was neither good nor bad, it was in the middle. It badly needed someone of Arthur's stature to give it a lift', Interview, 8 January 2012.

12. Lewis (1965b), Preface, p. 12.
13. This was emphasised in Cruise O'Brien (1967), pp. 95–6.
14. Lewis's contribution to this debate, (Lewis, 1949c), is described in Chapter 2 of this book. Lewis's book is concerned with how the state can improve the allocation of resources under democratic governance in the environment of post-war Britain. It turns to developing countries only in its Appendix II, which says that 'planning requires a strong, competent and incorrupt administration', which 'is just what no backward country possesses, and in the absence of such an administration it is often much better that governments should be *laissez-faire* than that they should pretend to plan' (p. 121). This is fascinatingly at variance, not only with the position taken in *Development Planning*, but also with what Lewis had already written in the 1940s for the CEAC and CEDC.
15. Lewis's 1959 talk 'On Making a Development Plan' is in the Lewis Archive at Princeton, Box 12.
16. Lewis Archive, Princeton, Box 38/6: *On Making A Development Plan*, by W. A. Lewis. Transcript of a paper delivered from notes to the 1959 National Conference of the American Society for Public Administration.
17. Lewis had a very quiet speaking voice (Deaton interview, 3 January 2012; Warke interview, 30 May 2012) and thus found the mass-lecture mode very uncomfortable. He felt much more at home in conversational mode, in classes and workshops.
18. Lewis Archive, Princeton, Box 34/1: Economics 566 'Modern Economic History' and Boxes 34/2, 34/3 and 34/4, 'Economic Growth in Developing Areas', Lewis's lecture notes, 'Surplus Labour in India: A Pedagogical Note'.
19. Lewis Archive, Princeton, Box 6/6: Hansen to Lewis, 27 January 1969.
20. Jorgensen wrote to Lewis that he regarded Lewis's view that some rural people had zero or near-zero labour productivity as 'a red herring, for which I am afraid you must bear some responsibility', Lewis Archive, Princeton, Box 8/1: Jorgensen to Lewis, 23 January 1969.
21. Schultz (1964), ch. 3.
22. Lewis Archive, Princeton, Box 34/3: Lewis's lecture notes.
23. The successive versions of the *Economic Growth in Developing Areas* reading list can be inspected at Lewis Archives, Princeton, Box 34/2.
24. Telephone interview, Henry Bienen, 10 January 2012.
25. Lewis (1966), p. 22.
26. Lewis (1966), p. 87.
27. 'The rise of one new profitable industry, capable of paying very high wages, can have a devastating effect on employment throughout the economy, since, as wages everywhere chase the leader, not only the traditional sector, but also existing industries in the modern sector, dispose of labour, and throw it into open unemployment in the labour market. Jamaica's case is classic: during the decade of the 1950s net investment averaged 18 per cent of national income, real output doubled, and 11 per cent of the labour force emigrated; yet open unemployment was as great at the end as at the beginning of the decade. Several countries of Latin America have had similar, if not so spectacular, experiences', Lewis (1966), p. 78. This is also the essence of South Africa's high-wages-plus-unemployment-plus-rising poverty problem at present.

28. 'It is now clear that little more than a decade of rapid growth in under-developed countries has been of little benefit to perhaps a third of their population. Although the average per capita income of the Third World has increased by 50 per cent since 1960, this growth has been very une-qually distributed between countries, regions within countries, and socio-economic groups. Paradoxically, while growth policies have succeeded beyond the expectations of the first development decade, the very idea of aggregate growth as a social objective has increasingly been called into question' (Chenery *et al.* (1974), p. xiii).
29. Lewis (1966), p. 60 .
30. Baumol interview, 8 January 2011.
31. Ibid.
32. See Baumol (1971). Baumol, in conjunction with the President of Princeton, William Bowen, produced, in Lewis's description, a 'huge tome' on the economics of the American theatre and classical music in the 1960s; Lewis Archive, Princeton, Box 4/5: Lewis to Werner Dannhauser, National Humanities Centre.
33. Mark Gersovitz, personal communication, 19 June 2012.
34. Ibid.
35. Interview, Gustav Ranis, New Haven, CT, 13 January 2012.
36. I asked Bienen why this was so (interview 10 January 2012). He replied that it might be because some political scientists failed to apply rigorous reasoning to the development process, and let themselves get carried away into arguments based on emotion, or simply consisting of narrative, rather than logic. (Lewis seems to have been particularly underwhelmed by Uphoff and Ilchman's recently published *The Political Economy of Growth*; see Lewis Archive, Princeton, Box 13/5: Uphoff to Lewis, 26 January 1969). At the time that Bienen was appointed, in the late 1960s, it was becoming clear to Lewis from his first-hand experience in West Africa in particular that much of the developing world was being afflicted by the failure of its political and administrative institutions, as described in *Politics in West Africa*, and in Bienen's view, Lewis saw this before many political scientists did. Interview, Bienen, 10 January 2012.
37. Lewis Archives, Princeton, Box 2/8: F. W. Blackman to Lewis, 26 June 1967.
38. Lewis's contempt for calypso music and steel bands continued unabated: 'My exclusion of West Indian topics at this stage was deliberate. The reason is that the students on the Mona campus seemed very well versed in West Indian cultural life – our novelists, our dances, our steel bands – and also very knowledgeable about current Anglo-American pop culture – Beatniks, Beatles and whatnot – but seemed almost completely ignorant of the great stream of world culture, extending backwards over thirty centuries, which we West Indians have inherited along with the rest of the human race. No prize was needed to encourage the students to find out more about the West Indies, but a substantial incentive was needed to encourage them to find out more about this external cultural heritage. Consequently, West Indian topics were deliberately excluded from *this* prize' (Lewis Archive, Princeton, Box 2/8: Lewis to F. W. Blackman, University of the West Indies, 6 July 1967). What he would have made of reggae and rap, one can only wonder.

39. Lewis Archive, Princeton, Box 8/7: Lewis to Professor Robert Lively, 14 September 1966.
40. Lewis Archive, Princeton, Box 6: Lewis to Professor David Walker, University of Exeter, etc.
41. Ranis interview, 13 January 2012.
42. Lewis (1952), pp. 105–38. As shown in Chapter 3, this paper estimated (by simple OLS methods) that the elasticity of the volume of trade with respect to the rate of growth of world manufacturing from 1881 to 1987 was 0.87 (ibid., p. 111): in other words, that world trade grew very nearly, but not quite as fast as world manufacturing. Measurements of this kind had not been made before.
43. Lewis and O'Leary (1955), pp. 113–52.
44. Lewis (1978a), p. 16.
45. These include Baran (1968), Frank (1974), Palmer and Parsons (1977) and Perrings (1979).
46. Interviews, William Baumol, 8 January 2012; and Henry Bienen 10 January 2012.
47. Lewis (1978a), p. 16.
48. Lewis Archive, Princeton, Box 34/2: Public Affairs 531, *Economic Growth in Developing Areas*, class handout, 'A Possible Seminar Book'.
49. Lewis (1970a), p. 21.
50. Lewis (1978a), p. 208.
51. Lewis Archive, Princeton, Box 8/6: Arthur Lewis to John P. Lewis, 30 January 1973.
52. Lewis (1969c), pp. 1, 18–22.
53. In his Janeway Lectures at Princeton, Lewis put the proposition in this way: 'The remedy follows. The way to create a new international economic order is to eliminate the 50 to 60 per cent of low-productivity workers in food by transforming their productivity. This would change the factoral terms of tropical trade and raise the prices of the traditional agricultural exports. It would also create an agricultural surplus that would support industrial production for the home market' (Janeway Lectures), Lewis (1978b), p. 37.
54. Lewis Archives, Princeton, Box 6/4: Aggrey–Fraser–Guggisberg Memorial Lectures 1968, second lecture on 'The Economics of Education', p. 3.
55. Ibid., p. 2.
56. Lewis Archives, Princeton, Box 12/3: W. A. Lewis to Edward Shils, 11 June 1975 and 2 January 1979.
57. Lewis (1971a), p. 8.
58. Ibid. ..
59. For a discussion of asset-based welfare policy, see Sherraden (1991) in the US context and Emmerson and Wakefield (2001) in the UK context.
60. This banner is reproduced on p. 198 of Oberdorfer (1995).
61. Lewis(1969a), p. 10. Later reprinted in *Princeton Alumni Weekly* in Lewis Archive, Princeton, Box 39/8.
62. Ibid., p. 11. Lewis proceeded to take his idealization of African principles back into child-rearing: 'The most successful minorities in America, the Chinese, the Japanese and the Jews, are distinguished by their close and highly disciplined family, with its undisciplined and uncontrollable children reared on what are alleged to be the disciplines of Dr Spock. African

families are warm, highly disciplined structures just like Jewish or Chinese families. If black Americans are looking to Africa for aspects of culture which will distinguish them from white Americans, let them turn their back on Spockism, and rear their children on African principles, for this is the way to the middle and the top' (ibid., p. 12)

63. Reply: 'Notes on Black Studies', attached to Lewis Papers, Princeton, Box ¾: Lewis to McGeorge Bundy, president, Ford Foundation, 28 May 1969.
64. Ibid.
65. Lewis Papers, Princeton, Box 13/7: Lewis to J. Allen Wallis, president, University of Rochester.
66. The letter is to be found at Lewis Archives, Princeton, Box 4/6: Lewis to Vernon Dixon, 1 October 1969. It is fully summarized and discussed in Tignor (2005), ch. 7.
67. W. Arthur Lewis, 'The Economic Status of Women', Commencement address, Rosary College, Illinois, May 1970. Lewis Papers, Princeton, Box 39/8, p. 1.
68. Ibid., p. 5.
69. Ibid., p. 6.
70. Lewis Archives, Princeton, Box 10: John P. Lewis (Dean, Woodrow Wilson School) to W. A. Lewis, 20 November 1973.
71. He had put considerable effort into trying, and failing, to secure a large Ford Foundation programme grant in the 1960s (see Tignor, 2005, ch. 7).
72. Lewis Archives, Princeton, Box 8/6: Beatrice Miers (Administrator, Woodrow Wilson School) to Lewis, 1 April 1974; and reply by Lewis to Dean of the School (John P. Lewis), 4 April 1974.
73. Chenery *et al.*, (1974), p. xiii.
74. Lewis papers, Princeton, Box 8/6: W. A. Lewis to John P. Lewis, 30 January 1973. In his detailed comment to John P. Lewis, Arthur Lewis adds: 'I know of no development economists who "presumed that growth would bring distributional benefits to the weakest sections in its wake". The majority of theoretical economists since Ricardo and of economic historians since the Hammonds, had argued exactly the opposite'. This would have appalled the World Bank, which especially since the rebirth of pro-poor strategies in the 1970s has put enormous efforts into researching the relationship between growth and poverty, reaching the result that overall it is significantly and strongly negative (Dollar and Kraay (2001), and World Bank (2006), esp. fig. 4.2). True, the growth–poverty link appears to be weaker for the poorest groups, which only goes to show that supplementary measures are required for the chronic poor and extreme poor (Mosley (2004b). The real issue is the need for action, even more than the need to research and not take for granted the shape of the relationship, which Lewis seems to treat as quite obvious and scarcely requiring research.
75. Interview, Gustav Ranis, New Haven, 13 January 2012.
76. Lewis papers, Princeton, Box 31/9: meeting of panel with Mr Chenery, 28 October 1978.
77. Lewis papers, Princeton, Box 31/9: Reply to Bela Balassa, 27 October 1978; and Box 31/10: S. Bery and W. A. Lewis, Report of Advisory Panel on Research, June 1979, p. 17.
78. Lewis papers, Princeton, Box 31/10: Comments by T. N. Srinivasan on Bery/Lewis report, May 1979. Balassa too was critical of the Bery/Lewis

report, saying that it was 'long on definitions and categorisation, but short on discussions of the character and orientation of Bank research'. Lewis papers, Princeton, Box 31/10: Comments by Bela Balassa on Bery/Lewis report, May 1979.

79. Our evidence for making this claim is given above. Others do not agree. William Baumol writes: 'To me he seems to have been well acclimatised in Princeton, and was warmly welcomed when he returned from his efforts in the Caribbean, and the process of return was welcomed by him' (Personal communication, 29 May 2012).

80. Lewis Archives, Princeton, Box 8/6, John P. Lewis to W. Arthur Lewis, 12 May 1971.

81. In the sixth Janeway Lecture on the 'Evolution of the International Economic Order', Lewis outlines this idea as follows: 'The way to create a new international order is to eliminate the 50 to 60 per cent of low-productivity workers in food by transforming their productivity. This would change the factoral terms of trade and raise the prices of the traditional agricultural exports. It would also create an agricultural surplus that would support industrial production for the home market. These countries would then be less dependent on the rest of the world for finance or for their engine of growth', Lewis (1978b), p. 37.

82. 'The factoral terms of trade can be improved only by raising tropical productivity in the common commodity, domestic foodstuffs,' Lewis (1978b), p. 16. Emphasis in text added.

83. Ibid., p. 12.

84. 'In my last book, on Baumol's suggestion, [I] put a summary of each chapter at the beginning of each chapter, so that the reader can see what you are driving at, and the steps you use, before he plunges into the text', Lewis Archives, Princeton, Box 4/1: Lewis to Hollis Chenery, 7 September 1978.

85. One very perceptive review of *Growth and Fluctuations*, by George Rosen, shows that *Growth and Fluctuations* 'follows in the same classical tradition' as *Unlimited Supplies of Labour*, extending the dualistic model of 'modern' and 'traditional' sectors presented in *Unlimited Supplies of Labour* to depict, in the later publication, the relationship between North and South as the relationship between the modern and the traditional parts of the global economy. (Lewis Archives, Princeton, Box 40/4: review of *Growth and Fluctuations* by George Rosen, University of Illinois at Chicago Circle.)

86. Lewis (1978a), p. 214.

87. See note 81 above.

88. Lewis (1954), p. 410.

89. Lewis (1978a), p. 167.

90. Ronald Findlay, 'On W. Arthur Lewis' Contributions to Economics', published by Almquist and Wiksell, Stockholm. In Lewis Archive, Princeton, Box 1/1, 22 January 1980.

91. But, as Skidelsky points out, harsh to Keynes. The Keynesian achievement of full employment with price stability lasted, in Britain and most industrialized countries, from the implementation of the Kingsley Wood budget of 1940 through to Keynes' death in 1946, and indeed as far as the 1960s. If it fell apart into 'stagflation' thereafter, this was because industrialized country governments did not have at their command the agencies of restraint

(on effective demand, and thence on prices and wages) which Keynes had devised in *How to Pay for the War*, and which the Treasury implemented thereafter. See Skidelsky(1998), paperback 2000, pp. 498–504.

92. Lewis (1978a), p. 28.
93. Lewis's salary in 1974 was US$27,000 (Lewis Archives, Box 6); by 1983 it had risen to US$62,500 (Lewis Archives, Princeton, Box 8/6: Aaron Lemonick, Dean of the Faculty, to Lewis, 2 February 1983). At both dates this was in the top 10 per cent of what Princeton full professors were paid at the time.
94. On 5 June 1977, Lewis went into hospital for three weeks with gastrointestinal trouble (Lewis Archives, Box 7/5: Lewis to Barbara Ward, Lady Jackson, 1 June 1977.
95. Interviews, Michael Hodd, 5 July 2004; Thomas Warke, 30 May 2012. Robert Tignor, in an interview with us, stressed that 'he was not admired as an undergraduate teacher at all'. Tignor interview, 18 January 2012.
96. Johnson and Johnson (1978), pp. 211–12.
97. See passages keyed by Footnotes 22 to 24 above.
98. They might say, 'It's unfortunate that he chooses to express himself purely in that way (i.e. purely in prose),' but they would also concede, 'Like Jacob Viner, who also did, there is great wisdom in what he says.' Interview, William Baumol, 8 January 2011.
99. The paper by Krugman (1993) sets up a model in which modern-sector (industrial) production does not become profitable until multiple modernsector enterprises have been induced to set up in production simultaneously, which is an idea not of Lewis's but of Rosenstein-Rodan (1943, 1984). But it does for good measure add the remark that Lewis's article on unlimited supplies of labour was 'probably the most famous paper in the literature of development economics' [but] 'in retrospect, it is hard to see exactly why'. Krugman (1993) p. 21.
100. Lewis Papers, Princeton, Box 2/7: Lewis to Errol Barrow, PM of Barbados, 1966.
101. Lewis Papers, Princeton, Box 7/4: H. C. Holness to Lewis, 10 October 1969.
102. Lewis Papers, Princeton, Box 6/1: Lewis to Charles Furth.
103. Lewis Papers, Princeton, Box 2/3: Lewis to Sir Walter Adams, Association of Commonwealth Universities.
104. Lewis Papers, Princeton, Box 1: Lewis to Charles Furth, George Allen & Unwin, 1975.
105. The detailed empirical argument of Little *et al.* (1975), was crucial in changing the public mood against the idea that state-financed industrialization was essential for development.
106. Apart from Bauer, the main agents in the counter-revolution were Bela Balassa, discussed above, and Lal (1983). An important critique of the development counter-revolution is by Toye (1987)
107. Lewis Archive, Princeton, Box 1/10: *WWS Newsletter,* Princeton University, Woodrow Wilson School of Public and International Affairs, p. 2.
108. Baumol interview, 8 January 2012.
109. Telephone interview, William Baumol, 8 January 2012.
110. Gersovitz interview, 11 January 2012.
111. In 1963, in *Transforming Traditional Agriculture,* Schultz had shown that there was a substantial reduction in agricultural output in rural India after

the influenza epidemic of 1918, which he interpreted as a disproof of the surplus labour hypothesis.

112. The recommendations by John Lewis and by Stokes are reproduced in Tignor (2005), pp. 269–70.

113. Lewis Archives, Princeton, Box 2/8: Bhagwati to Lewis, 24 October 1979.

114. Lewis Archives, Princeton, Box 12/4: H. A. Simon to Lewis, 23 October 1979. Lewis reciprocated: 'I much enjoyed your Nobel lecture and have been recommending it to my students. The economic theory we teach is in a cul de sac', Lewis Archives, Princeton, Box 12/4: Lewis to Simon, 30 November 1979.

115. Lewis Archives, Princeton, Box 9/6: L. T. Melling, chairman, Eastern Electricity Board, to Lewis, 3 March 1952; and congratulating him on his Nobel award, 21 July 1980.

116. Lewis Archives, Princeton, Box 12/2: N. K. Sethia to Lewis, 30 April 1981.

117. One correspondent with a more radical disposition than either Hicks or Robbins – we leave it to readers to guess who – was to intimate, in the process of congratulating Lewis, that the award to Hayek had been a disgrace; Lewis Papers, Princeton, Box 8/2: letter of congratulation to Lewis, 17 October 1979.

118. By 1979 things had deteriorated from the decolonization-related problems described in Chapters 5 and 6 of this book. Jamaica and Guyana, in particular, had built up budget deficits which they were unable to service once the economic crisis at the end of the 1970s took hold. Emergency loans from the World Bank and the IMF were required, and there was substantial political violence in both cases. For more detail, see Harrigan, 'Jamaica' and 'Guyana', chs 17 and 18 in Mosley *et al.* (1995).

119. Lewis Archives, Princeton, Box 6/7: Hicks to Lewis, November 1979.

120. For Lewis's similar complaint about the Princeton Economics Department, see passage keyed by note 70 above.

121. Italics in original. Robbins, 20 years before, had produced the 'Robbins Report', which had recommended a big expansion of the British higher education system, which, it was feared, the new fees regime would put at risk, as well as being prejudicial to students from poorer developing countries, which Lewis had once been.

122. Robbins has mistaken Gladys Lewis's name.

123. Lewis, *Colonial Development in British Territories,* Rhodes House Oxford: Mss. Brit. Emp. s. 350, Jan. 1948, p. 10. For further discussion see Chapter 4 above.

124. Email/interview, Angus Deaton, professor, Woodrow Wilson School, 3 January 2012. Material taken from this interview is reproduced with permission.

125. One exception to this is that Ernest Stern, senior vice-president for operations at the World Bank, did invite Lewis to help him prepare a shortlist of individuals for the post of vice-president, economics and research. Lewis Archives, Princeton, Box 12/8: Lewis to Stern, 12 January 1982.

126. Lewis Archives, Princeton, Box 8/6 Lewis to Uma Lele, 21 October 1980.

127. As original. Keynes was actually born in January 1883.

128. Lewis Archive, Princeton, Box 5/2: Lewis to Elizabeth Durbin, 11 August 1981.

129. Lewis Archives, Princeton, Box 40/6: *Economic Inequality in the United States,* Report to Rockefeller Foundation, April 1981, p. 8.

130. Ibid., p. 27.
131. Lewis acted as an adviser for the NAACP. In his report for Rockefeller he wrote: 'At present, the NAACP takes employment discrimination to court, but it can handle only a few highly spectacular situations which serve to establish and expand the law ... Here we are thinking of an organisation which would aim at settling 95 per cent of its cases out of court, while leaving the big cases to be handled as they are now. The NAACP seems the obvious organisation to do this as a major development of its existing procedures', Lewis Archives, Princeton, Box 40/6: *Economic Inequality in the United States,* Report to Rockefeller Foundation, April 1981, p. 11.
132. Ibid., p. 23.
133. Ibid., p. 40.
134. Lewis Archive, Princeton, Box 12/3: Lewis to Sir Philip Sherlock, 1 November 1979.
135. Lewis Archive, Princeton, Box 12/6: Exchange between Lewis and unidentified Trinidadian correspondent, 4 May 1981.
136. Lewis Archive, Princeton, Box 12/5: M. G. Smith to and from Lewis, 12 September 1982.
137. Handwritten notes for farewell speech, July 1983, Lewis Archives, Princeton, Box 34/6.
138. 'To allow academics to continue to teach on flexible contracts beyond the retirement age is something which Princeton [normally] "never does"'. Interview, Robert Tignor, Princeton, 18 January 2012.
139. *Outlook for Development.* Inaugural Lecture of the Dr Eric Williams Memorial Lecture Series by W. A. Lewis, 27 August 1983, p. 4 of printed transcript.
140. Ibid..
141. Ibid., p. 6 of printed transcript. Chile at that time was under the dictatorship of Augusto Pinochet, and Uganda and Zaire (DRC) were in the midst of civil wars.
142. Today this does not read as a very-well chosen example, and one might prefer to substitute Malaysia or Indonesia.
143. *Outlook for Development.* Inaugural Lecture of the Dr Eric Williams Memorial Lecture Series, 27 August 1983, p. 6 of printed transcript.
144. Lewis (1985a), p. 121.
145. 'The weather keeps me away from Western Europe from then [October?] until April', Lewis Archives, Princeton, Box 6: Lewis to Charles Furth, 11 April 1985.
146. For example, Lewis's correspondence with Barbara Solow (wife of Robert), who attended Lewis's Harvard lectures in 1982, and now reports that she 'has become so involved with these subjects that [she] has resigned from Boston University to come to the DuBois Institute as a Research Associate'. 'Are you still interested in any of this stuff?' she asked. Lewis's reply was short but encouraging. Lewis Archive, Princeton, Box 12/6: Barbara Solow to Lewis, 22 May 1986.
147. Lewis Archive, Princeton, Box 13/3: correspondence with Commonwealth Caribbean Medical Council, October 1986.
148. Interviews, Mark Gersovitz, 10 January 2012; and Gustav Ranis, 13 January 2012.

149. The St Lucians were very upset in 1979 and 1980 that Lewis took more than a year to visit the island after he had been awarded the Nobel Prize in October 1979. Lalljie interview, 18 June 2012.
150. Interview, Robert Lalljie, 18 June 2012.
151. Readers will recall (Chapter 1) that Lewis had been brought up on an island speaking an Anglo-French patois. Lewis was always proud of these elements of French cultural heritage and had even attempted to teach French to Kwame Nkrumah (Chapter 6) and, later, to Kofi Annan, the future Secretary-General of the United Nations.
152. Lewis Archive, Princeton, Box 6/4: Lewis to and from Prof. R. Granier, University of Aix-en-Provence, 6 May 1987.
153. Lewis Archive, Princeton, Box 7/1: Harrison? (signature illegible) to Lewis, 17 October 1988.

9   'The Fundamental Cure for Poverty Is Not Money but Knowledge': Lewis's Legacy

1. Lewis (1939), p. 9.
2. Lewis (1949e), p. 18.
3. See Chapter 7 above, p. 194.
4. See letter to Director of the LSE, 20 January 1946; reproduced in Chapter 3, p. 78 above.
5. Banerjee and Duflo (2011), p. 269. Their poverty traps – from which the likelihood of escape depends on how the poor respond to conditions in the markets in which they trade – are depicted formally on p.12.
6. Lewis (1949e), p. 18.
7. The main textbook of new growth theory, Barro and Sala-i-Martin (1995) does not mention Lewis at all. John Toye suggests that this neglect is not only because the Solow model is more mathematically tractable but because 'it opened out an attractive research programme around topics such as the global convergence of growth rates, the sources of growth, and the existence or otherwise of a technological gap between developed and developing countries (Personal communication, 29 August 2012). Lewis made things difficult for himself by not engaging with the applied economics literature on growth, taking the view that econometrics was simply not applicable to the analysis of long-term growth processes (Lewis, 1955, ch.6). But his attempts, especially in *The Theory of Economic Growth*, to widen the scope of growth analysis by incorporating the political determinants of growth are in our view still worth taking further. For an exploration in this direction, see Mosley (2004a).
8. Angus Deaton goes further, and suggests, in a commentary on what is argued here, that:
'One line you take is to summarize the Lewis oeuvre by the contribution it has made and is making to modern development economics. But to me, that is to assign a value to modern development economics which it is far from meriting. A lot of what Arthur did is just straight better than what is going on now, and I am not sure there is any net progress.

In my view, modern development economics is internally doomed because it is tied to the vision of developing other countries from the outside, something that I do not believe can be done, and that leads to an endless succession of foolish fads and worthless intellectual forays. Perhaps Arthur's experience in Ghana taught him something of this, I don't know. I think Arthur would have appreciated some of what is going on now. Young scholars are seriously interested in poverty and inequality in a way that was not true in 1985. There is a return to history though I suspect Arthur would have been rightly sceptical of colonial mortality as an instrument for anything! [For the allusion see Acemoğlu *et al.*, 1991] Yet there is world class work going on in economic history more generally, with scholars like Bob Allen and Joel Mokyr leading the way. I think Arthur might have liked that too. And there is growing appreciation of the centrality of politics in economic development – Nkrumah was right! – that is new (at least for now) with contributions by Besley and Persson, Boix, van de Walle, Acemoğlu and Robinson, and many more. So I think that, if we are making progress, it is because we are turning our back on the last quarter century, and returning to the themes to which Arthur devoted his life.' (Personal communication, 12 June 2012)

9. The World Bank of the 1980s and 1990s took this view mainly because of pessimism about African governance – in other words, it assumed almost axiomatically that the benefits of any government actions to promote industrialization would find their way into the pockets of rent-seekers, rather than forming the basis for an industrialization programme on the Far Eastern model.

10. These are Lewis and Meyer(1946), Lewis and Martin (1956) and Lewis and O'Leary (1955), to which should perhaps be added the paper he wrote with Durbin's collaboration for the Colonial Economic Development Council – listed here as Lewis in consultation with Durbin (1944).

11. Mark Gersovitz demurs from the description 'father', on the grounds that he developed his research programme independently of Lewis, and we take the responsibility for using the word here. Gersovitz elucidated the inspiration he got from Lewis as follows: 'When I think of Arthur, I think of the contrasts between him and most of the contemporary professoriate at even the best departments – he was a thinker who left people with a perpetual inheritance of understanding of very important economic and therefore social questions; most academics produce articles, it's how they see their job. Arthur was an adviser of people who had the authority to take decisions at the very highest levels ... and a public servant who tried to influence social outcomes through reason, most of all, he was engagé; most academics are consultants who worry about their consulting fees. Being with someone like this is a very special, almost unique gift to have been given by the good luck of being in the right place at the right time, and the memory of him keeps my own courage up when I am discouraged' (Private communication, 19 June 2012).

12. One exception to this is Richard Allsopp, a lexicographer and senior administrator at the British Guiana campus of the University of the West Indies who then moved (reluctantly) to join Lewis at UWI, first in

Jamaica and then in Barbados, and who was Lewis's most long-standing West Indian friend. With Eric Williams, prime minister of Trinidad, Lewis formed a close friendship during the 1950s, but that relationship fell apart for political reasons at the beginning of 1962, and subsequently the two men were barely on speaking terms. The important friendship with Neville Nicholls of the Caribbean Development Bank was formed in the 1970s.

13. As noted above, this was a highly unusual departure from Princeton's rules, which normally required staff to retire at 68.
14. Probably Brother Bernard of Community House (see Figure 5.4 above); Weatherby does not name his informant.
15. W. J. Weatherby, contribution to obituary of Lewis by Maurice [later Lord] Peston, 'Sensible Tendency and the Lessons of Moss Side', *The Guardian*, 24 June 1991.

References

Interviews

William Baumol, Professor of Economics, Stern School, New York University, formerly at Princeton University. Interviewed by Mosley (by telephone), 8 January 2012.

Henry Bienen, former President, Northwestern University, and formerly Professor of Political Science and Director, Development Research Program, Princeton University. Interviewed by Mosley (by telephone), 10 January 2012.

Phyllis Deane, Emeritus Professor of Economic History, University of Cambridge. Interviewed by Mosley, Cambridge, 2 April 2004; and by Ingham, Cambridge, February and September 2006.

Angus Deaton, Dwight D. Eisenhower Professor of International Affairs and Professor of Economics, Princeton University. Interviewed by Mosley, Princeton, New Jersey, 2 January 2012.

Andrew Downes, Professor of Economics, The University of the West Indies, Barbados. Former student of Arthur Lewis. Interviewed by Ingham at Cave Hill, Barbados, 11 and 14 November 2005.

Gisela Eisner, formerly Lewis's research assistant at Manchester University and author of *Jamaica 1830–1930: A Study in Economic Growth*. Interviewed by Ingham, Buxton, Derbyshire, 5 May and 22 November 2006.

Mark Figueroa, Professor of Economics, The University of the West Indies. An authority on the works of Arthur Lewis. Interviewed by Ingham at The University of the West Indies, Mona, Jamaica, 6 September 2006 and in the UK, 4 January 2007.

Mark Gersovitz, Professor of Economics, Johns Hopkins University. Interviewed by Mosley (by telephone), 11 January 2012.

Michael Hodd, Senior Lecturer, University of Westminster. Interviewed by Mosley, Manchester, 5 July 2004.

Robert Lalljie, freelance journalist on *Caribbean Chronicle* and author of biographical memoirs on Lewis. Interviewed by Mosley (by telephone), 18 June 2012.

Kari Polanyi Levitt, former student of Lewis at the LSE, and now living in Montreal, Canada. Interviewed by Ingham (by telephone) 12 October 2006.

Sir Neville Nicholls, 3rd President of the Caribbean Development Bank. Interviewed by Ingham, Barbados, 16 November 2005.

Greta Payne, of the Barbados Historical Society. Interviewed by Ingham, Barbados, 15 November 2005.

Gustav Ranis, Professor of Economics, Yale University. Interviewed by Mosley, New Haven, Connecticut, 13 January 2012.

Mark Rosenzweig, Professor of Economics, Yale University. Interviewed by Mosley, New Haven, Connecticut, 13 January 2012.

Robert Tignor, Professor of History, Princeton University (and previous biographer of Lewis). Interviewed by Mosley, Princeton, New Jersey, 18 January 2012.

Thomas Warke, PhD student and teaching assistant at Princeton, 1963–7, and now Lecturer in Economics, University of Sheffield. Interviewed by Mosley, Sheffield, 30 May 2012.

Audine Wilkinson, founder member and documentalist at the Institute of Social and Economic Research, Cave Hill, Barbados. Family friend of Sir William and Lady Lewis. Interviewed by Ingham in Barbados, 15 November 2005.

Archival sources

Lewis Archive at the Seeley G. Mudd Library, Princeton University, New Jersey: 55 boxes of personal papers, mainly covering the period from 1950 to 1986. Donated by Gladys Lewis, widow of Arthur Lewis, in June 1992, with an addition in November 1992. The papers have been arranged in seven series:

1. Biographical, 1938–89 (boxes 1 and 2)
2. Correspondence, 1942–90 (boxes 2–14)
3. Country files, 1892–1989 (boxes 15–24)
4. Organisational affiliations, 1946–88 (boxes 24–32)
5. University career, 1947–89 (boxes 32–37)
6. Writings, 1936–89 (boxes 37–54)
7. Audiovisual materials, 1978–90 (box 55).

Cambridge University Archives: London Colleges; Minutes of the Colonial Development Course, 1928–57; Papers relating to University Arrangements during the Second World War, 1939–1949.

Greater Manchester County Record Office. This archive contains the papers of the Manchester City Council Education Department.

John Rylands University Library, Manchester. This archive contains the papers of Max Gluckman, also Lewis's staff record while a professor at Manchester. The archives of *The Manchester Guardian* and *Manchester Evening News* are also held here and, in a more complete form, in the Manchester Central Library.

Ahmed Iqbal Ullah Race Relations Resource Centre, University of Manchester (in Sackville St. Building). Transcripts of 43 interviews with members of the West Indian, African and White communities of Moss Side, Manchester, collated in two waves in 1983 and 2000.

LSE (London School of Economics) Archives, LSE Library and Special Collections. These papers contain Lewis's personal file while at the LSE, and a number of unpublished papers by Lewis from the 1940s; also the School's Calendars, annually from 1933–49.

National Archives (formerly Public Record Office), Kew, London. This archive contains the records of the Colonial Office.

Rhodes House Library, Oxford. This archive contains the Arthur Creech Jones Papers and Fabian Colonial Bureau Papers, and a number of unpublished papers by Lewis from the 1940s.

Senate House Library, London. This archive contains unpublished papers by Lewis, pamphlets such as his *Labour in the West Indies* (1939) and a copy of his Ph.D. thesis (Lewis, 1940).

The Archives of University of the West Indies, Mona Campus, Jamaica. They include files relating to Arthur Lewis' appointment and tenure as Principal. The

Barbados Campus of UWI at Cave Hill holds material relating to the Institute of Social and Economic Research (ISER). The Barbados Museum and Historical Society holds an important press archive for the East Caribbean.

Printed sources (published and unpublished)

Abbott, G. (1976) 'Why Visiting Economists Fail: An Alternative Interpretation', *Public Administration*, 54(1): 31–43.

Abrahams, P. (2000) *The Coyoba Chronicles: Reflections on the Black Experience in the Twentieth Century*, Kingston, Jamaica: Ian Randle Publishers.

Acemoğlu, D., S. Johnson, and J. Robinson (2001) 'The Colonial Origins of Comparative Development: An Empirical Investigation', *American Economic Review*, 91: 1369–401.

Agarwala, A. N. and S. P. Singh (eds) (1963) *The Economics of Underdevelopment*, Bombay: Oxford University Press.

Akerlof, G. (1970) 'The Market for "Lemons"', *Quarterly Journal of Economics*, 84(3): 488–500, MIT Press; repr. in G. Akerlof, *An Economic Theorist's Book of Tales* (Cambridge: Cambridge University Press): ch. 2: 7–22.

Armitage-Smith, Sir S. (1931) *Report by Sir Sydney Armitage-Smith on a Financial Mission to the Leeward Islands and St Lucia, 31 October 1931*, Cmnd 3996, London, Her Majesty's Stationery Office. (Copy at Rhodes House, Oxford: 525s.15.)

Arrighi, G. (1970) 'Labour Supplies in Historical Perspective: A Study of the Proletarianisation of the African Peasantry in Rhodesia', *Journal of Development Studies*, 6(3) (April): 198–233.

Austin, D. (1964) *Politics in Ghana, 1946–1960*, London: Oxford University Press.

Banerjee, A. and E. Duflo (2011) *Poor Economics: A Radical Rethinking of the Way to Fight Global Poverty*, Washington, DC: Public Affairs Press.

Baran, P. (1968) *The Political Economy of Growth* (first published 1957), New York: Monthly Review Press.

Barber, W. J. (1961) *The Economy of British Central Africa*, Oxford: Oxford University Press.

Barro, R. and X. Sala-i-Martin (1995) *Economic Growth*, New York/London: McGraw-Hill.

Baumol, W. J. (1971) 'Economics of Athenian Drama: Its Relevance for the Arts in a Small City Today', *Quarterly Journal of Economics*, 85(3): 365–76.

Beckford, G. (1984) 'A Struggle for a More Relevant Economics', *Social and Economic Studies*, 33(1): 47.

Besley, T., S. Coate and G. Loury (1995) 'The Economics of Rotating Savings and Credit Associations', Boston, MA: Boston University, Institute for Economic Development, 24.

Bianchi, A. M. (2011) 'Visiting economists through Hirschman's Eyes', *European Journal of the History of Economic Thought*, 18: 217–42.

Boserup, E. (1965) *Woman's Role in Economic Development*, London: Allen & Unwin, 1965.

Bowden, S. and P. Mosley (2012) 'Four African Case Studies: Ghana, Uganda, Kenya, and Zimbabwe', in Mosley (2012), ch. 13.

Bräutigam, D. and S. Knack (2004) 'Foreign Aid, Institutions and Governance in Sub-Saharan Africa', *Economic Development and Cultural Change*, 52: 255–85.

Breit, W. and R. Spencer (eds) (1986) *Lives of the Laureates: Seven Nobel Economists,* Cambridge, MA: MIT Press.

Bruccoli, M. J. (1981) *Some Sort of Epic Grandeur: The Life of F. Scott Fitzgerald,* London: Sphere Books.

Chenery, H., M. Ahluwalia, C. Bell, J. Duloy and R. Jolly (1974) *Redistribution with Growth: Policies to Improve Income Distribution in Developing Countries in the Context of Economic Growth,* New York/ Oxford: Oxford University Press.

Clarke, A. (2003) *Growing Up Stupid Under the Union Jack,* Kingston, Jamaica: Ian Randle Publishers.

Coase, R. (1977) Review of Sir Arnold Plant, *Selected Economic Essays and Addresses, Journal of Economic Literature,* 15 (March): 87.

Coase, R. (1986) 'Professor Arnold Plant: His Ideas and Influence', in M. A. Anderson (ed.), *The Unfinished Agenda: Essays in Honour of Arthur Seldon* (London: Institute of Economic Affairs).

Coleman, P., P. Drake and S. Cornish (2007) *Arndt's Story: The Life of an Australian Economist,* Canberra, Australia: ANU Press.

Collier, P. and A. Hoeffler (2004) 'Greed and Grievance in Civil War', *Oxford Economic Papers,* 56: 563–95.

Colonial Office, *see* UK Colonial Office.

Craig, S. (1977) 'Germs of an Idea', Afterword to W. Arthur Lewis's *Labour in the West Indies: The Birth of a Workers' Movement,* Port of Spain, Trinidad and Tobago: New Beacon Books.

Creech Jones, A. and R. Hinden (1945) *Colonies and International Conscience,* Report to the Fabian Colonial Bureau, London: Victor Gollancz.

Cruise O'Brien, D. (1967) review of W.A. Lewis, *Politics in West Africa, Journal of Development Studies,* 3: 95–6.

Cumper, P. (2004) *One Bright Child,* new edn, Southport, UK: BlackAmber Books.

Dahrendorf, R. (1995) *LSE: A History of the London School of Economics and Political Science, 1895–1995,* Oxford: Oxford University Press.

Deane, P. (2011 [1953]) *Colonial Social Accounting.* Cambridge: Cambridge University Press for National Institute of Economic and Social Research.

Deane, P. (1959) 'The NIESR: Memoirs of a Survivor', Unpublished paper, National Institute of Economic and Social Research.

Deane, P. and W. A. Cole (1962) *British Economic Growth,1688–1959: Trends and Structure,* Cambridge: Cambridge University Press.

Dollar, D. and A. Kraay (2001) 'Growth is Good for the Poor', *Journal of Economic Growth,* 7(3): 195–225.

Durbin, Elizabeth (1985) *New Jerusalems: The Labour Party and the Economics of Democratic Socialism,* London: Routledge & Kegan Paul.

Durbin, Evan (1933) *Socialist Credit Policy,* London: New Fabian Research Bureau. Republished in revised form, 1935.

Durbin, Evan (1935) *The Problem of Credit Policy,* London: Chapman & Hall.

Durbin, Evan (1940) *The Politics of Democratic Socialism,* London: Routledge & Kegan Paul.

Durbin, Evan (1949) *Problems of Economic Planning: Papers on Planning and Economics,* London: Routledge & Kegan Paul.

Easterly, W. (2006) *The White Man's Burden: Why the West's Efforts to Aid the Rest Have Done So Much Ill and So Little Good,* Oxford: Oxford University Press.

Eisner, G. (1961) *Jamaica 1830–1930: A Study in Economic Growth,* Manchester: Manchester University Press.

Einthoven, W. and M. Smagorinsky (1992) *The Tigers of Princeton University*, Princeton NJ: Office of Communications/Publications, Princeton University.

Ellis, G. and L. Bhajan (1987) *Sir Arthur Lewis*, School textbook published in *National Heritage Series of Caribbean Heroes*, Bridgetown, Barbados: Inprint Publishing Caribbean Publishing, p. 2. (Copy in Lewis Archives, Princeton University, Princeton, NJ: Box 1/8.)

Emmanuel, P. (ed.) (1994) *Sir William Arthur Lewis Collected Papers*, Vols I and II, Barbados: Institute of Social and Economic Research (Eastern Caribbean), University of the West Indies.

Emmerson, C. and M. Wakefield (2001) 'The Saving Gateway and the Child Trust Fund: Is Asset-Based Welfare 'Well Fair'?, *IFS Commentary*, 85, London: Institute for Fiscal Studies.

Fei, J. C. H. and G. Ranis (1964) *The Development of the Labour Surplus Economy*, Irwin, Homewood, IL.

Fields, G. (2004) 'Dualism in the Labor Market: A Perspective on the Lewis Model after Half a Century', *The Manchester School*, 72: 724–36.

Figueroa, M. (1994) 'The Plantation School and Lewis: Contradictions, Continuities and Continued Caribbean Relevance', *Symposium on the Plantation Model 25 Years Later*, Department of Economics, University of the West Indies, St Augustine, Trinidad, April.

Figueroa, M. (2004) 'W. Arthur Lewis versus the Lewis Model: Agricultural or Industrial Development?', *The Manchester School*, 72: 736–51.

Figueroa, M. (2008) 'George Cumper and the Critical Tradition: Common Themes in Post World War II Caribbean Economic Thought', *Social and Economic Studies*, 57(1): 46–71.

Fishlow, A. (1972) 'Brazilian Size Distribution of Income', *American Economic Review Papers and Proceedings*, 62: 391–402.

Fitzgerald, F. S. (2000) *This Side of Paradise*, New York, Scribners(1919)/Oxford: Oxford University Press.

Frank, A. G. (1974) *Capitalism and Underdevelopment in Latin America: Historical Studies of Chile and Brazil*, London: Penguin.

Frankel, S. H. (1952) 'United Nations Primer for Development', *Quarterly Journal of Economics*, 66, (August): 301–26.

Girvan, N. and O. Jefferson (eds) (1971) 'Introduction' in *Readings in the Political Economy of the Caribbean*, Kingston, Jamaica: New World Group.

Gluckman, M. (1955) *Custom and Conflict in Africa*, Oxford: Basil Blackwell.

Gold Coast Government (1953) *Report on Industrialisation and the Gold Coast by Professor W. A. Lewis*, Accra: Government Printer.

Goldsworthy, D. (1971) *Colonial Issues in British Politics, 1945–1961*, Oxford: Clarendon Press.

Hagemann, H. (2006) 'Dismissal, Expulsion and Emigration of German-Speaking Economists after 1933', *Journal of the History of Economic Thought*, 27(4).

Hall, N. (1944) *Post-War Economic Readjustment*, National Archives, Kew: CO 990/2, Colonial Economic Advisory Council minutes, July.

Hammond, J. L. and B. Hammond (1911) *The Village Labourer: A Study of the Government of England before the Reform Bill*, London: Longmans, Green.

Hammond, J. L. and B. Hammond (1918) *The Town Labourer, 1760–1832: The New Civilisation*, London: Longmans, Green.

Hammond, J. L. and B. Hammond (1919) *The Skilled Labourer, 1760–1832*, London: Longmans, Green.

Harberger, A. (1984) 'Comment' on W.A. Lewis 'Development Economics in the 1950s', in Meier and Seers (1984): 138–49.

Harrigan, J. (1995) 'Jamaica' and 'Guyana', in Mosley *et al.* (eds), *Aid and Power*, Vol. 2 (2nd edn), London: Routledge, chs 17 and 18.

Hart, K. (1973) 'Informal Income Opportunities and the Structure of Urban Employment in Ghana', *Journal of Modern African Studies*, 11: 61–89.

Hayek, F. A. (1946) 'The London School of Economics 1895–1945', *Economica*, New Series, 13(49): 1–31.

Hendry, D. and H.-M. Krolzig (2004) 'We Ran One Regression', *Oxford Bulletin of Economics and Statistics*, 66(5): 799–810.

Hinden, R. (1941) *Plan for Africa: A Report prepared for the Colonial Bureau of the Fabian Society*, London: George Allen & Unwin. (Copy at Rhodes House Oxford: 600.14 r.13.)

Hinden, R. (1971) Obituary of Rita Hinden, *The Times*, 20 November.

Hinden, R., W. A. Lewis and A. Creech Jones, MP (1942) *Freedom for Colonial Peoples*, Peace Aims Pamphlet No. 11, UK: National Peace Council.

Hintzen, P. C. (1991) 'Arthur Lewis and the Development of a Middle Class Ideology', in R. Premdas and E. St Cyr (1991).

Hirschman, A. O. (1958) *The Strategy of Economic Development*, Cambridge, MA: Harvard University Press.

Hirschman, A. O. (1963) *Journeys Towards Progress*, Washington, DC: Brookings Institution.

Hirschman, A. O. (1981) *Essays in Trespassing: Economics, Politics and Beyond*, Cambridge: Cambridge University Press.

Hirschman, A. O. (1984) 'A Dissenter's Confession: "The Strategy of Economic Development" Revisited', in G. M. Meier and D. Seers (eds), *Pioneers in Development*, New York: Oxford University Press.

House of Commons (1935) *Papers Related to the Disturbances in St Christopher (St Kitts), January–February 1935*, Cmd. 4956, His Majesty's Stationery Office, London. (Copy at Rhodes House, Oxford: 525 r.15/1935.)

Hudson, M., J. Phillips, K. Ray and H. Barnes (2007) *Social Cohesion in Diverse Communities*, York: Joseph Rowntree Foundation. Available at: www.jrf.org.uk/sites/files/jrf/2036-social-cohesion-communities.pdf.

Hulme, D. and P. Mosley (1996) *Finance against Poverty*, 2 Vols, London: Routledge.

Huff, G. and G. Caggiano (2007) 'Globalization, Immigration and Lewisian Elastic Labour in Pre-World War II South-East Asia', *Journal of Economic History*, 67(1): 33–69.

Hussain, J. and P. Mosley (2012) 'Achieving Financial Inclusion Among Ethnic Minority Communities: A Case Study of Birmingham', Unpublished paper, Birmingham City University and University of Sheffield.

ILO (International Labour Organization) (1973) *Employment, Incomes and Equality: Report on a Mission to Kenya*, Geneva: ILO.

Independent Group on British Aid (1981) *Real Aid: A Strategy for Britain* (London: Oxfam/Overseas Development Institute).

Ingham, B. (1987) 'Shaping Opinion on Development Policy in Africa: The Lewis and Seers and Ross Reports of the Early 1950s', *Manchester Papers on Development*, 3 (November): 68–89.

Ingham, B. (1992) 'Shaping Opinion on Development Policy: Economists at the Colonial Office during World War II', *History of Political Economy*, 24: 689–710.

Ingham, B. (2010) 'Policy Advice in the Transition to Independence: The Role of External Policy Advisers at the Colonial Office, 1943–1951', Paper Presented at the History and Economic Development Conference, London University, School of Oriental and African Studies, June.

Ingham, B. and M. Figueroa (2009) 'Lewis and the Legacy of the Caribbean Development Bank', *Journal of East Caribbean Studies*, 34(4).

Ingham, B. and P. Mosley (2013) 'Marvellous Intellectual Feasts: Arthur Lewis at the London School of Economics' *History of Political Economy* (Duke University Press), Summer.

James, C. L. R. (2009 [1963]) *Beyond a Boundary*, London: Stanley Paul & Co. ltd.

Jay, M. (1973) *The Dialectical Imagination: A History of the Frankfurt School and the Institute of Social Research 1923–50*, Boston: Little, Brown & Co.

Johnson, C. (1982) *MITI and the Japanese Miracle*. Stanford, CA: Stanford University Press.

Johnson, E. S. and H. Johnson (1978) *The Shadow of Keynes: Understanding Keynes, Cambridge and Keynesian Economics*, Oxford: Oxford University Press.

Jorgensen, Dale W. (1969) 'The Role of Agriculture in Economic Development: Classical versus Neoclassical Models of Growth', in C. Wharton (ed.), Subsistence Agriculture and Economic Development (Chicago: University of Chicago Press): 320–47.

Joseph, T. S. D. (2009) 'Decolonisation, Democracy and Development: The Political Ideas of W. Arthur Lewis', Paper delivered at the Sir Arthur Lewis Memorial Conference: Development Challenges in the 21st Century, University of the West Indies, St Augustine Campus, Trinidad and Tobago.

Kanbur, R. (2001) 'Economic Policy, Distribution and Policy: The Nature of Disagreements', *World Development*, 29: 1083–94.

Killick, T. (1978) *Development Economics in Action: A Study of Economic Policies in Ghana*, London: Heinemann.

Kimble, D. (1963) *A Political History of Ghana: The Rise of Gold Coast Nationalism, 1850–1928*, Oxford: Clarendon Press.

King, B. (2000) *Derek Walcott: A Caribbean Life*, Oxford: Oxford University Press.

Krueger, Anne O. (1974) 'The Political Economy of the Rent-seeking Society', *American Economic Review*, 64: 291–310.

Krugman, P. (1993) 'Towards a Counter-Counter Revolution in Development Theory', Proceedings of the Annual World Bank Conference on Development 1992, Supplement, Washington, DC, World Bank Economic Review: 15–38.

Labour Party (1941) 'Colonial Economic Policy During the War', International Department, Document 234a, July. Unpublished paper, Rhodes House, Oxford: Fabian Colonial Bureau papers, box 48.

Lal, D. (1983) *The Poverty of Development Economics*, Institute of Economic Affairs, London: Hobart Paperback.

Lalljie, R. (1997) *Sir Arthur Lewis, Nobel Laureate: A Biographical Profile*, privately published, Port of Spain, Trinidad and Tobago.

LaGuerre, J. (1991) 'Arthur Lewis and the Moyne Commission', in R. Prendas and E. St Cyr (eds) (1991).

Lee, J. M. and M. Petter (1982) *The Colonial Office, War and Development Policy*, London, Institute of Commonwealth Studies.

Leeson, P. F. and F. I. Nixson (2004) 'Development Economics in the Department of Economics at the University of Manchester', *Journal of Economic Studies*, 31(1): 6–24.

Lenton, P. and P. Mosley (2011) *Financial Exclusion and the Poverty Trap*, London: Routledge.

Lewis, W. A. (1939) *Labour in the West Indies: The Birth of a Workers' Movement*, London, Fabian Society Research Series 44. (Copy at University of London, Senate House Library, Special Collections.)

Lewis, W. A. (1940a) *The Economics of Loyalty Contracts*, PhD thesis, University of London.

Lewis, W. A. (1940b) *Economic Problems of Today*, London: Fabian Research Bureau.

Lewis, W. A. (1941) 'The Two-part Tariff', *Economica*, 8(29): 52–76.

Lewis, W. A. (1942a) 'The Economics of Loyalty', *Economica*, 9(36): 333–48.

Lewis, W. A. (1942b) 'Some Aspects of the Flow of Capital into the British Colonies', Unpublished paper. (Copy in LSE Archives; also in National Archives, Kew; Colonial Economic Advisory Committee Papers.).

Lewis, W. A., (1944) 'An Economic Plan for Jamaica', *Agenda*, 3(4). Reprinted in Emmanuel (1994).

Lewis, W. A. (1946) 'Fixed Costs', *Economica*, 13(49).

Lewis, W. A. (1949a) *Economic Survey, 1919–1939*, London: George Allen & Unwin.

Lewis, W. A. (1949b) *Overhead Costs: Essays in Economic Analysis*, London: George Allen & Unwin.

Lewis, W. A. (1949c) *The Principles of Economic Planning*, London: George Allen & Unwin.

Lewis, W. A. (1949d) 'Developing Colonial Agriculture', *Three Banks Review*, 2, (June).

Lewis, W. A. (1949e) 'Colonial Development', Paper presented at a meeting of the Manchester Statistical Society, 12 January (copy in University of Sheffield Library).

Lewis, W. A. (1950a) 'Industrial Development in Puerto Rico', Unpublished Colonial Office report.

Lewis, W. A. (1950b) *The Industrialisation of the British West Indies*, Unpublished Colonial Office report.

Lewis, W. A. (1951) 'Were We Better Off in the Nineteenth Century?', *Manchester Guardian*, 27 June.

Lewis, W. A. (1952) 'World Production, Prices and Trade, 1870–1960', *The Manchester School*, 20(2): 105–38.

Lewis, W. A. (1953a) *Report on the Industrialisation of the Gold Coast*: see Gold Coast Government (1953).

Lewis, W. A. (1953b) 'United Nations Primer for Development: Comment', *Quarterly Journal of Economics*, 67 (May): 267–275.

Lewis, W. A. (1954) 'Economic Development with Unlimited Supplies of Labour', *The Manchester School*, 22: 139–91. Reprinted in Agarwala and Singh (1963).

Lewis, W. A. (1955) *The Theory of Economic Growth*, London: George Allen & Unwin.

Lewis, W. A. (1959) 'On Assessing a Development Plan', *Economic Bulletin of Ghana*, 3(6/7), University of Ghana Department of Economics.

Lewis, W. A. (1960) 'Address on the Occasion of the Matriculation of New Students at the University College of the West Indies, Mona, 7 October. University of the West Indies, Kingston, Jamaica.

Lewis, W. A. (1965a) *The Agony of the Eight*, Barbados: Advocate Commercial Printery. (Date not specified on title page.)

Lewis, W. A. (1965b) *Politics in West Africa*, Whidden Lectures for 1965 delivered at McMaster University, Hamilton, ON, Canada, London: George Allen & Unwin.

Lewis, W. A. (1965c) *Progress Report on the Institute of Social and Economic Research (Eastern Caribbean)*, University of the West Indies.

Lewis, W. A. (1966) *Development Planning*, London: George Allen & Unwin.

Lewis, W. A. (1968) 'Epilogue', in J. Mordecai (1968).

Lewis, W. A. (1969a) 'Black Power and the American University', *University: A Princeton Quarterly*, 40 (Spring): 10. Later in 1969 repr. in *Princeton Alumni Weekly*.

Lewis, W. A. (1969b) *Some Aspects of Economic Development*, Accra: Ghana Publishing Corporation.

Lewis, W. A. (1969c) *Aspects of Tropical Trade 1883–1965*, Stockholm: Almqvist & Wiksell.

Lewis, W. A. (1970a) *Tropical Development 1880–1913: Studies in Economic Progress*, London: George Allen & Unwin.

Lewis, W. A. (1970b) 'The Economic Status of Women', Commencement address, Rosary College, Illinois, (May). (Copy in Lewis Papers, Princeton: Box 39/8, p. 1.)

Lewis, W. A. (1971a) *Socialism and Economic Growth*, Speech delivered at The London School of Economics and Political Science, Pamphlet published by London School of Economics.

Lewis, W. A. (1971b) 'On Being Different', *BIM Magazine*, 14(3), Barbados. Repr. in Emmanuel (ed.) (1994) *Collected Papers of Arthur Lewis, Vol. 3*.

Lewis, W. A. (1972) 'Annual Report of the President of the Caribbean Development Bank'.

Lewis, W. A. (1973) 'Annual Report of the President of the Caribbean Development Bank'.

Lewis, W. A. (1978a) *Growth and Fluctuations 1870–1913*, London: George Allen & Unwin.

Lewis, W. A. (1978b) *The Evolution of the International Economic Order*, Janeway Lectures 1977, Princeton, NJ: Princeton University Press.

Lewis, W. A. (1985a) *Racial Conflict and Economic Development*, W. E. B. Du Bois Lectures 1982, Cambridge, MA: Harvard University Press.

Lewis, W. A. (1985b) *The Economics of Racial Inequality*, New York: Columbia University, Centre for the Study of Human Rights.

Lewis, W. A. (1986) 'Autobiographical Account', in W. Breit and R. W. Spencer (eds), *Lives of the Laureates: Seven Nobel Economists*, Cambridge, MA: MIT Press.

Lewis, W. A. (1988) 'The Roots of Development Theory', in H. Chenery and T. N. Srinivasan (eds), *Handbook of Development Economics*. Repr. in W. Arthur Lewis, *Collected Economic Papers, Vol. 3* (ed. Patrick Emanuel), Barbados: Institute of Social and Economic Research.

Lewis, W. A., in consultation with E. F. M. Durbin (1944) *Colonial Economic Development*, Colonial Economic Advisory Council, CO 990/2, CEAC, *Agenda*, (44) 7, 23 June, National Archives, Kew.

Lewis, W. A. and F. V. Meyer (1946) *The Analysis of Secondary Industries*, National Archives, Kew, CO 990/2: Colonial Economic Advisory Committee, Industry Sub-Committee, CEAC, Industry (46) 26.(Note anomaly in the printed date: Lewis resigned from the Committee in October 1944.)

Lewis, W. A. and A. M. Martin (1956) 'Patterns of Public Revenue and Expenditure', *The Manchester School*, 24: 203–44.

Lewis, W. A. and P. J. O'Leary (1955) 'Secular Swings in Production and Trade 1870–1913', *The Manchester School*, 23: 113–52.

Lin, J. Y. (2009) *Economic Development and Transition: Thought, Strategy, and Viability* (Marshall Lectures). New York: Cambridge University Press.

Lin, J. Y. (2011) *From Flying Geese to Leading Dragons: New Opportunities and Strategies for Structural Transformation in Developing Countries*, WIDER annual lecture 15, Helsinki: UNU-WIDER.

Lin, J. Y. and C. Monga (2011) 'Growth Identification and Facilitation: The Role of the State in the Dynamics of Structural Change', *Development Policy Review*, 29: 264–90.

Little, I., T. Scitovsky and M. Scott (1975) *Industry and Trade in Some Developing Countries*, London: Heinemann.

Macmillan, W. M. (1938) *Warning from the West Indies*, 2nd edn, London: Macmillan Publishers.

Manchester City Council (2012) *Strangers in Our Midst, 1958*, Report by Ahmed Iqbal Ullah Race Relations Resource Centre based on coverage by *Manchester Evening News* and *Manchester Evening Chronicle* of 1958 race riots. See www.manchester.gov.uk/libraries

K. Mandelbaum (Martin) (1945) *The Industrialisation of Backward Areas*, Oxford: Oxford University Press.

McClelland, D. (1971) *The Achieving Society*, Cambridge, MA: Harvard University Press.

Meade, J. E. (1950) 'Review of *Problems of Economic Planning* by E. F. M. Durbin and *The Principles of Economic Planning* by W. Arthur Lewis', *Economic Journal*, 60: 117–22.

Meier, G. M. (1993) 'The New Political Economy and Policy Reform', *Journal of International Development*, 5: 381–9.

Meier, G. M. and D. Seers (1984) *Pioneers of Development: Development Economics in the 1950s*, Baltimore: Johns Hopkins University Press.

Meier, G. M. and D. Seers (eds) (1985) *Pioneers in Development*, New York: Oxford University Press, for World Bank.

Mill, J. S. (1994[1848]) *Principles of Political Economy*, (with *Chapters on Socialism*), Oxford: Oxford University Press World's Classics.

Mills, D. (2002) 'British Anthropology at the End of Empire: The Rise and Fall of the Colonial Social Science Research Council, 1944–1962', *Revue d'Histoire des Sciences Humaines*, 6: 161–88.

Mine, Y. (2004) 'The Political Element in the Works of W. Arthur Lewis: A Black Fabian's Attitude to Africa', Paper presented at a conference on the Lewis Model after 50 Years, University of Manchester, 6–7 July.

Moggridge, D. E. (2007) 'Biography and Autobiography: Harry Johnson', in E. R. Weintraub and E. L. Forget (eds), *Economists' Lives*.

Mordecai, J. (1968) *Federation of the West Indies*, London, Allen & Unwin.

Morgenstern, O. and J. von Neumann (1951) *Theory of Games and Economic Behaviour*, Washington, DC: Brookings Institution.

Morrissey, O., B. Smith and E. Horesh (1992) *British Aid and International Trade*, Buckingham: Open University Press.

Mosley, P. (2004a) 'Institutions and Politics in a Lewis-type Growth Model', *The Manchester School*, 72: 751–74.

Mosley, P. (2004b) 'Severe poverty and growth: a macro-micro analysis', Manchester: Chronic Poverty Research Centre, Working Paper 51.

Mosley, P., with B. Chiripanhura, J. Grugel and B. Thirkell-White (2012) *The Politics of Poverty Reduction*, Oxford: Oxford University Press.

Mosley, P., J. Harrigan and J. Toye (eds) (1995) *Aid and Power*, Vol. 2 (2nd edn), London: Routledge.

Mosley, P. and B. Ingham (2012) 'Fighting Discrimination: W. Arthur Lewis and the Dual Economy of Manchester, 1951–58', Unpublished paper, University of Manchester: Brooks World Poverty Institute, Occasional Paper 179.

Moyne, Lord (1945) *The Report of West India Royal Commission* (The Moyne Report), Chairman Lord Moyne. Report of a Commission established in August 1938 to investigate social and economic conditions in Barbados, British Guiana, British Honduras, Jamaica, the Leeward Islands, Trinidad and Tobago, and the Windward Islands, Cmd 6607, London: His Majesty's Stationery Office.

Myrdal, G. (1967) *Economic Theory and Under-Developed Regions*, London: Gerald Duckworth.

Nafziger, W. and J. Auvinen (2002) 'Economic Development, Inequality, War and State Violence', *World Development*, 30: 153–63.

Naipaul, V. S. (1962) *The Middle Passage*, London: Penguin.

Nasar, S. (1998) *A Beautiful Mind*, London: Faber & Faber. (Publ. in paperback, 2001)

National Archives, Kew: Colonial Economic Advisory Council (1944) CEAC (Agenda) (44)7, 23 June 1944, memorandum on Colonial Economic Development by W.A. Lewis in consultation with E.F.M. Durbin. (Copy at Rhodes House, Oxford: Mss. Brit. Emp. s.350.)

Nicholls, N. (2005) 'Towards an Eastern Caribbean Federation' by a Group of West Indians meeting in Tobago, *Caribbean Studies*, 12 (June 1972): 98–102.

Nkrumah, K. (1957) *Ghana: An Autobiography*, London: PanAfrica.

Nkrumah, K. (1961) *I Speak of Freedom*, London: Heinemann.

Oberdorfer, D. (1995) *Princeton University: The First 250 Years*, Princeton University, Office of Communications and Publications.

Palmer, R. and Parsons, N. (1977) *The Roots of Rural Poverty in Central Africa*, London: Heinemann.

Perham, M. (1937) *Africans and British Rule*, Oxford: Oxford University Press.

Perkins, D. H. and M. Roemer (1991) *Reforming Economic Systems In Developing Countries*, Harvard Studies in International Development, Cambridge, MA: Harvard University Press.

Perrings, C. (1979) *Black Mine Workers in Central Africa*, London: Heinemann

Phelps Brown, E. H. (1951) 'Evan Durbin, 1906–1948', *Economica*, 18: 91–5.

Pimlott, B. (1992) *Harold Wilson*, London: HarperCollins.

Plant, A., Sir (1965) 'Review of *The Economics of the Colour Bar* by W. H. Hutt', *Economic Journal*, 75(3) (December): 827–8.

Plant, A., Sir (1974) *Selected Economic Essays and Addresses*, London: Routledge & Kegan Paul.

Polanyi, K. (1944) *The Great Transformation*, New York: Rinehart (republ. in 1957, Boston: Beacon Press; and in 2001 as *The Great Transformation: The Political and Economic Origins of Our Time*, Boston: Beacon Press.

Polanyi, M. (1964 [1946]) *Science, Faith and Society*, Current edn, Chicago: University of Chicago Press.

Premdas, R. and E. St Cyr (eds) (1991) *Sir Arthur Lewis: An Economic and Political Portrait*, Institute of Social and Economic Research, University of the West Indies, Mona, Jamaica.

Ranis, G. (2004) 'Arthur Lewis's Contribution to Development Thinking and Policy', *The Manchester School*, 72: 712–24.

Ranis, G. and J. C. H. Fei (1961) 'A Theory of Economic Development', *American Economic Review*, 51: 533–65.

Reid, J. (1955) 'Coloured Immigrants: Some Employment Problems', *Manchester Guardian*, 22 February.

Romer, P. M. (1986) 'Increasing Returns and Long-Run Growth', *Journal of Political Economy*, 94(5) (October): 1002–37.

Rosenstein-Rodan, P. (1943) 'Problems of Industrialisation of Eastern and South-Eastern Europe', *Economic Journal*, 53: 202–11.

Rosenstein-Rodan, P. (1984) 'Natura Facit Saltum: Analysis of the Disequilibrium Growth Process', in Meier and Seers (1984): 205–27.

Sachs, J. (2005) *The End of Poverty: Economic Possibilities for Our Time*, New York: Penguin.

Sala-i-Martin, X. (1997) 'I Just Ran Two Million Regressions', Papers and Proceedings of the Hundred and Fourth Annual Meeting of the American Economic Association, *The American Economic Review*, (May), 87(2): 178–83..

Saville, J. (1980) 'Hugh Gaitskell (1906–1963) An Assessment', *Socialist Register*: 148–69.

Schultz, T. W. (1964) *Transforming Traditional Agriculture*, New Haven, CT: Yale University Press.

Seers, D. (1962) 'Why Visiting Economists Fail', *Journal of Political Economy*, 70 (August).

Seers, D. (1963) 'The Limitations of the Special Case', *Bulletin of the Oxford University Institute of Statistics*, 25(2): 77–98.

Seers, D. and C. R. Ross (1952) *Report on Financial and Physical Problems of Development in the Gold Coast*, Office of the Government Statistician, Accra, July.

Sen, A. K. (1966) 'Peasants and Dualism With and Without Surplus Labour', *Journal of Political Economy*, 74 (October).

Sen, A. K. (1982) *Poverty and Famines*, Oxford: Oxford University Press.

Sherraden, M. (1991) *Assets and the Poor: A New American Welfare Policy*, New York: M. E. Sharpe.

Skidelsky, R. (1992) *John Maynard Keynes, Vol. 2: The Economist as Saviour 1920–1937*, London: Macmillan: 455, 603.

Skidelsky, R. (1998) 'Introduction', *John Maynard Keynes, Vol. 3: Fighting for Britain 1937–1946*, London: Macmillan) (published in paperback, 2000): xxii.

Stanley, J. (1998) 'Mangoes to Moss Side: Caribbean Migration to Manchester in the 1950s and 1960s', Manchester County Record Office; available at www.manchester.gov.uk/libraries

Sternlieb, G., R. W. Burchell and L. Sagalyn (1971) *The Affluent Suburb: Princeton* (New Brunswick, NJ: Transaction Books).

Stiglitz. J. (1976) 'The Efficiency Wage Hypothesis, Surplus Labour and the Distribution of Income in LDCs', *Oxford Economic Papers*, 28.

Stolper, W. (1966) *Planning Without Facts: Lessons in Resource Allocation from Nigeria's Development*, Cambridge, MA: Harvard University Press.

Tawney, R.H. (1926) *Religion and the Rise of Capitalism*, Holland Lectures 1922; 2nd edn,(publ. 1937) London: Penguin Books.

Tignor, R. (2005) *W. Arthur Lewis and the Birth of Development Economics*, Princeton, NJ: Princeton University Press.

Timmins, N. (2001) *The Five Giants: A Biography of the Welfare State*, 2nd edn, London: HarperCollins.

Toye, J. (1987) *Dilemmas of Development: The Intellectual Counter-Revolution in Development Studies*, Oxford: Basil Blackwell.

Toye, J. (2006) 'Hans Singer's Debts to Schumpeter and Keynes', *Cambridge Journal of Economics* (November): 819–33.

Toye, J. (2009) 'Herbert Frankel: From Colonial Economics to Development Economics', *Oxford Development Studies*, 37: 171–82

Toye, J. and Toye, R. (2004) *The UN and Global Political Economy: Trade, Finance and Development*, Bloomington, Ind.: Indiana University Press.

UK Colonial Office (1943) *Report of the Mass Education Sub-Committee: Mass Education in African Society*, Advisory Committee on Education in the Colonies; Rhodes House, Oxford: Creech Jones Papers (Mss. Afr. s.332).

United Nations (1951) *Measures for the Economic Development of Underdeveloped Countries*, New York: United Nations.

Walcott, D. (1973) *Another Life*, London: Jonathan Cape.

Weeks, J. (1973) 'Uneven Sectoral Development and the Role of the State', *IDS Bulletin*, 5 (October): 76–82.

Weintraub, E. R. and E. L. Forget (eds) (2007) 'Economists' Lives: Biography and Autobiography in the History of Economics', *History of Political Economy*, Special Issue, 39(5).

Wilford, H. (2000) '"Unwitting Assets"? British Intellectuals and the Congress for Cultural Freedom', *Twentieth Century British History*, 11(1).

Williams, B. (2005) '"Displaced Scholars", Refugees at the University of Manchester', *Melilah: Manchester Journal of Jewish Studies*, Vol. 2.

Williams, P. M. (1979) *Hugh Gaitskell: A Political Biography* (London: Jonathan Cape).

Wilson, F. (1973) *Labour in the South African Gold Mines, 1911–1969*, Cambridge: Cambridge University Press.

Woolcock, M. (1998) 'Social Capital and Economic Development: Toward a Theoretical Synthesis and Policy Framework', *Theory and Society*, 27: 151–208.

Woolcock, M. and D. Narayan (2000) 'Social Capital: Implications for Development Theory, Research and Policy', *World Bank Research Observer*, 15.

World Bank (1981) *Accelerated Development in Sub-Saharan Africa: An Agenda for Action*, Washington, DC: World Bank.

World Bank (1983) *World Bank/IFC Oral History Program: Transcript of interview by Robert Asher with Hollis Chenery*, 27 January.

World Bank (1989) *Sub-Saharan Africa: From Crisis to Sustainable Growth: A Long-Term Perspective Study*, Washington, DC: World Bank.

World Bank (1990) *World Development Report: Poverty*, New York/Oxford: Oxford University Press.

World Bank (1994) *Adjustment in Africa: Reforms, Results and the Road Ahead*, Washington, DC: World Bank.

World Bank (2000) *World Development Report: Attacking Poverty*, New York/Oxford: Oxford University Press.

World Bank (2006) *World Development Report 2006: Inequality*, Washington, DC: World Bank.

Wraith, R.E. (1967) *Guggisberg*, Oxford: Oxford University Press.

Index

Note: material appearing in the endnotes is suffixed 'n', e.g. 273n.21 = page 273, note 21.

Abbott, George, 163
Abrahams, Peter, 39, 43–4
Adams, Grantley, 52, 175, 190, 201, 267
  see also West Indies Federation
adult education, 50, 137
  see also mass education; technical training
agricultural credit, *see* rural credit
agricultural extension, 60, 69, 72, 110, 149, 153, 193–4, 230, 240, 270n.7
agricultural schools, 60, 230
  see also agricultural extension
agriculture
  agricultural mechanization, 72, 78, 107, 152
  agricultural research, 149
  Lewis's preoccupation with smallholder agriculture, 60, 69, 72–3, 81, 113, 118, 138, 149, 202, 220, 241, 263, 288n.85, 289n.105
  markets for agricultural inputs, 114
  policy in Caribbean Development Bank, 208
  underbudgeting in development plans, 69
aid, *see* overseas aid
Aix-en-Provence, University of, 259
Akerlof, George, 251, 286n.67
anti-imperialism, 8
  in general, 8, 83
  in Lewis, 8, 81
Appleby, Sir Humphrey, character in *Yes, Minister*, 55
Argentina, 116
Arndt, H.W. 17, 93–4, 272n.3
'asset-based welfare policy', 231
Attlee, Clement, 51, 71

Banerjee, Abhijit, 265
Bangkok, alleged scene of Lewis' 'Eureka moment', 104
Barbados
  establishment of Institute of Economic and Social Research, 24
  formation of Progressive League of Barbados, 47
  Lewis's attachment to the island, 172, 259
  US finance for 'responsible' trade unions, 53
  see also Barrow, Errol
Barlow, Sir Thomas, 121, 126
Barrow, Errol, 168, 199, 247
Bauer, (Lord) Peter, 117, 248
Baumol, William, ix, 214, 241, 246, 248, 268, 303n.11
  interest in economics of the arts, 221
bauxite, 149
Benham, Frederic, 25, 29, 36–8, 181
Beveridge, Sir William, 19, 27
Bevin, Ernest, 66
Bienen, Henry, ix, 219, 222–3
'big push', 105
  see also Rosenstein-Rodan, Paul
Bird, Vere, Prime Minister of Antigua, 205
Bolivia, 116
Board of Trade, of UK, 54
black people
  as depicted in the media, 38
  'black studies' programmes in US and Lewis's attitude to them, 232–4
  immigration into Manchester in 1950s, 289n.4

Lewis, Sir William Arthur –
  continued

  friendships and rivalries –
  nature of Lewis's personal
    relationships, 222, 267
  with Richard Allsopp, 259–60,
    313n.12
  with William and Hilda Baumol,
    214, 221, 267–8
  with Ely Devons, 95–6
  with Evan Durbin, 51–2, 267–8
  with Hugh Gaitskell, 139–41, 143
  with Mark Gersovitz, 221–2,
    313n.11
  with Rita Hinden, 45–6, 267
  with Manchester economics
    department, 95–8
  with Neville Nicholls, 206–8, 259,
    313n.12
  with Princeton economics
    department, 236–7
  with M.G. (Mike) Smith, 255–6,
    267
  with Eric Williams, 178, 198, 205,
    255–6

  miscellaneous –
  earnings at Princeton, 309n.93
  extravagance at UCWI, 191
  health problems
    duodenal ulcer (1942–44), 31, 57
    gastric and unspecified
      problems (1970s), 235, 246,
      309n.94
    stroke (1986), 259
  house in Manchester, 89
  winter migration to Caribbean, 247

Lewis, Sir Alan, governor of
    St Lucia and chancellor of
    UCWI, Arthur Lewis's brother,
    96, 259
Lewis, Barbara, Arthur Lewis's elder
    daughter, 89, 224
Lewis, Elizabeth, Arthur Lewis's
    younger daughter, 89, 223–4
Lewis, Gladys (*née* Jacobs), Arthur
    Lewis's wife, 18, 88, 248, 252,
    258

Lewis, John P., departmental
    chairman at Princeton, 236–7
Leys, Norman, 49
Lively, Robert, 223
Lloyd, Sir Thomas, 83–4
Lomax, Kenneth and Leah, 96
London School of Economics (LSE),
    Chapter 2 *passim*, 251
loyalty contracts, 25, 32

Machlup, Fritz, 213
macroeconomics, 51
  see also Durbin, Evan: Keynes, J.M.;
    von Hayek, Friedrich
malaria, 4. 182
Malaysia, 83, 104
malnutrition, 4, 59
Malthus, Thomas Robert, 111, 245
Manchester, 13, 157
Manchester City Council, 120, 122,
    136
Manchester Guardian, 22, 36, 38, 83,
    98, 181, 268
Manchester Statistical Society, 105
Manchester University, 1, 14, 18,
    93–9
  anthropology department, 98–9
  economics department, 93–8; feuds
    within, 94, 96–7, 282n.23
  see also Gluckman, Max
Manley, Norman, 52, 175, 197, 205,
    291n.6
  persuades Lewis to stay on as
    principal of UCWI, 189–90
maquiladoras, 48
  see also industrialisation
Marcus Garvey Association, 8
  see also Garvey, Marcus
marginal utility, 105–7, 262
market failure, 58, 105–7
  see also laissez-faire
Mars, John, 96–7, 111
Marshall Aid, 67
Martin (Mandelbaum), Kurt, 94–5,
    98, 111
Marx, Karl, 111, 141, 145
Marxism, 44, 94, 135, 226
'mass education', 49–50, 60–1, 69–72,
    229, 248, 266, 274n.12